SELF, SOCIETY,
EXISTENCE

SELF, SOCIETY, EXISTENCE

EXISTENCE

Human Nature and Dialogue

in the Thought of

George Herbert Mead and Martin Buber

by PAUL PFUETZE

WITH A FOREWORD BY H. RICHARD NIEBUHR

HARPER TORCHBOOKS   *The Academy Library*

HARPER & BROTHERS, NEW YORK

HARPER TORCHBOOKS / The Academy Library
Advisory Editor in the Humanities and Social Sciences: Benjamin Nelson

ACKNOWLEDGMENTS

The courtesy of the following publishers and journals in permitting the use of copy-
righted material is gratefully acknowledged:

University of Chicago Press, publishers of Mead's works; Schocken Books, Inc.,
Harper & Bros.; Charles Scribner's Sons; Philosophical Library; T. & T. Clark; Mel-
bourne University Press; Open Court Publishing Co.; Macmillan Co.; Farrar, Straus
and Young; *Journal of Philosophy; International Journal of Ethics; Philosophical
Review; Religion in Life; American Journal of Sociology; Psychological Bulletin;*
King's Crown Press; Henry Holt & Co.; Yale University Press; Prentice-Hall; *Review
of Religion; Commentary; Menorah Journal; New Palestine;* Behrman's Jewish Book
House; Abingdon-Cokesbury Press; Westminster Press; Rinehart; Willett, Clark &
Co., Student Christian Movement Press; Whittlesey House; Oxford University Press;
Longmans, Green and Co.; *The Christian Century;* Harcourt, Brace & Co.; Clarendon
Press; Ives Washburn; Routledge & Kegan Paul; *The Hibbert Journal;* Norton & Co.;
The Seabury Press; Columbia University Press; George Allen & Unwin, Ltd.; *Journal
of Religion; Sociology and Social Research;* American Psychological Assn.; Harvard
University Press; Rütten & Loening Varlag; Drei Masken Verlag; James Nisbet & Co.,
Ltd.; Insel-Verlag.

All direct quotations are used by permission of the publishers.

To LOUISE

*With this book the author pays tribute to
Vassar College on the occasion of its Centennial*

Foreword

FEW RECENT IDEAS have been so fruitful in so many areas of thought as the idea of the interpersonal nature of our human existence. That no self exists or knows itself save in the presence of another self is a thought that has doubtless occurred to men at many times in the past. Yet little use has been made of it in philosophy, psychology and theology. Even today the idea is more widely referred to than actually used. But what use has been made of it indicates that it holds great promise. With its aid light is being cast on many obscure places in our understanding of ourselves in our world. It is an idea that will doubtlessly be refined and developed as it is used, in the form of hypotheses, for the understanding of various human situations and events.

"It is most remarkable that this idea should have been brought to the attention of modern man mainly by two thinkers who operated in the context of different cultures and worked with very different intellectual tools. In this study Professor Pfuetze calls attention to the strange parallelism between the ego-alter dialectic of G. H. Mead's radically empirical philosophy and Martin Buber's religiously oriented reflections upon the I-Thou relation. Thus he makes a contribution to the history of ideas and also to the development of a most fruitful mode of thinking. I am indebted to Mr. Pfuetze for the light he casts on the meaning of a seminal idea.

H. RICHARD NIEBUHR

Preface to The Torchbook Edition

THIS ESSAY is an attempt to state and explore the concept of what I have called "the social self" from a philosophical, psychological, and religious point of view, especially as this heuristic idea finds expression in the thought of George Herbert Mead and Martin Buber. Its main concern is to examine this "dialogical" concept of human nature, to compare it with other relevant notions, and to see what we can learn from it about the self, its form, and its relations.

This investigation began with two basic assumptions: First, that the form of the person-in-relation is emerging as a crucial problem of contemporary philosophy and psychology. The problem is both old and new, and very much alive today. For one's understanding of the self will define one's entire outlook on man and society. Even leading Marxist theoreticians, (who previously have submerged the individual in society, in the class, and in the currents of history) are now, like Poland's Professor Adam Schaff, warning that Communism stands to lose "the struggle for men's minds" unless it comes to grips with the problems of the human person-in-community.

The second assumption initiating this study was that there are striking and significant similarities between the thought of Mead and Buber, two thinkers widely divergent and uncongenial in many respects. It occurred to me that American pragmatism had been saying some of the same things that European *Existenz-philosophie* was emphasizing. Whether the connection was logical and genuine or only historical, or both, to me the notion held great promise for illuminating many problems in our understanding of ourselves in our world. Mead and Buber seemed to live in such different worlds and speak such different languages. Nevertheless, I thought they should be brought together, placed at least on speaking

1

terms with each other. This I have tried to do, and I am grateful that some have found the results interesting.

Accordingly, one major purpose of this essay is to determine, on the basis of the available evidence, whether in fact this assumption of similarities and parallelisms is valid and verifiable as alleged. My reasons for accepting this assumption as a working hypothesis will, I trust, become clear in the following chapters. A related concern is appropriately an inquiry into the kind and degree of similarity or dissimilarity to be found in the thought of Mead and Buber.

It was a further initial belief that such an analysis and comparison would prove helpful in displaying the psychological, social, ethical, and religious meanings and applications of this "self-other" concept of self and society. It therefore appears in order to set forth some of the areas of practical application within which this new ego-alter concept finds cogency and practical verification. Such an exposition should yield some indication as to the psychological, moral, and religious adequacy of the self-other or I-Thou motif.

The publisher's decision to reprint *The Social Self* in the Harper Torchbook series is gratifying confirmation of the author's conviction that the themes, concerns, and contentions of this study are increasingly germane to the problems, both theoretical and practical, in which contemporary ethics, education, sociology, psychology, psychotherapy, and theology are interested. The central motif in the work of Mead and Buber, and the emerging heuristic doctrine concerning the interpersonal nature of human existence, provide us with a remarkably valuable instrument of analysis in understanding the human situation. Mead and Buber, in their different ways, have drawn attention to certain facts often, if strangely, overlooked or neglected, which are essential for our understanding of the distinctly human.

Here, then, is an idea which is very much alive in the thought of men today and is finding fruitful expression and application in many directions. Serious study of Mead and Buber have steadily grown throughout recent years, so that they have become commanding figures of our intellectual world.

Impressive evidence confirming this fact came to my attention only recently. By coincidence, within a single week, there came to my desk the following items: (1) A new paperback by Professor O. Hobart Morover: *The Crisis in Psychiatry and Religion* (Van Nostrand, 1961). In Chapter 10, entitled "Psychology, Theology, and the Social Self," given earlier as one of the Earl Lectures at the Pacific School of Religion,

Berkeley, California, the author refers specifically to the contributions of George Herbert Mead and Martin Buber. (2) *The Proceedings and Addresses of the American Philosophical Association* for 1959-60. Included in the volume is the Presidential Address by Van Meter Ames before the Western Division of the Association: "Zen to Mead," in which Professor Ames discusses the affinities and parallels he finds between Japanese Zen and American pragmatic philosophy. (3) A new book, *The Idea of Catholicism* (Meridian, 1960), edited by two eminent Jesuit scholars, Walter J. Burghardt and William F. Lynch. One of the essays in this anthology, "The Master Idea of Christian Morality," by Bernard Häring, C.S.S.R., is informed throughout by the I-Thou motif. (4) Information about numerous dissertations being written on various aspects of Buber's thought.

I first heard of Martin Buber and George Herbert Mead in Professor H. Richard Niebuhr's lecture hall at Yale University. This was in 1940. Mead was at the time somewhat under the shadow of his life-long friend and better known pragmatist, John Dewey. All of his significant extant literary remains were available, but nowhere brought together in systematic form. Buber was then little known in America, even among Jewish scholars and writers; and there had been no serious effort to gain for him an audience in the United States. Of his many books, only *I and Thou,* his now classic "philosophical-religious poem," was available in English translation. Everything else was in German or Hebrew; and many of these works were not directly relevant to this study because they dealt so exclusively with Jewish Nationalism, Zionism, Jewish religiosity, Biblical exegesis, and Hasidism. So far as I know, I was the first Christian student in America (excepting Professor Niebuhr) to give serious and systematic attention to the work of Martin Buber. Today many others are devoting earnest attention to Buber and writing books about him. Nearly all of his important books and essays have been published in excellent English translations, or soon will be. He has made three lecture trips to the United States, and is the subject of a forthcoming volume in *The Library of Living Philosophers* to which I have been privileged to contribute.

But even as I was beginning this investigation, J. H. Oldham in England was saying of *I and Thou:* "I question whether any book has been published in the present century the message of which, if it were understood and heeded, would have such far-reaching consequences for the life of our time." That perceptive prediction is in a fair way to being fulfilled. Today, if tardily, Martin Buber is recognized as one of the world's great thinkers—philosopher, theologian, prophet, poet. It is a testimony to the far-reaching influence and relevance of Buber's thought that what he says is heard with understanding and appreciation by persons of the most diverse creeds.

Increasingly, Jews and Christians alike are heeding Martin Buber's message of the "life of dialogue"; and in so doing are recovering a fresh and vivid understanding of Biblical faith as the encounter with God in history. The dialogue about "dialogue" is now carried on wherever one turns. Not only has Buber been the herald of a renaissance of spiritual Judaism, but he has been the agent through whom, in our day, Judaism and Christianity have been brought close together to their mutual enrichment.

Nowhere has the I-Thou relational theme and method of Buber's dialogical thinking had so marked an influence as in recent Protestant theology—both continental and American. Nor has contemporary Catholic discussion escaped the pervasive reach of his influence. For though Buber is a Jew, he seems to have articulated more clearly and persuasively than any other modern writer the "word" that speaks to our human condition in this "world-hour." As I have said elsewhere, he seems to possess a paradigmatic significance for the religious, moral, and sociological predicament of modern man. His thought springs from deep Jewish sources, but always against the background of a searching criticism of the axioms and values of contemporary culture.

Buber's spirit is so elevated and universal, his poetic gift so eloquent, that what he says to Jews is equally applicable to Christians. Moses said at Sinai to the people who listened to God: "Ye heard the voice of words, but ye saw no form." It doesn't really matter what you call the voice: all that matters is that you hear it and respond to it. Professor Buber is most concerned to express the eternal truth about God and his ways with men. But eternal truth has many rays, one of which has informed the teaching of Israel. This circumstance detracts little or nothing from the value which that, or any other, "ray of truth" has for others who take their inspiration from the doctrines, practices, and associations of other traditions. If one has something to communicate that is transparently authentic, transcendent, and of universal worth, he will be understood even by people of very different backgrounds. Martin Buber is such a one, for he has seen the Way himself, and walked in it. He has achieved in his writing and in his living a deep identity of truth and life. His personal history and religious experience have given him a vantage point from which he speaks to all of us in this historic hour.

There are also signs of a renewal of interest in the thought of George Herbert Mead. This thinker—whom John Dewey called "the most original mind in philosophy in America of the last generation"—has been dead for thirty years. His works deserve, and are getting, another careful reading—with some rather startling results, as will be seen in Van Meter Ames' attempts to relate Mead to Japanese Zen. Indeed, one need not now read Mead to encounter his germinal ideas; for they have found their way into many contemporary studies in social psychology, ethics, education, and social philosophy. As someone has observed: Mead has written many books of which other men are the authors.

In what follows, it should not be inferred that Mead and Buber are regarded as the only, or the primary, sources of this concept of the social self. But they do stand forth as pioneers in the contemporary discussions of the social theory of the self. They have given us exceptionally thorough, attractive, and fruitful expositions of a theme which has many other expressions—some of them historically not derived from either Mead or Buber. Indeed, it is difficult to trace this motif to any one thinker or school; the seeds of this germinal idea are scattered, windborne in many directions. It is a part of the *Zeitgeist*, and has opened up new vistas and fresh possibilities for further advance in many disciplines.

One other caution. In bringing Mead and Buber face to face, in order to display their remarkable similarities, I have not been unmindful of their equally significant differences in method, spirit, and metaphysical presuppositions. The reader should also keep this fact in mind. Mead worked within the frame of a scientific behaviorism, concerned as a social psychologist with the empirical study of mind, self, and society in their bio-social evolution. On the other hand, Buber, the Jewish existentialist, speaks the language of faith and revelation, of Hasidic mysticism, seeing the self (in the most real sense) as originating in the dialogue with a God who is both immanent and transcendent. Buber, like Judaism, cannot be understood at all save on the basis of a faith in and meeting with a particular, sovereign, living God, the Eternal Thou whom man meets and knows in the dialogue. In Buber one finds a spiritual tension unknown to Mead, a "holy insecurity," a seeking for a unity of contraries, which Buber himself has described as the "narrow ridge."

Furthermore, no claim is made that Mead's self-other relation and resulting "social self" is the *same* as Buber's I-Thou relation or embraces all the concrete meaning of Buber's "life of dialogue." *Similarity* is not *identity*. Indeed, the "social self" is *my* term—not Buber's or Mead's—and is employed simply as a convenient and adequately accurate term to mean that the self (in the thought of both Mead and Buber) is a product of social or inter-personal relations involving meeting, symbolic communication, or dialogue. Some readers may feel that my term, "the social self," is too general a linguistic form to cover accurately both Mead's self-other dialectic and Buber's I-Thou dialogic relation. For our purposes in this essay, the particular term is not for me important, so long as the meanings are kept distinct and clearly in mind throughout the discussion. Both Mead and Buber are saying, if I mistake not, that the essential and constitutive character of human life and selfhood is something that takes place *between* one person and another in a society of persons. It is social interplay, inter-human relation, reflected appraisal, concrete meeting with others, a life of dialogue that turn the human organism into full selfhood. The finite individual self is mutually dependent upon and mutually determinative of other concrete selves in a network of mutually supporting, dynamic, constitutive interpersonal relations. Within that network, some relations are more obvious than others; and some are ultimately more important than others. At this point, Buber's religious concern becomes crucial; for it is the revelation of God in history and in the community which becomes the source of man's responsible decision and faithful response.

The program of this essay is threefold. First, it attempts a clear statement of the nature and structure of the "social self" as seen in the writings of George Herbert Mead and Martin Buber. Second, it attempts a comparison and critique of Mead and Buber respecting their concepts of the social self with a view to displaying the significant similarities and differences in their thought. Third, it ventures a conclusion as to the validity and value of the self-other dialogic theory of the self.

An introductory chapter attempts to set the issue and to state the problem of modern man's predicament and crisis in his knowledge of himself. Chapter II sets forth an extended and systematic statement of Mead's genetic account of mind, self, and society. Here also is treated Mead's detailed analysis of the mechanisms of gesture, vocal symbol, speech, and "role-taking" as basic to the correlative development of the self and cognitive meanings. Chapter III explores Buber's original and subtle theory of the "personal." Against a background of European Enlightenment and Jewish mysticism, Buber develops the basis for man's status as a *person* in a world of persons, living in I-Thou dialogic relation. This calls for a consideration of the nature and meaning of "dialogue" and of the community which includes God.

Chapter IV brings the two thinkers together in a rather detailed comparison and critique in order to display clearly the likenesses and the differences between Mead and Buber, and suggests tentative amendments of Mead in the direction of Buber. Chapter V consists of an attempt to indicate the validity and the value of this ego-alter concept of the self by showing its fruitful applications to certain crucial problems in the fields of religion, ethics, social philosophy, psychotherapy, and education.

I am only too aware of the faults and failures in this book. One day, perhaps, I shall write another book which will correct or avoid the flaws in this one. For the present, this statement must stand. I have made but few changes in the text. I have brought the bibliography up to date, while adding two pages of representative works by authors other than Mead and Buber, but who are likewise concerned with the same or similar problems of inter-personal or I-Thou relation.

It is a pleasure to record here my appreciation to those who have contributed in various ways to the preparation of this book. I have received help and illumination from many others—authors, teachers, colleagues, students, and friends. A special debt of gratitude is due to Professors H. Richard Niebuhr and Albert C. Outler for their encouragement and for their help and criticism during the progress of this study. I am already beholden to Professor Niebuhr for so many things that I have placed myself further in his debt by asking him to write the Foreword to this volume. Professor Buber read Chapter III, corrected certain errors of fact or interpretation, and made other suggestions for improving the presentation of my material. Dr. Rubin Gotesky, my associate for ten years in the department of philosophy at the University of Georgia gave me many valuable suggestions. Professor Maurice Friedman has been a friend and critic for many years. My thanks also go to Professor Benjamin Nelson, who first suggested and has since encouraged the paperback edition of the book, and to the editors of Harper Torchbooks for their editorial assistance. The help of all these friends has made of this volume a far better book than it otherwise would have been.

I am, of course, most indebted to my wife, whose love and encouragement over the years have been too loyal, too constant, for appropriate tribute. To her, my partner in the "dialogue," I gratefully inscribe this book.

PAUL E. PFUETZE

Vassar College
April 1961

Preface

THIS ESSAY is an attempt to state and explore the concept of the "social self" from a philosophical and religious point of view, especially as this idea finds expression in the thought of George Herbert Mead and Martin Buber. Its main concern is to examine this "dialogical" concept of human nature, to compare it with other relevant psychological notions, and to see what we can learn from it about the self and its relations.

This investigation began with the assumption that there are striking and significant similarities between the thought of Mead and Buber, two thinkers otherwise widely divergent and uncongenial in many respects. One major purpose of this study, therefore, is to determine, on the basis of the available evidence, whether in fact this assumption of similarities and parallelisms is valid and verifiable as alleged. My reasons for accepting this assumption as a working hypothesis will, I trust, become clear in the following chapters. A second concern is appropriately an inquiry into the kind and degree of similarity or dissimilarity found in the thought of Mead and Buber.

It was a further initial belief that such an analysis and comparison would prove interesting and valuable in displaying the psychological, social, religious, and ethical meanings and applications of this "self-other" concept of self and society. It therefore appears in order to set forth some of the areas of practical application within which this new ego-alter concept finds cogency and practical verification. Such an exposition should yield some indication as to the religious and ethical adequacy of the self-other motif. Auxiliary to the major task, it will be appropriate to raise and attempt to answer certain critical questions which appear central to this study.

The programme of this essay is, therefore, threefold. First, it attempts a clear statement of the nature and structure of the "social self" as seen in the writings of George Herbert Mead and Martin Buber. Second, it attempts a comparison and critique of Mead and Buber respecting their concepts of the social self with a view to displaying the significant similarities and differences in their thought. Third, it ventures a final appraisal as to the validity and value of the self-other dialogic theory of the self.

An introductory chapter essays to set the issue and to state the problem of modern man's predicament and crisis in his knowledge of himself—this by way of justifying the inquiry. Here also are given the justifying reasons for centering on Mead and Buber for intensive study.

Chapter II sets forth an extended statement of the fundamental features and the background of Mead's genetic account of mind, self, and society as emergents out of a bio-social context. Here also is treated Mead's detailed analysis of the mechanisms of gesture, vocal symbol, and "role-taking" as basic to the correlative development of the self and cognitive meanings.

Chapter III explores Buber's original and subtle theory of the "personal." Against a background of European Enlightenment and Jewish mysticism, Buber develops the basis for man's status as a *person* in a world of persons, living in *I-Thou* dialogic relations. This calls for a consideration of the nature and meaning of "dialogue" and of the community which includes God.

Chapter IV brings the two thinkers together in a rather detailed comparison and critique in order to explore the likenesses and the differences between Mead and Buber, and suggests what, at this stage, must be regarded as only tentative amendments of Mead in the direction of Buber.

Chapter V consists of an attempt to indicate the validity and the value of the self-other, inter-personal concept of the self by showing its fruitful applications to certain crucial problems in the fields of religion, ethics, social philosophy, psychotherapy, and education.

The posthumous collection of Mead's unpublished writings, essays, and fragmentary notes consists of four volumes:

The Philosophy of the Present (Chicago: Open Court Publ. Co., 1932). The Paul Carus Foundation Lectures. Edited by A. E. Murphy.

Mind, Self and Society (Chicago: University of Chicago Press, 1934). Edited by Charles W. Morris.

Movements of Thought in the Nineteenth Century (Chicago: University of Chicago Press, 1936). Edited by Merritt H. Moore.

The Philosophy of the Act (Chicago: University of Chicago Press, 1938). Edited by Charles W. Morris.

Professor Charles W. Morris, of the University of Chicago, has assured me that all of the significant extant literary remains of Professor Mead are to be found in these four volumes and in the numerous articles which appeared in various journals over the years from 1899 until his death in 1931. In some respects these articles are to be preferred because they are Mead's own writing and not the edited classroom notes of his students.

When I began this investigation, hardly any of Martin Buber's major works had been translated into English. The one exception was his now famous classic "philosophical-religious-poem," *Ich und Du,* translated by Ronald Gregor Smith as *I and Thou* (Edinburgh: T. & T. Clark, 1937). A few articles by Buber and about Buber, and a few of his Chassidic legends, were to be found in such journals as *The Menorah Journal, Commentary,* and *The New Palestine.* The only studies of Buber which had been made in America were an academic, and not very sympathetic, presentation by Jacob B. Agus in his *Modern Philosophies of Judaism* (New York: Behrman's Jewish Book House, 1941) and a brief account by John J. Tepfer, "Martin Buber and Neo-Mysticism," in the *Yearbook* of the Central Conference of American Rabbis, XLIV (1934). Everything else was in German or Hebrew; and many of these works were not directly relevant to this study because they dealt so exclusively with Jewish Nationalism, Zionism, Jewish religiosity, Biblical exegesis, and Chassidism. Professor Hans Kohn generously made available certain material not otherwise known to me. His own intimate knowledge of Buber is presented in the splendid and exhaustive biography, *Martin Buber, Sein Werk und Seine Zeit* (Verlag von Jakob Hegner in Hellerau, 1930), the Appendix to which contains a complete bibliography up to 1930.

It is only recently that there has been any attempt to gain Buber an audience in the United States by the publishing of his works in translation. It is gratifying to be able to report that within the last four or five years there have appeared several English translations from his works. These consist in the main of collections of essays, addresses, and articles on a wide variety of topics dealing with Israel's religion, culture, and nationhood, its relation to the spirit and to the world, with an eye to the needs of the Jew (and the Christian, too) in a time of crisis. Of the major early works *Daniel* and *Königtum Gottes* have not been translated.

For the purposes of this study, the most valuable early works were *Die Frage an den Einzelnen* (Berlin: Schocken Verlag, 1936) and *Zwiesprache* (1929). These, along with *Was ist der Mensch?* and two addresses on problems of education, *Rede über das Erzieherische* (1926) and *Über Charaktererziehung* (1939) were brought together for English readers in 1947 by Kegan Paul, London, under the title *Between Man and Man*. They constitute a sequel to *I and Thou*, amplifying and applying what was said there about the reality of the mutual dialogic relation between man and man. Along with *Ich und Du*, these same writings have been published as *Dialogisches Leben*; *Gesammelte philosophische und pädagogische Schriften* (Zürich: G. Müller, 1947).

Aside from his translation of the Bible, in collaboration with Franz Rosenzweig, Buber's most notable Biblical studies are *Königtum Gottes* (Berlin: Schocken Verlag, 1936), *Moses* (Oxford: East & West Library, 1946), *The Prophetic Faith* (New York: Macmillan, 1949), a group of the essays in *Israel and the World* (New York: Schocken Books, 1948), and *Zwei Glaubensweisen* (Zürich: Manesse Verlag, 1950), a comparative study of Jesus and Paul.

A generous selection of the famous *Die Chassidischen Bücher* (Hellerau: Verlag Jakob Hegner, 1928) dealing with Chassidism and the lives of the Baal Shem Tov and his disciples is now available in translation in two volumes of *Tales of the Hasidim*: Vol. I, *The Early Masters;* Vol. II, *The Later Masters* (New York: Schocken Books, 1947-48). Other essays interpreting Chassidism appear in *Hasidism* (New York: Philosophical Library, 1948) and in *The Ways of Man According to the Teachings of Hasidism* (London: Routledge & Kegan Paul, 1950). Some of these same essays on Hasidism, plus five essays from *Kampf um Israel* (Berlin: Shocken Verlag, 1933) have also been brought together in a little volume *Mamre* (Melbourne University Press, 1946).

Professor Buber himself prefers the revised translations of the essays in *Hasidism* and *Israel and the World* to those in *Mamre*. Accordingly, while I also note certain *Mamre* references, I usually quote from the revised translations in *Hasidism* and *Israel and the World*.

Paths in Utopia (New York: Macmillan, 1950) is a study in social theory and social history dealing with "Utopian" and Marxian socialism. Four new books have recently been published: *Israel and Palestine: The History of an Idea* (New York: Farrar, Straus & Young, 1952); *Eclipse of God* (New York: Harper, 1952) which contains Buber's lectures at American universities together with some earlier pieces; *At the Turning* (New York: Farrar, Straus & Young, 1952) consisting of three addresses on Judaism delivered at the Jewish Theological Seminary in New York City; and *Good and Evil* (New York: Charles Scribner's Sons, 1953).

In this investigation I have received help and illumination from many others—authors, former teachers, colleagues, and friends. It is a pleasure to record here my appreciation to those who have contributed in various ways to the preparation of this volume. To all of my teachers at Yale University, I am indebted for the encouragement and challenge they presented to develop this study which, earlier and in somewhat different form, was presented to the faculty of the Yale University Graduate School in partial fulfillment of the requirements for the degree of Doctor of Philosophy. A special debt of gratitude is due to Professors Albert C. Outler, H. Richard Niebuhr, Robert L. Calhoun, and Julian Hartt for their help and criticism during the progress of this study. I am already graciously beholden to Professor Niebuhr for so many things that I have placed myself further in his debt by asking him to write the Foreword to this volume. Professor Raymond P. Morris, Librarian of the Yale Divinity School Library, and his able staff, contributed much by making books and journals so readily available. Professor Martin Buber read most of Chapter III, corrected certain errors of fact or interpretation, and made other suggestions for improving the presentation of my material. Dr. Rubin Gotesky, my associate in the department of philosophy at the University of Georgia, also read parts of the manuscript and gave many helpful suggestions. Dr. David Gelzer, of Basle, Switzerland, assisted me in translating certain difficult passages. Miss Marian Martin typed the final draft. The help of all these friends has made of this volume a far better book than it otherwise could possibly have been.

I am, of course, most indebted to my wife, whose love and help over the years have been too loyal, too constant, for appropriate tribute, and who gladly assumed additional family and financial responsibilities during the months and years of this research and writing.

PAUL E. PFUETZE

The University of Georgia

Contents

AJS   *American Journal of Sociology*

BMM   Martin Buber, *Between Man and Man*

DFE   Martin Buber, *Die Frage an den Einzelnen*

IATW   Martin Buber, *Israel and the World*

IJE   *International Journal of Ethics*

JP   *Journal of Philosophy*

MB   Hans Kohn, *Martin Buber: Sein Werk und Seine Zeit*

MSS   G. H. Mead, *Mind, Self and Society*

MT   G. H. Mead, *Movements of Thought in the Nineteenth Century*

PA   G. H. Mead, *The Philosophy of the Act*

PB   *Psychological Bulletin*

PIU   Martin Buber, *Paths in Utopia*

PP   G. H. Mead, *The Philosophy of the Present*

PR   *Philosophical Review*

ZS   Martin Buber, *Zwiesprache*

The notes are printed at the end of each chapter.

Chapter One

Introduction

THERE IS A CRISIS and revolution in modern culture and in man's knowledge of himself which has occasioned a revival of interest in anthropology both in philosophical and in theological circles. Modern man has become a problem to himself, and all over the world men are inquiring with fresh zeal into the nature of man. What is man? What is the meaning of human existence? In the confusion of voices, a deep disquietude has fallen upon the human race. On all sides one finds moral disaster, political confusion, spiritual discontent, mental breakdown, and a growing suspicion, now amounting to a certainty, that during the last few centuries man has so far misinterpreted his own nature as to make tragic and catastrophic use of his powers and technics.

Accompanying the re-examination and resulting disparagement of the doctrines of man which have been dominant in preceding periods, there is a feeling that if we are to get to the bottom of life's problem, if we are to diagnose with even a degree of accuracy the perilous times in which we live, and if we are to direct theory toward a successful solution of practical problems, we must deepen our understanding of the nature of man. The great struggle going on between totalitarianism and democracy, between individualism and collectivism, between capitalism and communism is, fundamentally, a struggle over the nature, meaning, moral responsibility, and the destiny of man. Thus it is that in our time, the question *What is man?* is again being raised with urgency, sometimes in hope, more often in despair. And any such inquiry leads inescapably into a consideration of the fundamental

19

nature of the "self"—its nature, origin, qualities, relations, and possibilities.

The cultural crisis of the twentieth century, besides philosophical
development itself, has forced upon modern man the conviction that
somewhere along the line his techniques of analysis and his philosophical constructions have missed the mark. Many of the older
mechanisms and traditional answers seem no longer entirely valid,
not adequate in their theoretical formulation to solve the problems of
the modern period, or not in accord with the best methods and data
which a critical empirical science can provide.[1] It is to be expected that
new theories and instruments of research will have emerged.

Indeed, a new hypothesis has come to hand and been developed
which is proving remarkably fruitful in such diverse fields as
philosophy, theology, ethics, social psychology, politics, education, and
psychotherapy. It is the concept of the "social self," the I-Thou
dialogic self, the self-other dialectical self, which sees the "self" essentially in its relations with the "other" variously conceived. This view
posits the origin and growth of the "self-system" in a community of
selves, the process of its formation involving the symbolic mechanisms
of language and role-taking.

Something of the wide-spread interest and influence of this new
concept can be seen in the fact that this attempt to articulate the
fundamentally "social" structure of man's nature and situation proceeds from such widely divergent starting points as American social
behaviorism and European existential personalistic theology. This
fact warrants our conclusion as a working hypothesis that the social
doctrine of the self can be developed and elaborated empirically,
independent of disparate methodologies and metaphysical viewpoints.
It appears that here is a case in which different approaches and perspectives brought to bear upon a given segment of human experience
converge into common principles of fruitful analysis. Here possibly
may be found a new standpoint and a unifying set of concepts for
philosophers, theologians, psychologists, and sociologists. Accordingly,
it appears to me worthwhile to examine the European *I-Thou* motif,
set in a frame of Jewish mysticism, and compare it with the American
pragmatic social conception of the self.

The new hypothesis represents a breaking away from the older
idealistic and scholastic traditions in epistemology and metaphysics,
and finds its home in the functional, pragmatic, and existential philoso-

phies of the early twentieth century. It also represents an attempt to come to terms with Darwinism, evolution, and the new physics with its stress on time, relations, relativity, and individual perspectives. Philosophical questions and answers are inevitably stated in terms of the conceptions, ideas, and *Zeitgeist* of the period. So here we find our discussion informed by a new motif and stated in terms of a new concept. Here is a new instrument of analysis, a new hypothesis capable of bearing the weight of a remarkable number of facts.

The thing which first attracted my attention to George H. Mead and Martin Buber was the fact—as it appeared to me—that, in spite of almost complete divergence in their background, methodology, and philosophical tradition, Mead and Buber came close to each other in numerous and remarkable respects, especially in their social philosophy. One is reminded of Kierkegaard's comment on Schopenhauer: "I am astonished to find an author who, in spite of complete disagreement, touches me at so many points."

Beyond that, these two thinkers have been selected because of their representative character, originality, influence, and because of their concern with crucial problems of philosophical, ethical, social, and religious analysis. The thought of Mead and Buber is attracting more and more attention in this country because they speak in novel and attractive terms of matters of deep concern to us all. In their differing ways and idioms, they are interested in the nature of the life of the spirit, and above all they are interested in the nature of man, and in the relations between men.[2] In their different ways, both Mead and Buber are humanists, and in our western tradition the great gifts of humanism, both Renaissance and Judeo-Christian, are still strong elements in our intellectual and spiritual situation. They both speak to those who are not prone to listen to the siren voices of authoritative, or authoritarian, dogma; they speak to those who might well be termed "the intellectually displaced persons" of our time. Our present situation presents a scene of confusion and negation where once notable and clear-cut doctrines of theology and philosophy held sway.[3] Pragmatism and Naturalism, as philosophies, gain increasing support from philosophers as well as from laymen. And the fad of existentialism is slowly passing into a real interest in what the serious existentialists have to say. The full import of Heidegger, Jaspers, and Sartre, of Buber and Marcel, and of Kierkegaard himself, the master of them all, is yet to come. Meanwhile, the influence of their ideas and ways of interpreting the human situation is growing.

It will become evident, I think, as the essay proceeds, that both Mead and Buber have gone beyond *Credo ut intelligam* and *Cogito ergo sum* as the starting point and guide of human endeavor.[4] They have raised the question of man and his truth, his knowing and his being, in another idiom: *Respondeo etsi mutabor*. Truth is vital and must be socially represented. Both Mead and Buber, in their differing ways, have realized the crucial significance of *relations* between persons and the fundamentally *social* nature of reality.

These and other facts have established Mead and Buber as pioneers in the contemporary discussions of the social theory of the self. It should not, however, be inferred from what follows that Mead and Buber are regarded as the only, or even the primary, sources of this concept of the social self. They have given two exceptionally thorough, attractive, and fruitful expositions of a theme which has many other expressions—some of them historically not derived from either Mead or Buber. As a matter of fact, their theory is not entirely new. Others have been groping in the same direction.[5] But to have stated with some completeness and persuasive clarity what others have been holding or seeking confusedly merits high honor in the field of thought— no matter how much of truth or error there may finally turn out to be in what they stated. Our gratitude and tribute are not measured accurately by our agreement nor by the final content of truth in their doctrine. One is reminded of Columbus, who thought he had discovered India. He was mistaken; but he made a great discovery just the same!

Thus it may be with this new concept and standpoint. Every new mode of philosophizing reveals some new aspect or facet of human experience. We need not claim for it that this new theory by itself contains the whole truth. Meanwhile, the germinal idea of these thinkers informs the writing of an increasing number of significant thinkers. Here is a concept which appears to have valid and productive applications and meanings in many directions.

Accordingly, this essay proposes, by an inspection of the theories of the self held by George H. Mead and Martin Buber, to establish the fact that they have an important contribution to make to contemporary discussions in this area. The apparently disparate, yet actually similar, positions which Mead and Buber occupy, judged according to historical period, cultural epoch, nationality, and philosophical viewpoint, make their understanding of the nature of man significant far beyond the intrinsic interest and merit of their thought. I trust that all of this will become clear to the reader as the argument unfolds.

HISTORICAL BACKGROUND AND PRESENT TENDENCIES IN PHILOSOPHICAL ANTHROPOLOGY[6]

The problem of the self is perhaps the most elusive, abstruse, and subtle problem in philosophy. We know, or think we know, so much about man, about human nature—and yet we know so little. The terms we employ are names to cover our ignorance; they are abstracted descriptions which never give us the concrete wholeness of human lives nor explain the rich complexity of human experience. Thus we are given many, and often conflicting, answers in each of which something of the truth about man is implied; yet each reveals that the others have not told what is essential, not the whole truth.[7] All of the special sciences and disciplines give us only partial views of man, while missing man in his totality.[8] Perhaps we shall never know the whole truth about man. This is precisely a part of what Buber calls the "problematic" of philosophical anthropology.[9] But man continues restlessly to push back the veil as far as possible. We may not know *The Truth* about man, but our partial answers may approach the goal. Mead and Buber, with their notion that the self is not only an "I" but also a "thou" and a "we," have grasped one of the very important, and sometimes neglected, truths about man.

Of course, this is not the first time in history that men have addressed themselves to this problem. It has been a recurring theme for the great thinkers of all ages. Man is the one creature who is continually in search of himself, seeking the conditions and the meaning of his existence. One of the most revealing things about man is that he asks the question at all: What is man? Who am I? What is the meaning of *my* existence?

Socrates, in Plato's *Phaedrus*, declared: "I devote myself to the study, not of fables, but of my own self." Plato and Aristotle set their search on a larger base—that of man viewed as a member of a political state, suggesting that man's essence is not to be grasped from what unrolls in the individual's inner consciousness, but from the distinctiveness of his relations to things and to other living beings. Descartes began his *Meditations* with a question as to his own existence, and since that time *man,* and not God, has been the chief starting point of most metaphysical thought. Malebranche, who continued the Cartesian investigations, wrote: "Of all human knowledge the knowledge of man is the most deserving of his study." [10]

But all of these missed the truth of the whole man, the essential "I." Conceptual and scientific thinking has tended either to split the original unity of man and nature into the epistemological oppositions of subject and object, or to erase any distinction between the two, thus losing both subject and object, man and nature, in some Absolute, be it idealistic or materialistic. To make an objective, scientific study of man is to *objectify* him, *de-humanize* him, lose the "subject" in its genuine wholeness.[11] "Objectifying knowledge," writes a modern noted scientist, confirming the conviction of Buber, Berdyaev, Bergson and others, "is self-oblivious. In the act of knowing I come to know the object, but I do not at the same time come to know the subject, myself." [12]

Professor von Weizsäcker has vividly shown that it makes a difference how we ask the question about man, how we approach the study of man.[13]

First, we encounter physical things in space. Here subject and object are physically separate. The other—stick, stone, animal, person—is "out there." But soon I discover among those physical bodies one that is myself. I, too, am an object in space. My physical self has been discovered.

But I am not only the physical body that is seen and touched. I am also the eye that sees and the hand that touches. I am also sense perception, emotion, thought process—a "psychic" self. I may even attempt to turn this psychic self into an object of knowledge. But any such knowledge is also knowledge gained by a subject. If I turn my attention to this "subject," I discover that I cannot know it through sense experience, but only intuitively or as a logical necessity, a precondition of any knowledge at all. Here I discover, with Kant and the idealists, the "transcendental" self.

But there is still another phase of the self of whose existence we are made aware when we ask the idealist, as Kierkegaard asked Hegel: "Where do *you* stand, *you,* the man who like a god thinks about the absolute? You affirm reality, existence, after the manner of your thoughts. But before you can think, you must first exist. What, then, are the norms and values by which *your* existence is measured?" This is the crucial question for man.

How then does man have knowledge of himself He may look at life from the outside; or he may view it from inside, as one experiences it in his own inner meaning. And he soon discovers that objective information about man, like speculative thought about man, does not always agree with one's own inner history; it may not truly interpret the life it would serve. In any event, theory never relieves one of responsible choice and decision, never frees one from the response he must make to the claims which life and death, love and hate, neighbor and God make upon him.

So we return to the question about the essence of existence itself. Buber believes that the most revealing answers to this basic question have come from "the times of spiritual history in which . . . a feeling of strict and inescapable solitude took possession of man." [14] In the history of the human spirit, Buber distinguishes between "epochs of habitation" and "epochs of homelessness." It is in the "epochs of homelessness" and "in the ice of solitude that man becomes most inexorably a question to himself." [15]

Buber declares that the first thinker in the Christian West to pose the genuine anthropological question, and in the first person, was Augustine. Aristotle's tidy world, in which man had his fixed place, had long since collapsed. In a world divided against itself, the possessor of a soul divided against itself, Augustine asked in the first person: "What is man that thou art mindful of him?" He asks for the answer from the only one who can give it: *quid ergo sum, Deus meus? quae natura mea?* And here Augustine does not mean only himself; he means also *man*, the *grande profundum*.

> "This wonder of man at himself, which Augustine demands as a result of his own self-experience, is something quite different from the wonder with which Aristotle in his metaphysics makes all philosophizing begin. The Aristotelian man wonders at man . . . only as a part of a quite astonishing world. The Augustinian man wonders at that in man which cannot be understood as a part of the world, as a thing among things. . . . It is not philosophy, but it affects all future philosophy." [16]

In the centuries following, faith built a new home in which the solitary soul might dwell and know redemption. Thus it was that Dante and Aquinas knew "no special problem and no special problematic of human life, such as Augustine experienced and expressed with trembling heart." [17] There did emerge a new seriousness about man as man. Bovillus cried to man: *homo es, sistere in homine,* as Cusa before him: *homo non vult esse nisi homo.* But it remained for Luther and Pascal, living in a world no longer secure, feeling the pathos of the human problem, to ask solitary man's question about man in deadly earnestness. In an agony of spirit, they perceived that in ourselves which we cannot explain to ourselves. They came to know man's exposed and uncanny position, man's limitations, his moral misery, and the casualness of his existence in the face of eternity: *qu'est ce qu'un homme dans l'infini?* This is the attitude of the person who feels homeless; yet it is also the attitude of a being who "faces the universe" and "knows the relation between the universe and himself." [18]

Spinoza answered the problem of post-copernican man, as mediated to us by Pascal, in such a way as to deprive it of much of its uncanniness: man is a being in whom God loves himself. For as Buber writes, "Infinite substance, also called God by Spinoza . . . loves itself . . . and especially in man, for the love of the human spirit for God is only *pars infiniti amoris, quo Deus se ipsum amat.*" [19] A man who knows this is no longer a burning problematic to himself: cosmology and anthropology are reconciled, and man finds a certain security. Gœthe, a true heir of Spinoza, was made happy by "the most blissful assurance of the harmony of existence." Yet, even in Gœthe, the problem secretly festers. He, like Werther, heard "the voice of the creature completely driven into itself, lacking itself, and falling irresistibly downwards." [20] The Faustian quest for redemption finds no lasting satisfaction. In the concrete living of life there is still essential tragedy, conflict, striving, ambiguity. Like the strange creature which Rodin portrays in "The Soul and the Body," Faust cries out in passionate distress: "Two souls, alas! within my breast abide."

In Buber's account, Kant next set the task for philosophical anthropology in his four famous questions: "What can I know? What ought I to do? What may I hope? What is man?" And Kant adds: "Fundamentally all this could be reckoned as anthopology, since the first three questions are related to the last." [21] Buber adds, however, that Kant neither answered nor really attempted to answer his basic question—What is man? Kant left this harder question for others to wrestle with. This legacy has laid the foundation for contemporary philosophical anthropology.[22]

Hegel claimed to have answered the question, but in reality with him the question is obscured, even eliminated, since he ends up not with man, but with universal reason. Hegel's influence, says Buber, "can be characterized as the dispossessing of the concrete human person and the concrete human community in favor of universal reason."[23] Man is now only the principle in which Absolute Reason reaches self-consciousness. Thus Hegel sought to give man a new security. "Man's new house is to be time in the form of history whose meaning can be perfectly learned and understood." "Hegel's system," continues Buber, "is the third great attempt at security within western thought; following Aristotle's cosmological attempt and Aquinas's theological attempt, it is the logological attempt."[24] The abysmal problematical and insecurity are eliminated. Yet, protests Buber, the Hegelian house proved uninhabitable. "Thought confirms it and the world glorifies it; but the real man does not set foot in it."[25] Hegel's universe never became the real universe for real modern man. Rebellion soon set in with Kierkegaard, Feuerbach, Marx, and Nietzsche leading the attack.

Feuerbach launched his attack against Hegel in his manifesto of 1843: *Grundsätze der Philosophie der Zukunft.*[26] Its central thesis is "not the absolute, that is, the abstract, spirit—in short, not reason *in abstracto,* but man's real, whole being." Feuerbach here "makes man . . . the exclusive, universal . . . object of philosophy, and thus makes anthropology . . . the universal science."[27] But Feuerbach, by his anthropological reduction, placed man at the center in such a way as to exclude all else, including the very question *What is man?* Therefore his reduction of being "is a reduction to unproblematic man."[28] It remained for Nietzsche to deepen and sharpen, with force and passion, the real human question as the subject matter of philosophy. He, avers Buber, more than any other previous thinker, brings man into the center of his thought as a "questionable," "problematic" being. This was Nietzsche's great concern and theme—and it was to become Buber's. This was Nietzsche's importance for Buber.

Feuerbach did, however, introduce another matter which is centrally significant for this investigation, which Nietzsche neglected, and which caused Buber to say of himself: "I myself in my youth was given a decisive impetus by Feuerbach."[29] For when Feuerbach talks about man in the *Grundsätze,* he does not mean man as an individual, but *"Mensch mit Mensch—die Einheit von Ich und Du."* [30] "The individual man for himself," wrote Feuerbach, prophetically, of the thought of our age about man, "does not have man's being in himself, either as a moral or a thinking being. Man's being is contained only in community, in the unity of man with man—a unity which rests, however, only on the reality of the difference between I and Thou." [31] Here Feuerbach points to the principle which Nietzsche, Kierkegaard, and Stirner overlooked—*man in community,* the fact that man who knows the world is *man with man.* Nietzsche failed to see this because he attempted to explain the fact and origin of man solely in terms of nature and the animal world. Without including "spirit" and "community" in the equation, the other factors lead only to fragmentary and inadequate understanding. Kierkegaard missed the significance of community because for him the "crowd" is "untruth"—impersonal, faceless, formless. And to become a real person, "a Single One," [32] meant, for Kierkegaard, the prerequisite to entry into essential relation with God. Max Stirner, a pathetic solipsist and nominalist, raised the concrete individual to the lonely eminence of pure egoism and total selfishness. In his book about "The Unique One" (*den Einzigen*) man becomes "the exclusive I," the only one who has primary existence. Thus the whole question of an essential relation between himself and another is eliminated.[33]

By virtue of his nature and situation, declares Buber, man has actually a three-fold living relation, and his essential nature can be fulfilled only if he lives with his whole self in all three of these relations. Man is related, first, to the world and to things; secondly, to his fellowmen; and thirdly, to the mystery of being which the believer calls God. For Kierkegaard, Buber holds, the relation to things is lacking: "he knows them only as similes." [34] And the relation to other men is a dubious one because, in Kierkegaard's view, *the essential relation* to God is obstructed by an essential relation to human companions. In his anxiety and dread Kierkegaard's man stands "alone before God," having renounced the essential relation to others, as Kierkegaard himself had renounced the relation to his fiancée, Regina Olsen.

Marx took society as the starting point and offered men security in a perfected society, and in so doing claimed to have answered the human problem in the form of a secularized Messianism based on

Hegel's historical dialectic. But in Marx the home in which man is to dwell is not a vision of the universe but "only an image of society," more precisely, "the image of the way by which human society is to reach perfection," and built on the conditions of production alone.[35] But it becomes increasingly evident that human society provides no final protection from convulsions of the cosmos, and that collectivism offers no real deliverance of men from their isolation. Rather it destroys the very living bonds which make them persons. Marx's promised security has perished in the chaos of historical convulsion.[36] There is no calm security. A new dread has arisen. "The question about man's being faces us as never before in all its grandeur and terror." [37]

"Only in our time has the anthropological problem reached maturity, that is, come to be recognized and treated as an independent philosophical problem." [38] In these words, Buber is referring not only to the crisis in man's understanding of himself, but also to the cultural crisis of our times which is the occasion of modern man's "burning problematic"—his feeling of solitude, estrangement, and cosmic homelessness. For in our epoch, "Man is sick, both in his relations to others and in his very soul." [39]

The archetypal spiritual problem of contemporary man, according to Buber, is called in another place "the eclipse of God, the eclipse of the light of heaven." We have forsaken God, or, like Job, we seem to be "forsaken of God," fated to spend our lives in a dreadful time of God's "hiddenness," of God's silence, when man either does not hear God's address or is unable to recognize and interpret God's word in history. Such, as Buber sees it, is the character, the purport, and the spiritual agony of the historic hour through which the world is now passing. This silence of the transcendent, in the face of the patent religious need and demand of modern man, is the problem which torments Nietzsche, Heidegger, Jaspers, Sarte, Jung,—and Buber.[40]

The ancient command, "Know Thyself!" still stands. This admonition appeared to Buber and to Mead as relevant in this time as it was to ancient Greece.[41] Thus it is that in our day Freud and Sullivan, Niebuhr and Sartre, to mention only a few, try to describe what Thomas Aquinas so differently and less ambiguously defined in his day. The medieval theologian knew well enough what he meant by the "soul" and its "salvation." Modern men are not so sure; indeed, they scarcely believe they have a soul. Still men ask, in divers accents: "What must I do to be saved?" For even after man's soul or mind is dissolved away under the merciless scrutiny of certain modern psychologies, he continues to be fretfully aware of himself and of the world around him,—to hope and plan and dare and suffer. When even second-rate novelists cast their stories in terms of an analysis of the nature of man, it is not surprising that theologians and philosophers write books about anthropology—especially with reference to the problem of how man is to live with himself and with his fellows. No other problem has in recent years been more frequently employed as the starting point and core of serious discussion.[42]

An increasing number of first-rate thinkers are confronting us with the proposition that man's essence is not to be found in isolated individuals, but in his bonds with his generation and his society. It is from this platform that Buber criticizes two notable contemporary attempts at an answer: those of Martin Heidegger and Max Scheler, one of whom considers man in his self-being, the other of whom does consider man's relations, but regards them as impairing his real essence. In Buber's own words: " . . . Scheler, who, though a sociologist, scarcely noticed man's social connections in his anthropological thought, and . . . Heidegger, who certainly recognized that these connections were primary but treated them essentially as the great obstacle to man's attainment of himself." [43] Thus Heidegger's system, in many respects, is a philosophical secularization of Kierkegaard.

In contrast to this individualistic anthropology, Buber holds: "Only the man who realizes in his whole life with his whole being the relations possible to him helps us to know man truly." And again: "The way to the answer lies through the man who overcomes his solitude without forfeiting its questioning power." [44] That is to say that the central subject of this renewed interest in man "is neither the individual nor the collective but man with man. That essence of man which is special to him can be directly known only in a living relation." [45] We must know what these bonds of relation really mean if we want to know the essence of man. This discovery of the *Thou,* first announced by Feuerbach, has been called "the Copernican revolution" of modern thought, "an elemental happening which is just as rich in consequences as the idealist discovery of the I," and "is bound to lead to a new beginning of European thought, pointing beyond the Cartesian contribution to modern philosophy." [46]

In America, traveling by a different route, and feeling little of the urgency born of cultural crisis, Mead arrived at a similar conclusion respecting the need for re-examining the theory and practice of modern man. But Mead called for a revision in the direction of a naturalistic and functional doctrine of mind, self, and society.

The realization of impending disaster and disintegration was borne in upon sensitive Europeans before it came to Americans like Mead. Indeed, the progress of the sickness of civilization was actually more advanced in Europe than in America; and the mounting despair and questioning of the visionary "prophets of doom" made little sense to people tanned by the sun of American optimism.[47]

Mead, as a matter of fact, had turned his back upon Europe, thinking that the "furniture" of the Old World was incongruous in the new home. Even Royce's warm and luminous idealism was, for Mead, "part of the escape from the crudity of American life, not an interpretation of it."[48] It was out of his attempt to formulate a philosophy indigenous to the spirit and practice of America that Mead's social idealism arose. And he turned to social psychology as a way of elucidating our experience, partly because American social psychology represented a reaction both from the abstract atomistic individualism of traditional English psychology, and from the social realism of continental psychology.

Mead died in 1931; so he never experienced deeply the period of paralyzing economic depression, unrestrained butcheries and enslavements, and the second world-ravaging war. Living in America, on the frontier,[49] Mead felt all the beneficent promises of the twentieth century, but few of its evil fulfillments. He believed that the creative forces of life and freedom were on the side of the men of science and intelligent good will; and furthermore, the means for building the good society exist naturally in the present. In his lectures, *The Movements of Thought in the Nineteenth Century,* Mead was centrally concerned with methodology throughout, using his theme of research science as the key for interpreting the entire period. There is the sense of "movement," of progressive change, of evolutionary development of ideas and systems; but little indication of impending catastrophe. Mead recognized that ideas and systems, including his own, have social roots, but in one sense his discernment of the "signs of the times" was very uncritical of those roots. Therefore Mead's interpretation of and response to the changes in thought and culture, and the resulting answers to the issues and discontents of our era, are very different from those of

Buber, the European Jew, as he wrestled with the Jewish problem and the larger spiritual problem of mankind.

Mead stood for many of the things which Buber condemned: the stress upon science and material progress as the starting point of man's endeavor, the value of the objective and analytical approach, the substituting of a secular moral relativism for the sense of transcendent and eternal values. In Buber's view, these were some of the very causes of the cultural sickness. From his standpoint, it would appear that Mead failed to see that his "remedy" only hastened the breakdown.[50] In his fight against Victorian ideals and romantic idealisms, Mead was unwittingly feeding the flames which his own humane and optimistic social philosophy was designed to quench.

But Mead was aware of no crisis so severe that failure to find a solution for the urgent problems of human relations would threaten man's very existence. It was Buber of the two who realized that "powers of darkness," both within and without, engage man in hostilities and perversions which may end in self-destruction unless there is a renewal within man and between man.

Still, if our thesis is tenable, these two thinkers of such divergent background, experience and method, succeeded in calling our attention to a simple and familiar reality to which we had been unaccountably blind: namely, the fact and significance of relations between persons and of the social nature of reality.

The fundamental problem of all men and all eras, and therefore of all philosophy, is the relation of the individual to the whole of things. It is also to the solution of this problem that Mead, along with Buber, devoted the earnest endeavors of his seminal mind. As Mead writes: "Stating it in as broad a form as I can, this is the philosophical problem that faces the community at the present time. How are we to get the universality involved, the general statement which must go with any interpretation of the world and still make use of the differences which belong to the individual as an individual?" [51] Martin Buber, the man of faith, would add: "We may come nearer the answer to the question what is man when we come to see him as the eternal meeting of the One with the Other." [52]

Against this background of cultural crisis and currents of thought, as sketched briefly in the preceding pages, Mead and Buber are to be viewed as they react in criticism and constructive suggestion. One is tempted to write at length of the cultural crisis, its sources and symptoms. But enough has been said to set the stage for our thesis; namely, that a significant new understanding of man is developing in which Mead and Buber play major roles. The collapse of the assumptions and systems of recent decades calls for re-examination. It remains to be seen whether and in what respects their views are more adequate in the face of the present crisis. We proceed, then, to an inspection of Mead's theory of self and society, to be followed in Chapter III by an analysis of Buber's *I and Thou* theme.

NOTES

1. See e.g., C. W. Morris, *Six Theories of Mind* (University of Chicago Press, 1932). Cf. John Dewey, *The Quest for Certainty* (New York: Minton, Balch & Co., 1929), pp. 290, 291; Arthur O. Lovejoy, *The Revolt Against Dualism* (Chicago: Open Court Pub. Co., 1930).

2. Buber's interest in the nature of man is most explicit in his inaugural lectures which he delivered in the Hebrew University of Jerusalem in 1938 under the title *Was ist der Mensch?* These lectures were later published as *Das Problem des Menschen* (Heidelberg: Verlag Lambert Schneider, 1948). Translated *What is Man?* they appear as Section V of *Between Man and Man* (London: Kegan Paul, 1947). A similar interest is also found in nearly all of Mead's writings, especially in his essays on education, sociology, social work, psychology, politics, ethics, and philanthropy.

3. See, especially, *Was ist der Mensch, loc. cit.,* and Buber's recent work, *Eclipse of God* (New York: Harper, 1952).

4. Buber, as a religious existentialist, would place the stress on the *sum* of Descartes' famous phrase. Buber is one of those who helped develop *das neue Denken,* the heart of which is the idea of "making" truth true (Bewahrung) by decision, commitment and venture, into its place of great influence in Europe. It is similar to what Emil Brunner means when he speaks of the "knowledge of faith" or "existential" knowledge. And Mead, in America, was one of the four outstanding pragmatists who developed the pragmatic "new thinking," the others being Peirce, James, and Dewey.

5. See e.g., John Cullberg's study, *Das Du und die Wirklichkeit; zum ontologischen Hintergrund der Gemeinschaftskategorie* (Uppsala: A.-b. Lundequistska bokhandeln, 1933). Buber claims no monopoly on his central thesis. He traces its source to Feuerbach, and before the publication of *I and Thou* Eugen Rosenstock-Huessy had begun to develop his very similar philosophy of *speech.* According to Cullberg's study, it was Ferdinand Ebner who rediscovered the I-Thou relation which we know through Buber's writings. Ebner was one of the most original religious thinkers of our time. An unknown Austrian school-teacher (1882–1931) he came to his germinal insight out of personal suffering and from the experience that the "I" of contemporary man is Thou-less. The isolation of the individual and his estrangement from his

fellows is regarded as the mortal malady of modern man. The search for God as a search for the Thou, and the conviction that in the relation between persons there is a unique spiritual quality, are Ebner's central themes. See his book, *Das Wort und die Geistigen Realitäten* (1921) and his recently published diaries, *Das Wort ist der Weg* (Wien: Herder, 1950). Ebner's work contains the seed in his fragmentary utterances; but Buber, whose *Ich und Du* was not published until 1923, gives us a much more complete and penetrating statement of the I-Thou theme. In America, as we shall see, James Mark Baldwin and Charles H. Cooley were among the pioneers.

6. This section follows the general tenor of Buber's extended and brilliant treatment in *Das Problem des Menschen* (Heidelberg: Verlag Lambert Schneider, 1948); see also *BMM*, pp. 118-205. These lectures are in the main an historical survey of some of the great thinkers who have raised the question seriously from Aristotle up to Heidegger and Scheler. He also gives, against this background, his own understanding of and wrestle with the problem.

7. *BMM*, p. 12f; see also *BMM*, pp. 119f.

8. *Idem*. See also Erich Fromm, *Man For Himself* (New York: Rinehart, 1947), p. 7. Cf. C. F. von Weizsäcker, *The History of Nature* (Chicago: University of Chicago Press, 1949); also Gardner Murphy, *Personality* (New York: Harper, 1947).

9. Cf. Rousseau's query, "Ne connaitrons-nous jamais l'homme?" or Pascal's "qu'est ce qu'un homme dans l'infini?" or the Psalmist's cry, "What is man that Thou art mindful of him?"

10. In the Foreword to *De la recherche de la verité* (1674).

11. Buber, *BMM*, p. 122. This is also a central theme in Berdyaev, with whose personalism Buber's affinities are many and remarkable. See e.g., Berdyaev, *Solitude and Society* (New York: Charles Scribner's Sons, 1937) which carried the original title of *I and the World of Objects*.

12. C. F. von Weizsäcker, *op. cit.*, p. 145.

13. *Ibid.*, pp. 145ff.

14. *BMM*, p. 126.

15. *Idem*.

16. *Ibid.*, p. 128.

17. *Ibid.*, p. 129.

18. *Ibid.*, p. 132.

19. *Ibid.*, p. 134.

20. Quoted by Buber, *Ibid.*, p. 135.

21. In the *Handbook* to his lectures on logic; quoted by Buber in *BMM*, p. 119.

22. See e.g., Bernard Groethuysen, in *Philosophy and History*, Editors, Raymond Klibansky and H. J. Paton (Oxford University Press, 1936), pp. 77-93. Groethuysen, like Buber, was a student of Wilhelm Dilthey, the founder of the history of philosophical anthropology. In his work *Philosophical Anthropology* (1931) Groethuysen says of Aristotle that while he recognized man as a social and political animal, he never really explored that special dimension in which man knows himself as he can know himself alone. Man is comprehended in the world, but the world is not comprehended in him. Man is known as a "he," an object of study, not an "I." Man, for Aristotle, was

a thing among things, a species beside other species, but not comprehended as "I myself," the "problematic."

23. *BMM*, p. 137.

24. *Ibid.*, p. 139.

25. *Ibid.*, p. 140.

26. The references which follow are taken from Feuerbach, *Philosophie der Zukunft* (Stuttgart: Fr. Frommanns Verlag (H. Kurtz), 1922).

27. *Ibid.*, #54.

28. Buber, *BMM*, p. 147.

29. *Ibid.*, p. 148.

30. *Op. cit.*, #60.

31. Feuerbach, *Philosophie der Zukunft*, #59.

32. The German which is here rendered "the Single One" is *der Einzelne*, which is a fairly precise parallel of Kierkegaard's *hiin Enkelte*. See *Die Frage an den Einzelnen*, translated as *The Question to the Single One* in *BMM*. The phrase is a bit odd and cumbrous, but closer to the true meaning than the customary "'individual."

33. An English translation of Stirner's book, by S. C. Byington, was published under the title *The Ego and His Own* (London: A. C. Fifield, 1913).

34. *BMM*, p. 177.

35. *Ibid.*, p. 143.

36. See Buber's study of the movements for the reform of society along collectivist lines in the 19th century, *Paths in Utopia* (New York: Macmillan, 1950).

37. *BMM*, p. 145.

38. *BMM*, p. 157. Cf. Max Scheler: "We are the first epoch in which man has become fully and thoroughly 'problematic' to himself; in which he no longer knows what he essentially is, but at the same time also *knows* that he does not know." (Quoted in *BMM*, p. 182)

39. *Ibid.*, p. 196. Cf. Lewis Mumford, *The Condition of Man* (New York: Harcourt, Brace & Co., 1944), pp. 391-423; also Nietzsche, *Beyond Good and Evil*, #208. Cf. also the writings of J. Maritain, Christopher Dawson, Elton Trueblood, Paul Tillich, Emil Brunner, and Albert Schweitzer. Arnold J. Toynbee, *A Study of History* (D. C. Somervell abridgement, p. 429) speaks of an "inward and spiritual rift" in the souls of men. The standard pattern of a sick society, he writes, appears to be a "schism of the body social" but the underlying and more essential concomitant of disintegration is the "schism in the soul." See also *PIU*, pp. 129, 130, 148, *passim*.

40. See *Eclipse of God*, esp. Chaps. II and V.

41. See Mead, in *IJE*, XXXIX (1929), 394. It is clear, however, that Mead never experienced this question as the dreadful "problematic" that Buber and the other existentialist thinkers feel with respect to it.

42. To list only a few titles: Martin Buber, *Between Man and Man;* Ernst Cassirer, *An Essay on Man;* Reinhold Niebuhr, *The Nature and Destiny of Man;* Ralph Linton, *The Study of Man;* J. Maritain, *Humanisme Integral;* E. G. Conklin, *Man: Real and Ideal;* Erich Fromm, *Man For Himself;* MacNeile Dixon, *The Human Situation;* Lewis Mumford, *The Condition of Man;* Charles Sherrington, *Man on His Nature;* N. Berdyaev, *Solitude and*

Society; The Destiny of Man; Elton Trueblood, *The Predicament of Modern Man;* C. G. Jung, *Modern Man in Search of a Soul;* Karl Menninger, *Man Against Himself;* Alexis Carrel, *Man the Unknown;* E. E. Aubrey, *Man's Search for Himself,* etc., etc.

43. *BMM,* p. 160.
44. *Ibid.,* p. 199.
45. *Ibid.,* p. 205.
46. Karl Heim, *Ontologie und Theologie* (1930), p. 133; also *Glaube und Denken* (1931), p. 405f. The English translation, *God Transcendent,* was made from this third, revised, and shortened, and more orthodox edition. For a similar judgment, refer to the works of Emil Brunner, especially *The Divine-Human Encounter* (Philadelphia: Westminster, 1943).
47. It must be noted, of course, that even in America there were voices of protest, calling for reform and predicting the approaching disaster. See e.g., *The Education of Henry Adams* (New York: 1918). Cf. also Vernon L. Parrington, *Main Currents in American Thought,* Vols. II and III (New York: Harcourt, Brace & Co., 1927–30).
48. *IJE,* XL (1929–30), 222-223.
49. Mead agreed with Professor Frederick Jackson Turner in his concept of the "frontier" and the "pioneer" as giving the key to the interpretation of the history of the American community and its unique development. See *The Frontier in American History* (New York: Holt, 1921).
50. Emil Brunner, in *Christianity and Civilization* (2 vols., New York: Scribner, 1948–49), Vol. I, also asserts that science has given us mastery over things, but we seem unable to turn away from the road to ruin.
51. *MT,* p. 417.
52. *BMM,* p. 205.

Chapter Two

Mead's Doctrine of Mind, Self, and Society

GEORGE HERBERT MEAD was an American philosopher and social psychologist, a pragmatist of the so-called "Chicago School," a brilliant lecturer and beloved teacher who, through his students more than through his fragmentary writings, has significantly influenced the development of American social philosophy.[1] His was "a seminal mind of the very first order,"[2] but he gave his views no written, systematic presentation adequate to their importance. An original and independent thinker, Mead developed a functional, bio-social theory of mind and self, based upon rigorous scientific, behavioristic methodology and the principle of continuity, which sees man as a distinctive expression of nature. Consequently, he is best remembered for his genetic analysis of mind, self, and society as emergents out of a bio-social process, his analysis of symbolic interaction, and his detailed empirical description of the *mechanism* of "role-taking" and language as basic to the correlative rise of the self and cognitive meanings. The major problem of social philosophy is to harmonize individual interests with the common welfare. And, for Mead, the new science of "social psychology" is "the study of the experience and behavior of the individual organism or self in its dependence upon the social group."[3] Mead thought that he could solve this and other related problems if he could show that psychologically the individual self is really "social" in essence; furthermore, that social amelioration (as well as a valid social philosophy) would flow differentially from his account of the self.

George Herbert Mead was born in 1863, in South Hadley, Massachusetts, into the home of a Yankee parson from whom he inherited a grim Puritan theology and a robust probing mind. In 1870 the family moved to Oberlin, Ohio, where his father was to teach homiletics in the new seminary. Mead entered Oberlin College in 1879, and was graduated in 1883. Graduate study took him to Harvard (1887-88) and on to Berlin to study philosophy and psychology. In 1891 he joined the Philosophy Department at the University of Michigan where John Dewey, James H. Tufts and Charles H. Cooley were also teaching. Two years later he accompanied Dewey to the newly-founded University of Chicago where he remained until his death, April 26, 1931.

An inheritance of the best in the New England tradition, life in the rugged democratic West, advanced study at Harvard, travel and study in Europe—all these contributed to produce a man of many interests, cosmopolitan culture, wide horizons, moral earnestness, and generous human concerns. Mead studied with Royce and James and Palmer. Tarde and Simmel and Wundt contributed to his thinking. He knew well the work of Bergson, Adam Smith, James Mark Baldwin, Giddings, and Thurstone. He taught with Cooley at Michigan and with A. W. Moore, Tufts, and Dewey at Chicago, the latter becoming his life-long friend and co-worker in pressing the claims of scientific pragmatism as the philosophical system most germane to modern life in America. In all important respects Mead's general position is the same as John Dewey's. There is, for example, the same notion of mind as social and functional; the same emphasis upon the instrumental functioning of thought in the service of conduct; the same conviction that mind is the symbolic functioning of events, "an evolution in nature in which culminates the sociality which is the principle and the form of emergence";[4] the same position that symbols are social in nature, and that language is the matrix of mind and meaning.

Mead's major academic interests were in Social Psychology, Ethics, History of Philosophy, and the Philosophy of Science. He gave brillian courses in Aristotle, Hume, Kant, and Hegel. But probably Dewey, Bergson, and Whitehead held the places of honor in his esteem, for these three he regarded as the vanguard of modern thought. All of these great figures whom he liked best to interpret were like facets of his own personality; yet he was no mere follower of any of them.

Mead responded to the optimistic moral challenge of the scientific age and the American frontier. In meeting that challenge he made much of scientific method and of its uses for philosophy. Trained in the Hegelian tradition, he soon transformed that idealism into a pragmatic "social idealism" which included reliance upon experimental science, the moral values of democracy, empirical naturalism, historical and psychological relativism, the primacy of experience, and the employment of biological and sociological categories in the consideration of philosophical and psychological problems.[5]

THE NATURE OF THE PSYCHICAL

In his remarkable but difficult essay on "The Definition of the Psychical," [6] Mead had early declared that the attitude and methodological presuppositions of the psychologist determine his definition of the "psychical," and with that the very material and subject-matter of Psychology as a science. One tends to find what he is looking for. Mead's own earlier rebellion against the traditional psychologies and philosophies (and theologies) which had prevailed since Descartes, and his preference for the ideas of men like James, Dewey, Peirce, and Bergson, had led him to try to clear his skirts of traditional metaphysics, epistemology, and formal logic. Metaphysics, certainly in so far as it implies meta-experience, was, for him, futile and without meaning. His concern was to develop a world-view in which science— particularly as it was complicated and enriched by the new concepts of evolution and relativity physics—might be used for purposes of human prediction and control, and toward the goal of an expanded good for all men. Taking a pragmatic standpoint, Mead, along with Dewey and Alfred Lloyd, had begun to develop a utilitarian and instrumentalist logic,[7] a logic which would describe and organize the effective procedures of working science as they could observe it in actual practice. "The problem of knowledge," Mead reiterated again and again, "is not to find out how we can get from a state of mind to an object outside the mind, but how an intelligence that lies within nature can so reorganize its experience that the activities of the inhibited individual can proceed." [8] The test of knowing is the test of the hypothesis—i.e., does it work? does it achieve successful adjustment? Logic is the "natural history of thought"; and it is derivative and continuous with other types of human activity. It grows out of something and for the sake of something.[9]

The effect of this general temper and movement in philosophy led Mead into a behavioristic approach to psychology, in terms of which the "psychical" is not a "content of consciousness," but the cognitive act of the mind. Sensations are not psychical; they are merely parts of the data which define the conditions under which any given problem is to be solved. The mind is not a substance and it is not located in the brain; rather, it is the functioning of significant symbols. Such symbols arise, Mead holds, only in a social process.[10] By the same token, the self is not a content, but an activity: an activity defined in terms of analysis and reconstruction. The Ego or the "I" is the analytic and synthetic processes of cognition; the "me" is the empirical self, the object of science.[11] In other words, the "psychical" is not a substance but a continuous process, a distinctive kind of purposive behavior, appearing within nature, within the conduct of biological organisms equipped with a certain kind of central nervous system. The psychical refers to no transcendent soul, entity, or spiritual stuff, rather to an emergent functional activity of the organism in the face of a problematic situation. The process of problem solving, or organizing conflicting tendencies into successful adjustment, is the work of the so-called "psychical."

But for Mead this psychical process is "social" in character. There is no signification without reference to both self and others.[12] That is to say that mind is socially constituted, at the level of cooperative behavior; but, on Mead's account, mind is restricted to *human* social behavior which involves the use of language ("significant symbol") beginning in play and gesture.[13] Thinking, on this view, is implicit speech, the internalized conversation of gestures and attitudes with one's self playing a dual inner role. "It is through the ability to be the other at the same time that he is himself that the symbol becomes significant." [14] Sociality, on Mead's view, is thus seen to be the ultimate explanation of mind, self, and society, and to be inseparably linked with the occurrence in nature of the novel—"sociality" being defined as the capacity for being several things at once or playing several roles simultaneously.

From this point of view, then, the ultimate unit of existence is the *act*[15]—the self-caused, self-sustaining, ongoing behavior of the organism, initiated by want or problem, and directed to the end of satisfying the want or solving the problem by means of the available elements in the environment. Consciousness, usually defined in vague, ambiguous, and static terms, is now conceived behavioristically as ongoing, purposive life-process and interaction. Mind is no longer viewed as a kind of spiritual stuff, a trans-empirical state or substance, or even a *tabula rasa* which receives sensory impressions from without.[16] Mind or consciousness is rather an "instrument" in the service of the organism's better adjustment to its environment. It is volitional as well as sensory. It seems to have likes and dislikes; it attentively selects and rejects its content.

Among Mead's chief mentors was William James, of whom he thought highly as being in line with the new orientation in psychology and philosophy.[17] Of the many things in James's thought which appealed to Mead,[18] there are two major items which need to be underscored: (1) James's ideas about "consciousness" or mind as selective, functional, and relational; and (2) his ideas about the nature and criteria of knowledge wherein thinking (ideas, hypotheses) is a part of action, and action finds its fulfillment, norm, and test in consequences. The organism operates interestedly and selectively within the total environment, and the manifold of elements selected make up the mind's content. This active unity of consciousness is teleological, willful. It attends to this or that within a "theatre of simultaneous possibilities" and thus "carves out" its own world from the stream of experience.[19] It then proceeds to express itself in whatever action may prove fruitful.[20] On this view, obviously, the mind is not a substance or state or entity which mirrors the environment; it is rather a certain grouping of contents derived from environment.[21] In a certain spatial system these elements constitute nature; in another system of relations, perhaps intersecting with the first, these same elements make up "the inner history of a person." This unique grouping of the elements or contents of experience constitutes the "individualized self," a specific experience-complex, a center of interest and activity which can be located.[22]

The *unity* of consciousness, upon which James insisted, consists in its complete "connectedness" or continuity. It is like a flowing stream in which the "substantive parts" flow into one another through the "transitive parts," and in which every object is accompanied by a "feeling of tendency" through which it passes over into another.[23] James's theory of knowledge was dominated by three main points: (1) it emphasized the categories of will, interest, selective attention; (2) it pointed to satisfactory working as the test of any idea or hypothesis; and (3) it reduced relations, substances, activities and other alleged transcendent elements to the continuities of sense-experience.

Of these three notions, the first led to James's *voluntarism;* the second to his *pragmatism;* the third to his *radical empiricism.*[24] Mead has his roots in the same soil.

Obviously, the whole orientation of knowledge was changed by these suggestions and concepts, and the repercussions produced a reconstruction within philosophy. The validity and efficacy—the *truth*—of any alleged knowledge can, on this new view, be determined not by its agreement with any pre-existent norm or reality, but by its solution of the problem within which the act finds itself.

Mead followed with gusto James's attack on the traditional concept of consciousness prevalent at the time.[25] He came to believe that much of what had been called "consciousness" must be returned to the objective world of behavior.[26] Psychology must be freed from its involvement with a philosophy of mental states.

So the world provides the data and materials and conditions for the act; the selective, impulsive, end-seeking organism provides the want, the hypothesis, and the end toward which the act moves. For Mead, the Ego is an *act.* "It is an act that makes use of all the data that reflection can present, but uses them merely as the conditions of the new world that cannot possibly be foretold from them."[27] The "I" appears to be free; it is an *activity,* not a *content.* "It is the self of unconditioned choice, of undreamt hypothesis, of inventions that change the whole face of nature."[28] The act is self-caused by the individual whose reasons for movement lie within himself, rather than in another.[29] But self-causation here means, not the cause of the act by a private inner being, but rather causation by the elements of the act itself. Therefore, this living process, which is presently incomplete and has a part of its action in the future, is a "process in which the later events in the experience control the acts which express the process."[30]

Such considerations prompted Mead to substitute *temporal* concepts and distinctions for the more familiar spatial ones; in other words, he defined the act in terms of *process* rather than in terms of structure, in terms of continuous, incomplete experience which unfolds as the act proceeds. The act, then, is an ongoing event in which the end toward which it moves defines the want, provides direction, and regulates its expression. It is important to note that the end of the act is present at the beginning as a want, a problem, a deficiency, an impulse to be released, a satisfaction to be found. The act is thus self-stimulating and self-sustaining, since it provides both the need or deficiency, the attempt to meet the need, and the repeated reinforcement of the need.[31]

Wants or impulses, writes Mead, "will be good to the degree that they reinforce themselves and expand and give expression to other impulses as well." [32] Thus not only in biology but also in ethics, Mead associated himself with the functional psychology and pragmatic philosophy which emphasize the ongoing continuum of experience and permit no separation between ends and means.[33] *Doing* is more fundamental than knowing, or being, certainly in the sense of function having primacy over knowing or being. Knowing is for the sake of action, for purposes of conduct and future control. Knowing begins in doing and has doing as its end. What is known must be true in the sense that it conforms to our experience. Ideas, according to Mead, have the character of actions directed toward the achieving of some goal or the attaining of some end. This, of course, is the familiar pragmatic notion that ideas are not true in themselves, but merely represent labor-saving devices for dealing with the varied and chaotic manifold of sensations. Ideas are only tools, plans of action. It is clear that, for Mead, mind is both instrumental and symbolic in its nature and functioning.

The teleological and instrumental nature of the act suggests its division into three phases or stages. As ongoing activity, the act falls, logically and temporally, into the stages of *impulse, stimulus,* and *response*—corresponding, respectively, to *want, interest,* and *satisfaction.* This relationship of the response to the stimulus, mediated by interest, becomes of very great importance in Mead's analysis of perception and behavior. Therefore, we must consider it in some detail.

We have just indicated that William James had called attention to the fact of selective interest in conscious activity. Later John Dewey elaborated on this thesis in his noted article on the stimulus-response concept.[34] There he pointed out that the attitude of being acted upon by a stimulus is continually affected by the response. The process of responding determines the way in which we receive our impressions. That is to say, the organism is not simply *receiving* impressions and then answering them. The organism is *doing* something; it is actively seeking and selecting certain stimuli. For example, when one is hungry, he is sensitive to the odors of food. Whatever one is doing, or whatever one needs, will determine the selection of the sort of stimuli which will set free certain appropriate responses which are there ready for release. The attitude or action determines what the stimulus will be. In our acting, we select those elements in the field of stimulation which will set the response free. This, says Mead, is the basis of behavioristic psychology.[35] "Stimuli do nothing more than enable (the person) to do what he is all ready to do." [36] The environment exists as means for the act. The stimulus is only an opportunity for the act, not a command.

An *impulse* is the felt want or the feeling of incompletion projecting the need of the organism into the environment, relating the organism to the environment both selectively and then responsively, both actively and passively. By the active aspect, Mead refers to the impulse seeking expression.[37] This means that, in a sense, the organism creates its own environment, defines its own world. The physical object is thus a mental construct and a percept is a "collapsed act." [38] By the passive aspect, Mead refers to the impulse as requiring release: "a congenital tendency to react in a specific manner to a certain sort of stimulus, under certain organic conditions." [39]

A *stimulus,* in Mead's analysis, is what he calls "an object of interest" because it is that in the environment which sets free the impulse, the tendency to act in a certain way.[40] A stimulus is any concrete particular which is of interest to the active organism because it falls within the general category defined by the impulse as capable of releasing it.[41] By thus regarding the stimulus as an answer to the impulse rather than as the first cause of a compulsive reaction, Mead tries to avoid the old mechanistic "stimulus-response fallacy." This fallacy, committed by Watson, is simply the mechanistic dogma that the behavior of the organism is completely determined by the environment. Over against this view is that of Mead who contends that the environment is, at least to a degree, determined by the selective sensitivity of the organism.[42]

The significance of Mead's quarrel with Watson can be seen at just this point.[43] Watson's version of behaviorism, in Mead's judgment, was too extreme, too mechanistic, dependent too much on data derived from the study of animals, and much too indifferent to the *fact* of *private experience.*[44] Mead wanted to retain the truth about the "inner" and creative aspects of consciousness, to bring it into the scope of behavioristic treatment, while purging it of its connotations of static structure and spiritual substance. Mind, he insisted, can be explained in behavioristic or non-mentalistic terms without reducing it to a mere stimulus-response arc, thus really explaining it away and denying its existence as such.[45]

Consequently, while Mead was a behaviorist, his behaviorism does not reduce the world to the visible and the overt, to movements of nerves and muscles. He does, however, insist that action and objective behavior are centrally important and that the objects of this world are functions of impulses seeking expression. Mind is not mere non-mental motor reactions, but a special type of behavior genetically emergent out of non-mental processes in social experience. Mead, then, was a *social behaviorist*,[46] in the sense that he starts with an observable activity of biological forms within a dynamic, ongoing social process. He starts from the outside and works in—emphasizing the act of the individual in its social setting while recognizing those parts of the act which belong to the individual *qua* individual and which do not come to external observation. Consequently his approach to human behavior and the resulting pragmatic naturalism was through the door of social psychology rather than by way of biology, ethics, or logic, as was true respectively of James, Dewey, and Peirce.

Mead was also critical of Watson's concept of language and thought as merely "implicit laryngeal behavior." As Professor Faris, Mead's noted student and interpreter, remarks: "It may provoke a laugh for a behaviorist to refer to his indecision by saying: 'On that point I have not yet made up my larynx.'"[47] For Mead, language is the highly developed and objective expression of symbolic communication within a social group. It is a complex gesture situation, and even when internalized in thought, it remains social, i.e., a way of evoking in the individual by his own gestures the attitudes of others who are implicated in the common activity. The difficulties of studying mind objectively are hardly warrant for the conclusion that man has no mind and therefore cannot think.

In the three phases of the act, the *response* is the reply to the stimulus terminating the chain of reactions set in motion by the impulsive act of the form in selecting its stimulus.[48] It is the attempted completion or the satisfaction of the want or need. Whereas the *impulse* is the initial and potential tendency of the organism in the direction of the object which may satisfy its want; and whereas the *stimulus* represents that environment which may effect the release of the impulse; the *response* is the actual verification of the interest in the stimulus by an external adjustment to it—and thereby satisfying the want or need. Impulse and response, on this view, are the subjective poles of a reciprocal relation in which the stimulus is at the objective pole. This fits in with the pragmatic doctrine that things are real only in so far as they constitute the objects of our desires. That is to say, objects are defined in terms of conduct; hence Mead's theory that *social consciousness* must precede *physical consciousness*. As Mead puts it:

> Whatever our theory may be as to the history of things, social consciousness must antedate physical consciousness. A more correct statement would be that experience in its original form became reflective in the recognition of selves, and only gradually was there differentiated a reflective experience of things which are purely physical.[49]

It becomes clear that, in Mead's analysis, the impulse functions as a "universal" for which the stimulus is a particular occasion. By the same token, the response also functions as a universal by remaining the same in spite of a variety of particular stimuli.[50] This "universality" is reflected in behavioristic terms in the "identity" of the response. "In the experience of individuals they (the identical responses) are the criteria by which we identify the universal character in things. Whatever one tends to sit down in is a chair." [51] It also is clear that it is the response which endows the environment with the *meaning* and *structure* which it has for the organism. The environment first exists merely as the external objective of the impulse seeking a means of satisfaction. In the response are integrated the universality of the impulse and the particularity of the stimuli.[52] The world provides the data and the self provides the hypothesis for the solution of the problematic situation. Stated in somewhat different terms, the two poles of this subject-object relation are the "I" and the "me." The "me" is the empirical self which belongs to the world which it is the function of this phase of consciousness to reconstruct.[53] But it is the "I" that effects the reconstruction. The result of the reconstruction will be a new empirical self, as well as a new social environment. The psychical is the name for this synthetic activity of the living form.

That the categories which organize and explain this development are reminiscent of the dialectic of Fichte and the social philosophy of idealism is made clear in Mead's treatment of Fichte, with whose thought Mead's "philosophy of the act" has obvious affinities. Thus Mead writes of Fichte:

> For the individual the world is always a task to be accomplished. It is not simply there by chance, as something that just happens. It is there because one realizes it as a field for one's endeavors. It is not a world simply in so far as there are sensations, in so far as there is the movement of masses of bodies. It is a world, a real thing, just to the extent that one constructs it, that one organizes it for one's action. The objects about one are means of conduct. They take on meaning in proportion as one uses them as means. The ground is something to tread upon. The objects about one are all implements. The universe is a field of action. It is organized only in so far as one acts in it. Its meaning lies in the conduct of the individual. . . . This is the only way in which he can achieve a self.[54]

THE NATURE OF THOUGHT

In his definition of the psychical, Mead is saying that *thinking* is the internalized carrying on of a social conversation with one's self: it is "talking to one's self." But beyond that it is the *beginning of the act.* By means of internalized inter-play of self and other, testing alternative solutions in an inner dialectic, the individual arrives at what may be considered the appropriate response. By functioning in this manner, the individual is able to anticipate the total problematic situation in advance of overt action.

This psycho-physico-social organism we call man is in constant and dynamic connection with his world, and within his complex experience there are dynamic functional connections between the most abstract-logical and the most concrete-emotional phases of experience and those more elementary factors which we call motor, sensory, perceptual, etc. There are no structural cleavages between environment and organism, nor within the conscious processes of the organism.[55] Content and process cannot be separated within this protoplasmic, neutral stuff which is neither physical nor psychical. Thoughts are continuous with sensations, conations, affections, etc. All thought is a way of behaving; specifically it is a mode of responding and adjusting to resolve a conflict between a new situation and old modes of action, between a present exception and an old "law" which is seen to be no longer adequate. And this, avers Mead, is essentially the method of science.

Thought always has its setting and source in a social situation. Thought is an inner conversation of gesture between selves, an internalization of the speech process, in which "selves" are a part of our own inner self-consciousness.[56] It is not necessary that we talk to another to have ideas and attitudes in our minds. We can talk to ourselves, and this is exactly what we do in the "inner forum" of thought.[57] Thinking is an inner, symbolic dialogue with one's self when one has himself taken the attitude or place of the other, or others, and has thus become an object to himself, and especially when the symbols used have a meaning common to the entire group.[58] "Thinking is simply the reasoning of the individual, the carrying-on of a conversation between what I have termed the "I" and the "me." [59]

By virtue of this importation of the social process of communication into oneself, the individual acquires the processes of reflective thought, of analysis and reconstruction. He has become a rational animal with the ability to control his actions in terms of the foreseen consequences of his action. Thought, in this framework, is only the internalized conversation of gestures by a self-conscious individual living in a common world of social experience and meaning. The "mechanism of introspection" is thereby provided in the social attitude which man necessarily assumes toward himself.[60]

Mead's conception of thinking is that of an internal, sublimated process of *acting* through the use of language symbols or by use of verbalization. The word or language symbol is viewed as a substitute stimulus, that is, it refers to some object in the environment to which an appropriate response might be made. Through the use of the language symbol (vocal stimulus) one may respond incipiently or actually as one would to the object which is symbolized. By such a schema, it is believed that we may explain thinking in terms of the stimulus-response formula. When one thinks, he is simply talking to himself, silently responding to his own talk in which vocal symbols serve as substitute stimuli. In terms of habit-formation and problem-solving, thinking is regarded as an interior trial-and-error procedure like that of a rat in a maze. In this process of thought, the individual is subject to the mechanisms of learning, conditioning, and habit-formation with which psychology is familiar. Gestures are also seen as instrumental in the development of the consciousness of meaning. The meaning of a gesture arises when one imagines the social consequences of a gesture. "One's own gesture could not take on meaning directly. The gestures aroused by them in others would be that upon which attention is centered. And these gestures become identified with the content of one's own emotional attitude." [61] In Mead's own words:

> There is a field, a sort of inner forum, in which we are the only spectators and the only actors. In that field each one of us confers with himself. We carry on something of a drama.[62] If a person retires to a secluded spot and sits down to think, he talks to himself. He asks and answers questions. He develops his ideas and arranges and organizes those ideas as he might do in conversation with somebody else. He may prefer talking to himself. . . . He is a more appreciative audience, perhaps.[63]

The process of thinking, then, is much the same as that of talking to someone else. Yet the activity is not the same. The man who talks to himself takes different roles. He asks questions and answers them; presents arguments and refutes them. But he doesn't do it out loud.

> He does it himself, and it lies inside of the man himself. It has not yet become public. But it is a part of the act which does become public. . . . The process which goes on inside of him is only the beginning of the process which is finally carried on (in public). It is just a part of the whole thing, and the fact that he talks to himself rather than to someone else is simply an indication of the beginning of a process which is carried on outside.[64]

We can now also see the logical basis of Mead's ethical assumption that the sharing of experience is the greatest good; for that which is "private" is "therefore subject to disintegration" and in fact exists only because of the incompleteness of social organization.[65] The subjective, the private, the psychical arises only as the result of disintegration and exists for the sake of redintegration. Subjectivity is the "homeless sprite" of that which is no more and of that which is not yet. But subjectivity loses any invidious significance when we realize that the sense-datum is functionally a stimulus which can be integrated with a response. By "mental" or "subjective" data Mead means, then, not a kind of substance or a location, but elements in an incompleted act.[66] And in Mead's view, it is the task of science and the burden of ethical science to complete this organization of society.

To summarize the argument thus far, we may say that mind is a natural process or activity within nature. In a certain sense, mind is Nature groping her way along, meeting and solving problems, redirecting activity by anticipating consequences, reconstructing environment in terms of needs and possibilities, finding out by trial and error what she can and cannot do. Therefore, the career of the human mind within nature has significance for nature as well as for man. The "self" is central to all so-called mental experience; and every self, as we shall see, is or has both an *I* and a *me,* is active and reactive with both an inside and an outside. The "I" is identical with the active, analytic and synthetic processes of cognition which, in conflicting situations, reconstruct out of the "protoplasmic" states of consciousness both the empirical self (the "me") and the world of objects. The objective world is a mental construction and is defined in terms of the needs and acts of the "I." [67] The perceptual object is an organization of responses. An object is not just a something with stimulus value to be *reacted* to; it is a thing with a past and a future to be *responded* to as something that is not only *there,* but as something that *will be there,* perhaps in altered form, as the result of one's response to it.[68] Perceptual reality is not something that exists in the present instant, but is realized in the perceptual act as a process taking place in time. The objective reality of the sense-datum is still in the future. "Taken as existing now, it is a subjective substitute for an objective reality that lies ahead of us." [69] The subjective or the psychical is that which is there as experience but not yet as perceptual fact.[70] By "subjective" data, Mead means elements in an incomplete act.[71] Therefore, man's reasoned response is directed as much to the future object as to the present object.[72] Men are not just "driven," nor manipulated like puppets, nor determined by external pressures. They transform their own drives and urges into anticipated satisfactions which "pull" them on to action. Thus men create values and forms, they actualize possibilities, which unaided nature could not develop. By such considerations, Mead is saying that the individual belongs to a system which determines him in part, and at the same time to a system which he determines in part. He belongs to two systems at once; he is a *social* individual.

PERSPECTIVES IN NATURE: THE ACT IN TIME

In our discussion of the "psychical" there have emerged certain features of Mead's later thought to which we will give fuller attention in subsequent sections of this essay. Indeed, the outlines of Mead's whole system are already faintly visible. For Mead, the *act* of the individual is the unit of existence. We have further seen how this practical, ongoing activity develops by a fracture of the act into a reflective and reconstructive activity in which the impulsive organism eventually becomes "rational." Both mechanism and static structure in both life and thought have been rejected in favor of living, functional process. Knowledge is a means to action. Subjective or psychical experience is prior to reflection and to perceptual fact. We have glimpsed something of Mead's stress on the "social attitude"; how the activity of the individual biological form becomes coordinated with others in a socially conscious sense, culminating in the reflective act which implies the assumption of the attitude of others, or the social attitude. The most apt meaning of "consciousness," according to Mead, is that which describes the awareness of the organism in relation to other physical objects and organisms,[73] developing finally into the experience in which the individual assumes the attitude of the other. In this way, the object (or other organism) acquires an inside, and the (first) organism acquires an outside. Only by taking the attitude of the other does one confer an inside upon the other and an outside upon one's self.

Thus early in our exposition we find Mead's insistence that all individual living forms are bound up in a social situation.[74] Mind is the functioning of socially derived symbols—symbol and mind arising together in those situations where one participant assumes the role of the other. In this complex of social inter-relationships and interactions, physiological differentiation of the forms is overshadowed, especially at the human level, by the social attitude and principle of organization. This attitude and principle is succinctly laid down in the following passage:

> That which creates the duties, rights, the customs, the laws and the various institutions in human society, as distinguished from the physiological relationships of an ant nest or beehive, is the capacity of the human individual to assume the organized attitude of the community toward himself as well as toward others.[75]

It is this principle and process which Mead develops at length, since it is the heart of his philosophy of experience.

All of this must come in for more extended treatment as we proceed. Our understanding of Mead's further development of this theme will be clearer, however, if we tarry long enough to consider more explicitly one other point which is basic to Mead's later doctrine of the social self; namely, his notion of perspectives in nature and in time. For here we see Mead's notion of the nature of history as well as his insistence upon the value of the individual.

In Mead's thinking, the relation between objects, events and organisms in nature is not only *spatial*, but, and more significantly, *temporal*. That is to say that the processes within nature are conditioned by the past, take place in the present, and are directed to and controlled by the future.[76] This means specifically in this connection (and it is crucial to Mead's whole theory of the teleological act) that the act has a temporal character: (1) it has continuity or duration; (2) it has direction; and (3) it has uniqueness or perspectivity.

An act stretches over a period of time, "beyond the stimulus to the response." [77] It requires a temporal span in order to be what it is. "The real is qualitative and you cannot get quality at an instant." [78]

It is the enduring character of the experience that contains in it the continuity of nature, that contains in it just that connection which Hume denied. There is something that continues. If there is something that continues, that which is there at the present time is responsible for what is going to be there in the future.[79]

A process is not a monotonous continuity, nor a succession of instantaneous presents or points such as is given in spatial extension.[80] The existence within the present of both the past as condition and the future as control is what gives the character of continuity to the present. An act, then, is a single whole of concrete time within which are distinct phases of duration, direction, and discreteness.

For Mead, "reality is always in a present," [81] since it is the ongoing act which is the unity of existence. The present, however, is not "a piece cut out anywhere from the temporal dimension of uniformly passing reality." [82] A present always implies a past and a future, although Mead denies that either past or future has any metaphysical reality as existence. "When the present has passed it no longer is." [83] The present is always becoming and disappearing; it is the occurrence or emergence of something new.[84] "Presents" are continually sliding into each other, marking themselves off from previous presents as qualitatively different, then disappearing to give way to future presents emerging as novel events. "All the past is in the present as the conditioning nature of passage, and all the future arises out of the present as the unique events that transpire." [85] Each "present" reconstructs a "past" peculiar to itself and also a "future" peculiar to the present-and-its-peculiar-past. We are always advancing into a future which is different from the past. Every individual and every generation re-writes its own history.[86] Novelty reaches out in both directions from each present perspective.[87] This emergent, evolutionary point of view is central to Mead's whole system, from which it follows that Mead believed in the reality of many perspectives and of many presents. Mead took time seriously, as do all process thinkers; and this view commits Mead to a pluralism and a qualified relativism.[88] This pluralism and objectivity of perspectives, plus his stress on the primacy of experience, adds up in Mead's case to what we have called a "social idealism." The individual is ultimate; but his reality is not complete if isolated. It must be achieved in part through being related to a wider process.

The nature of the past is that of conditioning the present; the form of the past is that of a cognitive structure in the present; and the function of the past is that of a remembered chronicle which is seen to lead up to, and thus explain, the present. Only a past which has its origin in a present can have meaning for that present, and only a present which has evoked its own past is one which can properly serve to determine its future. The past is purely cognitive and instrumental; it is only and always such as the present extracts in the interests of a selected future.[89] Each individual or event "slices the world from the standpoint of a different time system." [90] There is a relativity of the individual and its environment.[91]

If this all sounds strange as well as novel, it must be remembered that Mead is reacting against all those systems—particularly the naive materialism and the absolute idealism of the nineteenth century— which minimize the individual. He is trying to maintain a place of dignty and uniqueness for the concrete individual. His philosophy of experience which denies the rigidity of all forms and structures enables Mead to reject the presuppositions and propositions of both mechanistic materialism and objective idealism; namely, that reality, including man, is, on the one hand, only an aggregation of abstract parts, or, on the other hand, a simple all-inclusive rational whole. It is Mead's strong conviction that both mechanism and idealism fail to do justice to the individual's unique reality as an experienced and experiencing perspective in the present. In the case of mechanism, the present is conceived as completely determined by the past in terms of a cause-and-effect sequence. In the case of absolute idealism, the present is completely determined by the future. In other words, the world is defined and limited either by its beginning or its end; and either limitation implies a closed system. Mead is rather pleading for an open, dynamic, emergent system; and he hopes to accomplish this by setting up the present as the locus of reality.

In view of Mead's worship of Science, it may appear eccentric on his part and contradictory to find him criticizing science in this connection. But a careful review of Mead's notion of emergent and novel perspectives in time, and his theory of the teleological act as controlled by the future, will show that this view of science is integral to his whole viewpoint. Science has indeed been reared on *vis a tergo* theories. It has been the boast of science to describe and explain events in terms of preceding events. Thus for its own purposes of observation and exact measurement, science has abstracted time and has thus reduced the world to a "knife-edged present." [92] Mead defends this practice of science as a "methodological fiction" or an operational requirement while pointing out its dire results: (1) science has left out of consideration the *end* by which the act is controlled and has concerned itself exclusively with the antecedent factors of determination; [93] (2) by reducing the world to a series of points, or instantaneous presents, science has presented a world which has conjunctivity but no genuine continuity; and (3) this doctrine of knife-edged presents renders causality meaningless, as Hume's devastating analysis made clear. A series of non-extended factors could never influence each other causally. [94]

But in Mead's theory of the act as controlled by the future, the distinctive nature of this act is precisely that it contains within its present the *end* to which it is directed. [95] The existence within the present of both the past as condition and the future as control is what gives duration to the present. As was pointed out above, a process is not a monotonous continuity of spatial extension. [96] It is an emergent event in which there are distinct phases which nevertheless belong to a single whole. And as an emergent event, the present has a unique structure which sets it off from other events which are past or future. Thus, the act in time has duration as well as uniqueness.

Another important consideration here is that Mead developed his conception of the world (his ontology and his cosmology) from his methodology, i.e., from an analogy to scientific method. On Mead's account, science is essentially a process of meeting and solving problems.[97] Changes and problems occur, exceptional instances arise— "the common world is continually breaking down"—and the old habits of thought are continually revised to meet these exceptional and problematical situations.[98] "It (science) states its laws in terms of uniformities, but it is always ready to change any statement it has made." [99] It is "undertaking to set up another law in place of the one which has been overthrown." [100] Science is a method of continually adjusting itself to that which is new.[101] Science is evolutionary.

But so does the world evolve. It is no static thing in space. "Reality itself is in a course of evolution." [102] Furthermore, Mead regarded the process of evolution as the "process of meeting and solving problems." [103] The world has no linear development, but develops through conflict. In organic evolution, changes occur in the environment, "something happens in (the organism's) world which makes it run counter to the world in which it has been living." [104] The organism then achieves a more or less successful mutation; but in the process it reconstructs its environment in the sense of "cutting out" different values as means for its own survival. As the result of these changes, there arises a new type of animal or plant which is adjusted to a new world. Evolutionary advance means the solving of problems. And with the new form comes a new environment which is itself dependent upon the new form.[105] "We are always advancing into a future which is different from the past. . . . The point of view which comes in with scientific method implies that, so far as our experience is concerned, the world is always different. Each morning we open our eyes upon a different universe. Our intelligence is occupied with continued adjustment to these differences. . . . Novelty reaches out in both directions from each present experience." [106]

It now becomes clear that Mead was trying to present a picture of nature or reality as an organization of perspectives or percipient events, each of which would be characterized by persistence *and* uniqueness within a spatio-temporal process. Mead criticized most traditional theories for achieving only persistence *or* discreteness, but not both together.[107] Mead exploited the concepts of "emergence" and "relativity" and "interdependence" to enable him to accomplish this feat within a thorough-going naturalism. For emergence implies perspectives, and the world or any part of it illustrates numbers of perspectives organized or "socialized" by including a past and a future.[108] From this Mead deduced, as we shall later see in detail, that all experience, all events, even the universe itself, is *social*. Furthermore, Mead's analysis of the act in time led him to a conception of relativity similar to that of modern physics. Any object or event in nature is dependent upon a percipient individual, and what is seen from the perspective of one individual is not necessarily what is seen from the standpoint of another. "One of the great contributions of relativity has been that it has accustomed us to the recognition that the determining relation of the individual or percipient event to the consentient set is a fact in nature." [109]

The significance of Mead's doctrine of time, with its stress on the emergence and relativity of discrete and persistent factors, is made clear by pointing out the corollaries of this doctrine:

(1) Individuals are thus given exclusive identity as well as continuity—both of which are essential to individuality.

(2) Society is thus conceived as an organization of all the individuals in it.[110]

(3) The social and psychological processes are but instances of what takes place in nature, if nature is an evolution.[111] The "present" is emergent and it is social.

(4) Mead is thus committed to a relativism and a "standpoint" philosophy which approaches the existential view which he might be expected to reject as romantic and subjective nonsense.

Each perspective as an individual act has an independent identity and autonomy. Every individual has something that is peculiar to himself. Each one has his own value and his own standpoint. But, contends Mead, this does not mean "solipsism" and the defeat of a universal philosophy.[112] For to retain its identity, each individual (act, event, perspective, or person) must carry on a continuous and changing relationship to the rest of nature. Mead's monads are not without windows; they are not isolated from nor indifferent to their environment; indeed they imply and require the environment as a condition of their own existence.[113] "If no change were involved in its maintenance, it would disappear in a more extensive structure and lose its identity as an individual." [114] All of nature is in a process of continual flux; therefore each individual or perspective must change along with its environment as the price of its own existence.

Now the organization of many individual perspectives is precisely what Mead means by society, and by a "universal." [115] The individual is there only through cooperative interaction with others in the community. His own particular perspective arises in the community. The individual comes to himself in so far as he can take the attitude of the group to which he belongs. He stands on his own feet as he assumes his own perspective, criticizes it, reconstructs it. Other persons can likewise put themselves in his place. "They all belong to the same consentient set. But it is an organization of the perspectives of real individuals. Each one has his own perspective, and he can assert it against the group." [116] We have in social experience a real organization of perspectives in an attempt to find out what is universal, "but with the recognition that, when we do find that out, the very character of one's self as an individual lies in discovering some exception to the universal and going on to the formation of other universals." [117] This takes place in the present, and in nature, as well as in human nature.[118] This is the price of progress.

Let us pause long enough to point out the revolutionary implications of Mead's interpretation of the psychical process; for if Mead is correct, certain things seem to follow:

(1) Psychical or mental behavior *precedes* the object, and is not to be identified with it.

(2) Gesture and communication come before mind or self.

(3) The process is one in which objects are in continual process of disintegration and reformation. There are no fixed objects, no absolutes, no final entities; no complete conditioning from either the past or the future. Change is as ultimate as endurance and they mutually implicate one another.

(4) The process is in the form of social interaction carried on within the individual. Thought is only internalized conversation. Mental activity is *social*, and the individual, though ultimate, is really a miniature society.

(5) Out of the process arise the attitudes of the individual and the perceptual objects of his world.

(6) Only human beings can have "self-hood" and, consequently, objects and meanings.

These preliminary considerations and conclusions point to a more extended and detailed analysis, if we are clearly to grasp and substantiate Mead's doctrine concerning the nature and development of mind and self in gesture, role-taking and language. With the foregoing definitions and distinctions in mind, we may proceed in the following sections of this chapter to the examination of Mead's theory of the social self.

THE GENESIS OF MIND IN GESTURE AND SYMBOL

We now have to observe the emergence of mind and self; precisely *how*, in Mead's account, the biological form is transformed into a rational self or person. This further requires that we consider in some detail the nature of communication and the social attitude. We shall proceed by asking ourselves, and answering, the question: What are the conditions, on Mead's view, necessary to the rise and existence of the self? There are at least four such conditions: (1) There must be life in a social situation of cooperative association and communication with others. (2) There must be certain physiological capacities and neurological or cortical endowments necessary for the invention and use of significant symbols. (3) There must be a mechanism for self-stimulation, such as is found in the unique capacity of human beings for vocal gesture or language, and the vocal-auditory relations of human beings. The unique and crucial importance of speech is that it alone stimulates the speaker in the same manner in which it stimulates the hearer, and thus enables the individual to react or respond to his own utterances in the same manner in which another would respond. (4) One final factor is required: the ability to "get into" the experience of the other, to experience "from the other side." The human being, alone among the animals and insects, can fulfill this condition; and it is done, says Mead, by "taking the role of the other," i.e., by becoming an object to himself, by acting toward himself as he acts toward another, and as the other acts toward him. The individual has to "get out of himself," as it were, in order to come back to himself; and he does this by taking the place of the other who stands opposite him treating him as an object. In so doing he gets the *sense of himself as a self,* and therein he reaches the stage where he can carry on the conversation of attitude and gesture within himself. The following sections of this chapter constitute an analysis of these phenomena and mechanisms.

Assuming only the human organism, Mead starts with an objective social process. He does not begin with already existing minds or selves who then initiate the social process. This was his chief complaint against Aristotle's "substance-attribute" metaphysics, the "social instinct" theory of Hume and Adam Smith, the psycho-physical dualism of Wundt, and the idealistic, mentalistic, or subjectivistic taint which he detected in Kant, James, Royce, Baldwin, Cooley, and Boodin.[119] Mead assumes only a primitive and minimal society of biologic forms participating in a social act, impelled by the biological drives of hunger and sex (whch are in a broad sense social in character) and employing simple gestures to communicate meaning to guide the behavior of any one form with respect to other forms.[120]

Granted that the social organism is used by individuals whose cooperative activity is essential to the life of the whole: such organisms exist outside of and below the human group, among certain insects and certain animal groups.[121] Ants, bees, and termites, for example, exhibit a remarkable "social" organization. There are different types of individuals with corresponding functions, and a life-process which seems to determine the development of the individuals. One is tempted to regard such communities of hymenoptera as analogous to a human society. However, in such insect societies, there is no evidence of any system of communication, and the principle of organization is patently different from that found in human groups.

Cooperative activity among the ants, bees and termites is obviously carried to a high degree of complexity, but it finds its explanation in the physiological structure of the organisms, in a physiological differentiation of function comparable to the differentiation of different cells and tissues in a multicellular form.[122] Consequently, their contacts and interactions evoke cooperative reactions inherently embedded in the separate forms. Following a purely behavioristic stimulus-response pattern, the activity of each form evokes an appropriate mutually adjustive *but fixed* reaction from each other. There is no variation, no flexibility of pattern.

Among vertebrate animals there are loose "social" aggregations: the herd, the school of fishes, the flock of birds, etc. Moreover, certain animal groups do not depend upon physiological differentiation. But such groups are relatively insignificant; and we rarely find an organization of a large group of animals on the basis solely of the primary family group and the family functions.[123] Such herds and companies exhibit rather an "instinctive relationship" which keeps the group together for such activities as grazing, mating, defense against attack, et cetera. But, as Mead points out, such mechanisms give slight basis for community organization, and they do not enter into the life and conduct of the individual in such a manner as to determine his life completely.[124] Moreover, among the animals there is little evidence of significant symbolic communication.[125]

But in even the most primitive human societies, you find cooperative attitudes, combined with family functions, which supply the conditions out of which selves arise. Only in human groups do we find variation, pliability, novelty, differential adjustment, flexible organization and functional differentiation. This fact argues for a different form of interaction and organization among human beings than the physiological differentiation which obtains among insects.[126] There is, of course, the distinction of sex in human beings based upon physiological differentiation; but this is subordinate to the distinctly human principle of organization: the genuinely social attitude based upon language communication, role-taking and mutual adjustment.

> That which creates the duties, rights, the customs, the laws and the various institutions in human society, as distinguished from the physiological relationships of an ant nest or beehive, is the capacity of the human individual to assume the organized attitude of the community toward himself as well as toward others.[127]

Mention should be made of what might be called the physiological basis for human society in the use of the *hand* and in the development of a complex *central nervous system*.[128] The hand makes possible the analysis, isolation and control of physical things. And through the organization of the central nervous system an almost unlimited number and variety of reactions of the organism may be combined into all sorts of orders, spatial and temporal. So there is some physiological basis for human society; but more important is the capacity for symbolic communication. It should be further noted that if the individual were not sensitive to his own stimuli which are essential to the carrying out of the response to the other, such communications could not take place.

> In fact [Mead writes], we find that in the case of the deaf and dumb, if no care is given to the development of language, the

child does not develop normal human intelligence, but remains on the level of lower animals. . . . There is then a physiological background for language, but it is not one of physiological differentiation between the various forms. . . . It is out of this capacity for being influenced by our own gesture as we influence others that has arisen the peculiar form of the human social organism. . . . [129]

Among animal and insect societies there is no evidence of language. Social activities are incited and controlled by odor and contact. But in human communities the principle of organization is that of communication and participation in a universe of discourse by means of vocal gesture.[130] Only selves have minds. And the selves that are central to all mental experience have appeared only in the social conduct of human vertebrates who have the capacity to get the acts and attitudes of others into themselves so as to produce a common social act.[131]

It is, of course, better not to dogmatize about animal psychology, for it is always possible, and surely conceivable, that animals have "minds" and a social life of their own;[132] and that while we humans are referring to the complex activities of bees and ants to "instinct," they are making similar, even invidious, observations with regard to us—like the monkeys in the cartoons who are depicted as making acute and snide remarks about the follies and foibles of the human race.

It seems fair, however, to say that no animal can understand the mind of man; but man can, to a degree, understand the mind of the animal. So far as we can tell, animals do not have a highly developed capacity to look before and after, and to act rationally in the light of self-chosen ends. It is, for instance, hardly probable that dogs perceive any parental relation of cause and effect between copulation and the remote birth of puppies. One need not, therefore, dogmatically deny the presence in animals of morality and intelligence in order to argue that, as compared to men, their range of reasoning, including imagination and memory, is extremely limited.[133] If this be true, mind is a matter of degree, and only human animals have "selves." [134]

THE SOCIAL OBJECT AND THE SOCIAL ACT

In our previous analysis of the *act*, we pointed out that the object controls the act. The field of ongoing action is space-time. The selected stimulus or distant object has its value for the act as a guiding control and will realize its full promise only in the future when the act is completed.[135] Thus the perceiving organism "cuts out" its object. "The vision of the distant object is not only the stimulus to movement toward it. It is also, in its changing distance values, a continual control of the act of approach." [136]

In the social act, however, the act is distributed among two or more individuals. Mead defines the "social act" as one in which the stimulus which sets free an impulse is found in the character or conduct of the living form whose impulse it is.[137] Mead restricts the social act to that class of acts which involves the *cooperation* of more than one individual, and whose object, as defined by the act, is a social object. And he means by a "social object" one that answers to all the parts of a complex act. The "objective" or meaning of the social act, then, is to be found in the life-processes of the group, not in those of the various individuals alone. Social acts, according to this view, are the correlated activities of men living together in their efforts to perform ever more complex functions. The common world of men is all of their attitudes, meanings, percepts and values mobilized for action. So the act is "social" in a double sense: the pattern of the act in the individual is social, and the act itself becomes objectified in the social habits of the group. In this way, an individual becomes identified with his group, and his own actions are carried out through others, with the aid of others, and with the knowledge that others are also acting. The whole social act is in some fashion and to some degree present in the conduct of each individual involved.[138] The social attitude, therefore, implies a recognition that the ends and objects of others are pertinent to one's own ends. This being so, we must somehow get the ongoing acts and attitudes of others into ourselves if we are to make the common act possible.[139] This does happen, and can happen, only through communication.

The self-conscious human individual, who assumes the organized social attitudes of any given social group, enters into special sets of social relations with various other individuals.[140] It is the individual's membership in social groups or classes which makes possible his entrance into definite social relations, direct and indirect, with an almost infinite number of other individuals who also belong to, or are included within, one or another of these groups or classes. It also provides possibilities for the widening and enriching of the social relations among all the members of any given society as an organized whole, and defined by a universe of discourse (or universally significant symbols).

In this connection, Mead also asserts that the most universal social processes in human society, making for the development of a social attitude, are the *religious* and the *economic*.[141] In the case of religion, the process is characterized by "such fundamental attitudes of human beings toward each other as kindliness, helpfulness, and assistance."[142] Such attitudes as cooperative activity and aid to those in trouble are found in every human group and the generalization of them is found back of all universal religions. Such a simple act as breaking bread with another identified the individual with the other, even if he was an enemy. The classic illustration of this neighborliness is found in the parable of the good Samaritan.

Likewise, the economic process of exchange can take place wherever individuals who have a surplus are able to communicate with each other. "There is a participation in the attitude of need, each putting himself in the attitude of the other in the recognition of the mutual value which the exchange has for both."[143] One cannot cooperate or exchange goods in the market, otherwise than by putting oneself in the attitude of the other party to the bargain. Property is a tangible social object because all essential phases of property (its acquisition, conserving, protecting, etc.) appear in the actions of all those involved in exchange, and appear as essential features of the individual's action.[144] Buying and selling are necessarily involved in each other. Or consider a "right," property or civil: In claiming our "right" to the protection of life and property, we assume the attitude of assent and cooperation of every member of the community. "Value exists as an object only for individuals within whose acts in exchange are present those attitudes which belong to the acts of the others who are essential to the exchange."[145]

> In so far as this attitude is that of a number of others, and in so far as he can assume the organized attitudes of a number that are cooperating in a common activity, he takes the attitudes of the group toward himself, and in taking this or these attitudes he is defining the object of the group, that which defines and controls the response.[146]

Social control, on this view, will depend upon the degree to which the individual does assume the attitudes of those in his group.

This capacity of individuals to play their own role and at the same time assume the role of others, i.e., to be contemporaneously in different systems or dimensions, to be several things at once, is what Mead describes as "sociality." [147] The individual is "social" because he belongs to a system which determines him in part, and at the same time to a system which he determines in part. Mead's extension of this principle to the universe as a whole was perhaps his most original and daring postulation.[148] He came to believe that there is "sociality" in nature; and thus he made the claim that the highest and finest product of the whole evolutionary process is the ideal of human solidarity, cooperation, justice, and mutual service. The appearance of "minds" and "selves" is only the culmination of that sociality which is found throughout the universe.

Mead came to feel that a profounder interpretation of Nature as a whole would furnish support for his theory of the emergence and growth of "sociality" and for his conviction that the human self, because it is a social self, will increasingly identify itself with larger and larger groups until it finds itself completed and fulfilled in the larger Self, or Universal Other. Examples of the encouraging, if limited, success of his theory Mead found in the League of Nations and the World Court.

THE GESTURE

We must now observe the adjustment to one another of the acts of different human individuals within the human social process: an adjustment which takes place through communication—by *gestures* on the lower levels of animal evolution, and by *significant symbols* (gestures which possess meanings and are hence more than mere stimuli) on the higher level of human behavior.

The adjustment of one form to another begins as an adjustment to the gestures of the other, that is, to the early manifestations of an overt act—for example, as seen in the feinting and maneuvering of dogs in a fight, or in the thrust and parry of fencers. It was Wundt who, while seeking that in psychical experience which could be referred to in physical terms, hit upon the "gesture" as that which later becomes a symbol, but which is to be found in the initial stages of an act.[149] The gesture signalizes or stands for the whole oncoming overt act, and in this sense is regarded as a "truncated act." In signalizing the whole act, the gesture enables the actors to anticipate and grasp the meaning of each other's intended behavior, and thus respond appropriately.

In this sense, the gesture is a stimulus for the response of other forms. But, as we saw in analysing the act, this situation has three phases.

> A gesture by one organism, the resultant of the social act in which the gesture is an early phase, and the response of another organism to the gesture, are the relata in a triple or threefold relationship of gesture to first organism, of gesture to second organism, and of gesture to subsequent phases of the given social act; and this threefold relationship constitutes the matrix within which meaning arises, or which develops into the field of meaning.[150]

Consider the illustration of a dog-fight—an illustration which Mead is fond of employing. The actions of each dog become the stimuli to the other dog for his response; and as this act proceeds, it undergoes change. One dog changes his attitude or position; this in turn produces a change in attitude or position of the other dog. We have here what Mead calls a "conversation of gestures."[151] There is play back and forth, advance and retreat, attack and defense, "a field of palaver within the social conduct of animals."[152] Gestures are not complete acts. They are the glance, the posture, the growl, the thrust, the cry—and they all change with the answering attitudes, glances, movements, or cries which are the beginnings of the actions which they themselves arouse. These beginnings call out responses which lead to re-adjustments of acts perhaps already begun, and these re-adjustments lead to still others. A boxer gauges his actions in the ring by his anticipation of the action of his opponent. A feint is designed to create an advantageous situation to which the boxer will react after his feint has been reacted to by his opponent. Thus social behavior is an intricate system of stimulus and response in which *anticipated response is also a stimulus*. Another illustration of this is in the relation of parent to child: first there is the stimulating cry; then the answering voice of the parent, and the consequent change in the cry of the infant. Here we see a set of adjustments of two forms carrying out a common social act.

"Gestures are then that part of the act which is responsible for its influence upon other forms."[153] Gesture carries with it the *import* of the act itself—import, not in terms of reflective consciousness, but in terms of behavior. The clenched fist, for example, as a threat of violence, is a stimulus to the other form for defense or flight. The first function of a symbol then is to stimulate to action; secondly, to connote; and thirdly, to denote.[154] Communication advances from gestures, through exclamation to systematic language.

When, now, that gesture means this idea behind it and it arouses that idea in the other individual, then we have a significant symbol. In the case of the dog-fight we have a gesture which calls out appropriate response; in the present case we have a symbol which answers to a meaning in the experience of the first individual and which also calls out that meaning in the second individual. Where the gesture reaches that situation it has become what we call "language." It is now a significant symbol and it signifies a certain meaning.[155]

This play back and forth may be either instinctive and non-reflective (what Mead calls "unconscious" or "non-significant" conversation of gestures) or it may be deliberate and reflective (what Mead calls "conscious" or "significant" conversation of gestures).[156] A great deal of animal play and gestural interaction is clearly instinctive and not thought out.

The conversation of gestures is not significant below the human level, because it is not conscious, that is, not *self*-conscious (though it is conscious in the sense of involving feelings or sensations). . . . A gesture is not significant when the response of another organism to it does not indicate to the organism making it what the other organism is responding to.[157]

MEANING

Mind or consciousness emerges eventually from the interplay of gesture and symbol; but the central point here concerns *meaning*, not consciousness. From gestures, symbols are developed; symbols are gestures that indicate to another agent how he should respond. Meaning is not simply some nexus of ideas within a private consciousness; it is rather a gestural relation in which the *adjustive response* of one organism to another *is* the interpreted *meaning* of the gesture. And, as such, it determines the later phases of the social act. "Life becomes conscious at those points at which the organism's own responses enter into the objective field to which it reacts."[158] The relations in which the environment stands to our own response are its meanings. To respond to such meanings as stimuli for further action is to have imported into the world as experienced the promise of the future and the lessons of the past. In reacting to the meaning of his sensations and objects, the individual is in both systems at once. In social situations, we become conscious of interpreting the gestures of others by our own responses or tendencies to respond.

Indeed, on Mead's view, it is only in the context of mutual adjustment of social *stimulation* and *response* that the consciousness of meaning arises.[159] For example, one responds to the interpreted hostility of another's attitude by the aroused tendency to attack, defend, or escape. "We become aware of the direction of another's line of march by our tendencies to step one side or the other." [160] If this is true, it means that during the whole social process of interaction we are analyzing and interpreting the oncoming acts of others by our own instinctive or deliberate responses to their movements, postures, or other indications of developing acts. Similarly, we become conscious of our attitudes when and because they are responsible for the changes in the conduct of others. "The consciousness of meaning . . . is a consciousness of one's own attitudes of response as they answer to, control, and interpret the gestures of others." [161] Such consciousness implies: (1) a social situation of stimulation by the acts of others; (2) an awareness of the import of one's own gestures in terms of the change in the gestures of others; and (3) the feel of one's own attitude arising to meet the gestures of others.

Mead is careful to point out that meaning can exist on the subhuman level. *Self*-consciousness is not necessary to the presence of meaning in the process of social experience.

> The mechanism of meaning is present in the social act before the emergence of consciousness or awareness of meaning occurs. The act or adjustive response of the second organism gives to the gesture of the first organism the meaning which it has.[162]

The social process relates the responses of one individual to those of another, as the meanings of the latter, and is thus responsible for the emergence and existence of new objects in the social situation—objects dependent upon or constituted by these meanings. Behavioristically speaking:

> Meaning is thus not to be conceived, fundamentally, as a state of consciousness, or as a set of organized relations existing or

subsisting mentally outside the field of experience into which they enter; on the contrary, it should be conceived objectively, as having its existence entirely within this field itself.[163]

Now what is the basis or mechanism for such a response on the part of the second organism to a gesture of the first? What is the process or mechanism of this appropriate and adjustive response on the part of the second individual to the gesture or symbol of the first? How get this relationship between the idea and the symbol itself into the conversation of gestures?

Wundt and Tarde and Baldwin employed the concept of *imitation* in answer to the above queries. But Mead rejects any such explanation as inadequate.[164] There has been a good deal of study of this problem but the result of the study, concludes Mead, is to minimize the agency of imitation in the conduct of either men or animals. Monkeys, it has been found, learn very quickly, but they do not imitate. Likewise in dogs and cats, the responses are varied, and rarely identical copies of the act of the other. In human forms, and with certain birds, there does seem to be imitation in the case of certain vocal gestures. But imitation as a general instinct, avers Mead, is pretty well discredited in human psychology.[165] There is little evidence that young forms among the animals ever merely imitate or exactly copy the acts of the adult form. "They do acquire during their period of infancy the association of a set of more or less instinctive responses to a certain set of stimuli." [166] Imitation, by definition, involves a direct and identical reproduction of the stimulus by the response. But there is no sufficient evidence that one gesture generally or appropriately calls out the same gesture in the other organism. No, says Mead: "Imitation as the mere tendency on the part of an organism to reproduce what it sees or hears other organisms doing is mechanically impossible" and psychologically inadequate.[167] Indeed, concludes Mead, "It is a perfectly impossible assumption." [168] "It would mean that we have in our nature already all of these various activities, and that they are called out by the sight of other people doing the same thing." [169]

Such an assumption, declares Mead, is possible only in terms of an older "sensation" psychology which holds the mind to be made up of ideas and impressions; and if there is a motor tendency to react to these impressions, one might conceive of that tendency as being one which seeks to reproduce what is seen and heard. But this all seems very unlikely to Mead. In its place, he would put a behavioristic interpretation which would "recognize in the organism a set of acts which carry out the processes which are essential to the form." [170] Then sensory experience cannot be merely a stimulus to reproduce what is seen and heard, but a stimulus for carrying out the organic process. "They are acts which go beyond the organism taken by itself, but they belong to cooperative processes in which groups of animals act together, and they are the fulfillment of the processes which are essential to the life of the forms." [171] The advantage of Mead's theory over the imitation theory is two-fold: (1) it provides for the fact that the responses of animal forms are seldom or significantly exactly the same as the act or gesture which stimulated the response; and (2) it gives a solution, on behavioristic terms, for the origin of language.[172] This provides the next step in our developing exposition; for to understand Mead's treatment of language we must consider his definition of "significant symbol."

THE SIGNIFICANT SYMBOL

The key to this type of gestural and symbolic behavior, in Mead's analysis, lies in the human tendency to converse with oneself, that is, to stimulate oneself and to answer one's own stimulation, in which process one takes the role of the "other" and new attitudes from the other enter into one's own repertory. This analysis of the histrionic process of role-taking and conversing with one's self is surely one of Mead's most important contributions, and one which we must consider more fully.

The kind of gestural communication which we have been describing is not yet "significant" in the sense that the gesture made by an individual is understood by himself. Even if the gesture is a vocal gesture, it may be only a series of sounds signifying nothing in particular; it is not yet language, real speech, with explicable meanings attached to the words and symbols used. The organism is not yet a *self*-consciously communicating form. For these results to occur, the symbols or gestures must become what Mead calls "significant." [173] It is at the level of self-consciousness that a gesture becomes a significant symbol;[174] that is, when the gesture or symbol not only effects a change in the other but also within one's self, when the gesturer himself anticipates the change, and in so doing initiates a reaction or part reaction in himself. In other words, when the one making the gesture responds to it in the same way that the other responds. The gesture "does not become significant to the individuals involved in the act unless the tendency to the act is aroused within the individual who makes it." [175] The individual must be able to interpret the meaning of his own gesture, and then utilize his own response and that of the other for the further control of his conduct. The individual has thus turned round upon himself, he has taken the role of the other, he has indicated by means of his own gestures to other forms *and also to himself* those elements which are of importance in cooperative activity.

In general terms, then, "the significant symbol is the gesture, the sign, the word, which is addressed to the self when it is addressed to another individual, and is addressed to another when it is addressed to the self." [176] When each participant in a given situation responds to the same gesture or symbol in approximately the same manner, the gesture is "significant" in the sense that it has the same meaning for all of the parties to the act, for one's self as well as for the other.

Mead illustrates the difference between the significant and the non-significant symbol by citing the example of the man who calls out "Fire!" when smoke is seen in a theater.[177] The cry by itself would be only a non-significant symbol and part of the initiated act. But when the man tells himself of the danger as he tells it to others; when he excites himself in the same way that he excites the others, and controls his own actions by his cry, his vocal gesture has become a significant symbol. He has uttered a common meaning which is communicated to everyone and at the same time is communicated to himself. He is now using symbols instead of signs; he has reached the stage of language; *he now has acquired a mind*.

When this situation is further internalized, one becomes the "other" to one's self. And thinking, as opposed to vocal speech, as we have seen, becomes the conversation of the self with the other.

> Only in terms of gestures as significant symbols is the existence of mind or intelligence possible; for only in terms of gestures which are significant symbols can thinking—which is simply an internalized or implicit conversation of the individual with himself by means of such gestures—take place.[178]

It appears evident that an individual can thus stimulate himself. A person is both subject and object at the same time. Talking to one's self is a common phenomenon. In the reflection which follows some emotional experience it is normal to "live over again" the whole scene. I recall what the other said, then what I said, then his reply to me, after which I give my reply and his answer, and so on. . . . And in this way the conversation with one's self goes on, including the responses of the other, as the dramatic situation is lived over again. This is to take the role of the other, to play the other's part.

THE VOCAL GESTURE

The vocal gesture has an importance here which no other gesture has.[179] If a vocal gesture uttered by one individual leads to a certain response in another, it is simply a symbol of that act; but where it arouses in the speaker the tendency to the same response, Mead calls it a "significant symbol." But among all such significant symbols, Mead finds that the vocal symbol is the best suited to transform the biologic form into a minded individual. No other gesture or symbol is so successful in affecting the individual similarly as it affects others. The unique and crucial importance of speech is that it alone stimulates the speaker in the same manner in which it stimulates the hearer. The speaker can hear what he says and in hearing what he says he is enabled to respond to his own utterance in the same manner in which the hearer might respond. Here is the mechanism for self-stimulation as well as other-stimulation.[180] Such a mechanism or type of stimulus is found only in the vocal gesture in a human society. Vocal gesture, in Mead's system, is so extremely important because it is the real source of language, and so of mind. It has been the vocal gesture that has provided, more than any other thing, the medium of social organization in human society.[181] Language enters the picture at this point and has its great importance through being "verbal" or "vocal" and, therefore, can be heard by the speaker as well as by the listener, whereas visual symbols are often not seen. Furthermore, by means of language symbols in a logical universe of discourse, human beings have the capacity to indicate to themselves a whole series of possible responses; so when a gesture is made, they can easily select the appropriate response.[182] Each human being is thus able to engage in complex cooperative activity. It is this ability to respond to one's own symbolic behavior that distinguishes the human from the animal. The mechanism: communication, symbols, language. The result: mind.

LANGUAGE

We are human then, when and because we can talk. Without significant symbols, or language, man's life would be confined to his biological needs and practical interests; he could find no access to the higher reaches of symbolic reasoning, of reflective thinking, to the "ideal world" of art, religion, and philosophy. Somewhere along the age-old path upward man developed speech, pure symbolism, dealing with the sensible world of sticks and stones and stars, and dealing with the inner world by means of gestures, sounds and symbols which have no necessary relation, but only a symbolic one, to the objects they signify. All typically human behavior involves these significant symbols, usually in the form of vocal gesture or language.[183] Without a complex system of symbols, relational rational thought is not possible. Discriminating reflection is a human capacity. The processes of abstraction, generalization, reflection in terms of universals, appear to be lacking in animals lower than man.[184]

The genetic, behavioristic, child-study approach to the development of personality, employed variously by Baldwin, Cooley, and Mead, has led to a new method which has produced a shift in the basic assumptions underlying the nature and function of language and symbol communication. The older view, exemplified, for example, by Wundt, looked upon language as a means for the expression of ideas. Mead and Dewey, especially, have pioneered a functional approach in which the nature of language is not "expression" of antecedent thought. It is essentially communication, the establishment of cooperation in a social activity in which self and other are modified and regulated by the common act.[185] Language is a development within social intercourse. The older definition of man as "social animal" is not sufficiently comprehensive. On the new view, man cannot become himself save through the medium of social life.

Mead regarded language as the principle of social organization which has made the distinctly human society possible.[186] "Language implies organized responses and the value, the implication of these responses is to be found in the community from which this organization of responses is taken over into the nature of the individual."[187] It does not require for its explanation the positing of a special antecedent inclination in the human mind. Language—the symbolic form in which our meanings usually arise in consciousness—is but a highly specialized form of vocal-auditory gesture inviting response. And it is in these linguistic presentations of our own and other's attitudes and responses that we have the material out of which selves can arise.[188]

To *use* a symbol *is* to *be* a mind, and the "self" emerges when a mind is *self*-conscious, that is, conscious of itself as an object, indicating to itself its own role in a gesture situation. Symbols, in general, are linguistic and have the special virtue of affecting the individual who speaks in the same way in which they affect the one addressed. Therefore, there is "mind" where there is speech, and a "self" wherever self-communing occurs. The social group consists of those who attach the same meaning to the same gestures and objects. In such generalized agreement as to meaning and response of recognition, Mead believed he had provided for a behavioristic account of universals.

One cannot know what Mead's judgment would be, but I suspect he would find confirmation, or at least strong support, for his theory about the central importance of vocal symbol and language in Cassirer's work, despite what the latter says about "tactile language."

Vocal language has a very great technical advantage over tactile language; but the technical defects of the latter do not destroy its essential use. The free development of symbolic thought and symbolic expression is not obstructed by the use of tactile signs in the place of vocal ones. If the child has succeeded in grasping the *meaning of human language,* it does not matter in which particular material this meaning is accessible to it. As the case of Helen Keller proves, man can construct his symbolic world out of the poorest and scantiest materials. The thing of vital importance is not the individual bricks and stones but their general *function* as architectural forms. In the realm of speech it is their symbolic function which vivifies the material signs and 'makes them speak.' Without this vivifying principle the human world would indeed remain deaf and mute. With this principle, even the world of a deaf, dumb, and blind child can become incomparably broader and richer than the world of the most highly developed animal.[189]

Recent research in the field of the psycho-pathology of language has led to the conclusion that the loss, or severe impairment, of speech caused by brain injury is never an isolated phenomenon. Such a defect alters the whole character of human behavior. . . . They are at a complete loss as soon as the solution of the problem requires any specific theoretical or reflective activity. . . . They are no longer able to think in general concepts or categories. Having lost their grip on universals, they stick to the immediate facts, to concrete situations.[190]

Signals and Symbols belong to two different universes of discourse: a signal is a part of the physical world of meaning; a symbol is a part of the human world of meaning. Signals are 'operators'; symbols are 'designators.' [191]

Language, for Mead, is simply the process by means of which an individual who is engaged in cooperative activity can get the attitude of others involved in the common activity. If this be so, then language is the set of significant symbols or the set of gestures which the organism uses in indicating certain stimuli—thus calling out the responses of others and a similar response in one's self.[192] The effect of the gesture or attitude on others comes back on one's self. The result of this is that the individual who speaks in some sense takes the attitude of the other whom he addresses. It is in this way that *participation* arises out of communication.

One of the remarkable things about language is that which in grammar is called the "reflexive mood." This reflexive form in language, by recognizing the speaking self as both subject and object of the same experience, makes possible the mood of self-awareness. The self, through language and role-taking, can turn back upon itself, can become its own object, talk to itself, see itself as others see it, distinguish itself from other selves, judge itself from the standpoint of others.[193] The response which the first form makes is in turn a stimulus to him to direct his later action.[194] Language arises because the human being has the capacity to "indicate to himself what the other person is going to do and then to take his attitude on the basis of that indication." [195] A language symbol is the stimulus whose response is given in advance.[196]

We are all familiar with this phenomenon in giving directions to another person, and then "doing it ourselves." The orator or actor is able to produce in himself the same emotional effect he produces in his audience. He has imported the attitudes of the listeners into himself. Likewise we are familiar with the experience in which we find ourselves thinking out an argument by supposing that we are talking to someone who takes a particular side in the debate. We present our argument, and we know how he will, or may, reply. Then we counter in a certain way to him. Who has not lain awake nights going through some disturbing conversation or rehearsing some argument with an imaginary protagonist? It is this sort of reflexive participation, this taking the attitudes and roles of others, that, in Mead's account, characterizes and constitutes the peculiar character of human intelligence. Thus the individual who can speak in significant symbols is a self-conditioning individual who is also able to import into his own experience the social process.

UNIVERSALS AND THE GENERALIZED OTHER

The organization of the different individual attitudes and interactions in a given social act, with reference to their inter-relations as realized by the individuals themselves, is what Mead means by a "universal." [197] "What language seems to carry is a set of symbols answering to certain content which is measurably identical in the experience of the different individuals." [198] If there is to be communication as such, the symbol has to mean the same thing to all of the individuals involved. It must have the same, or approximately the same, meaning for all concerned, or there cannot be communication, nor similar response. Our symbols are all universal in this sense. "A universal may be interpreted behavioristically as simply the social act as a whole . . ." [199] You cannot say anything that is absolutely particular; anything you say that has meaning at all is universal. This functional identity in the social uses of a thing or a symbol is what Mead means by universality. It is the reliable response which gives us uniformity and univocal meaning. Or to put it somewhat differently: an act is universal when many objects can serve as appropriate stimuli. And this can happen only in a social process in which the individuals can assume the attitude of the "generalized other." A common world exists only in so far as there is a common experience.

We have said that approximate identity of response is necessary before we can say of an individual that he understands the meaning of his gesture. It should be noted, however, that such a similarity of responses can be present in situations where there is no reason to believe that the participants understand their acts. A logical universe of discourse (identity of meaning) is not at all essential to a simple "conversation of gestures" in cooperative social behavior[200]—as in an ant hill, in the play of animals, or the movements of people in a

crowd. There must also be present this *reflexive* behavior which we
find only among the users of significant symbols, in a social group
so constituted that there is a basis for communication by means
of vocal symbols.[201] This further implies the dependable organization
of responses which constitute the attitudes and values of a community or a "generalized other." The universality of thought, from
the behavioristic standpoint, is possible only as the result of a given
individual "taking the attitudes of others toward himself, and of his
finally crystallizing all these particular attitudes into a single attitude
or standpoint which may be called that of the 'generalized other.' "[202]
In such a group, every gesture and symbol comes to stand for a particular act or response. And when symbols and responses are thus
both indicated and organized, we have what Mead regards as a universe of discourse or a system of common meanings.

> The significant gesture or symbol always presupposes for its sig-
> nificance the social process of experience and behavior in which it
> arises; or, as the logicians say, a universe of discourse is always
> implied as the context in terms of which, or as the field within
> which, significant gestures or symbols do in fact have significance.
> This universe of discourse is constituted by a group of individuals
> carrying on and participating in a common social process of
> experience and behavior, within which these gestures or symbols
> have the same or common meanings for all members of that
> group, whether they make them or address them to other indi-
> viduals, or whether they overtly respond to them as made or
> addressed to them by other individuals.[203]

Insofar as individuals take the attitude of the generalized other
toward a given object or event, there emerges an object or event that
is universal. But this functional identity need not be, and Mead
argues that it should not be, an absolute identity. There can be
dependable responses, approximate sameness in the social uses of an
object or symbol, without an exact and monotonous likeness. For
Mead wants to make room for novel features in the object; he wants
to take into consideration the various individual perspectives. True
to his concept of "perspectives" in nature, he argues for a functional
generality which still takes account of particular perspectives. Here
again, he finds the formula for reconciling generality with uniqueness
in the theories of relativity and creative emergence which modern
science has substituted for absolute space and time.[204] Only thus,

thinks Mead, can the particular and emerging perspectives, which are both persistent and discrete, be combined with the common perspective. The generalized other which represents the universals and the uniformities of thought and action must not be conceived as absolute, but rather as a functional and plastic whole within which the multifold perspectives intersect. The locus of such intersection and correlation is in the reflective generalizations of a social process.

Something of Hegel's residual influence upon Mead becomes evident in this treatment of universals. Mead was not an idealist, but he was what an idealist becomes when he turns pragmatist and disregards or denies the problems of essence and transcendental reality—with thinkers like Dewey, Bergson, Whitehead and Alexander for neighbors. The dynamic character of Hegel's philosophy, its sense of history, its overcoming of dualisms in a dialectical synthesis, its vision of the freedom and creativeness of mind and the dominance of thought in the universe, its view of reality as an organic system of significant relations—all this appealed to Mead and never left him. His naturalistic version of Hegel (and of Berkeley)[205] produced in Mead what we have called a "social idealism." He clearly owed much to Hegel's doctrine of "concrete universals" [206] which dealt with species genetically and organically and differentially instead of generically, and this he adopted in preference to Aristotle's logical and "abstract" view of universals. Particular qualities and objects cannot exist in isolation; they presuppose opposite qualities and objects and exist only in relation with them.[207]

There are facts and experiences, Mead insisted, which are important only in so far as they belong to a particular individual. These experiences which lie in the biography of particular individuals may, in time, come to influence a larger number. Since the law, the universal, the generalized other, is not rigidly fixed and unalterable, the unique experience of the individual may become incorporated into the experience of the group. The non-conformity of the individual may through the evolutionary process bring about the revision of one law, theory, custom, or institution, and supplant it with another. Here, in Mead's scheme, is the agency of change and reconstruction. The individual exception, the individual experience, the novel emergent, may be "not only real but the possible source of fuller realities than the world of convention." The atypical individual, the revolutionist, the non-conformist is not necessarily the self-seeking anarchist but an inno-

vator or reformer.[208] Thus while it is over against the common "objective" world of common meanings that the individual sets his own
private experience and meaning, that individual may at the same time
become an agency of social change. And meanwhile, science, with its
claims to objectivity and impersonality based on empirical observation, endeavors to study and record the more universal, habitual, uniform, and invariable aspects of our common world.

THE SELF

We have now traced the biography of the mind in Mead's genetic
and naturalistic account of how the biological individual attains to
the status of a minded organism in a social process and through the
agency of language. The "self" is precipitated in the same process,
when the organism comes to respond to its own role assumptions as it
responds to the other. Self arises where the individual form has the
ability to take the attitude of the group to which he belongs, then to
come back upon himself, stimulate himself as he stimulates others,
talk to himself in terms of his community and lay upon himself the
responsibilities that go with the community life.[209] The individual conscious mind is, for Mead, the world of nature taken up into social relations and precipitated in a self which then goes out to reshape the world
of nature and social institutions. The distinctive nature of "selfhood"
is found in the capacity of the human "minded organism," employing
language symbols, to take the roles and attitudes of others and thus
become an object to itself, i.e., a "socius."

Here again we see that the pre-conditions of such an outcome are
a society of biologic forms endowed with certain physiological capacities and participating in social activity by means of language. Selves,
like mental activity, have appeared only in the social conduct of human vertebrates, within the evolutionary process.[210] The self is a
phase in the development of the social form, and is made possible by
the development of great and complex tracts in the human central nervous system.[211] This permits the human organism to act as well as
react; to respond and adjust flexibly, appropriately, instead of merely
reacting to stimuli in a rigid pattern.

But even given this remarkable equipment, it is only after months
of experience that a child can say "I" and "me." On the day he does
so, he becomes a real self.[212] For "we are in possession of selves just

in so far as we can and do take the attitudes of others toward ourselves and respond to those attitudes." [213] We *know* ourselves only in the presence of another,[214] seeing ourselves as others see us. But what is this gift that Robert Burns prayed for—"to see oursels as ithers see us!" Whence comes it? How does one individual "get into" the experience of another so as to experience "from the other side"? How can an individual get outside of himself in such a way as to become an object to himself, to get the sense of himself as a self from the standpoint of another? This is the essential psychological problem of selfhood.

The answer in Mead's theory is, in short: *Participation* and *Communication*.[215] The development of vocal gesture permits man to go beyond the stage of physical togetherness to the stage of socially conscious coordination of perspectives, which, in turn, enables the members of a social group to affect each other reciprocally. Gestures have no meaning unless one can assume the position and viewpoint of the other. And "the importance of what we term 'communication' lies in the fact that it provides a form of behavior in which the organism or the individual may become an object to himself." [216] He becomes the "other" to himself by responding to that which he addresses to another in the same way that the other tends to respond.[217] In giving directions to others, he gives them to himself, and thus arouses a similar response in himself which is understood by himself. Such a process, on Mead's view, makes for responsibility and self-control.

This self, says Mead, is not primarily the physiological organism, although the physiological organism is essential to it. "We are at least able to think of a self without it"—as people who believe in immortality, or primitives who believe in ghosts and a "double" which can leave the body.[218] Such a self is a social structure, arising in social experience. The individual experiences himself, as such, not directly, but indirectly, from the reflected standpoints of other members of the social group.

For he enters his own experience as a self or individual, not directly or immediately, not by becoming a subject to himself, but only in so far as he first becomes an object to himself just as other individuals are objects to him or in his experience; and he becomes an object to himself only by taking the attitudes of other individuals toward himself . . . [219]

The self is not something which is present at birth; it is something which has a development within a process of social experience and activity. "It is impossible to conceive of a self arising outside of social experience." [220] To say that society or the community *precedes* the individual is probably pure speculation. And at times Mead seems to say just that; certainly, he argues that the individual self is not the first term. At best, self and society are twin-born. Man comes to himself, becomes truly a person, in a dialogue, not in a monologue. The feeling of selfhood, self-worth, self-identity comes when one stands over against another. One cannot become a human being, that is to say, he cannot acquire that core of personality which we call the self-conscious, responsible, moral self without contact and interaction with other human beings. Not just action, nor even reaction, but *inter*action. Not only do one's actions and conversation influence others, but their acts and conversation influence the course of one's subsequent action. [221]

We are familiar enough with this process. It starts in infancy. Children, primitive savages, and poets, according to Mead, take a complete social attitude toward even physical objects, carrying on verbal intercourse with physical objects, at least in a limited sense. [222] And such an attitude is prior to the more sophisticated distinctions between the social world and the physical world.

> The mechanism of human society is that of bodily selves who assist or hinder each other in their cooperative acts by the manipulations of physical things. In the earliest forms of primitive societies, these physical things are treated as selves . . . [223]

Indeed, were it not for the fact that "the mechanism for the individual's acting toward himself as an object" [224] has already been set up in social conduct, human forms could not experience perceptual objects. Consciousness is a socially derived attitude, as we have already indicated.

It seems so obvious as hardly to warrant urging that man does not lead an independent or isolated existence in empty space. Moreover, it is clear that the object or other (alter) opposing the ego is not usually or typically a dumb thing of nature, but another conscious ego. Speaking has its counterpart in listening; just so conscious thinking and acting are correlative to the thought and action of other persons. More than that, we are always "playing" the role of others. The drama and the novel and the newspaper are familiar illustrations of how the individual reader (or writer) carries all the roles of the various persons involved.[225] Art is only a development of play. In writing a letter, the writer puts himself in the place of the one who is to read, anticipates the response of the other, carries on a running dialogue with the other. In the watches of the night, we go through inner conversations to preview and determine situations in advance. A child sees herself in the mirror and responds to herself in the same way that she might respond to her parents. In her play she assumes many and various roles: she "pretends," she "plays like," she puts on her mother's "glad rags," she "plays" mother or father with respect to her dollies, her small brother, etc.

We approve or condemn ourselves. "We pat ourselves on the back or in blind fury attack ourselves." [226] In moral conflict it is not unusual to be aware of an "inner conversation," one member of which is the voice of the desires and urges of the individual person, while the other member is the voice of the generalized other, the social phases of the self, the social habits and stereotypes and ideals of the other reflected in the "voice of conscience" or the "censor." Whenever a person acts in the light of "what people will say," the situation which Mead so carefully describes appears in clear lines. The social other seems necessary to the emergence of a self from organic and social play.[227]

It is, then, in the context of the social act that the self arises. The *social act* is, in its simplest form, an act of one individual qualified or modified in its course by the act of another individual. It may involve cooperation or conflict. In struggle and fighting, as well as in friendly intercourse, the counteracting behavior of others modifies and determines one's own act. In one way or another the individual is continually reacting back against his society.[228] To put it another way— the self-conscious, self-asserting individual needs an audience. Self-realization requires self-assertion plus recognition and reflected appraisal by others in order to possess those values and qualities which we associate with persons. "Being known" and, especially, *knowing that one is known,* is constitutive of self-hood. "One has to find one's self in his own individual creation as appreciated by others." [229]

Men's interests and duties, arising out of the environment and the world they are continually reconstructing, are often in conflict. This is to be expected, for there is a common process going on which differ-

entiates each individual in his functional participation, and at the same
time places certain restraints upon his activities. But this, says Mead,
is the way of growth, of evolution, through conflict, frustration, problem, maladjustment—into a higher redintegration. And selves can
be realized through conflict as well as through harmonious relation.
Social selves are developed by the active struggle of cooperating men
with their total environment. This is the pattern of evolution and of
historical development. For example, in a labor struggle the worker
and the employer may be hostile to one another; yet the laborer has
to realize himself in relation to the employer as well as in relation to
his fellow-workers. Individuals, it is true, realize themselves differently in their opposition to one another. But these very oppositions,
Mead argues, are the starting points for the development of the new
social order. This is true of all social development and has been evident in all the class conflicts of history. On Mead's view, men (e.g.,
the workers and the employers just cited) not only ought to, but
actually do, put themselves in the place of the others and thus can and
do develop a social consciousness as the normal thing. This is the
basis for Mead's empirical and optimistic ethics, "an ethics which
is simply the development of the intelligence implicit in the act,"
instead of an ethics from on high.[230]

ROLE-TAKING AND THE HISTRIONIC TENDENCY

It is Mead's conviction that the *histrionic tendency* runs through all
normal human imaginative experience; and he designates it aptly as
the tendency and capacity "to take the role of the other." By it the
impulsive and meaningless gesture is defined by the responses of the
other so that while our ideas are our own and the symbol may be
private, yet the soul of the symbol is its meaning, and the meaning
is the contribution of others.

It is because the individual finds himself taking the place and
attitudes of others who are involved in his world and in his conduct
that he becomes an object to himself. And the individual who thus
organizes his own attitudes and responses according to the tendency of
others to respond to his acts, *is a self*.[231] This particular mechanism
by which one becomes an object to himself, Mead designates as "role-
taking." "Taking the role of others" is synonymous with the process
of responding to the other's gestures in the same fashion as does the

other; or to put it another way, responding to one's own gestures in the same manner as the other tends to respond. Either way, he acquires the meaning of the other's and of his own activity as it appears in the mind of the other. This is the ability to "get into" the experience of the other, to experience from the other side, and then come back upon oneself. The human being, alone among the animals, can fulfill this condition—i.e., he can put himself in the attitude of the other party—"because the mechanism of the vertebrate brain enables the individual to take these different attitudes in the formation of the act." [232]

From observing the play of children Mead came to believe that it is when a child is able in his play to assume different roles, that he becomes aware of himself and of others in the mutual relations of social interaction. The continuing expansion and enrichment of the personality follows the same process. "The child will not succeed in forming an object of himself—of putting the so-called subjective material of consciousness within such a self—until he has recognized about him social objects who have arisen in his experience." [233] Anyone who has observed children closely will recall how a child may in play converse for hours with himself, creating imaginary companions whose various roles he will successively play.[234] What parent has not come upon his child ransacking an old trunk in the attic or going through the parents' closet or chest of drawers, putting on the adult finery, playing the various adult roles? But in thus trying to be someone else, Mead contends that the child discovers himself. We must be others if we are to be ourselves. When playing at being someone else, the self comes to realize its own nature at the same time it realizes the nature of the other persons whose role is being played.

Obviously, the mere capacity to talk to oneself and others is not the whole story of self-consciousness, otherwise talking parrots would have selves. What is lacking to parrots, declares Mead, are the social objects which can exist for the human baby and the complete mechanism for transplanting those social objects into an inner world.

THE GENERALIZED OTHER

From the many roles assumed successively and simultaneously, there gradually arises a sort of "generalized other" whose role may also be assumed. And it is this attitude of the generalized other or organized community that gives to the individual his unity of self and exercises control over him.[235]

This is one of Mead's most felicitous and suggestive concepts. The "generalized other" is a kind of corporate individual, a plural noun, a composite photograph which a self composes of the other members of his society. It is the universalization of the process of role-taking, since it is the general or corporate term to indicate any and all others who stand over against the self in his attitude of role-taking within the cooperative activity. The self which is here revealed is not the "I," but the empirical self or "me." And this "me" develops in the process of communication and participation as the individual sympathetically takes on the roles of others and enters the perspective of the community.[236] Within a society sharing a common milieu, a certain community of meaning arises. This kind of "social universality" or community consensus occurs whenever what is done or said or observed by one individual is understood and accepted as true by the other individuals in the group. Thus the individual transcends his merely private experience; he has gotten outside of his particular and limited world by taking the places of others, and has learned in this process that the world in general presents the same appearance to most, if not all, observers. In Mead's terms, the experience of the individual and the experience of others fall under the same "universal." This is the "generalized other" over against which the individual judges his own private experience and conduct. It is through the association of individuals in the everyday activities and relationships of life—in the home, school, club, neighborhood, church, and larger community—that the manifold "selves" or "others" of an individual personality are awakened, developed, correlated, and enabled to become moral.

In this connection it is interesting to note the affinities of Mead's "generalized other" with Adam Smith's "impartial spectator." [237] The problem set for themselves by Smith and Hume (and also by Mill and Bain) was to discover by what means the individual makes the welfare and happiness of others the object of his own self-transcending desire, judges himself disinterestedly, and sanctions his own good in terms of the common good. For Hume the answer was "sympathy," a concept which Smith elaborated in his doctrine of the moral sentiments. In the *Theory of the Moral Sentiments*[238] Smith gave an account of conscience by means of ejective consciousness: we disapprove of another's conduct when we fail to sympathize with the motives we read in his mind; we approve of it when we sympathize with his motives and with the happiness he causes in others. Conscience, Smith defined as sympathy with the judgment of an imaginary impartial spectator of one's own conduct. Speaking of the conscientious man, Smith wrote: "He has never dared to forget for one moment the judgment which the impartial spectator would pass upon his sentiments and conduct. He has never dared to suffer the man within the breast to be absent one moment from his attention. With the eyes of this great inmate he has always been accustomed to regard whatever relates to himself." [239] This notion of sympathy has contributed to the development in recent sociology of such varied interpretations as "imitation" (Tarde), "consciousness of kind" (Giddings), "group consciousness," etc.

In his *Wealth of Nations* (1776), Smith laid the foundations of classical political economy, based on the assumption of a kind of pre-established harmony between individual and social interest. But it is significant to remind ourselves that along with the freedom of the individual and the free market which Smith advocated, he asserted two other controlling ideas: (1) the *social* nature of the individual, so that in fulfilling his self-interest he automatically served the best interests of the greater society; [240] and (2) an order of law, akin to natural law, in social relations. In other words, in Smith's doctrine both the larger social good and the Moral Law qualify naked self-interest. The only trouble with the doctrine is that both human self-interest and social forces seem to be more recalcitrant to actual reconciliation than Smith realized. One suspects that Mead's optimism errs in the same direction.

Whatever the merits of this magic formula of "sympathy" in harmonizing the interests of self and society, it appears that the "generalized other" is a richer, more substantial concept. Smith's "man within the breast" might be compared to an altruistic guest in an egoistic home, kept there for purposes of prudence and respectability. Mead's "generalized other" is no guest; he is the landlord himself, a composite of all the roles which society has made available to each of its members.

It is true that without some element of sympathetic identification with others, one cannot even know that he exists as a self, much less develop a sense of justice. If Mead is correct, I cannot know myself, or continue as a self save in a dialectical situation in which I am confronted by another knowing self. I know myself only as I am known in the reflected appraisals of others. We have already observed how Mead provides for this event in his mechanism of "role-taking." On Mead's account, this process of role-taking is the basis for the sympathy which ethics and social theory require: only by being in the position of the other can one understand or evaluate his own conduct. The older psychology had had recourse to some vague "social instinct." Traditional morality had appealed to the dualism of "egoism" and "altruism." Mead believed that both of these alternatives involved serious difficulty. Furthermore, he thought that his theory would provide a natural solution to this problem of social sympathy. For in the process which he describes, we not only take the place of other selves, but in so doing, we become aware of their meaning and our meaning as persons. Having put ourselves in the other person's shoes, we are in a position to sympathize with him, to see his point of view, to know his troubles and limitations, to understand why he acts as he does, to make his interests our own interests. The more roles we thus assume, the wider will become our sympathy, the more sensitive and realistic will be our social responses, the more loving will be our attitudes. This is to make the Golden Rule the rule of social conduct. This is to "love the neighbor as oneself." And this law to love the neighbor is not simply a "command": it is rather a "law" of our very nature. It is the way of things. Thus Mead saw in social psychology and sociology an attempt to take up the larger scientific program of social analysis and reform which was implicit in Adam Smith's moral philosophy.

Since the "generalized other" is the symbol which stands for Society, for Humanity, for the Whole Community, and since Mead had his roots deep in the soil of humanism and positivism, and since he conceived of religion as the extension of social attitudes and relations to the universe at large, one may fairly raise the question as to why he did not see or why he was unwilling to grant the use of the Generalized Other as a religious equivalent for God. Indeed, Mead's friend and colleague Professor E. S. Ames, in a letter to me, remarked: "I differed with him in his unwillingness to encourage the use of the 'Generalized Other' in the interpretation of the concept of God." And Mead's student and interpreter, C. W. Morris, in commenting upon the fertility of Mead's basic ideas asks: "How far does the generalized other provide the psychological equivalent of the historical concept of God, and of the Absolute of the idealists . . . ?"[241] I raise these queries here only to indicate that, whereas Mead himself never conceived of the Generalized Other as more than the social universality of the human community, some of his friends among the religious humanists urged him to expand his concept to include the idea of God as a functional concept, after the manner in which E. S. Ames defined God as a symbol of "reality idealized," a useful concept analogous to such symbols as Alma Mater and Uncle Sam.[242] It may well be that in this matter Mead's secular bent produced a myopia which distorted his view of the total human situation, but which is corrected in Buber's theocentric personalism.

Be that as it may, the "generalized other" carried for Mead no connotations of a metaphysical ultimate. It remained for him a regulative and functional concept—the generalization of the process of role-taking within a common social activity.

PLAY AND THE GAME

In considering the social conditions under which the self arises as an object, Mead points to two other factors, in addition to language, which contribute to the full development of the self: play and the game.[243] The difference between play and the game is that in the latter the child must have the attitude of all the others involved in that game. In a game, also, there are rules and a regulated procedure. The game is thus an illustration of the social or generalized situation out of which a fully organized personality arises.

> At the first of these stages (in play) the individual's self is constituted simply by an organization of the particular attitudes of other individuals toward himself and toward one another in the specific social acts in which he participates with them. But at the second stage (in the game) in the full development of the individual's self that self is constituted not only by an organization of these particular individual attitudes, but also by an organization of the social attitudes of the generalized other or the social group as a whole to which he belongs.[244]

It may be helpful, by example and illustration, to reconstruct the actual situation in which the self arises, as Mead envisages it. A baby babbles and gurgles and coos to its mother; it is endowed with a vocal-auditory mechanism. The infant, born of the union of two persons, obviously and necessarily, lives in a group in more or less constant interaction with others. There is a play of gesture and rudimentary conversation of attitudes and gestures between the infant and his elders. To a baby the smiles of his parents or the outstretched arms are at first simply stimuli which call out instinctive reactions of his own. He cries or coos, he stretches out his arm, or tries to move toward the parent, to re-establish contact with the warm mother flesh. But when, over a period of time, these gestures in the parents immediately call up memory-images of his own previous responses and their results, the baby has the material out of which he begins to build up the social objects of his environment. The baby begins to recognize his parents and others in his little society. He learns to act with confidence (or fear) toward them since their gestures have come to have meaning for him. His own response to their gestures and its consequences are really an interpretation of the facial expressions and attitudes of body and tones of voice. "The awakening social intelligence of the child is evidenced . . . in the inner assurance of his own readiness to adjust himself to the attitudes of other." [245] "The child can think about his conduct as good or bad only as he reacts to his own acts in the remembered words of his parents." [246] Gradually, the child learns to participate in the experiences of his associates; he learns to get over to the other side—through imitation, copying, matching, role-taking, etc. He learns, in Mead's terms, to "take the roles" of the others, to see himself in their place, and to see himself, reflexively, as they see him. Into this response there naturally flows the memory images of the responses of those about him. He thus becomes *self*-conscious. At first the child takes separate roles, but gradually after taking many roles, he comes to assume the organized roles of his group—the collective or corporate role of all his "others"—the "generalized other."

The free play of a child is particularly marked by the playing of separate roles, serially, one at a time—that of mother, father, nurse, baby brother, grandpa, postman, Hopalong Cassidy, the "big bad wolf," himself as baby, etc. In this way the child is or has many selves. It is only later that these discrete, ephemeral, play-selves become organized into the relatively stable, mature self of experience. This true dependable self develops in what may be called the "game period" in which the individual boy or girl is engaged in cooperative activity with several other children and learns to take the roles of all the participants in the game. For example, in a baseball game, a boy must be familiar with all the nine positions on the field and be able to anticipate the simultaneous response of each player in order to play his own position successfully. Such behavior, Mead contends, necessitates taking the roles of all the other players at one and the same time, that is, taking the role of the group. The person has generalized the attitude of role-taking.

> The attitudes of the other players which the participant assumes organize into a sort of unity, and it is that organization which controls the response of the individual. . . . What he does is controlled by his being everyone else on that team, at least in so far as those attitudes affect his own particular response.[247]

By thus participating in the behavior of many others, the self gets an "other" which is an organization of the attitudes of those involved in the same process. By the progressive participation and role-taking in ever larger groups and more complex configurations of adjustment, the developing self acquires the relatively stable, complex, and organized "character" that we know in common experience. When this occurs, the stage of true self-hood or personality is reached.

THE "I" AND THE "ME"

We have now discussed at some length the social origins and foundations of the self, and have implied in various connections that the self does not consist merely and only in the internal organization of social attitudes. We must therefore examine and make explicit another interesting distinction which Mead makes between what he calls the "me," which is the organized set of attitudes which I assume and which I introject into my own private self, and the "I" which is the organism's response to the attitudes of others as this appears in his own experience.[248] The "me," as the organized attitudes of the group which one assumes, limits the "I" and thus provides for social control; while the "I" asserts itself within the limits of its community and thus makes for novelty, social change, and reconstruction. Taken together, the "I" and the "me" as phases of the self, they constitute a personality. In Mead's conception of these two phases, the potential psycho-physical assertive organism is the *given,* or the "I"; the "me" is the introjected other. The "self" or personality, then, is the *given as socialized* through the experiences and interplay of living in a group. In order to examine Mead's theory concerning these two aspects of the social individual, let us raise some specific questions and attempt to answer them on Mead's terms.

Exactly what is involved in the self being an object, a "me" which can also appear in consciousness? What is the nature of the "I" which is aware of the social "me"? What is the nature of this self as revealed by introspection and subject also to factual analysis? For analysis does reveal, in the memory and thinking processes, an attitude of observing oneself in which both the observer and the observed appear. We are all familiar with the experience of "talking to oneself," judging oneself, scolding oneself, or priding oneself—in quite the same manner as we address our fellows.

We have already seen how the self arises in the process of conversation or symbolic communication when the individual takes the role of another and acts toward himself as others do. This self, on Mead's account, comprises two phases in so far as the "I" consists of the relatively free, unpredictable, self-initiating responses of the organism to the attitudes of others, while the "me" consists of the set of attitudes of others which the individual himself assumes. The attitudes of others constitute the organized "me," and then one reacts toward that as an "I." [249] The one is unique, idiosyncratic, more or less uncertain, subjective, giving a sense of freedom and initiative; the other is objective, empirical, more or less dependable, existing for the group. The "I" is the active agent in the solution of problems and in the reconstruction of experience because of his unique perspective. "The objective self of human consciousness is the merging of one's responses with the social stimulation by which he affects himself. The 'me' is a man's reply to his own talk." [250] In other words, the "me" is an importation from the field of social objects and social conduct into the realm of what we call inner experience.

Perhaps the simplest way to conceive of the problem here is in terms of memory. For example, I talk to myself, and I recall what I said and felt. The "I" of this moment is present in the "me" of the next moment or hour. I cannot turn back quickly enough to catch myself; but I can remember what I said and did, and this historical figure becomes a part of the "me." The "I" is thus given a functional relationship. And perhaps that is all it is; for Mead is quick to deny that he is raising a metaphysical question of how a person can be both "I" and "me." [251] He is concerned only over the distinction from the point of view of conduct itself; for the individual *does* have the feeling of himself as having a particular position and function in society.

In Mead's account, then, and with what may be regarded as poetic or methodological license, the "I" is that part of the self, rooted in the biological equipment of the organism, which we identify with impulse, freedom, creativity, subjectivity; those aspects of individual behavior and experience which are over against the social or objective situation and which can and do change society. The "me" is all of the attitudes, roles, meanings, pressures and values of others organized and taken over into one's self through the agency of role-taking which is involved in the language symbol. Both "I" and "me" are essential to the self in its full development.[252] An object involves and implies a subject, and vice versa. One without the other would give an extreme and one-sided self. If the self were only a "me," the self would be nothing but a reflection of the social other. Yet a "me" is inconceivable without an "I." In other words, "the self-conscious, actual self in social intercourse is the objective 'me' or 'me's' with the process of response continually going on and implying a fictitious 'I' always out of sight of himself." [253]

There are certain difficulties here which Mead never completely harmonized and which we will discuss in a later section. It should be clear, however, that Mead is trying to do justice to both self and society, the private and the public, the particular and the universal. In the process of becoming an object to itself, the self knows itself in the same way it knows things other than itself. It is within a social field of common meanings that certain contents come to be referred to the self as subjective, while others establish themselves as objective. The complete self includes both "I" and a "me."

> (However) the fact that all selves are constituted by or in terms of social process and are individual reflections of it . . . is not in the least incompatible with, or destructive of the fact that every individual self has its own peculiar individuality, its own unique pattern.[254]

In terms of these two aspects of the self, Mead explains social control (the "me" limits and checks the "I") and social change (the "I" asserts itself within the limits of his society).[255]

It seems clear, if I mistake not, that Mead has accepted the distinction between the "I" and the "me" found in the transcendental philosophy of Kant and the post-Kantian idealists. He agrees with Kant that the "self cannot appear in consciousness as an 'I,' and that it is always an object, i.e., a 'me,' and that the 'me' is inconceivable without an 'I.' "[256] He further supports the Kantian view "that such an 'I' is a presupposition, but never a presentation of conscious experience."[257] The "I" is the necessary result of cognitive inference or intuition of a creative and active *subject* behind the scenes. But this "I" can never exist as an object of conscious knowledge, for the moment it is presented as such it becomes an "object," a "me," to an observing subject. This "I" is the transcendental self or unity of Kant, the soul that James conceived behind the scenes holding on to the skirts of an idea to give it an added increment of emphasis.[258]

> The individual enters as such into his own experience only as an object, not as a subject; and he can enter as an object only on the basis of social relation and interaction, only by means of his experiential transactions with other individuals in an organized social environment.[259]

Even though we must presuppose some sort of an "I," we cannot say anything about it until it is considered in conjunction with the "me." And, as we have said, the *me* is the aspect of the self which we know through others; it is the generalized other, the self in its universal character, organized and imported into the self.[260] Still, if and when Mead ventures into metaphysics he must say something about this hidden or transcendental agent.

THE RELATION OF THE "I" AND THE "ME" AS PHASES OF THE SELF

There are some sociologists and behaviorists who think that the "me" is all there is to the self: the self merely reflects and incorporates the social forms and contents—nothing more. And while Mead is not always clear on this point, and some of his phrases suggest a subordination of the *I* to the *me*, his consideration of the "I" as a phase of the self with status equal to that of the "me" seems to support his dismissal of any mechanistic and deterministic view which holds that the self is entirely molded by the social situation. One of the reasons why Mead also rejected Hegelian idealism was that it, too, appeared guilty of denying the individual's unique reality as experienced in the present. Modern social psychology, as represented by Durkheim, Simmel, Cooley and Mead, has usually repudiated the classical formulation of both *social nominalism* and *social realism,* and has insisted that the individual and society are twin-born, that they are inseparable aspects of the same reality. Personality develops only in a social context, and society exists only in and through persons. By implication, what is good for one is good for the other.

It needs to be pointed out, however, that Mead's attempts to stay within the bounds of a radical empiricism and naturalism put a severe strain on his own argument—for he seems to say in some places that the self is only a moment or phase *within* experience. The contrast between self and other become, in this setting, extremely soft, fluid, attenuated. Some of Mead's critics also contend that he (and pragmatists generally) has lost the individual autonomous self in society, just as the Hegelians were accused of swallowing up the person in the Absolute Self. And it must be admitted that certain passages and emphases in Mead's writings convey this impression and justify the criticism. For example, he writes: "The attitudes of the others constitute the organized 'me,' and then one reacts toward that as an 'I.' " [261] The structure of the society lies in its social habits and only in so far as we can take these social habits into ourselves can we become selves.[262] The whole is greater than the parts, precedes the parts, indeed creates the parts. "The form of the social object must be found first of all in the experience of other selves." [263] "The self-conscious actual self in social intercourse is the objective 'me.' " [264] "Inner consciousness is socially organized by the importation of the social organization of the outer world." [265] And again:

> Every individual self within a given society or social community reflects in its organized structure the whole relational pattern of organized social behavior which that society or community exhibits or is carrying on, and its organized structure is constituted by this pattern . . . [266]

From such passages as these it might appear that Mead's social behaviorism had at times forced him into compromising his oft-repeated assertion that nature and society are organizations of individual perspectives, and that these perspectives are primary.[267]

But, in all fairness, it must be remembered that Mead was aware of this problem and sought to disarm any such criticism by his recognition of the impulsive, creative, outgoing biologic individual, the "I" in contrast to the "me," that active principle which changes the social structure and reconstructs the environment from its own peculiar perspective. The self does not merely reflect the social structure; the complete self is both an *I* and a *me*. Of course, selves presuppose a prior social process which forms, and is reflected by, the individual selves. But Mead insists that selves, in turn, are distinguishable "reconstructive centers of society" (Dewey's term) making a truly human and progressive society possible. The self does more than merely mirror the social content. The self constitutes and changes society as really as society constitutes and molds the individual. The self is what it is both because of its own nature and because of the community's reciprocal action upon it. Mead's intention in this regard can perhaps best be conveyed by quoting again some typical passages:

> There is nothing that has suffered more through loss of dignity of content in modern positivistic psychology than the "I." The "me" has been most honorably dealt with. It has waxed in diameter and interest, not to speak of number, with continued analysis, while the "I" has been forced from its metaphysical throne. . . .[268]
>
> He is a member of the community, but he is a particular part of the community, with a particular heredity and position which distinguishes him from anybody else.[269]
>
> Each individual stratifies the common life in a different manner, and the life of the community is the sum of all these stratifications.[270]
>
> Each individual self within that process, while it reflects in its organized structure the behavior pattern of that process as a whole, does so from its own particular and unique standpoint . . . just as every monad in the Leibnizian universe mirrors that universe from a different point of view. . . .[271]

Whether or not we conclude that Mead's analysis is consistent, convincing and valid, it is clear that he is asserting that the individual self is constituted by an *I* and a *me*; and that the self-realization of this social individual is accompanied by at least a partial reconstruction of the environment and of the social patterns. The socially nurtured self is not wholly at the mercy of the existing mores, societal conventions, and institutional pressures. Mead believed that each individual variously responding to his environment, changed it to a degree; the genius or great man changed it to a greater degree. Self and Society are mutually conditioned and causally interdependent. The self thus assimilates reality to its own pattern, creates, as it were, its own environment.[272]

What is the cause of this apparent ambiguity in Mead's theory? Is there any way in which the apparent contradiction can be reconciled? It can be done, I think, but in so doing we become aware of one of the limitations of an "operational," descriptive method. In *Mind, Self and Society* and in most of his journal articles, Mead's concern was primarily scientific, behavioristic, descriptive: he was attempting to articulate a social psychology. And necessarily his emphasis fell on the empirical data and organized structure of the social process which Mead identifies with the "me." So he writes:

> For social psychology, the whole (society) is prior to the part (individual), not the part to the whole; and the part is explained in terms of the whole, not the whole in terms of the part. The social act is not explained by building it up of stimulus plus response; it must be taken as a dynamic whole—as something going on—no part of which can be considered or understood by itself—a complex organic process implied by each individual stimulus and response involved in it.[273]

As a scientist he began with observable behavior, with the organized social process as a whole, the generalized other, the "me." For only that is apprehended in empirical knowledge. Yet Mead was not content with the mechanistic behaviorism and determinism to which a merely descriptive positivism leads—e.g., in Watson. Mead wanted to account for the "cutting out" of the individual and private consciousness from the ongoing flow of experience. So while keeping his allegiance to pragmatism and behaviorism and objective methods, in the essays collected in *The Philosophy of the Act,* and especially in the later years of his life, Mead began to grope toward and to sketch the outlines of a metaphysics. As a metaphysician he began with the primary and ultimate unit of existence, with the individual; and he found that the whole is an organization and rationalization of these many individual acts and perspectives. "It is this employment of both the metaphysical and the scientific approach which gives Mead's philosophy the features of both a monadism and a monism." [274] But Mead repeatedly warns that scientific theories are postulates, not dogmas; that the social whole for social psychology is not an Absolute of which the individuals are partial representations. He disclaims any part-whole identity. It is rather a *social* universe, or a universe of discourse, which develops from the individual's assumption of the roles and attitudes of the generalized other in communication and participation. It is an emergent and scientific community, and explained on the basis of emergent evolution and relativity. So Mead argued that in explaining the origin and nature and development of individual selves in terms of a behavioristic social psychology, he was entirely justified in making such postulates, so long as he did not dogmatically assume that there is no meaning in the world beyond this behavioristic and operational statement of it. "The result is that research science has been able to take over a mechanistic theory of the world and postulate such a theory without committing itself to any philosophy based upon it." [275] Similarly, just as the scientist has no right to deny the primacy of the perceptual experience of color and sound in relation to its reflective analysis, the social psychologist may not deny the primacy of the individual. Mead's answer to this problem was to posit the "I" and the "me" as given together: both together constitute the individual personality.

Mead's definition of the existential social self has implications for the moral situation of man in his society. To a consideration of the self in society we turn briefly.

SELF AND SOCIETY

The normal situation is one which involves a reaction of the individual in a situation which is socially determined, but to which he brings his own responses as an *I*. Society (or its institutions; the *me*) gives form and content to the *I* without which the individual would have no meaning in nor control over his conduct as an *I*.[276] For Mead, the *form* as well as the *content* of consciousness is of social origin.[277] Inner consciousness is socially organized by the importation of the social organization of the outer world. There is a constant factor of awareness of what we do and say and think. But this "inner observer" or censor is not to be confused with the "I," or the implied object of our actions. "The observer," writes Mead, "who accompanies all our self-conscious conduct is then not the actual 'I' who is responsible for the conduct in *propria persona*—he is rather the response which one makes to his own conduct." [278] "Social control is the expression of the 'me' over against the expression of the 'I.' It sets the limits, it gives the determination that enables the 'I,' so to speak, to use the 'me' as the means of carrying out what is the undertaking that all are interested in." [279] In Freudian terms, the "me" is the *censor* or the "super-ego" which modifies the instinctive psychic energy of the "id." It determines the sort of expression which can take place, sets the stage, and gives the cue.[280] Under normal conditions the way in which an individual acts will be determined by his taking the attitudes of the others in the group. In the process of education the social mores, values, and institutions are inculcated into the consciousness, the inner pattern, the "conscience," of the individual. The *I* is given a *me*; the individual is taught his rights and his duties. Self-criticism, as we have indicated already, is really social criticism." And thus it is that social control, as operating in terms of self-criticism exerts itself so intimately and extensively over individual behavior or conduct." [281]

Since each component individual carries within himself the roles and attitudes and behavior patterns of the others implicated in the common life, society has in this fact a powerful technique for control and thus regulates the activity and behavior and ideas of its members in terms of the effect on others of any contemplated action. But while impressing the "me" on the individual, it must, under penalty of stagnation, accept the changes which the creative, ever novel, rebellious "I" forces upon society. Social control is far from absolute, on this view. The individual response is sometimes that of violent rebellion instead of acquiescence.

Take the situation of self-assertion where the self simply asserts itself over against others, and suppose that the emotional stress is such that the forms of polite society in the performance of legitimate conduct are overthrown, so that the person expresses himself violently. There the "me" is determined by the situation. There are certain recognized fields within which an individual can assert himself, certain rights which he has within these limits. But let the stress become too great, these limits are not observed, and an individual asserts himself in perhaps a violent fashion. Then the "I" is the dominant element over against the "me." [282]

Social control there surely is: the law must be obeyed; the constitution must be hallowed; the institutions such as family, courts, churches, morals, must be recognized and supported. We have to have an order of society. We cannot afford to let that order decay.[283] But we must not forget the other capacity of *talking back* to the community and, at times, insisting upon changing the significant symbols and behavior patterns of the community—thus changing the community itself.

> We can reform the order of things; we can insist on making the community standards better standards. We are not simply bound by the community. We are engaged in a conversation in which what we say is listened to by the community and its response is one which is affected by what we have to say.[284]

As a rule, we conform to the general will of the community; we assume that the organized institutions and customs represent the considered morality of the community. The things one can and cannot do, are those which everybody else would approve or condemn. But every man is entitled to his "day in court." Especially in critical situations, "the individual has not only the right but the duty of talking (back) to the community of which he is a part," and thus perhaps bringing about possible and desirable reforms. This is the way society gets ahead; and it is made easier if the individual can speak not only with the voice of reason, but also with the voices of the past and the future. From the historical perspective, from the standpoint of "a higher sort of community," the individual may speak with a voice which is greater than the present voice of the group.[285] This is the method of social progress; and it is modelled after the procedures of the research scientist. The scientist, confronted with a problem, "is not looking ahead toward a goal and charting his movement toward that goal. That is not the function of the scientist. He is finding out why his system does not work, what the difficulty is. And the test of his solution of the difficulty is that his system starts working again."[286] Mead found in the democratic, socially-minded community the finest example of, and the most favorable opportunity for, this correlative and full development of self and society, permitting individual expression while maintaining social order. Thus, teleology and mechanism, freedom and necessity are reconciled. In several places Mead referred to the way in which social and political revolution may, in constitutional nation-states, become incorporated into the regular processes of the state itself.[287] This is Mead's experimental and scientific answer to the problem of individuality within the social order.

Given Mead's faith in an evolving and teleological social intelligence competent to cope with social problems, and his pragmatic stress upon direction rather than destination, it is not surprising that he came to the rather utopian and romantic belief that history was on the side of automatic progress. Eventually, but inevitably, the democratic and cooperative commonwealth, the brotherhood of man, would emerge in the socio-historical process. Proposals for change and reform will always come from individuals, especially from exceptional geniuses, for "problems can appear only in the experience of the individual." [288] But Mead assumed that the solutions of these individual problems would become the new "universals," institutions, mores, conventions which would represent the interests of the majority. While this assumption is open to criticism, it is easy to see how Mead would make the assumption since he believed that any given social order already represents the organization of the perspectives of the many as over against the few. The novel experiences and the proposals for social innovations of the exceptional individuals must be given free expression and the opportunity to win acceptance, but without upsetting the prevailing social order.[289]

Mead believed that these same principles of social psychology provided a fruitful basis for aesthetic experience, ethical theory, social reform, economic practice, democratic political theory, and international relations. All of these areas of human activity involve a similar integration of impulses at the level of interacting selves. Here is the key to a society "in which everyone is going to recognize the interests of everybody else—for example, in which the golden rule is to be the rule of conduct, that is, a society in which everyone is to make the interests of others his own interests, while actually each person seems to be pursuing his own interest." [290] As social, the self has become the other, and the values of the other are his own. Thus the self escapes the egocentric predicament, both epistemologically and ethically. A social self has "social" impulses that demand fulfillment as imperatively as any other impulses. Moral ends are social ends. Moral action is intelligent, socially directed action, guided by consequences and experiment and by all the knowledge that science can give, and in which the interests of others are considered equal, indeed, identical with, one's own. It is in a society of such selves that Mead finds the social ideal; for there self-expression and social control are balanced for persons who are both individual and social. The implications of democracy and of moderate non-doctrinaire socialism are that each person should realize himself through moral participation in a cooperative enterprise.

SUMMARY

Such is the course and issue of Mead's reasoning about the problem of the self. And since our over-long attempt to describe the distinctive social nature of the self is now at an end, it is appropriate that we summarize what it all adds up to.

Mead's effort was to state a pragmatic philosophy and social psychology, reinterpreting the concepts of mind and self in the biological, psychological and sociological terms which post-Darwinian thought made prominent, but in such a way as would provide for the expression of individual experience without upsetting the social order. He believed that his analysis of self and society did in fact maintain such a balance, and as such provided the conditions for the development of selves who are both individual and social—"social individuals." While the precursors of this genetic theory of personality and society are James, Baldwin and Cooley, the clearest statement of this "symbolic interactionism" is found in Mead's account.

Mead's starting point is social experience. Men live together in a world of meaning only because there is a prior undergirding social process within which their biologic lives are set. Both rationalism and empiricism have traditionally tended to regard experience as individual, subjective, and mental; and the consequent problem of epistemology was to show how starting from such experience an opposite objective world could be grasped. The usual answer was that it could not be done. Mead therefore shifts the starting point, and points out that "my" has no meaning except over against "your," that unless there was a social interaction and a common dimension of experience the notion of individual private experience would be without meaning. The primary situation for observation, therefore, is a field in which one's self is present in the same way that other selves and physical objects are present. Experience of one's self is always in a field in which other things are experienced, and the self has no way of knowing itself different from the way in which it knows things other than itself. It is within such a context that certain contents (givens, meanings, truths, etc.) come to be referred to the self as private or subjective, while others establish themselves as objective and common. In symbolic communication on the higher conscious level, man achieves, paradoxically, a greater sense of individuality. Mind is a product of communication within a social process, in organisms endowed with certain neurological capacities which permit self-stimulation and imaginative role-taking. What we term "reason" arises when an organism takes into its own responses the attitudes of the other organisms involved. So far as we know, this is possible only for human beings, because they have reached the stage of evolution where the invention and use of language (vocal gesture and symbol) is possible. The human animal acquires a mind when he can use significant symbols and not merely respond to signs. It is through the ability to be the other at the same time that he is himself that the symbol becomes significant. And among gestures thus capable of becoming significant symbols, and so transforming the biologic individual into a minded-organism, the vocal gesture (speech) is preeminent. Speech makes this possible because in talking to others one stimulates himself at the same time and in the same way that he stimulates others. At this point the self appears—precipitated, as it were, together with mind and significant symbol.

The distinguishing characteristic of the self is that it is its own object. This in genesis requires that an organism must be able to get outside of itself, so to speak, in order to respond to itself as an object. The mechanism for this development, in the behavioristic approach, Mead finds in language and role-taking. In virtue of the cooperative interaction in which organisms participate, and because through speech an organism can hear itself talk and so affect itself as it affects others, the organism can "take the role of the other," i.e., respond to itself as others would. To the degree that this is so, the egocentric predicament is avoided, since the self as social can take the attitudes of others implicated in the common activity. Man is the role-taking animal. This situation can be internalized so that one becomes the other to one's self. Thinking, as opposed to speaking, is the conversation of the self with itself in the role of the other.

This process of role-taking, like any act, is capable of generalization, and in so far as one takes indifferently any and all of the roles of those engaged in the common activity, one takes what Mead calls "the role of the generalized other." This generalized other—the roles of others organized and taken over into one's self—constitute the "me." Now the world is common in so far as it appears in a plurality of perspectives. Thus the individual form (the "I") gets a "me," is conditioned by the social structure, and develops a self which is largely a reflection of the social patterns. The self is derivative of society, yet the "I" provides for novelty and change in society. Thus self and society are mutually interdependent and reciprocally conditioned. He is an object to himself because he can take the roles of others. To be oneself, one must first be another, be related to another.

The structure and continuity of society is qualified by the membership in it of free individuals whose future is not yet determined, yet the novelty of whose action is ever qualified by their relations to society. Thus is reconciled freedom and structure, individuality and sociality. The universal is nothing if the particular is nothing; the richness of the concrete universal depends upon the reality and variety of its constituents.

Individual selves, yes! But not absolute nor exclusive individuals. Society, yes! But not absolute nor exclusive society. The self is a "social" self.

NOTES

1. Mead experienced difficulty in finding a clear, felicitous, or even adequate expression for his thought. But one need not now read Mead to encounter his germinal and most valuable ideas; for they have found their way into many contemporary expositions of social psychology, philosophy, ethics, and education.

2. John Dewey said of his friend: "His mind was deeply original—in my contacts and my judgment the most original mind in philosophy in the America of the last generation." See Dewey's Memorial Address, "George Herbert Mead As I Knew Him," in the University of Chicago *Record*, XVII (1931), 174-75. This estimate is one with which A. N. Whitehead agrees.

3. G. H. Mead, *Mind, Self and Society*, p. 1.

4. G. H. Mead, *The Philosophy of the Present*.

5. Mead's naturalism and pragmatism are not entirely consistent, and there is evidence of a tendency in the direction of idealism. Indeed, it would appear that naturalism and humanism, in so far as they venture toward a comprehensive system, move in the direction of idealism. Mead never completely lost his early idealism.

6. In *The Decennial Publications of the University of Chicago* (First Series), III, 1903, pp. 75-112.

7. Alfred Lloyd's *Dynamic Idealism* appeared in 1898. Lloyd's thesis was that the relation between a self, an organism, and the world is a dynamic one,

not a formal one. "Parts are more than mere component parts; they are related parts, being related to each other with reference to the same end to which all are means." On this account, any physical object is a "system of relations" and relations are dynamic, not formal. See also John Dewey, *Outline of Ethics* (1891) and *Studies in Logical Theory* (1903). It was the decade between the appearance of these two books that witnessed, for both Dewey and Mead, their shift from idealism to pragmatism. One should perhaps mention the entire "Chicago School" who were busily at work on the new social psychology and its implications for a genetic logic: A. W. Moore, Albion Small, J. H. Tufts, W. I. Thomas, Thorstein Veblen, *et al.* These men, aided by the genetic approach derived from Darwin, launched a reconstruction of idealism in which ideas and concepts, like species, are plastic, variable, functional, and practical.

Peirce, who may be regarded as the logical father of pragmatism, also gave Mead valuable clues to the general position later assumed. Peirce was the first among modern writers to make inquiry and scientific method the primary source of logical subject matter. Peirce's "laboratory habit of mind" and his introduction of experimental logic into the process of knowing were inherited by Mead. (See *IJE*, XL, 1930, 225, 228). And in his science of meanings, elaborated in mathematical terms, Peirce showed in empirical terms the reality and utility of "universals." See *The Philosophy of Peirce, Selected Writings*, ed., J. Buchler. New York, 1940, pp. 36-7, 28-9, *passim*.

8. *IJE*, XLVI (1935-36), 77. Cf. also "A Pragmatic Theory of Truth," in *Studies in the Nature of Truth, University of California Publications in Philosophy*, XI (1929), 65-88.

9. *IJE*, XLVI (1935-36), 75-76.

10. "A Behavioristic Account of the Significant Symbol," *JP*, XIX (1922); also *MSS, passim*.

11. "The Definition of the Psychical," *op. cit.;* see also "The Mechanism of Social Consciousness," *JP*, IX (1912), 401-406; "The Social Self," *JP*, X (1913), 374-78; "What Social Objects Must Psychology Presuppose," *JP*, VII (1910), 180f; *MSS*, Sections 2, 3, 11, 13, 17, 22, 25.

12. "A Behavioristic Account of the Significant Symbol," *JP*, XIX (1922), 162. Cf. "The Objective Reality of Perspectives," *Proceedings of the Sixth International Congress of Philosophy* (1926), pp. 75-85. Reprinted in *The Philosophy of the Present* (Chicago, 1932).

13. *MSS*, pp. 121, 125, 133, *et passim*. Cf. John Dewey, *Experience and Nature*, pp. 177-87, 290-99; also C. W. Morris, *Six Theories of Mind*, pp. 320ff. Animals lower than man are regarded as using gestures; such gestures are significant to others but not to themselves.

14. *JP*, XIX (1922), 161.

15. G. H. Mead, *The Philosophy of the Act*, p. 65, *passim*.

16. Mead traces the shift to the behavioristic scientific approach to mind in *Movements of Thought in the Nineteenth Century*, pp. 387ff.

17. E.g., in "The Definition of the Psychical," p. 17, he writes of James: "If we take this (James's) description of the mind which presents outer reality and does so much more . . . we have by all odds the richest statement of

the psychical consciousness that philosophical literature has yet presented. . . ." Mead was also intrigued with the concept of the "stream of thought" and I suspect that it may have influenced his later theory of the dynamic overlapping flow of life, thought, history, and nature. See *MT*, p. 389.

18. The things which, it seems to me, most appealed to Mead were James's theory of consciousness, his theory of emotions, the selective attention of impulse, the general theory of volitional pragmatism, the theory of knowledge and verification, and the idea of process or flow of experience.

19. William James, *Principles of Psychology*, Vol. I, pp. 288-89, 298, 336. Cf. Mead, *IJE*, XL (1930), 223f.

20. James, *op. cit.*, Vol. II, Chaps. 19, 21, esp. p. 295.

21. See James's famous article, "Does Consciousness Exist?" (1904) in *Essays in Radical Empiricism* (New York: Longmans, Green, 1912).

22. The word 'I,' then, is primarily a noun of position, just like "this' and 'here.' Activities attached to 'this' position have prerogative emphasis. . . . The 'my' of them is the emphasis, the feeling of perspective-interest in which they are dyed." *A Pluralistic Universe*, p. 380.

23. James, *Principles of Psychology*, Vol. I, Chap. 9.

24. James's radical empiricism became an interpretation of nature as "identifiable with mental terms." What James did, in effect, was to extend his psychological doctrine of continuity in consciousness into a metaphysical doctrine of continuity in being between "things and thoughts." The common world is a world of pure experience.

25. *MSS*, pp. 18f, 27f. It should be added, however, that Mead could not accept James's lofty individualism—the precious individual with his freedom, his potentialities, his will, his feelings. Mead was the *social* psychologist relying on applied intelligence, a controlled environment, communal life, and co-operative social planning. Mead was afraid of that slippery term "satisfaction" as a test of truth, believing that it weakened James's analysis of knowledge in conduct. (*IJE*, XL, 1930, 226). Mead suspected that James retained enough of a Kantian taint to conceive of the individual as having a "soul" and to base his ethics on *a priori* foundations. And while James did include the idea of a "social self"—the knowledge of one's self as reflected from the attitudes and reactions of others—it was not such as to satisfy Mead. (See the *Principles of Psychology*, Vol. I, pp. 293-94, and cf. pp. 333-34, 339-40, 343-47). Mead might well have followed Royce, his idealist teacher, in what he called "the grandiose undertaking to bring the whole of reality within experience," and set up a theory of reality based on an absolute community. But he did just the opposite: he explained the emergence of minds and societies as instances of a general process of natural emergence.

26. *MSS*, pp. 329-336.

27. "The Definition of the Psychical," *op. cit.*, p. 35.

28. *Idem.* By contrast, as we shall explain later, the "me" is the empirical self, the object of scientific study, or, in other words, the attitudes of others organized and taken over into one's self.

29. *PA*, p. 417.

30. *Ibid.*, p. 343.

31. *PA*, pp. 303-4. Mead considers the nutritive process of an organism as an illustration of this circular activity of creating and supplying a want or need.

32. *MSS*, p. 385.

33. William James, perhaps more than the other pragmatists, stressed the continuous uninterrupted activity; and in so doing he laid himself open to Mead's criticism, to the effect that James failed to take account of the problems and inhibitions which inevitably fracture and frustrate the unity of experience. (*MT*, p. 396; *PA*, p. 631). Contrary to James's view, Mead had early expressed the notion that the psychical is a discontinuous characteristic of that continuing process. In other words, mind is a temporary phase of the empirical interaction of an organism with its environment concomitant with the interruption of that interaction by a problematic situation. (See "The Definition of the Psychical," *loc. cit.*, p. 93).

34. See *MSS*, pp. 125-131; 337ff; *MT*, pp. 389ff.

35. *MT*, p. 389; *PA*, p. 3; *MSS*, p. 129.

36. G. H. Mead, "The Relation of Play to Education," *University of Chicago Record*, I (1896-97), 145. See also *IJE*, XLVI (1936), 72-73, where Mead discusses Dewey's educational theory. It is the psychological analysis of impulse and interest which led Dewey into his educational theory and practice. It was his conception of the interest as presenting the object as it arises in the act and attitude of the child that furnished him with his basic tool. The child's mind can be trained only with respect to those objects in the child's own experience which arise out of its own interests, needs, and problems. Education is nothing but guiding the child in the exercise of his own intelligence. Mead agreed with this thesis; he too believed that education is a matter of so arranging the stimuli that they will answer to the natural growth of the child's organism.

37. *MSS*, p. 129; *MT*, p. 318.

38. "The Mechanism of Social Consciousness," *JP*, IX (1912), 401.

39. *MSS*, pp. 337, 328.

40. In value theory, also, Mead held to the familiar pragmatist "interest theory of value": That is good which satisfies an interest or impulse. But here too Mead's statement is in objective relativistic terms: value is the character of an object in its capacity to satisfy an interest—value resides neither in the object alone nor in an emotional state of the subject.

41. In hunger, for example, the goal of the impulse is usually of a general character, that is, for food rather than for a particular kind of food.

42. The logical corollary of this is that the self-realization of a social individual is accompanied by at least a partial reconstruction of the environment and of the social patterns, customs, and values.

43. Mead's emphasis grew out of James's theory of emotions and the James-Lange theory of visceral and motor responses, as amended by Dewey, and attempted to retain something of the active, creative side of human experience.

44. *MSS*, pp. 6-12, 100ff. See *MT*, pp. 387-91, for a brief discussion of the behavioristic movement in psychology; also E. Faris, "Behaviorism as a Movement in Psychology," in *AJS*, XXXIV (1938), 271ff. Miller and Dollard, (*Social Learning and Imitation*, New Haven: Yale Univ. Press, 1941)

are of the opinion that Mead did not grasp the basic elements and the full import of the Pavlovian experiments, especially the factors of *drive* and *reward* which are the essential conditions for inter-stimulation and response.

45. *MT*, pp. 386ff, 396, 404; *MSS*, pp. 2-8, 33-41.

46. The term "social behaviorism" is not Mead's; it was coined and used by C. W. Morris, the editor of *MSS*, to characterize the relation of Mead to Watson.

47. E. Faris, *loc. cit.*, p. 272.

48. *MSS*, pp. 125ff, 131.

49. *JP*, VII (1910), 180. It is perhaps noteworthy that in this instance Mead concurs with the views of the idealists. See J. Royce, *PR*, III (1894), 513-45; IV, (1895), 473. Mead, however, appears here to be in opposition to Cooley and Bergson in regard to *social* and *physical* consciousness. According to Cooley, our rational and conceptual knowledge develops in dealing with the material world. See C. H. Cooley, "The Roots of Social Knowledge," *AJS*, XXXII, 66f). And cf. Bergson's argument that the intellect "feels itself at home among inanimate objects." (*Creative Evolution*, English translation, p. ix).

50. *MSS*, p. 125; 83ff.

51. *PA*, p. 371.

52. *MSS*, p. 247.

53. "The Definition of the Psychical," *loc. cit.*, p. 34.

54. *MT*, pp. 89-90.

55. Cf. A. W. Moore, "The Reformation of Logic," in *Creative Intelligence*, pp. 82-84.

56. Cf. Irwin Edman, "The Private Thinker and the Public World," *JP*, XLIII (1946), 617-29. Thinking is a soliloquy which becomes a conversation, and then soliloquy again.

57. *PP*, pp. 189-90.

58. *MT*, pp. 380-81. It is this inner thought, this inner flow of speech and response, this reciprocal communication and participation, which becomes or constitutes the mind.

59. *MSS*, p. 335; *MT*, pp. 401-02; *JP*, X (1913), 377-78; *PA*, p. 89. See also *PB*, VI (1909), 406-07.

60. *JP*, X (1913), 377.

61. G. H. Mead, in *PB*, VI (1909), 406-07.

62. Cf. Buber's emphasis on the drama as illustrating the dialogic life.

63. *MT*, p. 401.

64. *Ibid.*, p. 402.

65. G. H. Mead, in *PR*, IX (1900), 5; see also "The Definition of the Psychical," *loc. cit.* Cf. John Dewey's views on this point as expressed in *Experience and Nature*.

66. *PA*, p. 71; cf. also pp. 218, 227, 122, 21. Mead writes, "I find myself in agreement with Professor Bode in identifying the future with consciousness, although I have reached the conclusion by a somewhat different path." (*PA*, 348n). See Boyd H. Bode, "Consciousness and Psychology," in *Creative Intelligence* (New York, 1917), pp. 228-81, esp. 242ff.

67. It should be noted that here Mead is stressing the "I" side of the self, the impulsive, initiating, creative, free aspects of the form. In other places, as we shall see, he seems to over-stress the "me" side of the self, almost to the point of losing the *I*. Mead tried to maintain the *I* of the self in order to provide for individuality and for novelty. The self develops in society, but Mead tried to reconcile the derivative aspects of the self with its creative aspects. In the passages here he is emphasizing the latter.

68. *PA*, pp. 65, 70, 647, 122, 227.

69. *Ibid.*, p. 122.

70. *PA*, p. 227.

71. *Ibid.*, p. 71.

72. *MSS*, p. 129.

73. *PA*, p. 428; *MSS*, pp. 27-30.

74. *MSS*, p. 228.

75. *PA*, p. 625.

76. *PA*, p. 351.

77. *Ibid.*, p. 65.

78. *MT*, p. 316.

79. *PA*, p. 647.

80. *Ibid.*, p. 344.

81. This is the theme of Mead's Carus Lectures, *The Philosophy of the Present*, in which he deals at length with the nature, the form, and the function of the present, past and future. For similar views, see Hobbes, *Leviathan*, I, Chap. 3; Lotze, *Metaphysics*, sec. 65; Laird, *A Study in Realism*, p. 50; S. Alexander, *Space, Time and Deity*, I, p. 71. See also Alfred Tonness, *JP*, XXIX (1932), 599-606, in which he makes a distinction between the *metaphysical* and the *epistemological* aspects of the past.

82. *PP*, p. 23.

83. *Ibid.*, pp. 1, 28.

84. *Ibid.*, pp. 1, 23.

85. *Ibid.*, p. 33.

86. Mead was fond of saying that for each age a new and different Caesar crosses a new and different Rubicon.

87. *MT*, p. 291.

88. See *PP*, Chap. I, pp. 1-31; *MT*, pp. 290-291, 408-412. Whitehead, too, has attempted to present an interpretation of the organization of perspectives. But Whitehead's suggestion of one vast specious present which could take in the whole temporal reality seemed to Mead to do away with a genuine past-present-future, and hence with existence itself.

89. *PP*, pp. 33, 177-78, *passim*.

90. *Ibid.*, p. 176.

91. *Idem.*

92. *PA*, pp. 225-26; *PP*, pp. 176-77.

93. *PA*, pp. 318-19, 343-44.

94. *Ibid.*, pp. 647-50.

95. *Ibid.*, pp. 343, 344, 351.

96. *Ibid.*, pp. 344, 649, 650, 647.

97. *MT*, pp. 264ff.

98. "A Pragmatic Theory of Truth," *loc. cit.*, p. 85.

99. *MT*, p. 275. It is at precisely this point, however, that Mead lays himself open to criticism. In ignoring the stable "structure" of the world, and by declaring that "each morning we open our eyes upon a different universe," Mead thought that he was providing for greater flow, freedom, novelty, and creativity. (*MT*, p. 325). But he left himself open to the charge of "irrationalism," of defending a philosophy of "gush and go" which in some respects goes beyond Bergson (see *MT*, p. 325). Scientific method, upon which Mead set such store, implies a high degree of stable structure in the universe—if we are to learn anything that stays learned, and if scientific method is to include reliable prediction and control.

100. *Ibid.*, p. 285.

101. *Ibid.*, p. 290.

102. *MT*, p. 154. Here Mead parts company with Aristotelian science, for which forms were eternally given.

103. *Ibid.*, p. 143.

104. *Ibid.*, p. 140.

105. *Idem.*

106. *Ibid.*, p. 290-291.

107. E.g., Mead criticizes Bergson as having failed to provide uniqueness or discreteness along with continuity and direction. Likewise, Descartes, in order to obtain persistence for his spatially discrete units, had to introduce a God who continually recreated his souls. (*Meditations*, III, tr. Haldane and Ross, Cambridge Univ. Press, 1931, V, I, pp. 168-9). In order to get discreteness in his world of becoming, Plato provided ideas or forms. (*Timeaus*, 37ff.) Man for Aristotle is the eternity of the species and, in spite of his inductive method, his notion of man is universalized by abstraction. See also E. Gilson, *The Spirit of Medieval Philosophy* (London: Sheed and Ward, 1936), Chap. VIII, pp. 166-67, where he contrasts the Christian and the Greek view of man. Cf. also the conclusions of Miss Lee in her study of *George Herbert Mead* (New York: King's Crown Press, 1945), pp. 24-25.

108. "Sociality," on Mead's definition, means the capacity of being several things at once, or belonging to more than one system contemporaneously.

109. *PA*, p. 325.

110. *MT*, pp. 413, 415.

111. *PP*, pp. 173-74.

112. Professor E. B. McGilvary does accuse Mead of solipsism, a solipsism of the present moment. It is not a solipsism which asserts the *solus ipse* of the *subject* of experience, but a novel solipsism which asserts the *sola ipsa* of the *experientia* consisting of a present situation in which there is nothing but an organism reacting to its environment. See *IJE*, XLIII (1932-33), 348.

113. In this connection, there are aspects of Mead's thought that suggest the monadism of Leibniz and other pluralistic systems, and which seriously qualify the monistic tendencies in Mead. On the other hand, his stress on social behaviorism and social control causes him at times to take a position which appears difficult to reconcile with his views of nature as an organization of

acts or discrete perspectives. Certain passages suggest a monism in which the individual is completely subordinate to the social whole. (See e.g., *MSS*, pp. 201, 202, 174, 87, 210; *PA*, pp. 606ff; *PP*, pp. 161-71). We shall have a fuller discussion of this ambiguity in Mead's thought in a later chapter. What Mead desires is not the absorption of the individual into any absolute, nor the isolation of the individual. What he wants is a community of social selves.

114. *PA*, p. 318.

115. *MT*, pp. 413, 415; *PP*, pp. 48, 49, 63-67, *passim.*

116. *MT*, p. 415.

117. *Idem.*

118. *PP*, pp. 48f, 58, 62-67, 85, *passim.*

119. Cf. C. W. Morris, *Six Theories of Mind,* and A. O. Lovejoy, *The Revolt Against Dualism.*

120. *MSS*, pp. 227-28.

121. *Ibid.*, pp. 227-37, 238-44; *PP*, pp. 178ff.

122. *MSS*, pp. 230-31.

123. C. H. Cooley is especially noted for his studies in the "primary group," by which he means those characterized by intimate face-to-face association and cooperation, like the family. They are primary in the sense that they are fundamental in forming the social nature and ideals of the individual. Under the influence of kindness, sympathy, and mutual identification, the I-feeling becomes a We-feeling which seeks no good that is not also the good of the group. (See *Social Organization,* Chap. XVII, esp. pp. 23f, 33f, 189f, 193, 298). All larger units or forms of *human* social organization are developed from or are extensions of the family. In this Mead agrees with Cooley. (See *MSS*, p. 229). See also C. H. Cooley, *Human Nature and the Social Order; Social Process;* and Mead's article, "Cooley's Contribution to American Sociological Thought," *AJS*, XXXV (1929–30), 693-706.

124. *MSS*, p. 239.

125. *Ibid.*, pp. 61-65, 359-60, 119-20, 347-48. There is the one possible exception of the "talking birds' and singers who stimulate themselves to sing by their own notes: parrots, mocking birds, canaries and sparrows.

126. *Ibid.*, p. 231.

127. *PA*, p. 625; *PP*, pp. 179ff.

128. *MSS*, pp. 237, 240ff, 347-53.

129. *Ibid.*, p. 234.

130. *MT*, pp. 377-78, 384.

131. *PP*, pp. 178-79.

132. See e.g., Vance Packard, *Animal IQ* (New York: Dial Press, 1950); *The Human Side of Animals* (New York: Pocket Books, 1951). Cf. H. Munro Fox, *The Personality of Animals* (New York: Pelican Books, 1947).

133. For similar conclusions on this issue see E. Cassirer, *An Essay on Man,* (New Haven: Yale University Press, 1944), pp. 29-41; W. Köhler, *The Mentality of Apes,* (New York: Harcourt, Brace & Co., 1925), pp. 317, 277; E. G. Conklin, *Man, Real and Ideal,* pp. 128-29; C. F. von Weizsächer, *The History of Nature,* p. 154.

134 *MT,* p. 384. Mead has little or nothing to say about the meaning or the nature of "spirit" which many other philosophers associate with human nature. Berdyaev, Niebuhr, and Buber, e.g., mean by spirit the capacity for devotion to ideal values, the capacity for love, the capacity for self transcendence and freedom.

135. *PP,* p. 190f; see also *PA,* pp. 216, 264. Mead speaks of value as "the future character of the object in so far as it determines your action to it."

136. *PP,* p. 191.

137. *IJE,* XXXV (1924-25), 263; also *PP,* pp. 180, 185.

138. *PP,* p. 185.

139. *Ibid.,* p. 179.

140. *MSS,* p. 157.

141. *Ibid.,* pp. 258ff.

142. *Ibid.,* p. 258.

143. *MSS,* p. 258. This is all very true, but it hardly does justice to the "market orientation" which has become so dominant in the modern capitalistic era. (See E. Fromm, *Man For Himself,* pp. 67ff). Here we have not simple barter and exchange between persons on the basis of mutual human need, but a complex mechanism characterized by abstract and impersonal demands and the laws of supply and demand. Value is determined not in terms of "use" or "need" but "exchange value." And men come to treat themselves and others as mere commodities, as "means" rather than as "ends" (in Kantian terms), to "objectify" persons (in Berdyaev's terms), to treat persons as "It" (in Buber's terms).

144. *PP,* pp. 183-84, 192.

145. *Ibid.,* p. 192.

146. *PP,* p. 192. It appears to the writer that Mead has over-simplified the actual situation. Property is, indeed, a "human" category, and is designed to satisfy the needs of man for security, recognition, and the other normal satisfactions of life. And property "value" is largely a "social" increment. But reduced to money-factors, in a system which proclaims the political freedom of economic power (such as we see in the theories of Locke, Hobbes, Smith, Ricardo, Harrington, Mill and Bentham), private property can and does become de-humanized, competitive, ambivalent, and the means of man's *isolation* from his fellows. It then determines man's activities as a purely external, functional force. Man's labor, truly an expression of personality, becomes de-personalized, treated as a mere commodity, degraded into a means of property. Too much of modern life has become the concomitant of an economic and scientific philosophy which places economic and material considerations at the center, and regards persons with what Buber calls the "It-attitude," as mere things.

147. *Ibid.,* p. 49, *passim.*

148. In his Carus Lectures, *The Philosophy of the Present,* Mead made a belated thrust in the direction of a systematic presentation of his ideas which would include the hint of an emerging metaphysics. Up until that time, Mead had eschewed metaphysics. Of the four prominent pragmatists (James, Peirce, Dewey and Mead) only Peirce really recognized the need for metaphysics

and first principles. For, said Peirce, "Find a scientific man who proposes to get along without any metaphysics . . . and you have found one whose doctrines are thoroughly vitiated by the crude and uncriticized metaphysics with which they are packed." *Collected Works of Charles Sanders Peirce,* edited by Charles Hartshorne and Paul Weiss (Cambridge: Harvard Univ. Press) Vol. I, p. 129.

149. *MSS,* pp. 42ff, 76ff. Wundt had given considerable attention to the social aspects of gesture, symbol, language, and religion. It was undoubtedly Wundt who helped Mead see the nature of the gesture and how it functions in a social context. Wundt saw that language is a social phenomenon, but he was unwilling to concede the instrumentalist theory that language is only a social product having its basis in use. So far as I am aware, Mead, with the possible exception of Dewey, was the only American philosopher of his generation to take seriously the conception of the origin and development of gesture-language. And few, if any, went so far as Mead in considering both language and self genetically, and positing language as the principle of social organization as well as of social beings.

150. *Ibid.,* p. 76.

151. *Ibid.,* p. 43.

152. *PB,* VII (1910), 398.

153. *MSS,* p. 53.

154. *PB,* VII (1910), 398. Darwin's notion that gestures express the emotions of animals is, on this view, clearly inadequate.

155. *MSS,* pp. 45-46.

156. *Ibid.,* pp. 46, 81.

157. *Ibid.,* p. 81.

158. *PP,* p. 73.

159. *PB,* VII (1910), 399f.

160. *Ibid.,* p. 403.

161. *Ibid.,* p. 397. See also *MSS,* pp. 75-76.

162. *MSS,* pp. 77-78. In other words, the fact that a gesture and its response have meaning does not necessarily imply that the gesture is "significant" to the individuals involved.

163. *MSS,* p. 78.

164. *Ibid.,* pp. 51ff.

165. *Ibid.,* pp. 51, 52, 58 *et passim.*

166. *Ibid.,* pp. 52-53, 59.

167. *Ibid.,* p. 60.

168. *Ibid.,* p. 58.

169. *Idem.*

170. *Ibid.,* p. 60.

171. *Idem.*

172. *MSS,* pp. 59-60. Mead may be correct. But one wonders if there is not more to the concept of imitation than Mead finds, especially in light of the work by Woodworth, Thorndike, E. B. Holt, F. H. Allport, and more recently by Dollard and Miller who appear to have modified, enlarged and enriched the term to include a four-fold pattern which includes the drive, the cue, the response, and the reward.

173. *Ibid.*, p. 61f.

174. *Ibid.*, p. 78.

175. *Ibid.*, p. 81.

176. *JP*, XIX (1922), 162. It seems to me that a similar distinction is made by W. Köhler in his study of chimpanzees, *op. cit.* There he reports that chimpanzees show a considerable degree of emotions by means of gesture. Nevertheless one element, which is characteristic of and indispensable to human language, is missing: there are no signs which have an *objective* reference or meaning. "It may be taken as positively proved," writes Kohler, "that their gamut of phonetics is entirely 'subjective' and can only express emotions, never designate or describe objects." Köhler believes that speech is beyond the power of apes. And E. Cassirer concludes that "the difference between *propositional language* and *emotional language* is the real landmark between the human and the animal world." And again, "animals possess a practical imagination and intelligence whereas man alone has developed a new form: *a symbolic imagination and intelligence.*" *Op. Cit.*, pp. 30, 33. Man's ability to use abstract symbols, universals, makes the difference. So Cassirer speaks of men as *animal symbolicum*: his capacity to invent and use symbols opens the way to civilization.

177. *MT*, pp. 380f.

178. *MSS*, p. 47.

179. *MSS*, pp. 65ff; *MT*, pp. 378-80; *PP*, pp. 187-88.

180. *PP*, p. 187.

181. *Ibid.*, p. 188.

182. *Ibid.*, p. 182; *MSS*, p. 96.

183. Cf. Ernst Cassirer, *Language and Myth* (New York: Harper & Bros., 1946), and *An Essay on Man* (New Haven: Yale Univ. Press, 1944). Mead and Cassirer appear to have much in common. But Mead represents a radical behavioristic interpretation, while Cassirer neglects language as behavioral response, adjustment between forms. For him language reflects an "inner process," springs from a basic mental activity, and expresses subject impulses and excitations. In Cassirer there is not the sense of a reciprocal mutually conditioning interaction between man and his world as it is expressed in Mead's writings.

184. Cf. W. Köhler, *The Mentality of Apes*, p. 27. Köhler insists that speech is definitely beyond the powers of the apes.

185. Cf. John Dewey, *Experience and Nature*, pp. 166-207.

186. *MSS*, p. 260.

187. *Ibid.*, p. 268.

188. *PB*, VII (1910), 404.

189. E. Cassirer, *An Essay on Man*, p. 36.

190. *Ibid.*, p. 40.

191. *Ibid.*, p. 32. This is a distinction made by Charles Morris in "The Foundation of the Theory of Signs," *Encyclopedia of the Unified Sciences* (1938).

192. *MSS*, p. 335, 97; *MT*, pp. 379-80.

193. In this fact Mead finds the root of the socially cohesive virtue of sympathy and fruitful implications for all manner of sociological and moral problems.

194. *MSS*, p. 73.

195. *Ibid.*, p. 244.

196. *Ibid.*, p. 181.

197. *Ibid.*, p. 146n.

198. *Ibid.*, p. 54.

199. *Ibid.*, p. 146n.

200. *Ibid.*, p. 55.

201. *Ibid.*, p. 57, 47.

202. *Ibid.*, p. 90.

203. *Ibid.*, p. 89.

204. *PA*, p. 523. According to Mead's definition, relativity is an instance of his general theory of role-taking and perspectives in nature. Relativity physics seeks a formula that is true to the physical world whatever the point of observation; while mathematics is the result of the search for structural and relational invariance. From such considerations Mead postulates the social and relational nature of reality.

205. See Mead's article, "Bishop Berkeley and his Message," *JP*, XXVI (1929), 421-30.

206. It is perhaps significant that this logical innovation came just at the time when Darwin's *Origin of Species* was calling into question the Platonic world view which provided the metaphysical background of the Aristotelian logic. (See John Dewey, *The Influence of Darwin on Philosophy*, Chap. I). It is especially Mead's account of the universals in pragmatic functional terms that gives him the status of what someone calls a "post-Darwinian Aristotle," that is, an Aristotle equipped by the growth of the biological sciences to amend the inadequacies of Platonism. On the whole, Mead found in Aristotle a kindred spirit.

207. *MSS*, p. 31.

208. "Scientific Method and Individual Thinker," *Creative Intelligence*, p. 189.

209. *MT*, pp. 366, 335, 375.

210. *PP*, pp. 182ff.

211. *MT*, pp. 382-83.

212. It was with good reason that Fichte thus celebrated the *birthday* of his son.

213. *PP*, p. 189. Professor H. Richard Niebuhr enters a caution in suggesting that it is better to leave out the "in so far as," since it is always risky to argue from silence. *JP*, XLII (1945), 353.

214. It is, of course, quite another matter to argue on this ground that we *exist* only in the presence of another.

215. Here Mead follows Cooley. Cooley, too, had seen that selves appear in a bi-polar process. The mind is not first individual and then social. The mind itself arises through communication. This, in Mead's eyes, represented a great advance over Baldwin, Tarde, Bagehot, McDougall, and even James. "The superiority of Cooley's position lies in his freedom to find in consciousness a social process going on, within which the self and the others arise." (*AJS*, XXXV, 1929-30, p. 700). Self and society are in the same field.

216. *MSS*, p. 138.

217. *Ibid.*, p. 139.

218. *MSS*, pp. 139-40.

219. *Ibid.*, p. 138.

220. *Ibid.*, p. 140.

221. *MSS*, p. 140. Cf. F. S. Chapin, *Introduction to the Study of Social Evolution* (New York: Century Co., 1913); see also Park and Thomas, "Participation and Social Assimilation," in K. Young, *Source Book for Social Psychology* (New York: Alfred A. Knopf, 1937), pp. 47-53, 35-37.

222. Ibid., Cf. Martin Buber's notion of addressing an "It" as a "Thou," of imputing personal qualities to physical objects.

223. *PP*, p. 169.

224. *PA*, p. 427.

225. The insatiable curiosity of journalism, the reader appeal of the "human interest story" seems to confirm this phenomenon. The curiosities of people about how other people live and work and fight and love follow from this more fundamental curiosity which is the passion of self-consciousness. "We must be others if we are to be ourselves." (*PP*, p. 194).

226. *Ibid.*, pp. 189-90.

227. *PA*, p. 312.

228. *MSS*, p. 202.

229. *Ibid.*, p. 324.

230. *IJE*, XL (1930), 230.

231. *PP*, p. 184.

232. *IJE*, XXXV (1924-25), 262.

233. *JP*, IX (1912), 404.

234. *Ibid.*, p. 403.

235. *MSS*, pp. 154-55.

236. "The Objective Reality of Perspectives" in *Proceedings of the Sixth International Congress of Philosophy*, 1926, p. 80.

237. T. V. Smith saw so much resemblance that he once jokingly accused Mead of having "stolen his thunder from Smith." Mead replied genially "that he had come under the influence of Adam Smith while studying at Harvard, and had there written a paper on Smith." See "The Social Philosophy of G. H. Mead," in *Am. Journal of Soc.*, XXXVII (1931–32), 378, 379.

238. Significantly, this work bears the sub-title: "An Essay towards an Analysis of the Principles by which Men Naturally Judge Concerning the Conduct and Character, First of Their Neighbor, and Afterwards of Themselves."

239. *Theory of the Moral Sentiments* (1759), Part III, Chap. 3. The point is that it is only as one imagines himself to be in the position of a disinterested spectator that one can understand and evaluate his own conduct.

240. I suspect that no theory has been so thoroughly discredited as this one: that the sum of men's selfishness would somehow add up to the common weal. Yet as Smith stated it, it contains the germ of truth. It is one of those half-truths which is worse than a lie, precisely because it contains so much of the truth. Smith himself would probably have been very unhappy at the subsequent use of his theories to justify and glorify "rugged individualism." He sincerely thought that he had reconciled self and other in his ethical doctrine of "sympathy," although he also introduced a kind of natural moral

law (an Invisible Hand) to preserve the harmony in case sympathy failed to do so.

241. In the introduction to *MSS*, p. xxx, Morris also raises the question whether the extension of role-taking toward physical things might permit one to transcend human observers altogether, so that one can meaningfully pass from the social positivism, which Mead seems to regard as the limit of meaningful metaphysics, to a philosophical realism. Morris further discusses this issue in "Pragmatism and Metaphysics," *PR*, XLIII, 1934, pp. 549-64.

242. E. S. Ames, *Religion*, pp. 24, 133, 149f, 176f, *passim*.

It is interesting to recall in this connection that Mead had friends and colleagues within the "Chicago School" of empirical and naturalistic historians and philosophers of religion: E. S. Ames, Eustace Haydon, Gerald Birney Smith, Shailer Mathews, H. N. Wieman, et al. This distinctively American philosophy of religion developed out of James's pragmatism, Dewey's instrumentalism, and contemporary cosmological speculation, and has as its goal an empirical theology analogous to the method of the natural sciences and interpreted religion in terms of human adjustment to environment.

243. *MSS*, pp. 152-64, 364-65; *PP*, pp. 186-87.

244. *MSS*, p. 158.

245. *JP*, IX (1912), 403.

246. *Ibid.*, X (1913), 377.

247. *MSS*, p. 154.

248. *MSS*, pp. 173-77, 192-99, 209-13, 272-80. See also "The Definition of the Psychical," *op. cit.*; "The Mechanism of Social Consciousness," *JP*, IX (1912), 401ff; "The Social Self," *Ibid.*, X (1913), 374ff.

249. *MSS*, p. 175.

250. *JP*, IX (1912), 405.

251. Mead's distrust of metaphysics appears to commit him to a positivism or operationalism. Mead declines to consider or defend whatever metaphysical assumptions may be involved; and he justifies his stand as being legitimate for the scientist who, allegedly, does not maintain a world-view. (See *PP*, pp. 117-18; *MSS*, p. 332; *MT*, pp. 397, 400, *passim*). But in this connection one recalls the warning of Peirce: "Find a scientific man who proposes to get along without any metaphysics . . . and you have found one whose doctrines are thoroughly vitiated by the crude and uncriticized metaphysics with which they are packed." (*Collected Works of Charles Sanders Peirce*, edited by Charles Hartshorne and Paul Weiss, I, p. 129).

252. *MSS*, p. 199.

253. *JP*, IX (1912), 406.

254. *MSS*, p. 201, also p. 163.

255. One immediately thinks of the "individualism" and "group control" which is present in a Quaker Meeting. The Inner Light (the "I") is constantly restrained, examined, corrected, and disciplined by the meeting (the "me" or the "we").

256. *JP*, X (1913), 374.

257. *Idem.* This conclusion is supported in psychology by the assertion that we cannot be conscious of motor processes although we are conscious of sensory

processes. "We are conscious only of what we have done, never of doing it. We are always conscious directly only of sensory processes, never of motor processes; hence we are conscious of motor processes only through sensory processes which are their resultants. The contents of consciousness, therefore, have to be correlated or fitted into a physiological system in dynamic terms, as processes going on." (*MSS*, p. 22n.)

258. *JP*, IX (1912), 406.

259. *MSS*, p. 225.

260. *Ibid.*, p. 255.

261. *Ibid.*, p. 175.

262. *MT*, p. 375.

263. *JP*, IX (1912), 404.

264. *Ibid.*, p. 406.

265. *Idem.*

266. *MSS*, p. 202.

267. The main burden of *PA* is to establish the primacy of the act or perspective.

268. "Definition of the Psychical," *op. cit.*, p. 30.

269. *MSS*, p. 200.

270. *IJE*, XXXV (1924–25), 260.

271. *MSS*, p. 201.

272. *MSS*, pp. 328; *MT*, p. 318; *PP*, pp. 70, 129; *PA*, pp. 127, 144, 212, 327, 428, 77, 129, 247.

273. *MSS*, p. 7.

274. Grace Chin Lee, *op. cit.*, p. 70. In agreeing with this position, I am glad to acknowledge my debt to Miss Lee for this insight.

275. *MT*, p. 273.

276. *MSS*, pp. 209f.

277. *Idem.*; see also *JP*, X (1913), 374-75; *Ibid.*, IX (1912), 404f.

278. *Ibid.*, X (1913), 376.

279. *MSS*, pp.210-211.

280. *Idem.*

281. *MSS*, p. 255.

282. *Ibid.*, p. 210.

283. See *MT*, pp. 361ff.

284. *MSS*, p. 168.

285. *Ibid.*, pp. 167-68. One wonders, however, since society is the real locus of values and there is no recognition of laying hold on a super-social good, how Mead gets his "higher community"? Where does he find the higher loyalty which will transcend both individual and group egoism, especially where there is an idolatry to some absolutized and vicious social system? Mead's view is dangerously unprotected at this point.

286. *MT*, p. 363.

287. *Ibid.*, pp. 225-36, 361ff.

288. *Ibid.*, p. 411; also pp. 373-74.

289. *Ibid.*, p. 363.

290. *Ibid.*, p. 362.

Chapter Three

Martin Buber's Philosophy
of the Personal

MARTIN BUBER'S religious philosophy derives its stimulus from two main sources: West European Enlightenment and East European Chassidism.[1] These were the two great streams which cleansed and energized modern Jewish life. The Enlightenment had made possible the emergence of the progressive Jew from the medieval ghetto into the spacious freedom and humanistic learning of European civilization. Chassidism had opened to the Jew the mysticism, religious wisdom, and joyous peace of a life lived deep in God: it taught that men could best worship God through joy, exaltation of spirit, and loving service.

Buber was born in Vienna, in 1878, of an old and famous Galician rabbinical family,[2] and in his own development he absorbed and synthesized both the culture of the West and the Chassidic religiosity of the East. His early youth was spent in Lemberg where, in the intensely pious Jewish world of his grandfather's circle, he acquired a thorough knowledge of the Hebrew language, religion, traditions and folkways. There it was also that he came in contact with the Chassidim, and was eventually initiated into their mystical piety and lore. Living among these humble "friends of God," Buber not only learned the language of faith, but he experienced a deep and abiding understanding of genuine community, of the strong spirit of brotherhood, of the joyous service of God in the world.

As a cultured, German-speaking European, Buber was educated in the tradition of Kantian and post-Kantian idealism. Kant stands at the bridge between the world of Descartes and the contemporary

117

world to which Buber belongs. In his *Critique of Pure Reason*, Kant explains how the mind "mechanizes" experience; in his *Critique of Practical Reason*, he shows how the mind "mysticizes" experience; in the *Critique of Practical Judgment* he explains how these two may be reconciled.[3] This was also Buber's problem and achievement. In Kant's *Prolegomena to all Future Metaphysics* which Buber read as a lad of fifteen, Buber learned that space and time are only the forms in which the human view of things works itself out; that is to say, space and time were not necessarily attached to the inner nature of the world, but to the nature of man's senses. It further taught him that it is just as impossible to all human concepts to say that the world in infinite, as to say that it is finite, since the world is given to us in experience, as appearance. Both can be asserted with equal justification; both are unimaginable. Between the two lies an irresolvable antinomy. From Kant's answer to this riddle, Buber began to get an inkling of man's problematic situation, and of the possibility of a connection between man and the eternal.[4]

So Buber came close to agreement with Kant in that the ultimate transcendental reality, the *Ding an sich,* cannot be derived from discursive logic, nor defined; it can only be "realized" in the lived life.[5] The Unconditioned, God, cannot be expressed, but only *addressed.* Ultimate reality is unknown, save as an inference from moral experience and the action that proves by faith. Nor have we any knowledge of the self as substance or cause in the empirical sense; any "knowledge" of the self as subject is intuitive and noumenal. Kant's antinomies, like the mysteries of Chassidism, are, from the human standpoint, insoluble paradoxes. Buber's doctrine is likewise "meta-logical" because it does not eliminate all contrast, but allows the paradoxes and antinomies and mysteries to stand. The ultimate secrets of God and of Life are rationally non-understandable. Yet the believer *knows* out of his own life. The antinomies and the paradoxes which bedevil philosophy and theology: the immanence and transcendence of God, Divine determinism and human freedom, time and eternity, nature and grace—all these are no longer in contradiction. God is not identical with the world, yet He somehow dwells within it. The ultimate ground of being transcends experience and knowledge, though it is that to which all experience and knowledge refer. Man is at once conditioned, and free.[6] Man is in God's hand, yet each one must go his own way responsibly. Man's action is real action.[7] And in the doing, in the deed, in the lived-life, is to be found the proof.[8] Furthermore, in Kant's famous dictum about the dignity of persons, is pre-figured Buber's contrast between the *person* and the *thing* (the Thou and the It).[9]

Buber's student years at the Universities of Vienna, Berlin, Leipzig, and Zurich gave him a rich background in philosophy, art and literature. He studied the great philosophers of the Greek and Western world. Dilthey was his teacher, Simmel both teacher and friend; and the influence of their "Lebensphilosophie" and method of thinking never left him. Among all of his teachers, these two made the most enduring impression on young Buber.[10] He knew Freud, attended the lectures of Mach, Wundt and Stumpf, and was an eager student in the psychiatric clinic. He felt a deep kinship with Dostoevsky, Tolstoi and Ibsen, and felt with them that he had been born into a period of spiritual decadence and cultural disintegration. The romantic rebellion of the late 19th century strongly affected his thinking. He was acutely aware of the polemic of Marx and Engels, but was more sympathetic to the so-called "utopian socialism" of Owen, Fourier, Proudhon, Kropotkin, and especially of Landauer, who was the leader of a group of young men trying to find the inner springs of ideal community and organic unity with mankind.[11] To all of these he owed much, but not too much. He was no slavish follower of any of them; and some of them like Hegel, Marx and Kierkegaard, he later severely criticized. It should be noted that Buber's thought clearly has affinities with many of the motives and themes of *Existenzphilosophie,* and was definitely influenced by Kierkegaard, Nietzsche, and the romantic poets of the period, remaining all the while independent of any of the schools or leaders of this current philosophical fashion. Similarly, there appear connections with that movement of thought in Germany—relatively unknown in America—which stems out of Husserl's Phenomenology, and which stresses the factors of time and the personal standpoint *(Standpunkt)* in all observation of the universe and human experience. This new philosophy, among other things, asserts the difference between the living lived-present, in which I stand, with the responsibility of deciding what new values and realities are to come into being, and the past of fixed, decided events and objects on which science depends.

At the age of 20, Buber joined the Zionist movement, then emerging under the leadership of Theodor Herzl and Achad Ha'am. Buber himself became the leader of a group of young idealists, artists and writers in Prague and Vienna who conceived of Zionism neither as a political party, a legalistic orthodoxy, nor as an ascetic puritanism, but as a cultural movement and renaissance of authentic Jewish life, fertilizing all things Jewish.[12] Consequently he soon broke with the moralism of Achad Ha'am and with the political Zionism of Herzl. There was and is a kind of antinomianism about Buber which expresses itself in his refusal to abide by a narrow acceptance of any creed, dogma, party or rule. In this respect he seems to follow the tradition of German mysticism, particularly as we find it in the anti-dogmatism and anti-ecclesiasticism of Eckhardt and Silesius.

For a time he turned exclusively to scholarly pursuits, and gave himself to the study and translation of the mythology and religious classics of the Nordic, Finnish, and Chinese people. In the religious *myth* Buber believed he had tapped a source of elemental wisdom about man and his world, a wisdom not given in science or in rational categories.[13] This is a traditional German distinction between *Vernunft* and *Verstand* deriving from Boehme, Kant, and other German philosophers. Buber also found the mystics, Eastern and Western, translated their writings, meditated deeply on their message, and finally came back to Chassidism, whose myths and legends revealed the deep authentic wisdom of the Jewish people.[14] Buber believed that the moments in history when the pure flame of "submerged Judaism" burned most brightly were in the period of the Hebrew prophets,[15] in early Christianity, and in the Chassidic movement; and that every genuine and redeeming revival of Judaism must stem from or attach to them. The distinctive essence of the Jewish faith is to be found in immanent spirituality, the sanctification of all life, and the reality of loving community.[16] "The Chassidic teaching," wrote Buber in 1907, "is the most powerful and unique phenomenon which the Diaspora has produced." "Indeed, nowhere has the spiritual power of Judaism so manifested itself in recent centuries as it has in Chassidism."[17] This emotional and religious world of Chassidism, with its ready acceptance of immanent divinity along with divine transcendence, its belief that ritual without "intention" is valueless, its pan-sacramentalism, and its deep sense of human community founded on divine truth exercised a strong fascination upon Buber. The fusion of Judaism and natural, ethical mysticism which he had found in Chassidism became the central theme in his own life and thought and literary activity.[18]

It is to Chassidism, then, as seen through the eyes of a cultured modern European Jew, that we must now turn if we would understand Martin Buber. For it was the force which, more than any other, shaped his philosophy, his interpretation of religion, as well as his sociological and educational theories. And it was he who first recreated in modern form the spiritual atmosphere and message of this vital pietistic movement which, welling up from deep Jewish springs, had, in the words of Hans Kohn, "restored spontaneity to the human heart, filled the darkness with joyous confidence, recognized and exalted the uniqueness and the value of personality." [19]

THE CHASSIDIC INFLUENCE

Chassidism was a burst of spontaneous and creative religious enthusiasm in a popular revivalist movement which flamed through the villages and ghettos of Eastern Europe in the 18th century, and came to embrace half of Jewry. Its founder was one Israel ben Eliezer to whom the faithful gave the name Baal-Shem-Tov (Master of the Good Name) or more simply, the "Besht." The spiritual leaders of the Chassidic communities became known as "Zaddikim" (righteous ones, masters); and the devotees whose lives centered round these religious "illuminates" were known as "Chassidim" (pious ones, faithful keepers of the covenant). Chassidism is surely one of the most remarkable and appealing manifestations of intense religious spirit of modern times.[20] It was not a monastic order, but a great popular movement concentrated on spiritual perception.[21] Drawing its strength from the common people, and from the creative interaction between the soul-leaders and their disciples, this mystical folk-movement established a neighborly communal life on the basis of a common search for divine truth. It was a kind of "revolt of the masses" against rabbinic legalism and sterile scholasticism. Like the early Christian movement, it was an appeal from the "letter" to the "spirit" of the Torah.[22] It was an authentic Jewish movement and culture with unique points of emphasis and practice. For the Chassidim redemption lay in devout works, loving deeds, fervent prayer, and single-hearted devotion to God and man in the common life. The Besht counseled against asceticism and self-mortification. The world was not to be fled, but hallowed through the service of God and neighbor. God's glory was to be found in all things; consequently a life of holiness and joy and purity was to be lived within the world. The union (yichud) to be sought is not the union of the soul outside the world but, in Buber's words, "the union of God with His Glory, as expressed in man and his works, dwelling within the world." [23] Rapture and fervor (hitlahabut), intensity and inner motive (kawwana), service and worship of God in the community (aboda), humility and simplicity (shiflut), and unity between faith and action (achdut): these were the main tenets of Chassidism.[24] The teachings of the Chassidim can be summarized even more briefly: God can be seen in everything and can be reached by means of every innocent and hallowed act.[25] Thought and deed must have one direction—toward God. *Loving the world in God and loving God in the world*—this was their secret.

There is much more one would like to say about this astonishing folk movement so concentrated on spiritual perceptivity and holy intention. We must content ourselves with a brief consideration of those features in Chassidic piety and teaching which struck so deeply into Buber's life and which were to affect so strongly his own convictions about *community* and true *dialogue*.

1. Chassidism represents a form of mysticism, derived in part from Kabbalism,[26] which does not deny the world nor seek seclusion from the community. Chassidism was not a monastic order, but a powerful and multiform popular movement, "a mode of life which shapes a community, and regulates a community in accordance with its own nature." [27] It is "Kabbalism turned Ethos," to use Buber's own words: a practical, ethical mysticism translated, paradoxically, into a social folk-movement.[28] This intense and brotherly communal life planted in Buber's young mind the seed of his mature thought concerning the ideal community of all men, *man with man,* living together in spiritual concord. *"Hier ist alles Ein Reich, Ein Geist, Eine Wirklichheit."* [29]

2. The Chassidic communities were centered around the religious personality of the Zaddik; their spiritual power was generated in the mutual quickening relation between the religious hero and his disciples. The life and character of the saint-mystic took the place of the learned rabbi and doctrine as medium and sanction of revelation. The Zaddik "had become a Torah." For this reason Chassidism has been called

the "cult of the great religious personality." [30] And it is clear that the example of the Zaddik was later to affect Buber's unusual ideas of leadership and of education.

The Zaddik, remarks Buber, is "the man who leads the community in God's stead." [31] The Chassidic movement educated such leaders, leaders who "undertook responsibility for the souls entrusted to them, while at the same time they kept alive in them the spark of responsibility." [32] "The Zaddik helps everyone, but he does not relieve anyone of what he must do for himself. . . . The teacher helps his disciples find themselves, and in hours of desolation the disciples help their teacher find himself again. The teacher kindles the souls of his disciples and they surround him and light his life with the flame he has kindled." [33]

3. Not unrelated to what we have just written, is another contribution of Chassidism: its interpretation of the values of individual personal existence. Personality takes the place of doctrine and convention and law. The Chassidim were free, uninhibited, undecorous, directing their service and worship to God, each in his own way. Each man must walk his own way, bear his own responsibility, even within the community—"all his walk and conversation a Torah."

Chassidism was thus a training of individuals in the discovery and re-creation of the self and in the development of all its powers. To become oneself was the moral goal of the Chassid. In one of the legends, Rabbi Zusya said, "In the world to come they will not ask me, 'Why were you not Moses?' They will ask, 'Why were you not Zusya?'" The human task is "to choose one's own way with all his strength." This attitude produced an almost daring sense of individuality and explains Buber's words: "No other religious movement of the modern era has produced so many and so varied independent personalities in so short a time." [34] The self is precious—not as viewed by bourgeois "rugged individualism" nor by Nietzsche's "superman"—but simply because every son of man is a son of God, and carries within him God's glory as a "spark" *(nitzotz)*. Therefore, all that warps and hurts and defeats human life must be put away.[35]

Here again we meet one of the paradoxes of Chassidism: the unique relation of the individual to the community. Singularity and completeness are one. Whoever is whole, authentic in his individuality, lives out of his inner self, in answer to the One Voice which comes out of himself. Each man has been given a realm of responsibility; but this realm includes the neighbor, the daily round, the natural environment. Thus the individuality of man verifies itself in his life with others. The single one completes himself in the community. *(Der Einzelne vollendet sich in der Gemeinschaft)*.[36] True individualism, the unique manhood of each single one, is his own greatest aim; and it is precisely the place where he is tied together with the community and with God.

4. There was a "protestant" and "democratic' 'insistence upon a direct approach to God, a faith which implies trust and loyalty, a sense of the omnipresence of God, and of man's ready communion with God. These simple folk *(am ha-aretz)* found a "life of fervor" and spiritual exaltation through a complete turning to God.[37] Theirs was a gospel of joy, of the hallowing of every day and every deed, of serving God through gladness, and of bringing joy into the lives of others. Religion for them is not merely a body of doctrine, cultus, ritual, or even moral law, but a condition of the heart and mind expressing itself notably in the feeling of meeting with God in a constant dialogic relationship.[38] It is "pure faith without any sophistries," a movement of concentration and holy intention (kawwanah),[39] an experience of direct face-to-face confrontation with God. "Man is truly free to choose God or to reject Him." [40] And "the unity of the contraries is the mystery at the innermost core of the dialogue," [41] for it is not contained in any pantheistic profession, but a living "in the reality of the impossible, . . . in the *imitatio Dei*." [42]

5. Another theme which Buber stresses in his accounts of Chassidism, and which he has taken up into his own philosophy of religion, is its intensified reinterpretation of Jewish messianism.[43] Traditionally messianism was the dream of a coming earthly "golden age" of perfection in which justice, peace, and plenty would obtain, and in which the children of Israel would be gathered in the Holy Land under the leadership of one anointed by God. There were different "schools" of interpretation as to just how and when this great event would take place; indeed the whole concept was rather vague. But to some degree it was believed that everyone could help to bring in the messianic age by obeying the Torah and perfecting his own life. In times of persecution and despair, or after the collapse of pseudo-messianic movements, the people were tempted to turn to magic, gnosis, or apocalypticism as methods of achieving the kingdom.

With a mind set toward Chassidism, Buber interprets Judaism as an age-long struggle against Babylonian "gnosis," Egyptian "magic," and Iranian dualism.[44] These are the great enemies of true religion, of living monotheism. For the gnostic "secret which can be learned," Judaism affirms a revelation which sets bounds to what men can learn, but no bounds to the number of men who can learn it. In Judaism, the constant temptation of gnosis is answered by the Law (Torah). Revelation does not concern itself with the secret things of God, but rather with a way of life for all men, a way of life which can and should be lived facing toward God.[45] "God is incomprehensible, but he can be known in the bond of mutual relationship with him. God cannot be fathomed by knowledge, but he can be imitated." [46] This is made possible from the fact that man is created in God's image and is destined to be like him.[47]

For magic, "the knowledge of the secret which can be coerced," Judaism substitutes the word of God from out of the burning bush and the faith that without cajolery or coercion God will be present to those who are turned to Him as His people.[48] Thus in Judaism there is a fusion of the religious and the ethical, the *Is* and the *Ought,* like a turning round the two centers of an ellipse: (i) an utterly transcendent God who is yet present in immediate relations with finite men, and (ii) God's redeeming power which is at work everywhere and at all times, but without a state of redemption existing in any time or place.[49] Similarly, the Iranian and Marcionite dualism, with its sense of the tragic evil in the world process, which alienates man from his natural, trustful faith in life is in Judaism "experienced in the dialogical situation, which means that it experienced *the contradiction as theophany*." [50] The contradiction is not simply overcome, but *consummated*, "while every unification of contraries would prepare it. It is a redemption not *from* the evil, but *of* the evil, as the power which God created for his service and for the performance of his work." [51] Revelation and redemption tarry "until the turning creature answers and his answer is accepted by God's redeeming grace. Then the unity emerges, formed out of the very elments of contrariety, to establish amidst all the undiminished multiplicity and manifoldness the communion of creatures in the name of God and before his face." [52] Thus Judaism holds together "the threefold chord in the triad of time: Creation, Revelation, Redemption." [53] And thus these dangers to true religion which came together in Kabbalism were overcome by Chassidism by reinterpreting its gnostic and magical elements into aspects of the true dialogic situation.[54] In its anti-dualistic gnosis Kabbalism attempted to deprive the "other" of its independence; whereas Chassidism trustfully endures the contradiction and thus is able to redeem it.[55] For Chassidism, agnostic in Kantian fashion with respect to objective and schematized knowledge, "is concerned with the vital, the biblical 'knowledge' of the fundamental, mutual relationship to God." [56] Thus Chassidism achieves the *yichud* (unity) with its insight into the dialogical relationship of "the undivided human being to the undivided God in the fulness of this earthly present," [57] and the constant rediscovery of the Divine Unity in the heart of multiplicity, while collecting oneself into a unity moving toward God. At the same time Chassidism "drains sorcery of its poison" by not attempting to deny the influence of humanity on deity.[58] Chassidism renews the insight into meeting and reciprocity.

Over and over again, like variations on a theme, Buber emphasizes the fact that for Chassidism, the messianic redemption of the world is to be prepared by men, not in extraordinary exploits, not by asceticism, not by theurgy, but by the hallowing of the deeds of everyday. Every act can be a way of serving God and preparing for the coming of the Kingdom of God—if the intention (kawwanah) is pure, if the man has given himself up to God and his redeeming work, if "he accomplishes his act with the whole of his being directed towards God." [59] All actions may be "messianic" in the sense of helping to make the Kingdom a present reality.

The burden of the unredeemed world rests on the Jew. This is the demand for the impossible which torments the Jew: the experience of the world's lack of redemption and the knowledge that the fate of God and of the world somehow depends upon his acting in a certain way.[60] This is the source of the polarity in the Jew, the source of his striving for unity.[61] And it is the source of his creativeness. Here is one of Buber's accounts:

> The intention of the divine revelation is to form men who can work for the redemption of the world. By this is not meant one single messianic act, but the deeds of the everyday, which prepare for the messianic fulfillment. . . . He who does a *mizwah* with complete *kawanah*, that is completes an act in such a way that his whole existence is gathered in it and directed towards God, he works on the redemption of the world, on its conquest for God.[62]

This language will sound too bold, intemperate, presumptuous, even blasphemous to some readers. But if this usage suggests that God needs man's help, it does not mean that God could not have redeemed his world without man's aid, but that God "wills to have need of man." [63] God specifically wills to use man for the completion of his work of creation, and since God intends to use man's cooperation, "the use of man for this work becomes an effective reality." [64] "God made no tools for himself; he needs none; he created for himself a partner in the dialogue of time and one who is capable of holding converse." [65] This is no proud blasphemy which rejects God's grace and erases the distinction between the creature and the Creator. Man must ever experience both limitation and grace in every act. But it attests to Judaism's profound sense that man has been appointed "as an originator of events," as a real legitimate partner in a real dialogue with God, "empowered to speak his own independent word from out of his own being." [66] As man has the power to fall so he also has the power to help effect the work of redemption. Creation is continuous, and so is Redemption and Messiahship.

It is, of course, futile to try to measure man's part in the work or God's share in the work; it is senseless to ask at what point man's action and God's grace begin and end. There is no sharp borderline. "God and man do not divide the government of the world between them; man's action is enclosed in God's action, but it is still real action." [67] Every deed of man done with simple heart is messianic action and brings "the downflowing of the blessing." Every moment is thus filled with all time; and God in his own time will harvest the fruit of the seeds of redemption which fall from the lives of men in this unredeemed world. [68]

How this can happen, Buber simply confesses, is a mystery which belongs to God, "the Creator and Redeemer, not more mysterious to me than that he is; and that he is, is far less mysterious to me than that I am." [69] Does it mean that God, by making room for a co-determining power, has surrendered his power to determine the course of events? Buber replies: "We only ask that question, when we are busy subsuming God under our logical categories." [70]

6. Finally, Buber discovered in Chassidism (as in Kabbalism) a metaphysically positive attitude toward language as God's own instrument. [71] The holy tongue is not simply a means of expressing thoughts, not just an instrument for contact between human beings. Speech is

communication itself. "Language," writes Scholem, "in its purest form, that is Hebrew . . . reflects the fundamental spiritual nature of the world; in other words, it has a mystical value. Speech reaches God because it comes from God. Man's common language . . . reflects the creative language of God. All creation . . . all that lives, is an expression of God's language, and what is it that Revelation can reveal in the last resort if not the name of God?" [72] Speech is the deepest secret of the Creator and His creation; and it is here that man "finds himself standing in the furrows which the living God himself has made on his way through the world." [73] God's act of creation is speech, but each lived moment is also. It is in these terms that "the whole history of the world . . . is a dialogue between God and his creature." [74] It is not just the world that speaks to man in everything that happens; the world is the word which is spoken. Thus is man addressed. And further to emphasize this dialogic nature of the relation between God and man, Buber translates both creation and theophany into speech. The word is before everything else the form of creation.

This emphasis upon *speech,* upon "the Word," is an old Biblical idea. [75] It is interesting in this connection, and significant for all of Buber's later work, that in some of his earliest writing on the nature of Judaism [76] he put forth the opinion that the basic difference between the Orient and the Occident, between the Hebrew and the Greek, is that the Hebrew is more the "ear-man," while the Greek is more "eye-man." [77] The Hebrew is more "motor-being," while the Greek is "visual-being." The Hebrew lives in time, with a sense of history, of the deed, of dynamic movement in time. [78] The Greek lives more in space, contemplating things in their spatial and formal arrangements. The Greek is the "thinker"; the Jew the "pray-er." The Hebrew did not "see" God so much as he "heard" His Word. He listened to God's voice, conscious of what ought to be done, aware of God's "No"! to his own self-will, eager to actualize the ideal in the real world, responsive to God's Word as pledge, promise, faithful covenant. *Shema! Yisroel!* Whenever God reveals Himself to His servants and His pledged people, He does it by His voice. It is the Word which comes to man, bridging the gulf between God and man; it is the creative and redeeming Word that God speaks to man which overcomes his sin and solitude and self-love. God calls to man; and man answers—and becomes his real self. He is a self because he is bound in loyal covenant to the Other who addresses him.

During the years when Buber was immersed in his study of Chassidism, he spent a season (1905) in Italy. There he saw the great Eleonora Duse in the theatre, and the theme and problem of *I* and *Thou* came to him again: the contrast-effect between actor and audience, the tension between the self and the other.[79] The importance of drama as over against the epic or mere pantomime, the moving dynamic dialogue between persons, the secret of speech and answer, the gulf and clash between *I* and *Thou* which can be bridged over only by speech—all this began to take shape in his mind. This experience in the theatre confirmed his studies in the life of Baalshem: Man and God face each other in dialogue. The Infinite who needs the finite recalls the finite, who then becomes dedicated through that call.[80] This call of the Infinite, *Die Unbedingtheit*, to whom the finite answers responsibly: this is the meaning of the religion of Israel. "Israel lives as one who is addressed and who answers, as one who speaks and receives answers; even more lives it." This is the source of the particular character of Hebrew *myth*. The Jews have never ceased to produce myth.[81]

His understanding of Chassidism became for Buber the understanding of Judaism—the life of men before God in responsible meeting and dialogue. "A call into nothing and the answer of things through their existence, the speech of creation continuing in the life of all creatures, the life of each being as dialogue, the World as Word: to proclaim this is Israel's mission." [82] The relation between God and man is double and reciprocal: there is real opposition and meeting, call and answer, summons and sending, prayer and listening. From the reality of this opposition develops the mystery of man, his "cosmic-metacosmic responsibility." "The World was created for this choosing. The shells are there so that one can break through them. The spheres are separated so that they can come together again." The creature waits before God, and He waits before man. From man, from below, this impulse for release must start. "Grace is God's answer." And in this process, the central act is the Word. In all being, the creative word rules.[83]

This recognition of *speech* as the means of grasping all being was a momentous event in Buber's maturing thought.[84] For he clearly saw that when concrete thinking becomes speech, it always turns to an "other." It becomes a dialogue-process in which something unpredictable happens. One can never know what the other will say, nor rehearse one's reply. Thus dramatic speech-thinking takes the place of abstract monologic thinking. It is a thinking of relationship, of meeting, of speech.[85] Truth is revealed through speech which expresses the intercommunication of one mind with another. It is not the formal truths of logic in their timeless, abstract, systematic character that are vital and relevant, but the truths emerging in the relationships of human beings with God and with one another—truths which are rooted in time yet reach toward the eternal. Speech is the carrier of the creative dialogue between man and God. "In the beginning was the Word." God creates by speaking. "We are the sounds which the Original Mouth speaks. And yet we are only isolated words, forming no context *(nur Wörter, Worte nicht)*. When will we become words which fit into a connected sentence, so as to satisfy the Original Pronouncement?"[86] In speech one has to stand his ground and answer to whomever he meets. To the spiritually aware, and within that sphere of the world entrusted to him, every concrete moment and event is speech.[87] It is precisely in speech, in being addressed *(angeredet)* and answering, as nowhere else, that *relation* becomes evident. In real difference, in opposing points of view, lies the meaning of conversation. Both speakers step into a mutual engagement, and yet retain their individuality.

In the giving of a name to something or someone, you differentiate it from yourself, you address it asking for an answer. The named being answers to the name. The nature of the thing is implied in the name. An object or person is at once something for itself and for me; therefore I am not a solitary self. "The reality in which we live is the reality of the relation between the things of the world, and myself, man. Reality is a 'between,' and Name is a 'between.'"[88] And in this dialogue the Word is superior to the Logos of philosophy; for the "word" springs from meeting and response and pledge. In this exchange truth is born, something new happens, and man knows the truth of concrete reality. "One should speak the words as though the Heavens were in them," according to an old Chassidic saying.

EMERGING PHILOSOPHY OF RELIGION

From his relation to and interpretation of Chassidism Buber began to articulate his own philosophy of religion. In the development of his mature thought Buber has generalized and applied the relationship which we have described between Chassid and Zaddik, and amplified it into a theory of the mutual relation between man and man which serves also as the basis of his philosophy of speech, his ethics, his social philosophy, and his anthropology.

Buber began to see that neither the "single one" nor the social aggregate is the fundamental fact of human existence. The fundamental fact is *man with man*. What is uniquely characteristic and constitutive of the human world is something that takes place *between* one person and another. It is in meeting, in bi-subjective communication, that man *is* or *becomes* truly man. The essence of human life is *what happens between* man and man in community. For human existence is essentially dialogue, claim and counter-claim, demand and response. Man does not become a whole self by virtue of a relation to himself, but only by a relation to another self. This real self, this whole self, is a unity of tension, an embracing of polarity. This polar situation is in all of life: self and other, being and becoming, knowing and doing, spirit and matter, life and death. Whoever has truly experienced the world, has experienced it as a duality. To overcome this duality, to find a unity in this tension; this is man's problem. When man lets the barriers of the ego fall, these oppositions flow together. The tensions should not be abrogated, but encircled, embraced, reconciled. "The true *I* is the *I* of tension which is formed together; not a pole or a thing, but only a stream of polarity floating in between the poles. The connecting stream becomes the *I*." [89]

The living soul lives as a duality. Whoever achieves unity must first live through the tension of the world as a tension in his own soul. Many analogies can be found in life for this essential polarity which Buber feels is so basic to man and the world: e.g., the ebb and flow of the tides, male and female. Perhaps the duality of male and female is the clearest and truest example of Buber's thesis.[90] The single man is not fully man; only with woman is he whole. Man must live through woman, and woman must live through man. Male-thinking and female-thinking *together* are *man* thinking. *Animus* needs *anima*; spirit develops in Yin and Yang, as it ripens in its ties and togetherness. *Consecrated* to each other sacramentally in marriage, their love becomes a means of grace. The *I* of which one usually speaks is only an expression of a grammatical necessity. But the *I* of this tension is deed and reality. For the *I* is then laid hold of and demanded in the core of its wholeness.

Buber's earliest attempt to formulate his philosophy of religion is to be found in the untranslated work *Daniel*.[91] Many, if not most, readers of this work will get no very clear sense of what Buber is trying to say, partly because he fails to say it lucidly, couched as it is (like so many of his works) in subtly elusive and allusive poetic prose, and partly because he seems to be saying something that is essentially ineffable to anyone who has not had a similar mystical experience.

The five dialogues in *Daniel* present various basic concepts dealing with his central existential experience: the concepts of *direction, actuality, meaning, duality,* and *unity.* These ideas deserve brief consideration because in fragmentary and incomplete form they represent a preliminary attempt to comprehend the nature of religious experience and to show how mystical experience can help in resolving problems in the lives of men. These elements were later incorporated into the *I-Thou* concept as expressing the heart of his philosophy.[92]

1. In the first dialogue Buber is concerned to show that the realm of space consists of an infinity of directions, but that each person is endowed with a definite direction of consciousness. And man possesses the faculty of viewing things as cutting across the kind of space which is formed by the radiation of lines of direction from himself as the center. Absolute space results from a particular human attitude or perception; therefore, he is able to assume a spaceless orientation of the soul along a line of direction peculiar to it. In ordinary experience we apprehend objects without particular reference to any of these directions. But in the mystical experience there is a concentration of apprehension, a directional intensity and selectivity in our perceptions. Here Buber is trying to distinguish between a space in which all points are equally significant and one in which a particularly luminous point or direction shines out.

As illustration, he relates an early experience of looking into the dark night. There was a feeling of dread associated with the darkness; but this fear gradually lifted when he managed "to tear out of the infinity of directions" the one which corresponded to his own direction. He now felt himself to have a "brother," and he was able to feel the sadness of the night without being afraid of it. The word "brother" is significant as indicating both the intimate nature of the relation felt, and his urge and need to enter into personal connection with the universe. Another example is given which shows that "direction" is the immediate way from being to being. A man looks at a pine tree "with all his directed powers" and identifies himself so completely with the tree that he feels its bark as his own skin and its cones as his own children.[93] Through such experiences man receives true knowledge;[94] he is removed to the spiritual realm of direction, "from the earth of space" to the "earth of the soul." However, mark this! in this realm of directional spirit, Buber insists, the true self is not dissolved, for the unity and consciousness of the direction are maintained.

To live this life of direction is to find blessedness, as contrasted with the life lived within the ordered world of science and commonsense. And each soul must seek its own direction. In the later I-Thou concept, the emphasis is placed on the *dialogue*, on mutual response, rather than simply on the individual seeking his own direction.

2. Still searching for a more adequate way of expressing this sense of unity, in the second dialogue Buber proposes that the two types of perception are paralleled by two fundamental attitudes toward life: those of *orienting* and *actualizing*. The former is the viewpoint of common sense and of science, in which things are placed in their spatial, temporal, and causal order. The latter consists in going out to *meet* all things, events, and persons with the whole of one's being. In this meeting things and persons are "actualized" in their real, unique meaning. "All actuality is filled connection; nothing individual is itself actual." [95] Here for the first time, Buber advances his notion that children and primitive men live in this realm of "actuality," while civilized man has grown away from, become stranger to, this realm. The false, unblessed reply of most men to the call from eternity is, "Ich weiss Bescheid."

Buber recounts another boyhood experience of grieving over the loss of a dear friend. One day he happened to peer from the height of a Tatra mountain into a deep lake below, and he was oppressed by the utter strangeness of the abyss below. But, as he continued to gaze into the dark liquid surface below, it suddenly came to him that the lake was not a stranger to him, that it had indeed an animate, almost personal aspect.[96] This experience is another illustration of Buber's growing conviction that it is possible to enter into living, even personal, relations with all things. A tree, a lake, a mountain, anything can be transformed into living reality by the power of intention, direction, and social imagination.

3. The third dialogue takes up the subject-object duality under the concept of *Sinn*, which here refers to the intuition of the *meaning* of life. Buber relates the story of a young man who, while peacefully rowing one evening, is suddenly overcome with the dread feeling that an abyss was yawning beneath him. Even after the hallucination had passed, the youth was oppressed with the anxious presentiment of impending danger. He was also obsessed with the doubleness of the "bright One" and the "dark Other," the fissure between the subject and object. None of the known philosophical schemes was adequate to bridge this gap. Daniel then assures the young man that this experience of the abyss really marked his entrance into the spiritual life.[97] For the nature and origin of religion are associated with this experience of duality, with fear, awe, and anxious fascination in the face of the Great Mystery. The world of orientation is the world of security; it is the world of experience, knowledge, use, stable order. The life of actualization, on the other hand, knows no such security; it is attended with uncertainty, danger, surprises. The failure to recognize that there is a deep chasm between the self and the other gives the orienting mind confidence in a dependable regime. The life of actualization, on the other hand, is lived in freedom, in creativity, and necessarily involves the taking of risks, the possible infliction of soul-wounds, the unexpected creative task. But in this form of life, every thing and every event takes on new meaning. And in these experienced antinomies and dualities of life, man ever finds his task: "To create unity out of his and all duality." [98] The deed and decision of man assume cosmic significance; for thereby man helps God to be realized.[99] Here is also expressed the notion, later developed in the I-Thou relation, that everything in the universe calls to us and we should receive it as a message, as though, looking up into the night, you felt a star saying to you, "all the time I was turned toward you."

4. The fourth dialogue is given over to the attempt, obscure at best, to clarify the meaning of the dualities which seem to comprise the world. Buber advances the theory that the being of the spirit is two-fold (*urzweiheit*). Being consists of two poles—*Wesen* and *Gegen-Wesen*—between which unity never is, but is always becoming. Man's spiritual deeds are informed with the desire to "establish

the rainbow bridge from pole to pole." [100] And here Buber avows with eloquence the certainty with which he felt that "the streams that ran from pole to pole ran through (his) heart." [101] Buber explains this feeling of duality as a revelation of the Real,[102] that world of Spirit which abides behind the veil of phenomena and which eternally sends forth pulsations of activity and meaning from pole to pole. The currents of reality run through the heart of man;[103] he alone can close the circuit through his own will and activity.

5. In the final dialogue, Buber continues his inquiry into the problem of unity. Man must first become aware of duality; then his task and way to blessedness is to overcome that duality by action. Unity must be lived; logic alone cannot bridge the gap. Buber is convinced that the world presents a double-aspect; that the different parts of the world need each other, and that this need can be satisfied only by the living of unity in the risk-taking life of freedom and action. Buber confesses that he felt these dualities, tensions, and cross currents in his own soul until, by means of a supreme effort, he achieved the strength to collect himself so that he was no longer inwardly separated. "I have torn down within me," he wrote, "the eternal wall, that wall within me." [104]

BUBER'S MYSTICISM

This mild form of mysticism, if such it can be called,[105] obviously does not lead to absorption in the Absolute. With its stress on *Innerlichkeit*, romanticism,[106] intuitive personal experience, and aesthetic awareness, Buber's mysticism and existentialism do not reside in nor result in a pantheistic union which destroys essential relation, with an attendant reduction of either self or Other. The fault that Buber finds in Spinoza is that his mysticism does tend to do away with real relation. In Buber's thought the center of gravity falls outside the self, in the "between." Buber's mysticism leads, rather, to a quick reverent awareness of and a receptive attitude toward all of God's creation.[107] It signifies an intuitive, but comprehensive and realistic, venture of faith toward communion with the creative depths of life, and a readiness to devote one's energies to the creative task which we cannot know until we have entered the I-Thou situation. For the situation as Buber describes it is one of meeting, of relation between "subjects" without deliquescence or appropriation either way. Buber wants to see life intensely and see it whole; he wants to reconcile the estranged "objectivity" as well as the empty "subjectivity" of recent philosophy. The sharp Cartesian hiatus between the thinker and his thoughts, between the subjective and objective realms, is transcended; and, paradoxically—in keeping with the paradoxical character of life and truth—the essence of objectivity is found in the depth of subjectivity. Buber's way is that of the poet, the artist, the man of faith, the "natural mystic"; from the insights and values of these disciplines comes the force with which Buber tries to break through the limitations of a scientific and rationalistic humanism. Mysticism is a perpetual return to reality, to the vision of God. The great problem of religion is that of how man can attain to spiritual and moral communion with Infinite Being. Mystical religion lives in the abiding conviction that the universe is friendly at heart and will support man's efforts to realize his ideal ends, achieve personal unity and cosmic adjustment. When such a mysticism is realistic and ethical it recognizes that "All being is life, and that in loving self-devotion to other life we realize our spiritual union with Infinite Being." [108] The religious person seldom seriously doubts that the universe is his friend. He enters the realm of religion when he takes his own stand in friendly relations to the universe. Thereafter he explores and enjoys the fruits that may come from that spirit.[109]

It is important to remark, however, that Buber's views on the nature of mystical religious experience underwent a noticeable change over the years. His youthful experiences and his early writings display no clear or consistent view of mysticism, but there is the hint of the ineffable ecstasy of union of God. Around 1900 Buber was under the influence of German mysticism (i.e., Eckhardt, Boehme, Silesius) which is often charged with being neo-platonic and anti-personalistic.[110] But it is also clearly in the record that after his deep study of Chassidism, Buber turned his back upon all mysticism of the extreme monistic, pantheistic type. That kind of mysticism is silent. And man's spirit withers in the air of soliloquy. Buber wants to say *Thou* to God, to *address* God as a real Other. A mysticism of the practical, ethical type—mild rather than extreme, pervasive of daily living, into which moral discernment and discipline enter, not as a means to induce the ecstatic vision, but as a condition of the practice of the presence of God—such, as I read it, is the kernel of Buber's mysticism.

There are different types of mysticism, of which the Hindu and Neoplatonic types tend to be extremely monistic, losing man in the Godhead. The classical extreme mysticism claims to effect a fusion between man and God. In the ecstatic vision the world, time, space, and self-consciousness disappear—and are counted well lost. The mystic is absorbed into the Absolute. "That Soul! That art thou!" "Whoever knows 'I am Brahma' becomes this all,"—this is typical of Hindu mysticism. To achieve this "union" the mystic turns away from this world which is only an illusion, blocking the way to Reality.

Not so with the Chassidim, and with Buber. Man cannot seek out God by a renunciation of the world, any more than he can find God by an exclusive devotion to the world.

> To step into pure relation is not to disregard everything but to see everything in the *Thou*. . . . Men do not find God if they stay in the world. They do not find Him if they leave the world. He who goes out with his whole being to meet his Thou and carries to it all being that is in the world, finds Him who cannot be sought.[111]

The world is neither evil nor illusory. It is to be lived in and enjoyed and loved. There is no sharp separation between the created world and the spirit, between man and God, between ethics and religion. Those frontier-lines Buber wants to keep fluid, provisional. The world is the reality wherein man finds God, and the neighbor. And other persons, instead of obstructing man's relations to God (as Kierkegaard believed), are the means by which man comes to God.[112] The Kingdom of God is between us, among us *(mitten unter uns)*. So Buber writes:

> The fundamental attitude of Jewish religiosity and the core of that Jewish monotheism which has been so vastly misunderstood, so cruelly rationalized, is to regard all things as manifestations of God, all events as revelation of the Absolute. Whereas for the other great monotheist of the Orient . . . sensory reality is an illusion to be sloughed off in order to enter into the world of truth, for the Jew sensory reality is a revelation of the divine spirit and will. Hence for the Indian, as later for the Platonist, all myth is metaphor, while for the Jew it is an authentic record of God's revelation on earth. . . . Hasidism teaches that the divine in things lies dormant and can be awakened only by him who approaches things with dedication and sanctifies himself in them.

Sensory reality is divine, but it must be *realized* in its divinity
through the man who authentically experiences it. . . . And thus
to each man it is given to affect God's destinies by his own
life. . . . [113]

In another place, writing of the Baal-Shem-Tov, he says: "The
world is the concrete embodiment of the creative message of God to
man and of man's responsive service to God; it was created for no
other purpose than to offer man redemption through its confluence of
divine and human activity." [114] Such a mysticism, declares Buber, is
a mysticism which preserves the immediacy of the relation, the concreteness of the Absolute, and the pledging of the entire being. The
individual ceases to exist if he cannot say "I" or if he is not engaged
with a Thou.[115] God and man are both subjects in the relationship.
True to his Jewish heritage, Buber refuses to suppress either the
transcendence or the immanence of God. In no case is the real distinction between the Creator and the creature erased. In Jewish (and
Christian) mysticism there must be free, autonomous persons in a
genuine meeting of *I* and *Thou* which preserves the integrity of both
self and Other. Any mysticism which denies the essential two-ness
of the dialogic relation is false, for it either cancels out the self by its
absorption into the Absolute, or it negates God by asserting the all-
embracing character of the self. In either case it permits an escape
from reality and from human responsibility.

It becomes clear from all this that Buber teaches and practices a
moderate, critical, active, and natural mysticism which stresses the
personal and the ethical and which does not confuse the intensity of
ecstasy for the fact of union. Buber's mysticism belongs to what
Pringle-Pattison called the "higher Mysticism" of real communion with
God, bringing a sense of a presence or reality which is immediately felt
to be valid, objective, and Divine. And while it emphasizes the
intuitive insights of religion as more precious than the intellectual and
institutional aspects, it does not overlook the communal and rational
elements. It therefore has strong appeal to those who are more concerned with vital religious experience than with theological argument.
Buber's existential mysticism involves a total operation of the whole
self in its encounter with reality.[116]

There was a time in his earlier years, Buber tells us, when religion
was for him something exalted and separate from life. But now, he
writes:

I possess nothing but the every day out of which I am never taken. . . . I know no fulness but each mortal hour's fulness of claim and responsibility. Though far from being equal to it, yet I know that in the claim I am claimed and may respond in responsibility, and know who speaks and demands a response. . . . If that is religion, then it is just everything, simply all that is lived in its possibility of dialogue.[117]

The constant renewal of this confrontation with the Eternal Thou, the living Center, both creates community and confirms that there is meaning in life.

THE I-THOU DIALOGUE

Buber's understanding of Chassidism, his re-discovery of Judaism, his search for the mysticism and philosophy of Orient and Occident, his interpretation of the cultural crisis of our times, and his own maturing thought—all came together in the now famous little book *Ich und Du*. This was not a break with what had gone before, but only a ripening, an explanation, and a summary. In this work, and in the several sequels to it,[118] Buber has attempted to rescue the "personal" from oblivion, as he recovered and preserved for posterity the life and legends of the Chassidim. This "philosophy of the personal," the emphasis upon the *sui generis* nature of persons and their relationship to God and to one another, has received its most original and subtle contemporary statement in Martin Buber's writings. Traditional ontology, logic and ethics overlooked these as apparently self-evident, and had thus neglected the real human problem. Buber has made himself the philosopher of the "personal." [119] He has set forth in fresh poetic terminology and vivid symbolism, the whole world of the personal—the facts, attitudes, dimensions, and laws by which it is constituted and differentiated from the world of things. We must, therefore, undertake the exposition of his conception of the personal in the *I-Thou* dialogic relation. For this is the primal category to which Buber arrives in his mature thought. The crucial importance of *relations* between persons is, he believes, the redeeming message for our sick, de-humanized world.

Life, says Buber, is in essence a complex of personal relationships. Personality, in a vague but real sense, may be imputed by man to the objects of his attention.[120] It is possible to enter into living personal relation with all things: with nature, man, and God. This has been the experience of man since the days of his childhood, individually and racially. But more of this later. The important thing is man's capacity to *address* and *be addressed* by natural objects, by other men, and by God. This is Buber's profound insight, the corollary of which is that knowledge of oneself is pre-eminently knowledge of oneself in relation to another. The meaning of existence is revealed to man only when he hears himself addressed, and answers with his whole being out of responsible decision.

Buber's whole life and effort have been dominated by the belief that true existence can be had only by entering into genuine personal relations with the environment. Life, reality, the world, is essentially a system of intimate relationships. The central fact of life, though not restricted to it alone, is love, the total direction of one's life and will toward the being and the need of the other *(der Mitmensch)*. It is a voluntary and ethical concentration of all one's being and interests on the "other" who is conceived as returning this outgoing devotion. *I* and *Thou* are two poles of an inter-personal relation: love is between *I* and *Thou*. Perfect relation is always mutual *(Beziehung ist Gegenseitigkeit)*. My *Thou* affects me as I affect him.[121] For life is not in man, but man is in life. Life is *between* persons and *between* things, not in them. "Spirit is not in the I, but between the I and Thou. Spirit is not like the blood which circulates within you, but like the air in which you breathe." Man lives in the Spirit whenever he can answer his Thou. There is no *I* in itself, but only the *I* which stands facing a *Thou* in the reality of relationship. "Through the *Thou* a man becomes *I*."[122] "The *I* is real in virtue of its sharing in reality."[123] The man who stands apart from true relation in lonely or proud isolation is doomed to loss of life, futility, and unreality.[124] For Buber is here not merely expressing a pretty moral sentiment; he insists that he is stating a law of human nature and existence—namely, that we cannot become selves or live as selves except in relationship. Man must give himself, meet the other, bind himself to the other in order to find selfhood. The fuller the sharing, the more loyal the bonds, the more real the self becomes.[125] For man's true self is "social."[126]

Buber's main theme in *I and Thou* is that there are two fundamental relations, attitudes, or dimensions in human experience. "To man the world is twofold, in accordance with the twofold nature of the primary words which he speaks."[127] There are two types of environment: the human and the physical. And there are two corresponding attitudes with which we may confront the external world: the personal and the functional. The intelligence of man is both intuitive and rational, personal and functional. Thus our relationships to environment fall into two classes: first, *personal response,* mostly made toward our fellowmen; and secondly, mechanical manipulative *adjustments,* which are mostly made toward the things about us. The latter is the attitude in which the object is a "thing" which serves my purpose or advantage; the former is the attitude in which I enter into and "realize" the essence of the other in a relation between persons. There is, Buber thinks, a world of difference between one's attitude and response to other persons and one's attitude to things; indeed there are two different attitudes, be it to persons or to things. The one is a *personal relation* of a subject standing over against another subject; the other is a mere *connection* with experienced objects. The first Buber designates as the *Ich-Du* (I-Thou) relationship; the second, the *Ich-Es* (I-It) relationship. These are the two primary words which man speaks: the combined words, *I-Thou* and *I-It*.[128]

There are, then, two basic situations or orders of living: the "world of Thou" wherein exist personal I-Thou relations; and the "world of It" wherein exist impersonal or mechanical connections. The difference may be illustrated as that between a man's whole bearing toward other men as "men," and his attitude toward things as objects. For primary words do not signify or describe things; they intimate relations.[129] In the living personal relation a "subject" confronts another "subject" in an *I-Thou* dialogue, facing and engaging another person; in the connection with things the subject experiences, judges, arranges, appropriates, uses an object. The other person is of course a datum to the *I,* but the *I* is never merely an experiencing subject, nor the *Thou* merely an experienced object.

These spheres are, of course, not water-tight compartments. We may, for instance, take the mechanical, functional It-attitude toward men, and treat them as things. And in our technological era it is all too easy to treat men as things. Indeed, this is a part of the intrinsic tragedy of life. On the other hand, it is inevitable that sometimes we take a social, personal attitude toward the non-human environment. This is the sphere of religious experience—taking social, personal attitudes towards the non-human environment as it has been "personified" by spiritual and social imagination.[130] In Buber's words: "As experience, the world belongs to the primary word *I-It*. The primary word *I-Thou* establishes the world of relations." [131] When under the aegis of the *I-It* mentality, living beings, works of art, and other persons can be regarded as mere objects of experience, to be classified, judged, used. But another relation is possible. Man, living things, and works of art can speak to us, so that we go out to them in their unique totality, and they become to us, not *It*, but Thou.[132]

How does the biologist look at a flower? And how does the artist or poet respond to the same flower? The biologist may take a very objective, dispassionate, scientific pose; he may dissect the plant, analyze it, classify it, study its histology, anatomy, ecology, etc. And that is important, and supplies a certain kind of data. The artist or lover, on the other hand, does not think of its usefulness, its biological form or function. He regards it concretely as a living and beautiful whole, he responds to it as a unique totality: he sings his rapture. He enters into it with empathy. It says something to him, it stirs his being, and he answers. It is not merely an *it*, a thing to be perceived, an object to be studied or used. It becomes a *thou*, to be enjoyed, to be loved; and the artist or lover mingles his soul, as it were, with the soul of the flower. He is filled by its presence, and he may desire to recreate its beauty. "The primary word *I-Thou* can only be spoken with the whole being." "The primary word *I-It* can never be spoken with the whole being." [133] In the *I-Thou* relation I *meet* the other. But "in the act of experience Thou is far away." [134]

The same differentiation must hold between what the scientist does in his laboratory and what he does in his home; between the way he handles his instruments and materials in the laboratory and the way he treats his wife and children.[135] The same distinction is found between a man's attitude toward a prostitute (or, indeed, any woman) as a mere sex object, to be used and discarded, and the husband's attitude toward his wife as the unique and beloved person. I do not "experience" the person to whom I say "Thou." Rather, "I take my stand in relation to him, in the sanctity of the primary word." [136] Merely to say the word "Thou" or even to whisper an amorous "Thou" with the lips is by no means the same as speaking the primary word, so long as "experience" and "make use of" are really intended.[137] To have dealings with people is not necessarily to have *relation between persons*.

A person can enter into either the *It* or the *Thou* relation with all things. Since men live in the world of *It,* they naturally must apply their intelligence and their powers to the *It*-world. But they may transform it through love and social imagination into a *Thou*-world. The *I* always stands on the edge of the *It*-world, the world of orientation in time and space, and yet one's attitude may transform the relational character of that world. And the "particular *Thou,* after the relational event has run its course, is bound to become an *It*." [138] Even love itself cannot persist continuously in the immediacy of the *Thou*-relation. Love endures, but in the inter-change of actual and potential being. Every *Thou* in the world at some time becomes a thing for us.[139] But "the particular It, by entering the relational event, may become a Thou." [140] "To step into pure relation is not to disregard everything but to see everything in the *Thou*." [141] One can learn to love the world as *Thou*. In this relation we touch reality. For real living is not lived in isolation, nor in a union which swallows up the other, nor in an annexation which exploits the other. The substance of the world is not separation, and not undifferentiated unity—it is *relation*. And true relation is mutual and reciprocal. So Buber warns, "Guard against wishing to remove it into your soul," for then you annihilate it.[142] Real living is a *meeting, eine Zwischenmenschlichkeit,* which involves mutual claims, sacrifices, promises, and risks: The claim of complete and vital engagement; the sacrifice of other possibilities, since the mutual relation requires a kind of exclusiveness; the promise that binds one to another; and the risk especially of giving oneself wholly into the keeping of another, withholding nothing.

When two men met as comrades, or when man and woman meet as lovers, their love encompasses them without destroying their integrity as persons. *I* and *Thou* are the two poles of a relation; love is the reality of the relation between them. Each retains his identity and autonomy and responsibility. In this situation we also discern the real difference between "community" as over against mere "organization" or "association" which is only a connection between an aggregate of things.[143]

It should be underlined that, in Buber's thought, there is no evil in things as such. Nor, indeed, is man evil and depraved. Buber sees man as essentially neither good nor evil, nor even as possessing only the indeterminate possibility of either. In a more precise sense, man is somehow "good and evil together." [144] Only as against God can radical evil be ascribed to man, "because God is God and man is man and the distance between them is absolute." In man, it is the feeling for this tension of polarity that generates the dynamic of spiritual life.

By the same token, the *I-It* world is in itself not evil. Man must live on the earth, in the natural order of physical objects. The world-of-Thou and the world-of-It are not absolutely incompatible. But to live in the world of *It* alone is not real life; it is a delusory, counterfeit, irresponsible, pseudo-life. Yet it *seems* to be the world of security, knowledge, certainty, use. "Without *It* man cannot live. But he who lives with *It* alone is not a man." [145] The real, joyous, manly, meaningful life springs from the *meetings* between I and Thou. Yet despite all this, man has a tendency to treat other men as *It*; and when that happens, when man forsakes the *Thou,* evil results. This is the situation, for example, when the scientist, the politician, the propagandist, the employer treats men and women as things, commodities, pawns, objects to be manipulated, used, pushed around. This is to treat persons as abstractions, as perceived in parts only, or in the mass. So to speak and act toward other persons is immoral; it is to reject the rule of God; it is to fail in our loyalty to the meaning of the "personal." [146] This is to be blind or disloyal to the meaning of *Thou* and to the truth of the dialogic relationship.

There is however, says Buber, one *Thou* which can never become an *It,* the eternal *Thou,* or God. Though we speak of God as *He,* the true meaning of His approach to man and His "address" to man is found only in the sense of the relation of an *I* and a *Thou.* God lets himself be spoken to personally, and speaks only to persons. God, by his nature, never ceases to be *Thou* for us.[147] He who knows God may at times know remoteness from God and the pain and barrenness of the tormented heart; but he does not know the absence of God: it is only man who is not always there, not always faithful to the truth of meeting with the *Thou.* We cannot, declares Buber, define or measure or use God. God cannot be expressed; He can only be *addressed.* We can hear His voice, and answer Him in loving obedience. God is ever confronting us. In each genuine Thou we address the eternal Thou. In every true meeting with a Thou we catch a glimpse of the eternal Thou.[148] In the eternal *Thou* the extended lines of relation meet and are consummated.

Religion consists in confronting the physical-seeming It-world with the attitudes, concepts and feelings of our socio-personal nature. Here there are call and answer, initiative and response, revelation and faith. This is the source of myth, says Buber. Faith is the *meeting* with the *Eternal Thou* who is both Other and the Present One who addresses man and makes a claim upon him.[149] Out of this meeting, Brunner agrees, "truth comes into being," and man becomes most truly a person.[150] Man is constituted in full self-hood when as an *I* he is able to know and answer God as *Thou.* "I become through my relation to the *Thou;* as *I* become *I,* I say *Thou.*" [151] "There is no *I* taken in itself, but only the *I* of the primary word *I-Thou* and the *I* of the primary word *I-It.*" [152] In the act of true dialogic relation, man becomes a *self.* And the fuller its sharing in the reality of dialogue the more real the self becomes.[153]

Religion is the dialogic life in history; the summons to man and his response.[154] The Bible is the age-old record of this dialogue between God and man. Judaism is the Jew's experience of this "heavenly discourse"—unique in the annals of history—with its continuing address and answer, revelation and response. No people has so comprehended its history and destiny under this perspective as have the Jews. Man is called by the world and by his fellowmen—and he must give answer. Nature, beauty, neighbor, God—everything speaks to man, crying for release, for the right word. God speaks and the world answers— and it is created. God speaks and man answers—and he becomes a "person," a "self." *Shema!* Hear, O Israel! The *Thou* meets man. This relation means being chosen and choosing, pledge and promise, binding and being bound, suffering and action in one. In this sense, every people is a "chosen" people. What every saint and prophet has done, what every truly religious person or race does, is to reply in faith to God in this meeting of God and man in the world. It is not a call that comes from within; this is likely to be mere self-deception, hallucination, escape from responsible answer. It is a call that comes thundering from without, from the neighbor, from God—crying for justice and mercy in the land, demanding a loyal pledge and promise.

The Bible is the story of the tortured Jewish soul in its historical development toward unity, deed, and the future kingdom. Through the Bible, Israel has taught mankind to know and address God as the *Eternal Thou.* Prayer is uttering the words which affirm and confirm this relation.

Having anticipated the fuller argument by this more summary statement of the nature of the "I-Thou-It" world, we may now retrace our steps and examine in more detail the nature of the relations and qualities characteristic of the "world of It" and the "world of Thou," the procedure by which the self develops, the circumstances under which man most fully realizes himself, and the self's relations to the larger community and to God.

THE NATURE OF THE I-IT WORLD

Buber is convinced that there is an obvious difference between the relation brought about when an *I* meets an *It*, and when an *I* meets a *Thou*. It is not that there are two kinds of man, but two poles of humanity, two dimensions within which the same man may dwell, two attitudes with which the individual may face his environment. Every man lives in the twofold dimension. But there are some men so defined by their attitudes that they may be called "persons," and there are other men so defined by their attitudes that they may be called "individuals." [155] And the more a man, or humanity, is mastered by the attitudes of "individuals" living in the "world of It," the deeper does the real self sink into unreality, discord and death. Even though we may speak in both cases of "meeting" or "relation" or "confronting," such terms mean different things in the two situations.

The uniqueness and reality and blessedness of the true *I-Thou* relation is incomprehensible to those who have never experienced it, or come close to it. Despite his varied and subtle analysis of the two different primary words or relations (*I-It* and *I-Thou*), Buber is really appealing to us to find an echo of his words and experience in our own lives. It is poetry, if you like; some will call it "subjective." Still it is his earnest attempt, from the standpoint of life, to tell the truth. A child cannot judge the experiences of an adult; an unmusical person can never quite understand the spell of great music; Narcissus and Don Juan will ever be incapable of love; the unbeliever can never quite comprehend the nature of faith nor the grounds of faith. Yet faith is not just a talent: it is possible for all, open to everyone. The proof lies not in the logical construction of universally valid propositions or scientific observations,[156] but in the actual *experience of relation in the "world of Thou."* Perhaps the I-Thou relation will be comprehensible only to those who have experienced it or have been close to it. Others may find the concept interesting but they will not be able to apply the insights to themselves.

Let us first be very clear about Buber's interpretation of the "world of It" in contrast to the "world of Thou."

"I perceive something. I am sensible of something. I imagine something. I will something. I feel something. I think something." [157] Whenever, in the relation of man to his world, the accent falls on *experiencing, possessing, using, talking about* something, we are in the objective-subjective realm of I-It. [158] What precisely do we mean when we say that a man experiences his world? The *I* is separated from the *It* in the subject-object antithesis. In "experience" one travels over *(befährt)* the surface of things and experiences *(erfährt)* them; one abstracts a knowledge of their qualities. [159] The individual is differentiated, isolated from other entities. He *has* things, he *sees* something or someone, he *knows* something, he *grasps* something, he *disposes* of something; he wins an experience from them; he has inner feelings related to those objects. His knowledge is thereby increased, but these somethings or someones do not essentially change him, or penetrate to the core of his being. *Die Erfahrung ist ja 'in ihm' und nicht zwischen ihm und der Welt.* [160] "You perceive it, take it to yourself as the 'truth,' and it lets itself be taken; but it does not give itself to you." [161] Nor do you give or pledge yourself to it.

The world of *It* is set in the context of space and time and causality. [162] Common sense and science share this attitude. This is the world of security, of predictable events, of fixed laws and understood connections which enable men to form a reasonable plan by which to build, sustain and equip organized social living. This is, in Kantian terms, the realm of knowledge. The scientist seizes upon an object of perception; he studies it, compares and classifies it, establishes it in its proper order, and sets up a general statement to cover its appearance in space and time. "Only as *It* can it enter the structure of knowledge." [163] Such knowledge enables man to "make progress," to "get one's bearings" in the world, to conquer and control nature. But with the development of these functions and powers, Buber notes a decrease in man's power and in his longing to enter into relation. For man now lives in a world of the pronouns *It, He, She, They,* and *It* again. *Thou* and *We* are the pronouns of true relation, genuine correspondence, giving and receiving.

Buber is equally opposed to both mere mechanical manipulative activity and sentimental egoism. The first leaves the "heart" out of living and deals only with the surface and from the surface. The latter never gets beyond the private boundaries. For *feelings* revolve upon themselves and are savored, without ever passing over into the common life.

When we concern ourselves with *institutions* and *feelings,* we are also in the world of *It.* How symbolic of *It* and *Ego,* respectively! Institutions are "outside" where a man works, organizes, conducts his business, officiates, governs, bears influence, controls. And when tolerably well ordered, with the aid of hand and brain, they are the places where the affairs of the world are handled, the work of the world done. Feelings are "inside" where man's inner life is lived and where he recovers from institutions. Here he may relax, in the citadel of his own house, and indulge his emotions. "Institutions are a complicated marketplace; feelings a boudoir rich in ever-changing interests." [164] But an institution is only an animated aggregation without a soul, and the separated withdrawn ego of feelings is "an uneasily fluttering soulbird." Neither of them knows man or mutual life. "Institutions know only the specimen, feelings only the 'object.' " [165] Both are necessary; "but put together they do not create human life: this is done by the third, the central presence of the *Thou.*" [166]

Causality reigns as king in the world of It. Material progress, scientific knowledge, human development are all regarded as subsumed under the scientific ordering of nature. This makes the empirical fact of free will an unsolvable problem. It also makes known the mechanistic tendencies in all such views of life. The world of Newtonian physics was a machine, marvelously complex, but still a machine. And this is why it was considered the task of science to reveal its secrets. The object of science, however, is determined by the laws of cause and effect. Science recognizes not only no creation, but no novelties, no unique creative acts, either in finite moral life, nor in the totality of the living; [167] it recognizes only a new grouping of old elements. But that means that it recognizes only what is dead and gone, in the past, and therefore fixed, determined. When man, the human person, becomes an "object" of scientific study, he is made tacitly, in the last analysis, into a machine, into a dead thing. The quasi-biological and quasi-historical methods have worked together to establish a tenacious belief in fate more oppressive than that of Karma. Many powers and formulae claim control of man's destiny. But whether it is the "law of life," "social law," "cultural law," or the faith in inevitable progress —whatever form it takes, it always means that man is set in a frame of inevitable happening and causal sequence which he cannot resist. Man misuses the name of destiny; *fate* is the correct term. The dogma of gradual process and of inevitable progress is the abdication of man before the world of It; for the dogma of process and progress leaves no room for freedom.[168] And man is finite freedom, "the crystallized potentiality of existence,' "the centre of all surprise in the world." [169]

Fate does not recognize genuine freedom and responsibility. No one is responsible for a fate brought about by "drives." On the other hand, what one is responsible for cannot be explained by causes. Likewise, in the realm of science there is neither freedom nor responsibility, and for that reason, precisely taken, there is no life. The free, responsible, creative human being ceases to be a "scientist" as such. He has caught sight of the other side of human existence—the world of persons, the world of relation—which must forever remain not-quite-accessible to science. He knows that man, the "great amphibian," lives in two elements and when he tries to make his home in one alone something goes wrong with him. The realm of the It-orientation is not enough for the creative spirit of man. If his spirit is to live, it must take periodic journeys into another realm.

The reign of causality need not weigh heavily on the man who is not limited to the world of *It*, who can and does leave it frequently for the world of *Thou*. For as he returns to the world of *It*, he carries with him the spark of freedom, the vigor of a healthy trust in life, the breath of the world of *Thou*.[170]

What Buber seems to be saying is that men, like migratory birds, cannot fulfill their lives in one climate but must take seasonal flights to another clime. Even this simile of migratory birds does not quite render Buber's meaning. He is pointing to the tragic fact that man cannot endure in the atmosphere of I-Thou; he is not allowed to do it; he is even duty bound to leave it again and again.

More specifically, in the I-It situation there is connection with and manipulation of things without ever really facing them or inter-penetrating them. Of course, when a man is using or investigating a thing, this is, in a sense, an affair between him and the object. But the connection does not go deep, it is detached, objectified, impersonal, held off, easily entered and left. Buber reminds us, however, that even in this situation there is a waiting potentiality of the *Thou*—in the *Between*. For the Spirit dwells in the *Between*—in what happens between man and his fellows *(Zwischenmenschlichkeit)*, between man and nature, between man and the Idea which seeks his service, between man and the God who addresses him. If man is to become truly a self, he must once and again enter the world of relations where persons meet as *I* and *Thou* and where are mutual self-disclosure and fellowship together.

THE WORLD OF I AND THOU

There is, then, another world and another relation possible, where the concepts of Space and Time and Casuality are irrelevant, at least not primary. Our existence is not made up simply of activities which have a "something" or a "someone" for their object. "When the *Thou* is spoken, the speaker has no thing for his object. . . . But he takes his stand in relation." [171] Spirit can penetrate and transform the world of It. This "someone-something" can become a *Thou* in intersubjective relation. The perfection of dialogic relationship constitutes the reality of God in his approach to man. For "every particular *Thou* is a glimpse through to the eternal *Thou;* by means of every particular *Thou* the primary word addresses the eternal *Thou.*" [172] In the eternal *Thou* the extended lines of relations meet.

When we use the basic I-Thou word, we are not designating a new object. Rather, a new kind of relation has come into being, a relation radically different from all that we mean by "experiencing" or "knowing" or "using." The I-It world is a world of subject-object connection, of separation, of I-solitariness. And though we may talk of "inner" experiences as well as of "outer" experiences, it makes no difference. Nothing in the situation is really changed. Inner things or outer things: they are still things.[173]

But when the "uncanny foundation word," the *I-Thou* word, is uttered, a new mode of relation is made accessible to us. Now we do not experience and use; we enter into mutual engagement and dealings in which each one reciprocally "says" himself to the other, discloses himself to the other, surrenders himself to the other, and receives the other.[174] Here the *Thou* meets me, and I step into direct relation with it. In one sense the relationship does not exist until one has entered it, but in another sense it is already there, waiting to be "realized." This means choosing and being chosen with the whole being.[175] This is the cradle of life, the source of art, the womb of the self. An illustration from the field of art may help to clarify Buber's vision of the Thou-world.

The artist is faced by a form which desires to be made through him into a work of art. It says something to him; and if he speaks the primary word out of his whole being to the form which appears, then the work beings. This act of meeting between the artist and the form involves a sacrifice and a risk—the sacrifice of endless possibility to the exclusiveness of that particular relation; the risk of giving himself wholly to the form which faces him. It commands, and the artist either breaks it or is broken by it. Of course, once the work is done it becomes a thing among things, capable of being experienced, described, appraised, compared. But it was not so for the artist when he was filled by its presence, and it can again and again become a Thou to the man who meets it and beholds it with the wholeness of his being and in the wholeness of its form.[176] And thus it is between man and man.

The *I* of the word *I-Thou* is a different *I* than the *I* of the word *I-It*. The *I* of the *I-It* world appears as an individual entity, conscious of himself as the subject of experiencing and using. The *I* of the *I-Thou* world appears as a *person,* conscious of himself as *subjectivity* (without a dependent genitive). The *individual* makes its appearance by virtue of differentiating itself from other entities. The *person* makes his appearance by virtue of his relations with other persons.[177] The person is concerned with reality, with the true Self, with the full *I*. The individual is concerned with "me" and "mine"—my experience, my kind, my race, my work of art. The stronger the *I* of the word *I-Thou,* the more personal is the man.[178]

It was pointed out in the previous section that neither institutions nor feelings have access to real life. "Institutions yield no public life," says Buber, "and feelings no personal life." [179] That institutions yield no genuine communal life is realized with distress by increasing numbers of men: this is the problem of our age. But surely it is mistaken to assert that feelings yield no personal life! The most personal life of all seems to reside in the feelings. But here also, Buber insists, lies much of the cause of the human ills of our time. For modern man, concerned with his own feelings, will hardly be instructed in a better way by despair over their unreality, since—as Buber aptly remarks—despair is also an interesting feeling.

Consider, for example, the modern State. The men who are in rebellion over the fact that institutions yield no genuine community have hit upon what appears to be a fruitful expedient: institutions must be loosened or burst asunder by the feelings themselves. If the modern state links citizens together without establishing a "being together," then let the State be replaced by the community of love, perhaps the classless society, which will arise when men, out of free abundant feeling, approach one another. But this will not do, argues Buber.

> The true community does not arise through people having feelings for one another (though indeed not without it), but through, first, their taking their stand in living mutual relation with a living Centre, and second, their being in living mutual relation with one another.... Living mutual relation includes feelings, but does not originate with them. The community is built up out of living mutual relations, but the builder is the living effective Centre.[180]

In other words, in true community, God enters as a *member*. Buber's social philosophy is of a piece with his religious thought: the dialogue of religion has its starting point, its center, and its culmination in the dialogical society. Or, Buber seems to say in *Paths in Utopia*, work at the building of actual organic communities, and a sense of the "metaphysical Thou" will follow.[181]

Similarly, institutions of the so-called "personal life" cannot be given new life by free feeling (though again not without it). This is the tragic fallacy of the whole erotic philosophy of our times. Men appeal to *Eros* because they have forgotten the meaning of *Agape*. The lover makes an *object* of the other. He (or she) degrades the other by using the marriage partner as a means to gratify his (or her) desires. The one is really loving himself through the other. The very phrase, "object of love," illustrates the error and shows why so many so-called "love" relationships are unhappy, inhibited, unfulfilled, or even poisoned. The partners have not learned the meaning of meeting as equals, and converging their two lives into a new "we." Egocentric demands, either of tyrannical exaction or of timid withdrawal, will never make for happy love and marriage. For in that case, there is only feeling, experiencing, taking, using; there is nothing of genuine engagement, meeting as equals, risk, surrender. Love and marriage will never be restored to their true meaning except by that out of which true marriage arises: "the revealing by two people of the *Thou* to one another. Out of this a marriage is built up by the *Thou* that is neither of the *I's*. This is the metaphysical and metapsychical factor of love to which feelings of love are mere accompaniments." [182] Here the *I* and the *Thou* take their stand not merely in relation, but also in the solid give-

and-take of "speech." True relation is here, immersed in the element of speech. The primary word goes backwards and forwards; address and response live in one language. "Here alone, then, as reality that cannot be lost, are gazing and being gazed upon, knowing and being known, loving and being loved." [183] This is also the main portal to the eternal Thou. Nature, thought, and mankind are all potential fields for the Thou, but the meeting between person and person is the clearest simile of the relation of man with God; in it true address receives true response.[184]

In the world of Thou, man is not proud of his ability to know and to use; rather is he humble about his ability to love. He does not say to the other (be it God, man or nature): "Help me to get this or that." Rather he says, "I seek not thy goods, but thee alone." He yields to the real situation and its demands. He accepts the hard truth rather than the easy fraud as truth. He is bound, like the true prophet, by the situation of the historical hour in which God is preparing the work He has in mind. (The false prophets, by contrast, "are entangled in the delusion of the world of wish." They dream dreams, and out of the "phantom of their heart" they announce what men want to hear, what will please the men who inquire of them.)[185] In the world of Thou, man sacrifices his puny, arbitrary, unfree will to his grand will. "He listens to what is emerging from itself, to the course of being in the world; not in order to be supported by it, but in order to bring it to reality as it desires, in its need of him, to be brought." [186] Even a tree stands over against me as an equal, with its own rights and claims to be respected.

We are now in a position to summarize the qualities or characteristics of the *I-Thou* relation in the world of *Thou*.

(1) First, we should mention "wholeness." In the *I-Thou* relation, in contrast to the *I-It* connection, the whole of one's being is involved and one is conscious of meeting the whole. In the I-It world we face things with only a part of our being, our senses or our calculating mind; we grasp them only in particular aspects, according to our need or purpose, never in their totality. But "the primary word I-Thou can only be spoken with the whole being." [187] All partial actions are suspended, the whole being becomes a unity as he goes out to the meeting.

(2) Meeting a *Thou* conceived as a whole involves an "exclusiveness," a sacrificing of other possibilities to the demands of this particular relation. There must be no abstractions, no diversions, no irrelevancies. In

genuine meeting, i.e., when one meets the other in his unique totality, one must be really *present*. The *Thou* is not just a thing among things. "He is *Thou* and fills the heavens. This does not mean that nothing exists except himself. But all else lives in his light." [188] Relation means choosing. The one thing that matters is full acceptance of the present. "The Thou is freed, steps forth, is single, and confronts you." [189] To step into pure relation is not to disregard everything else but to see everything in the *Thou*.

(3) The I-Thou relation is "direct." The *Thou* is an end in itself, and no mediation of sense, idea, or fancy is necessary. In the I-Thou relation, every means is an obstacle, everything indirect irrelevant. If I am considering a tree, for instance, and by will and grace become bound up in relation to it, the tree is no longer merely an It. Everything about the tree—view and movement, species and type, form and structure, colors and chemical composition—is immediately present and united in a single whole. "The tree is no impression, no play of my imagination, no value depending on my mood; but it is bodied over against me and has to do with me, as I with it." [190] Buber is here plunking for a stubborn realism, for the concrete. There is no rigid boundary between experience and non-experience, between what is given and what is not given, between the world of being and the world of value, between the ideal form and real appearance. More precisely, perhaps, Buber means only the concrete, and therefore values, forms, and appearances only in so far as they are embodied in the concrete. The real boundary, in Buber's thought, cuts across all these borders and lies between *Thou* and *It*. The real is apprehended directly as personal, as a *Thou*. God, too, in order to speak to man, must become a person and must make man a person. If I mistake not in my reading of Buber, the duality here is not so much metaphysical (between spirit and matter) as it is moral and ontological (between freedom and objectified necessity). The other person is an independent reality, and although the other is a datum to the *I*, it does not depend upon the *I*, nor can it be fully bounded by the *I*. The duality is ultimately one between the two modes of being, being in connection and being in disconnection, and therefore an ontological one (in Buber's terminology).

(4) In temporal terms, the quality of "presentness" belongs only to the Thou-world. "The *I* of the primary word I-It . . . has no present, only the past." [191] He lives in the past; he deals with objects. "But objects subsist in time that has been." [192] Not so, in the Thou-rela-

tion. "The real, filled present, exists only in so far as actual present-ness, meeting, and relation exist. The present arises only in virtue of the fact that the Thou becomes present." [193] The present is that which is continuous and enduring. An object, an *It*, on the other hand, exists in the past, when real duration has ceased, broken off, hardened, when real relation is absent.[194] It is evident that Buber has accepted Berg-son's general view of time; he qualifies Bergson only to the extent of saying that duration is felt only in the *Thou*-relation.[195]

(5) Not only does the *Thou*-world transcend mathematical time to endure in presentness; it is also not set in the context of Space. In the Thou, both space and time fade in the background. I do not meet my Thou in some time and place. I can, of course, place him in time and space; indeed, I continually do just that. But each time I do it, I transform our person-to-person relation into an understood connec-tion. I do violence to the truth of the meeting with *Thou*. The con-text of the *Thou*-world is the center, "where the extended lines of relation meet—in the eternal *Thou*." [196]

(6) In the world of *Thou*, the self is exempt from the reign of causality.[197] Again Buber echoes Bergson in holding that determinism obtains only for the past. The man of the I-Thou realm does not be-lieve in fate; he knows freedom, struggle, decision, responsibility. He lives in the Spirit. "Prediction from objectivity is valid only for the man who does not know presentness." [198] "So long as the heaven of Thou is spread over me the winds of causality cower at my heels, and the whirlpool of fate stays its course." [199] Only the *It* can be arranged in order. Buber insists further that "a world that is ordered is not the world-order." [200] On the other hand, "the Thou knows no system of co-ordination." Each Thou is unique, and precious.

(7) All genuine *I-Thou* relations are characterized by love. Not *Eros*, not subjective feeling. Buber has in mind an ethical principle, even a kind of ontological principle, akin to what the Bible calls *agape*. "Love is responsibility of an I for a Thou." [201] Love is *between* I and Thou, in the communion between person and person. Love is not to be confused with any "feelings." "Feelings are 'entertained': love comes to pass. Feelings dwell in man; but man dwells in his love." [202] This is no mere metaphor; it is the truth. Is love, then, the only true relationship between men? What of hate? Buber believes that hate is blind; only a part of a being can be hated. Hate does not see the whole being of the other. But the man who genuinely hates another

is nearer to real relation than the man who is indifferent, disdainful, condescending, or exploitive. Thus Buber does not restrict the total and immediate relationship to love alone.

(8) The *I-Thou* relation involves genuine response and responsibility. There is mutual obligation, pledge and promise, binding and loyal bonds. The *I* of the *Thou*-world is a loyal self, a bound self, pledged to the other in the bonds of covenant, one who has exchanged vows of fidelity, one who makes claims upon the other and at the same time puts himself under claim. Here man is free, yet bound to another. He cannot escape. He can, of course, reject the claim of the other, sever the ties, refuse to make the vow or default on it once made—but he is still conditioned by it. It has become a part of his history. Here there is not just one will; there are at least two wills at work which check and limit each other. Here the other is not a passive instrument of the *I*, but an independent *Thou* in whose independence the *I* rejoices.

(9) In the world of *Thou*, knowledge of oneself is pre-eminently knowledge of oneself in relation to another. The highest expression of this situation in which man comes to himself appears when God steps into the lived and living relationship as *Thou*. The world of *Thou*, then, includes the infinite personal God as well as the finite persons of men. By the very nature and constitution of the world of *Thou*, every person stands in a dual personal relationship: he is related at one and the same time to the infinite Person and to finite persons. This is not two relationships, but a *dual* relationship. Indeed, it is truer to say it is a *triadic* relationship. For the relation to my neighbor is always a part of my relation to God. God meets me in and through the neighbor. "Every particular *Thou* is a glimpse through to the eternal Thou." [203]

(10) In every true meeting with a *Thou* we are aware of the ultimate reality and meaning of life. In each Thou we catch a breath from the eternal Thou; in each Thou we address the eternal Thou.[204] These moments are immortal; they are moments of revelation. Revelation brings no definite command, no precise content. *But it brings assurance as to the meaningfulness of life.*

(11) In the I-Thou relation with God unconditional exclusiveness and unconditional inclusiveness are one; everything is gathered up in relation. There must ever be an inevitable antinomy in man's relation with God.[205] He is the one *Thou* which never becomes an *It*. We cannot speak of God, we can only live through Him. There is no

knowledge expressible to men about God, no name to define Him, no quality to bound Him. "I Am That I Am!" "I will be present as I will be present." And yet man can enter in relation with the eternal *Thou*. And when this happens the antinomies are resolved, the paradoxes reconciled. What were unsolvable mysteries, are now reconciled in the lived-life of relation. Man, in his personal relations with God, and only thus, can become the agent of reconciliation. Man's religious situation cannot be demonstrated in logic; it can only be lived. The paradoxes can never be solved by reason: God's immanence and transcendence; man's freedom within necessity; nature and grace— these can only be reconciled by living the life of relation.[206] "To look away from the world, or to stare at it, does not help a man to reach God; but he who sees the world in Him stands in His presence."[207] Of course God is the "wholly Other," but He is also the Present One. Of course God is the "Mysterium Tremendum," but He is also nearer than hands and feet. "If you hallow this life you meet the living God."[208] If you take the antinomies to yourself, to be lived together, in being lived they are one.

The Three-fold Living Relation.—Buber does not restrict the meeting and dialogue of relation to man's relations with his fellowmen. He is very explicit on this point. There are three spheres in which the world of relation may be built.[209] More than that, man's whole essential nature is fulfilled only if he lives with his whole self in all three of these relations.

1. *Our life with nature.* We are related, first, to the world and to things. Man may address nature or natural objects as *Thou*. But here the relation must be conducted only at the threshold of speech.

2. Second, *our life with other men.* A man may address another person as his *Thou*. Here the relation naturally is open, clear, and in the form of speech. Here language is consummated in the give and take.

3. Third, *our life with intelligible forms*—ideas, Deeds, Works of Art. Man may regard ideal forms and essences as *Thou* and address his whole being to them. This relation is without speech, yet begets speech. "We perceive no *Thou*, but none the less we feel that we are addressed and we answer—forming, thinking, acting. We speak the primary word with our being, though we cannot utter *Thou* with our lips."[210]

In and through each sphere, in its own way, we are really addressing the eternal Thou, "we look out toward the fringe of the eternal Thou." [211] The mute approach of the creature, man's loving speech, the form's silent command—all are gateways leading into the presence of the Word. "But when the full and complete meeting is to take place, the gates are united in one gateway of real life, and you no longer know through which you have entered." [212] This is the perfection of dialogic relation, of divine immanence.

It is centrally relevant to mention here that for Kierkegaard man's sole essential relation is with God, to the exclusion of all other relations with nature or persons. In regard to this exclusion Buber parts company with Kierkegaard. Buber makes no claim that man's often clumsy and inhibited relations with his fellows can plumb the depths of life's mystery; but he does contend that objects in nature and other human beings can mediate man's approach to God, can provide glimpses of the Eternal. It will be remembered in this connection also that Mead restricts man's essential relation to the human, social sphere. Nature and God are excluded or denied, as holding possibilities of relation which help to constitute the self. In including Nature and God in the possibility of genuine relations with men, Buber's concept is richer—and perhaps truer.

The Relational-Event among Primitive Men.—"In the beginning is relation." Buber contends that the *I-Thou* attitude precedes the *I-It* attitude in the development of children and in the history of the race. In other words, the Thou-attitude and response is native and habitual with primitive men. The early impressions and emotional stirrings, the first responses to the natural environment, the persistent animism of the savage and the child which awaken the spirit of the natural man, all arise from and within situations that are *relational* in character.[213] The primitive lives in a world filled with "spirits," "demons," and powers which are unpredictable, often inaccessible, which confront him and take shape as the willful doer and bringer of the experienced effects. Buber believes that this initial and continuing relational character of phenomena makes it easier to understand the "spiritual" element of primitive life—that mysterious, super-sensuous power or *anima*, the idea of which has been given the name of *Mana*.[214] The moon and the ghosts of the dead which visit him at night, the sun and the hunted beast and the sorcerer whose glance constrains him—

all these and more have the power to stir his body and leave behind in him a stirring image. "Mana is simply the effective force, that which has made the person of the moon, up there in the heavens, into a blood-stirring *Thou*." [215] Thus savages "personalize" things and events, imputing life and will and intention to natural objects and events, even to inanimate objects. Here is a crude, primitive example of the conviction that some "quality" of the universe is speaking in these situations, and man can answer.

Anthropomorphism is commonly acknowledged of primitives as well as of most civilized men. It is essentially the carrying over of the terms, meanings, and attitudes of the human world into the natural or non-human world, and vice versa. There is, of course, a certain obdurateness and independence of nature, a structure of reality, which will assert itself and which we must respect. Therefore, we speak of an "outer-world" or a natural world in contra-distinction to the "inner world." The words designed for use in the two realms are different; yet there is an inevitable inter-change of terms and meanings. This transfer of meanings is never exact or absolute, yet we do carry over terms and interpretations from one world to the other.

When we review the qualities and characteristics of the *I-Thou* relation (*supra,* pp. 153-57) we notice that they correspond rather nicely with the pre-scientific and pre-conceptual life of primitives. Of course, in the life of primitives only an elementary form of the relation is to be found, not the developed one. Their knowledge (i.e., beliefs) is direct, intuitive, non-analytical. Persons, as expressed in nouns and pronouns, are embedded in everything. The lived relation of early man is charged with wholeness, unity, presentness. Their speech is marked by directness, naivete, and vivid simplicity. The pre-grammatical form of their speech indicates the wholeness and directness, even the direct bodily contact, of a relation.[216]

The pre-natal life of a child is one of natural combination, of constant bodily inter-action with the mother. As the child grows, the desire for connection is gradually translated into spiritual terms as the yearning to meet the universal *Thou*. This is not to be interpreted in Freudian terms, as the infantile and parasitic longing to return to the mother's womb, but "the yearning is for the cosmic connection, with its true Thou, of this life that has burst forth into spirit." [217] This represents what Buber calls "*a priori* of relation, the inborn Thou." [218] The inborn Thou becomes realized, in personal actualized being, in the lived relations with that which meets it. In the instinct to make contact (first by touch, then by visual "touch," later by speech) the inborn *Thou* is gradually brought to full powers in relational behavior. Thus out of the primal world of the "primitive We," the bodily individual gradually enters into relation, makes "conversation" with the personified environment, and thus becomes a self. "The development of the soul in the child is inextricably bound up with that of the longing for the *Thou*, with the satisfaction and the disappointment of this longing, with the game of his experiments and the tragic seriousness of his perplexity." [219]

This does not happen automatically; nor does the child possess it at once. He must win it for himself, draw it out, make it into a reality for himself; he must find for himself his own world by seeing and hearing and touching and shaping it. "Creation does not spill itself into expectant senses, but rises up to meet the grasping senses": it must be wooed and won by the developing self. "For no *thing* is a ready-made part of an experience; only in the strength, acting and being acted upon, of what is over against men, is anything made accessible. Like primitive man the child lives between sleep and sleep . . . in the flash and counter-flash of meeting." [220] Buber believes that this primal nature of the effort to establish relation can be seen in the earliest behavior of the child. Before anything is perceived and identified as differentiated object, timid glances move out into the environment, hands stretch into the air, little disjointed sounds go out into the void. This behavior is not experience of an object, not yet; it is the instinct to make everything into a *Thou*, to enter into relations with what is alive and effective over against him. And one day, these movements and sounds become "conversation"—with a toy, the pet, a simmering kettle, or a woolly Teddy-bear.

It is simply not the case, (argues Buber) that the child first perceives an object, then, as it were, puts himself in relation with it. But the effort to establish relation comes first—the hand of the child arched out so that what is over against him may nestle under it; second, is the actual relation, a saying of *Thou* without words, in the state preceding the word-form; the thing, like the I, is produced late, arising after the original experiences have been split asunder and the connected partners separated. In the beginning is relation—as category of being, readiness, grasping form, mould for the soul. [221]

In the beginning is *relation*. First the *I-Thou;* not the *I* or the *Thou*, but their spiritual ties. And then comes the *It*, and the *I-It*. It is the lot of mankind that every *Thou* must at some time become an *It*. The progress of civilization is characterized by the consistent enlargement of the It-world at the expense of the Thou-world and the power to maintain true relation. As mankind advances from childhood, it takes up more and more of the It-world, with a corresponding lessening of the Thou-attitude. "The development of the ability to experience and use comes about mostly through the decrease of man's power to enter into relation—the power in virtue of which alone man can live the life of the spirit." But man feels, even so, that this direction leads to a blind-alley instead of into freer, more creative life. This is the cause of the pain and despair of our times,[222] with its accompanying sense of the loss of community.

The fundamental difference between *I-Thou* and *I-It* comes to light in this experience of early man: the experience in which the *I* emerges out of the primal *I-affecting-Thou* and *Thou-affecting-I*, and having been split off begins to give eminence to its objects as *It*. In other words, in the original relational event the organism has not yet recognized himself as "I." But the primary word *I-It* is made possible only by means of this recognition, i.e., separation of the *I*. As Buber himself puts it: "The first primary word can be resolved, certainly, into *I* and *Thou*, but it did not arise from their being set together; by its nature it precedes *I*. The second word arose from the setting together of *I* and *It;* by nature it comes after *I*." [223] After the *I* has stepped forth in its conscious separate existence, it moves toward a functional activity which awakens the sense of separation from the world round about it.[224] Here is the beginning of the *I-It* form, when the *I* declares itself to be the bearer, and the world to be the object of its perceptions. Of course, at this primitive stage, the situation is not regarded as a "theory of knowledge." "But whenever the sentence 'I see the tree' is so uttered that it no longer tells of a relation between the man—*I*— and the tree—*Thou*—but establishes the perception of the tree as object by the human consciousness, the barrier between subject and object has been set up." [225] This is the world of *It*, the world of science, of knowledge, experience, and use. It is the world of order, but it is not the world-order. Through the *Thou* a man becomes *I*. Then comes the *It* and the world of *I-It*.

The Other.—The *I-Thou* relation is unique; yet this relation can be found or achieved in different spheres of experience. A man may say "Thou" to other men, but also to a tree, a lake, an animal, a work of art, an idea, God. Any "It" may be regarded as a "Thou" through the power of imagination, intention, and insight. Buber, for example, relates a bit of autobiography in pointing up this claim.[226] As a boy he used to steal into the stable and stroke the neck of a horse.

> It was not a casual delight, but a great, certainly friendly, but also deeply stirring happening. . . . . I must say that what I experienced in touch with the animal was the Other, the immense otherness of the Other, which, however, did not remain strange like the otherness of the ox and the ram, but rather let me draw near and touch it. . . . When I stroked the mighty mane . . . it was as though the element of vitality itself bordered on my skin, something that was not I, was certainly not akin to me, palpably the Other, not just another, really the Other itself; and yet it let me approach, confided itself to me, placed itself elementally in the relation of *Thou* and *Thou with me*. . . . But once . . . it struck me about the stroking, what fun it gave me, and suddenly I became conscious of my hand. The game went on as before, but something had changed, it was no longer the same thing.

The It-attitude had entered and clouded the pure disinterested relation. "How powerful is the unbroken world of *It,* and how delicate are the appearances of the *Thou!*" [227]

To the critic who says that all this is pretty but indemonstrable poetry and would never work in the hurly-burly life of the modern industrial world, Buber replies that, while the *I-Thou* attitude is at times difficult to maintain and is not applicable in its purity in all circumstances, nevertheless it applies generally, if not absolutely, in all situations. Buber cites the case of the industrial worker who speaks to his tool or machine as if it were his friend in an I-Thou situation when, for instance, "a compositor tells that he has understood the machine's humming as a 'merry and grateful smile at me for helping it to set aside the difficulties and obstructions which disturbed and bruised and pained it, so that now it could run free.' " [228] Buber insists that in the public life of the community and in industry, men can be approached in this same personal attitude, and must be so approached if the spirit of man is not to be stifled by the swarm of things. One can and does find himself involved *with* the other. Sympathy, empathy,

Einfühlung are similar suggestive terms, but still not quite what Buber is saying. Once and again I make the discovery of the presence of a *Thou;* and as the artist says, "I put my own life into it," or, as the spectator might say, "I partake of its life." The leader of a great enterprise may live the life of dialogue, if and when he ceases to think of the business in terms of balance sheets and mechanical forces, and becomes aware of it as a human, personal, mutual association. When this happens, the leader will think of the human beings in the enterprise as persons, so that when he does happen to meet them in face-to-face encounter he will address them directly as *Thou.* The teacher, the preacher, the social worker, even the statesman, handling great affairs, may live the life of dialogue and thereby better fulfill his tasks.

Man and woman, together, are the clearest example of this elemental and fundamental relation which conditions both the perpetuation of life and structure of human society. "Marriage is the exemplary bond, it carries us as does none other into the greater bondage, and only as those who are bound can we reach the freedom of the children of God." "This person is other, essentially other than myself, and this otherness of his is what I mean, because I mean him; I confirm it; I wish his otherness to exist, because I wish his particular being to exist." [229] This is the basic principle of marriage and from this basis it leads, if it is real marriage, to insight into the right and legitimacy of otherness—even in contradiction and conflict—from which dealings with the public life receive their religious ethos. In the *I-Thou* relation there is no place for domination of one over the other. It is not a matter of subtraction for one and addition for the other. It should be a meeting of *equals,* in which there occurs a multiplication of interests and values and a division of responsibility, each for the other and to the other.

The general definition of "Mitwelt" [230] lies in the concept of the "other" and in that I meet the "Mitwelt" as the world of the others. The world of others is defined more or less through the fact that it is *my* "Mitwelt." In contrast to something else, the others distinguish themselves through the fact that they are beings like myself and exist in the same manner. Furthermore, the "mit" in "Mitwelt" means "fellowman" in the sense of being my equal. All others-than-myself become fellowmen. Their being different, just like their being like myself, is self-evident. Within the human world, the singularity of each person manifests itself as a general difference of each one. The very likeness that results from wearing a uniform or the likeness of twins only ac-centuates the fact of the unique and singular difference. When you meet someone who looks like you, that fact again only underlines the fact that you *are* different. This fact again bears evidence to the fact that the independence of the self is achieved only in a personal rela-tionship. Independence is reached within relationship. In a very real sense, one self is predestined through others. Independence is not ab-solute with respect to others; it is reciprocal and potential to relation.

The highest expression of this encounter is that between the self-revealing God and the human creature. For here again, if the testi-mony of the saints and prophets are to be taken at face value, God does not merely communicate "something" to man—but Himself! Not just a body of truths or propositions which I infer as logical implications from certain premises or experiences, but a Person who Himself comes to me, speaks to me, discloses Himself, and (as Brunner says) "takes over the role (so to say) which in thinking I have myself." [231] An *exchange* takes place, the sole analogy of which is found in the en-counter of two human beings. Hebraic and Christian truth has to do with acts, with historical events, with a divine-human encounter, some-thing that actually happened and happens in the personal meeting of God with man. A cogent passage from Brunner will help to make the situation clearer. [232]

> To see 'someone' is not essentially different from seeing some-*thing*. This someone says something to me. Someone saying 'something' to me is not essentially different from my saying 'some-thing' to myself—that is, thinking. But now let us put the case that this someone does not say 'something' but says 'himself,' dis-closes himself to me, and that I, while he 'says' himself to me, 'hear himself'; and more, that while he discloses himself to me, and so surrenders himself to me, I disclose myself to him and re-ceive him, while I surrender myself to him. . . . In this moment he ceases to be for me a 'someone-something' and becomes a 'Thou.' In that moment in which he becomes a 'Thou' he ceases to be an object of my thinking and transforms the Object-Subject relation into a relation of personal correspondence: we have fellowship to-gether.

Is it possible for some*thing* to exist for some*thing,* or for a some*one* to exist for a some*thing?* Buber appears not to have dealt with these possibilities; but it is perhaps not irrelevant to digress for a moment in order to consider the issue of means and ends as auxiliary to the personal-functional problem. Under the heading, *Etwas und Einer in ihren Dazudasein,* Löwith raises the question of existing for something or someone.[233]

(1) First, it may be asserted that something exists for someone in terms of its usefulness. Things exist in connection—e.g., pen, paper, desk, ink, etc.—only in so far as they are useful for someone.

(2) This existing for something else is really existing for someone. All useful things belong to the one who can make use of them. For example, ham and eggs belong together not in themselves, but because they have related meaning and function for someone.

(3) But can some*one* exist for some*thing?* Löwith thinks so, and he argues it thus: A merchant is there to sell something. The merchandise makes him a salesman; his relation to the merchandise makes him what he is. The merchant-customer relation is largely "functional," although it is not necessarily so. It may also be a "personal" relation. The real difference lies in the fact, which Buber stresses, that *things* have little or nothing to say about how they shall be used. A *person* does have a say so. Even a servant may not stand only in a functional relation without his consent. Here lies the real distinction between work and slavery. Man is not just a means to an end, but also an end, also a self, a "willing" tool, perhaps, or a servant only through his consent or purpose to be such. A "master" is not a personality, just as a "slave" is not a personality.

There is, then, in contrast to the pure *I-It* connection, a kind of relation in which the *wherefore* exists in the very relation itself. In other words, the relation is an end in itself. Furthermore, the purpose of the relation can identify the persons involved: e.g., father and son; confessor and priest; teacher and student; doctor and patient. Neither one is self-sufficient; each belongs to the other. It is in and through and out of this relation that the true independence of each one is established through the reciprocal recognition of *Thou.* It is precisely these functional wherefore relations, however, that so easily degenerate into purely *I-It* connections. Without the I-Thou attitude, without the inclusion of the *other,* without living through the common event from the "other side," there is ever the danger of the relation deteriorating into one of arbitrary dominating or using the other. The teacher's will to educate easily becomes the will to indoctrinate, to take advantage of the pupil, to disregard the pupil's own integrity. The doctor also, quite aside from any quackery, is in danger of falsifying the doctor-patient relation if he yields to the temptation to dominate or to enjoy his patient, or to treat the latter's neurotic wish to be dominated other than as a pathological condition.[234]

THE LIFE OF DIALOGUE

In *Zwiesprache*, published eight years after *Ich und Du* and comprising a post-script to the latter work, Buber describes the life of dialogue. It adds little that is new to the earlier book, but illuminates and embellishes and fills out the I-Thou concept like variations on a musical theme. Through example and commentary it explains the nature of the dialogic life: its characteristics, its elements, its limits, its difficulties, its true and false expressions.

This commentary, like the entire *I-Thou* concept, is obviously based upon a profound psychic experience which the author relates in the opening pages. He tells of the dream which, with few changes, recurred to him over several years. He calls it "the dream of the Double Call." It would always begin with some unusual occurrence of a frightening nature. Then followed a succession of events, mounting to a climax when there came a call, rhythmic and melodious, issuing from his own throat, with an answering call, another voice—"certainly no 'echo' of my cry but rather its true rejoinder." [235] This call would always be followed by the sense of certainty and of profound significance: "now, it has happened," he felt. Once it happened during a recurrence of the dream, that he called out and waited for an audible answer; but none came. Yet, strangely, he felt the silence itself respond and a final sense of certitude came over him as on previous occasions.[236]

Buber relates this dream-story in order to show how he came to the realization that "dialogue" can take place without words. There is a "silence" which is communication and which can become the embodiment of communion. The most obvious example of conversation is, of course, the speaking of one person with another. Here the relation is open and in the form of speech. Already in an earlier section, we have discussed the philosophy of speech.[237] Speech with men, and prayer with God, demonstrate that man has the capacity to seek connection with a truth and a reality more valid than his own existence, and that man has love lest his ego imprison his soul.[238] In the pain of speech, in the agony and leap of prayer, man's mind and self are born. Speech is the bridge over the distance between two poles; it is the act by which the potential between two poles (man and man, man and God) is enhanced. Conversation completes itself in one person speaking with another; when one person is heard understandingly by another person, and is answered in some way. Speaking, being heard, being answered, again speaking: these are the moments of conversation.

Silence Which is Communication.—While speech, involving sound and gesture, is the clearest medium of relation between persons, Buber contends that there is a kind of silence and solitude which can be communication.[239] "Just as the most eager speaking to one another does not make a conversation . . . so for a conversation no sound is necessary, not even a gesture. Speech can renounce all the media of sense, and it is still speech." Buber has already suggested how genuine communication can take place by the use of gesture, by the expression of the eyes, etc. Animals, too, can speak with their eyes, and can communicate certain meanings through their gestures. But Buber is apparently talking about something more than that. Not even the lovers' tender silence or the shared silence of the mystics is necessary. Even between strangers, on occasion, the word of dialogue may happen sacramentally; without gesture, communication may stream between them. The life of dialogue is not just limited to man's traffic with another; it is a *relation* of man to another man that is only represented in their dealings with one another. Therefore, even if speech and open gesture are absent, there may still be dialogue if there is present a mutuality of inner action; two men turned toward each other, exposed wholly to one another, mutually conditioned and limited by one another— and over-coming it together. As the result of some inner action, conscious or unconscious, "something happens to them which is called a covenant." One open-hearted person may so turn to another open-hearted person as to speak really to and towards him; and then genuine community will appear: not that of an identical content of ideology or faith, but "that of the situation, of anguish, and of expectation." [240]

Becoming aware.—Whatever occurs to me, whatever life brings to me, *addresses* me—unless I sterilize it by removing the "seed of address" from it. It is no superstition that cosmic and earthly happenings have for the life of men a direct meaning that can be grasped. "Signs happen to us without respite, living means being addressed, we would need only to present ourselves and to perceive." [241] But we build up an armour of protection, whose function it is to ward off signs, to protect us from "the soundless thunderings which seem to threaten us with annihilation." Confirmed by our culture, habit, and familiarity, we no longer notice this protective covering. Only occasionally does some unusual event or meeting penetrate to the heart and stir the soul awake. What Buber is saying, of course, is that the "signs of address" are not something extraordinary; they are what goes on all the time. Everything that occurs to me addresses me; but I usually disregard it as not really referring to me. I usually do not *see* or *hear* the other (person or object) because I know that if I were really to *see* or *hear* the plight of the other, I would have to do something about it. Love is the attitude of the soul which, in seeing and hearing, knows that it must help.

How then is the soul to be made aware? What does he mean by "being aware"? Buber distinguishes three ways in which we may perceive a man who is before us.[242]

First, by *observing*. "The observer is wholly intent on fixing the observed in his mind, on 'noting him.'" He probes him, notes his traits and expressions and movements. But when he does this, the other ceases to be a *Thou*.

Second, by *looking on*. "The onlooker is not at all intent." He does not take notes, he is not afraid of overlooking or forgetting something; he gives his memory no tasks. He merely regards the man or the object freely and awaits what will be presented to him.

There is, however, another and decisively different kind of perception, which we may call *awareness*. The onlooker and observer have only the desire to "perceive" the other. Consequently what they experience of the other—as existence or traits or expressions—"neither demands action from them nor inflicts destiny upon them." No claim is made upon them. Quite different is the situation when in a receptive mood of my personal life a man meets me about whom there is something that "says something to me." It does not say to me what manner of man this is, what is going on in him, and the like. It says something to *me*, addresses something to *me*, speaks something that enters into my life. It might be that it says he needs me. It might be something about myself. "The man himself in his relation to me has nothing to do with what is said . . . but *it* says it." [243] This is *real speech*. "In the house of speech there are many mansions, and this is one of the inner." [244]

For Buber, then, awareness is something quite different from observing or looking on. It is the difference between *Thou* and *It*. In awareness the *other* is not my *object;* I have to do *with him.* Whatever it is I have to do with him, " a word demanding an answer has happened to me." [245] The self-other antithesis is now at the same time a claim and a bond.

Each event, each person, each concrete hour which meets us, is speech for the man who is attentive. Attentive, expectant, for that is the beginning of awareness, and awareness leads to *responsibility.* For genuine responsibility exists only where there is real response. The responsive man will face all of life as it happens, as though it were laid upon him "to go up to and into it." [246]

To illustrate this Buber relates a profound personal experience which gave him insight into the true nature of dialogue and which, along with his Chassidic studies, turned him away from extreme mysticism.

> What happened was no more than that one forenoon, after a morning of 'religious enthusiasm,' I had a visit from an unknown young man, without being there in spirit. I certainly did not fail to let the meeting be friendly, I did not treat him remissly—I conversed attentively and openly with him—only I omitted to guess the questions which he did not put. Later, I learned from one of his friends—he himself was no longer alive—the essential content of his questions. I learned that he had come to me not casually, but borne by destiny, not for a chat but for a decision. He had come to me, he had come in this hour. What do we expect when we are in despair and yet go to a man? Surely a presence by means of which we are told that nevertheless there is a meaning.[247]

"Since then," Buber confesses, "I have given up the 'religious' which is nothing but the exception, exaltation, ecstasy; or it has given me up." The mystery, if it is disclosed, "has made its dwelling here where everything happens as it happens." [248]

When we are addressed by the signs of life, *who speaks to us?* God Himself, says Buber. Concrete revelation comes in the concrete situations of life. God employs as His mouthpiece different men, objects, animals, events, and situations. Each time we rise into this new life of complete awareness, each time we receive a message, God is apprehended in a new aspect— "the God of a moment, a moment-God" (*Augenblickgott*).[249] To clarify his meaning, Buber cites the analogy of the poet and his poems. All that we know of the poet is compounded out of the impressions and nuances we receive from reading several of his poems. "In such a way, out of the givers of the signs, the speakers of the words in lived life, out of the moment-Gods there arises for us with a single identity the Lord of the voice, the One." [250] To him who is aware and responsive, Gods speaks in all the happenings and meetings of our daily life. In this Buber echoes the strong Hebrew awareness of the concrete hour in its unique historical setting.

Monologue and Dialogue.—Buber goes to some pains to show the difference between the forms of true dialogue and false dialogue. There are forms of dialogue which are not truly the "dialogue of life," that is to say, they have the appearance of dialogue but not the real essence of dialogue.[251]

1. *Genuine dialogue*: whether spoken or silent, "where each of the participants really has in mind the other or others in their present and particular being and turns to them with the intention of establishing a living mutual relation between himself and them." Here there is readiness to receive the other into one's own being, while withholding nothing from the other.

2. *Technical dialogue*: which is prompted solely by the need of knowledge or objective understanding. This obtains in the world-of-It.

3. *Monologue* disguised as dialogue, "in which two or more men, meeting in space, speak each with himself in strangely tortuous and circuitous ways and yet imagine they have escaped the torment of being thrown back upon their own resources."

The first is rare nowadays, thinks Buber. The second, so much a part of modern technological society, occasionally "breaks surface" at unexpected times and places. But the third is the false, faceless spectre of dialogue. This latter (the monologue) may take the form of *debate* in which those spoken to are in no sense regarded as being present as persons, and in which the words expressed are pointed so as to strike home in the sharpest way. Or it may be in a *conversation* which is characterized by the need neither to learn something, to communicate something, nor come into connection with someone—but "solely by the desire to have one's own self-reliance confirmed by marking the impression that is made." [252] There are *friendly chats* in which one or both of the participants regards himself as absolute and the other as questionable. It may even be a *lovers' talk* in which the partners enjoy their own glorious soul and their precious experience.

Real dialogue involves a strong sense of reciprocity; monologue will not, even in tender intimacy, grope over the outlines of the ego-centric self.[253] That is why erotic love seldom rises to the test of true dialogue, although that may provide the occasions and instances of genuine communion. The life of dialogue is not one in which you necessarily have a lot to do with others, "but one in which *you really have to do with those with whom you have to do.*" [254] In other words, it is not necessarily the solitary man who lives the life of monologue; but he who is incapable of loving, incapable of streaming out to the other in the give and take of genuine community. The life of dialogue can be lived even in solitude if, in the solitude, one feels himself approached for an answer. Something confronts him, speaks to him, does not leave him, even on a companionless mountain tramp; he knows the deep intercourse with the incomparably real, with that which is not himself. In the monologic solitude, nature is only an *état d'âme,* a mood, or state of the soul, apprehended from within; or it is a mere object of knowledge. It does not become for him a "word" addressed to him.

Even solitude, then, may be a gateway to dialogue. There are two kinds of solitude, however, which must be carefully distinguished.[255] There is a kind of solitude which is only freeing oneself from the intercourse of experiencing and using things, in alternating rhythm. This is necessary in order that the act of relation may itself be reached. But if solitude means the absence of relation, it is illegitimate division. Stated in other terms: if solitude is the place of purification, necessary even to man who is bound up in relation, then to this solitude every fallible human being is disposed. But if solitude is "the stronghold of isolation, where a man conducts a dialogue with himself—not in order to test and master himself for that which awaits him but in the enjoyment of the conformation of his soul—then we have the real fall of the spirit into spirituality." [256]

The "basic movement" of the life of monologue is not simply turning away as opposed to turning towards; it is what Buber calls "reflexion." The self *curves back on itself;* the other has no objective status; it is not met and accepted as the other; it is idealistically brought within the self.[257]

On the other hand, the basic movement of the life of dialogue is the turning towards the other, really directing one's attention to the other, so that this one person steps out and becomes a concrete presence, is given form, is released from indifference. This is "essential action" done with the "essential being." [258] This is responsibility to and for the other.

One further qualification. Dialogue is not to be identified with "universal unreserve." Quite the contrary. He who can be unreserved with every passer-by has no real substance to pledge. "Dialogue between mere individuals is only a sketch; only in dialogue between persons is the sketch filled in." [259]

Thought as Dialogue.—To Buber it seems clear that all true art is essentially of the nature of dialogue. "All music calls to an ear not the musician's own, all sculpture to an eye not the sculptor's own, architecture in addition calls to the step as it walks in the building." [260] They all say something to him who receives them.

It would seem, at first glance, that *thought* was not of this nature, that it is essentially the life of monologue; it is conversation of one with another that seems best to fit the pattern of monologue. Communication presupposes the independent thinking of another, whose thought may not run parallel to mine. There is difference, strife, opposition, perhaps; and thus I differentiate myself from the other. "The thought in which I and Thou unite is a true one." [261] Yes, thought seems to arise in monologue; communication is a secondary concern. The solitary single one, in his private citadel, thinks, suffers, and triumphs in solitude. But is it truly so?

Plato called thinking a voiceless colloquy of the soul with itself. Every one is familiar surely with that stage of thought in which an "inner court" is questioned and replies. But Buber contends that the elements of dialogue are, or can be, present in thought.[262] For one thing, the character of monologue (at least as he defines it) is different from the insight into relations with which cognitive thought begins; it is different from the moulding of the materials of thought into conceptual forms; it is different from the final expression and clarification in language. Buber thinks there is real dialogue here.[263]

It is not really himself that the thinker addresses in the stages of thought, but, as it were, the basic relations and order of things in the face of which he has to answer for his insight and his newly articulated concepts. And surely in the trying and testing of the concept or argument dialogue plays a real part. First there is, says Buber, not the empirical self, but the *genius*, the image self, before whom the new thought is carried for approval. At the next step, comes a further testing, in which the Thou is "one that is thought and yet is felt as supremely living and 'other,' " or else is actually embodied in the role of a known person. At this point Buber quotes W. von Humboldt with approval.[264] "Man longs even for the sake of his mere thinking for a *Thou* corresponding to the *I*." Feuerbach, it will be remembered, said practically the same thing in his aphorism: "True dialectic is not a monologue of the solitary thinker with himself, it is a dialogue between I and Thou." [265] So Buber argues that in serious thought, the inner action takes place in relation to a genuine *Thou* and not merely an "inward" Thou. In philosophical thought, for example, I have the "other" in opposition because in such dialectic of discursive reasoning I truly must have the other who thinks differently than I do. In Buber's more colorful and poetic words:

> So, too, it is not a matter of a game of draughts in the tower of a castle in the air, but of the binding business of life on this hard earth, in which one is inexorably aware of the otherness of the other but does not at all contest it without realizing it; one takes up its nature into one's own thinking, thinks in relation to it, addresses it in thought.[266]

Thus in serious, honest thought of this dialogic kind, one really lives and thinks towards the "other" so that our thinking includes and refers to the presence of another man facing us.[267]

The contention of Buber concerning the dialogic character of thought finds support in Vossler's remarks[268] that "most primitive men, children, and drunks" very often speak with themselves, "where you can suppose that they believe that another one is present and speaks with them." According to Vossler, then, not the outward number of persons, but the constituting moment of dialogue is the crucial issue. Ordinarily, we suppose that there are two moments in conversation: an understanding speaker and an understanding listener. However, if the above argument is valid, these two "roles" may be contained in one person, in so far as they speak with themselves understandingly. "Who speaks is his own listener; who writes his own reader." [269]

It should be made clear, however, and underscored, that, in Buber's interpretation of this dialogic thinking, "we should also, with the thinking, precisely with the thinking, live towards the other man," not just as one framed by thought but in his concrete life. Without "otherness" standing over against me there is no real dialogue. "I can never be truly my own Thou," says Buber. We must not efface these essential boundary lines.

Love as Dialogue.—Dialogue is not to be equated with love. But love without dialogue, without reaching out to the other, and yielding to the other, is not love. It is then a chamber of horrors, not the mansion of intimate dialogue.

"The Kingdom of the lame-winged Eros is a world of mirrors and mirrorings." And the false Eros of monologue is legion; there is no end of the varieties of the "erotic man." [270] In true love, on the other hand, there is no mirroring, no Narcissism. Here the lover is turned to the other human being, the beloved, in his otherness, his equality, his self-reality, with eyes level and with all the power of intention. He turns to the other as to one who is also turning to him. "I do not assimilate into my own soul that which lives and faces me. I vow it faithfully to myself and myself to it; I vow, I have faith." [271] Here is true bi-polar experience. Lovers make and experience true dialogue, each receiving the common event from the other's side as well. "Only when two say to one another with all that they are, 'It is *Thou*' does the Eternal dwell between them." [272] Here the other, accepted by me, lives and faces me in the whole compression of existence. In such openness and full engagement I receive the world, all sexuality, all otherness, in him.[273]

Buber follows the Chassidic teaching of love and reverence for life as involving or including loyalty. Loyalty without love would cease to be ethical, for it would imply a dichotomy between thought and deed, a turning away from God. All love, ultimately, is love of God. So, unlike those who say that "religion" is beyond "ethics," Buber would affirm this mystical ethic to be the religion of the Jew. There is no distinction between the two. It is the manner and spirit of the act that makes it religious or profane. Love is that which binds all life together in God. Unity has the double meaning: unity of thought and deed, and unification of the world with its Source.

Community as Dialogue.—Although we shall have more to say about community and collectivism in a later section, it is fitting to mention in this place the relation of "community" to dialogue. For real community is but extending the circle of love to include a larger and larger number of other persons. And in contrast to the task of building community, Buber views the modern zeal for "collectivism" as an escape from the real task of community, escape from the commitment and testing of the person; it is a flight from vital dialogue in which the self is risked and given to the other.

Across the world there is a common view today, defined by political creeds, that the important thing is the group, the party, the class, the collective; and the important thing within the group is what they aim at and accomplish. This means a political pragmatism which declares that that is right and just and significant which benefits the party or the State. Significance is ascribed to the group's activities and programs only in so far as they further the group's aims. The group is cynical about the means employed to achieve its end. Thus, as Buber sees it, "it is conceded to a band conspiring to conquer the state power that the comradeship which fills it is of value just because it strengthens the band's reliable assault power." [274] This is true of revolutionary parties (Fascist, Nazi, Falangist, etc.) and could also be true of the "underground" resistance movements. Rigid obedience, or enthusiastic drill, may do just as well to accomplish the group's purpose—and the members can remain "strangers" to one another.[275] (Even to achieve a genuine, but premature, comradeship may actually blunt the edge of the effective and enduring impetus toward the new order.)[276] No other love or loyalty may compromise the will and aim of the group. The confusion and perversion of thought becomes compounded when the drivel is added about "sacrifice of being" and "renunciation of self-realization." For as Buber asserts, "Happiness, possessions, power, authority, life can be renounced, but sacrifice of 'being' is a sublime absurdity." [277] Buber sees all too clearly that the feeling of true community does not reign where perhaps desirable changes of institutions are violently wrested in common, but without community, from a resisting world. It does reign where the struggle that is made takes place from the position of community struggling for its own reality as a true community.[278] The "massed, mingled, marching collectives" have forgotten what it is they are striving for—which is true community. True community, which involves genuine dialogue, is not merely the being *side by side,* but the being *with* one another, "a turning to, a dynamic facing of, the other, a flowing from *I* to *Thou.*" [279]

Inclusion: Experience from the Other Side.—Can one ever really bridge the gap between *I* and *Thou?* Buber answers in the affirmative. It is precisely in man's ability to live through the common event from the standpoint of the other, and most clearly in the fact of speech, that one becomes confirmed in the life of dialogue. This capacity for "experiencing from the other side" is what Buber calls "inclusion." In discussing education and the role of the educator, Buber says: "The one who practices the experience of the other side and stands firm in it, experiences two things together, first that he is limited by otherness, and second that he receives grace by being bound to the other." [280] The "Mitwelt" is related to my world in the most explicit way when it is contained in one certain other, a Thou that for me contains the whole world. Only then can one really say with Feuerbach: "The world or Thou." This is the anthropological meaning of the world— in the logic of language. One comes to feel from "over there" the acceptance and the rejection of whatever is approaching.

> In learning from time to time what this human being needs and does not need at the moment, the educator is led to an ever deeper recognition of what the human being needs in order to grow. But he is also led to a recognition of what he is . . . able and what he is unable to give of what is needed. [281]

It is thus through the responsibility of some area of life allotted and entrusted to him, through constant responsibility for some (other) living soul, that one learns the meaning of self-education. For self-education cannot take place through one's being concerned with oneself, but only through being concerned with the other, with the world.

It is possible to experience from the other side. To speak, means implicitly to hold the presupposition that I may perhaps be able to think his thoughts after him. Buber is at great pains to point out by copious illustrations the possibility and the reality of direct and ingenuous participation in the life of the other, and especially by assuming responsibility which arises from such participation. [282] Taking part in the life of the other, and conscious of responsibility, everything that passes between man and man becomes fruitful. This does not mean *agreement* always, or the absence of conflict, between one and the other. It means being alive and intentional, able and ready to communicate oneself directly to the fellow-being.

It is perhaps especially in conversation or conflict with an opponent that the real test and proof of dialogue is to be found. Let Buber speak to this point:

> A man belabours another, who remains quite still. Then let us assume that the striker suddenly receives in his soul the blow which he strikes; the same blow; that he receives it as the other who remains still. For the space of a moment he experiences the situation from other side. Reality imposes itself on him. What will he do? Either he will overwhelm the voice of the soul, or his impulse will be reversed. [283]

Or consider the situation of two lovers.

> A man caresses a woman, who lets herself be caressed. Then let us assume that he feels the contact from two sides—with the palm of his hand still, and also with the woman's skin. The two-fold nature of the gesture, as one that takes place between two persons, thrills through the depth of enjoyment in his heart and stirs it. If he does not deafen his heart he will have—not to renounce the enjoyment but—to love.[284]

One such extreme experience makes the other person present for all time. A kind of "transfusion" takes place after which a mere elaboration of subjectivity is never again possible or tolerable. Inclusion means responsibility for the other; it means complete realization of the other, the partner, not by fancy but by the actuality of being.

It might appear, at first glance, that "inclusiveness" is the same as "empathy." But Buber is quick to point out that "inclusion" does not mean "empathy" quite; there is a basic difference.[285] Empathy means to glide with one's feelings and motor behavior into the other object or person, understanding the formation and motion of the object or person with the perceptions of one's own muscles. It means to "transpose" oneself over and into the other, a kind of altruism, or loss of self—an exclusion of one's own concreteness, an absorption in pure aestheticism of the reality in which one participates.

Inclusion, says Buber, is the opposite of this. It is the extension of one's own concreteness, the fulfillment of the actual life situation, the complete presence of both *I* and *Thou* in a dialogical relation.

> Its elements are, first, a relation, of no matter what kind, between two persons; second, an event experienced by them in common, in which at least one of them actively participates; and third, the fact that this person, without forfeiting anything of the felt reality of his activity, at the same time lives through the common event from the standpoint of the other.[286]

There are three chief forms, or degrees, of inclusion.[287] (1) Inclusion in its minimal form. This form rests on the abstract but mutual experience of inclusion. Consider, for example, a dispute between two men, different in nature and viewpoint; but suddenly, in an instant of illumination and acknowledgment it happens that each becomes aware of the other's full legitimacy, necessity, and meaning. The truth, the strength, the standpoint of each is in no way reduced; but there is "the essence of mortal recognition," the receiving all that is manifested of Present Being into the being of each. "We have become aware that it is with the other as with ourselves." [288] This form, however, leaves out much of the full reality of the being and life of the other. So we consider two other forms of the inclusive dialogical relation: *education* and *friendship*.

(2) *Education* involves the influencing of the lives of others with one's own life. And this always carries the danger that the teacher's will to educate may degenerate into egocentric arbitrariness, and that he may let his "selection of the world" proceed from his own self-will or his idea of the pupil and his needs, rather than from the pupil's own reality. The great teacher must and will experience "from the other side" ever anew. "Without the action of his spirit being in any way weakened, he must at the same time be *over there*, on the surface of that other spirit which is being acted upon—and not of some conceptual, contrived spirit, but all the time the wholly concrete spirit of this individual and unique being who is living and confronting him." [289] It is not enough merely to imagine the child's individuality and acknowledge it. "Only when he catches himself 'from over there' . . . how it affects this other human being, does he recognize the real limit, baptize his self-will in Reality . . . and renew his paradoxical legitimacy." [290]

But in education, the inclusion cannot be entirely mutual. The educator stands at both ends of the common situation, the pupil only at one end. The child or the pupil cannot participate completely as yet. "In the moment when the pupil is able to throw himself across and experience from over there, the educative relation would be burst asunder, or change into friendship." [291]

(3) *Friendship:* this is simply the concrete and complete and mutual experience of inclusion, the true and full inclusion of one another by human souls, the grateful and eager experiencing from the other side.

This relation of pure dialogue, in inclusion, should obtain in education, in friendship, in the political party, certainly in the family. The child, the pupil, the friend should know that he is "unceasingly addressed in a dialogue that never breaks off." [292] Trust in a human person, trust in the world because this person exists: this is the supreme achievement of the relation in education; it is the first step on the road to restored faith in God. Loyalty to a human person, loyalty to life, because of the child's trust in us is the first lesson in responsibility.

There is a "lofty asceticism" and self-discipline required in true community, true relation, enduring mutuality. In mutuality there obtains a kind of law of "counterpoint"—of giving and withholding, intimacy and distance, of loving without dominating, of helping without exploiting. This realm of true dialogue has a special objectivity which knows no ego-centricity.[293] The relation of the physician or therapist to his patient provides a good illustration and application of this principle. It is important that there should be a genuine personal relation between the two; but as soon as the helper is tempted to dominate or to enjoy the patient, or to cater to the latter's egocentric wishes, the danger of falsification arises, a danger more subtle and harmful than quackery.

Egoism and Altruism.—The life of dialogue is not to be confused with the contrast between egoism and altruism, at least as it is conceived by most moralists. There are some people who are busy in "social activity" who have never truly spoken with a fellowman as a person, from being to being. This is the curse of so much charity and "social work." Many who "love" mankind, find it impossible to love a particular man or woman. Yet we know that there are others who have little or no personal contact with others, except perhaps enemies, but who stand in such relation to them that it is the fault of the enemy if the relation does not flower into one of dialogue.[294]

It has often been asked whether man is naturally and inherently egoistic or altruistic. The answer is that neither one nor the other is "natural" to him; for both egoism and altruism involve behavior towards others with respect to oneself. Everything we do has a double-meaning. Everyone's actions are both egoistic and altruistic, i.e., in relation to others. My behavior has a double-meaning, but so also does the behavior of the other towards me have a double-meaning. In this way my conduct will be more or less determined by anticipation of his conduct. For example, consider the actions of opponents in a debate or a fight: one may and probably will anticipate what the other will say or do so as to invalidate or ward off ahead of time whatever the opponent may say or do.

The ethic of both egoism and altruism has its foundation in the distinction between "ego" and "alter." Both systems must assume that ego and alter are not indifferent to each other, but that they are first person and second person, the egoism or altruism of which expresses itself in the relation. All experience has a measure of altruism, of participation in the life or activity of others. We cannot avoid it. This is one of the common fallacies in any ethic of egoism; namely, that the very achievement of the "egoistic" aims depends for their realization upon the presence and help of others. Man is never, save in a limited sense, completely within the "egocentric predicament." He is always *with* others, active *and* passive, subject *and* object at one and the same time, affecting others and being affected by others. Certainly Buber's whole point of view is opposed to anything resembling epistemological solipsism, according to which direct experience discloses no active individual save the one having the experience. Experience, Buber keeps pointing out, is social and plural and objective,[295] involving the *givenness and concrete reality of persons and things to other persons.*

The discussion of existing ethical theories led Simmel to the conclusion that so-called egoism *assumes* the existence of society,[296] that the whole ethical problem rests on the real difference and connection between *I* and *Thou,* and that the very concept of egoism has meaning only in contrast to a concept of altruism. Egoism has meaning only as involving others in and through whom the egoist ascertains his own being. Feuerbach also emphasized that his new principle does not involve either ego or alter-ego, but ego *and* alter-ego, and that self-love does not exist without the love for another and vice versa.[297] The issue is one of *accent*—whether on the alter-*Ego* or on the *Alter*-ego.

It becomes clear that both egoism and altruism involve behavior of one with another. However, it is not always so evident that egoism does not necessarily express itself in "egoistic" conduct toward the other; it can also express itself in "altruistic" forms. It can, for example, express itself in extreme care and worry for the other. The self-deceptive egoism of a possessive mother may hide behind an apparently selfless love for her child. One goes to the other in search of himself. George Meredith in his "Bible of Egoism" exposes love as often having so little altruistic motive.[298] Hegel's concept of love (in contrast to a real *I* and *Thou* relation) is an artificial synthesis of egoism and altruism.

The two attitudes arise together, with the coming of consciousness of one's own selfhood and the independence of the other. The unconscious ego can hardly be egoistic toward another; and altruism must pre-suppose the recognition of another as one's alter-ego. For example, the ego-centric demands which a baby makes upon his world can hardly be called "egoistic," in contrast to the egoistic behavior of the adult who has become an *I* for himself. The egoism of the child is just as naive as his spontaneous generosity with his toys. Only I myself, conscious of my own independent being and the independence of the others, can be truly egoistic or altruistic. And I can then only be egoistic or altruistic in relation to others. Indeed, the egoist characteristically does not seek to find himself in himself, but in others. It might even be argued that the most typical form of egoism *is* "altruism"; not the Narcissus complex of self-love, but such a love for others that gives expression, status and power to oneself. One loves oneself, reflexively, through the other. And yet, one usually feels the resistance of the other, and becomes "other" to the other. In relation, the *I* and the *Thou* are mutually equal.

Responsibility.—It is only in the life of dialogue that responsibility becomes real and productive. This is the way that man comes to the truth about his own existence. For man is neither a solitary individual, nor a piece in the vast impersonal game of politics and economics. Man is not primarily an object, but a subject, who can claim and respond, choose and be chosen, make vows and receive vows, address and be addressed—one who can be, in the deepest sense, "respons-ible." Otherness rises up to meet you: the heart and fullness of life is a meeting which you cannot control, yet which you can continually expect, and for which you are "answerable." Man's real humanity, man's selfhood, consists both in his responding and in his being responsible. Like it or not, man is set in a situation in which he cannot deny the neighbor, without denying his own essential character. It is man's being-in-community that characterizes him as man. In a profound sense, man must live in love if he is to live at all.

Buber does more than re-state this truth in his own way. It is, after all, not a new idea in western thought, since it is in its various forms an amalgam of Christian and Stoic thought. It is the way he develops the nature of responsibility that gives Buber's thought such fertility in many fields of human action. Buber argues persuasively that the idea of responsibility must be brought back from the sphere of specialized ethics and mechanistic psychologies into the sphere of the lived life. Man must be rid of all fictitious responsibility—responsibility to whatever we are not truly answerable. Buber is equally trenchant in his treatment of false sentimentality and of false totalitarianisms. Where no primary address or claim can reach me, responsibility is a phantom. Responsibility exists only where there is address from a realm independent of myself and where there is real responding. Responding to what? To whatever or whomever addresses me; to what happens to me; to what is to be seen and heard and felt.[299] The real person is the one "who denies no answer to life and the world, but accepts responsibility for everything that he meets."[300] The responsible man is attentive to creation as it happens. It happens as speech, as the Word, directed to him. And the sounds of this speech are the events of the everyday life, this day, this hour, now! Here Buber preserves the Hebrew strain of intense concern for the concrete and the everyday.

On God's side it is written: *Be!* On man's side the same word reads: *Being is to be actualized!* The intoxication of the mystic, the search for tempting distances is gone. Remaining is this day, this hour, in its concrete and fateful destiny. It is given us, entrusted to us; we are bound to care for it loyally. It is our duty, our responsibility, our fate, our election.[301] Newly-created reality is laid in our arms every day. Responsibility means to respond to the person, the event, the moment; it means to be answerable to and for the person or the moment.[302]

Many of the contemporary psychological and sociological systems do not recognize or adequately provide for human freedom and responsibility. The individual, in certain accounts, is no longer the doer of his deeds; he is merely the battlefield on which biological drives and social pressures fight for supremacy. What is done is not what the human being wills, but what the conditioning urges strongest at the moment drive him to do. These urges and drives are formed by his inherited physical organism and childhood influences. If he has any luck, he acquires a well-integrated drive system; if he is unlucky, he is destroyed by conflicts. No one is, under such a system, responsible for a destiny brought about by drives. To the extent to which this view obtains psychology becomes a branch of physics. This was true, in large measure, of Freud's psychoanalysis. Based largely on physical and naturalistic assumptions, it does not adequately provide for human freedom and responsibility.[303]

On the other hand, such is the profound disparity between the world-of-It and the world-of-Thou, what one is responsible for cannot be explained by causes. A man who can explain his conduct by causes (which are not himself) is not responsible for his conduct. In the realm of physics (the world of It) there is neither freedom nor responsibility, and therefore, no life. But the free, creative, responsible human being is never comprehensible scientifically. In the world-of-Thou, in lived life where the possibility of novelty and creative acts prevails, all must and do acknowledge responsibility. The real reason for every deed is the doer himself.

Buber is, of course, not unaware of the influence of environment upon character development.[304] He is well aware that men are, in our era, more and more determined by circumstances and social forces and group objectives. And if we delude ourselves that nothing more is required of man than the technical mastery of every situation, we shall become the victims of sociological determinism and will have abdicated our position in creation as beings responsible to God for exercising dominion over the earth. Therefore, if one asks why he did *this* and not *that*, one must find the answer in the *goals* which the doer is seeking, in the attitude with which he approaches life, in the primary word which he addresses to life.[305] Life usually calls us to account not for our right conduct, but for our mistakes. Therefore, in the world of dialogue, the call is for man to bring his own self into being. Who calls? Existence itself; every situation which demands from us a complete engagement with reality. And every such situation is unique; it says something that has never been said before. It says it to me; and my response, even though it be a stammering venture, is an act of faith. "The Single One must answer, by what he does and does not do, he must accept and answer for the hour, the hour of the world, of all the world, as that which is given to him, entrusted to him." [306] No book of rules is at hand to tell me what I must do in this fateful hour and situation. It is *my* hour, and *my* act, for which I have to answer before God.[307] Even my group cannot relieve me of it. I may have to oppose my group and its decision and direction—if I become aware that God ordains otherwise.[308] This does not mean that a man must wrest the answer alone and unadvised out of his own soul. The materials and directions and suggestions out of which the decision is forged may come from many sources; but these directions and suggestions may not be substituted for responsible decision. "He who has a master may yield 'himself,' his bodily person, to him, but not his responsibility." [309]

Buber thus challenges our easy-going, liberal, religious thought, our shallow ethics, our thin social religion, our collectivisms, and forces us back upon the logic of individual decision and commitment, to the point of the individual's inescapable and irrevocable responsibility before God. To a generation intent on escaping from the demanding obligation of constant vigilance and responsibility, to an age seeking a "once-for-all" dictum, Buber reiterates the Biblical emphasis upon the sovereign *fact* and *action* and *command* of God without falling into the inviting arms of fatalism. Throughout he keeps faith with the fact of human freedom and responsibility.[310]

Even belonging to a group, or a party, or a *volk*, and rightly so, the individual must remain obedient to the One who is Lord. My group may not relieve me of my own responsibility; nor can it tell me how I, as I decide, have to do justice to my group before the face of God.[311] It is precisely in political life that the practical relevance of this principle of responsibility becomes apparent. Political activity and decision is generally understood to mean joining some political party. But it is a tragic mistake to suppose that when I have joined the "party" that my political duty is done, and that I am relieved of further responsibility. Not so, for the man of faith, for the man who knows the meaning of dialogue and responsibility. To remove any sphere of life from the realm of responsible decision is to cut it out from the rule of God over the world. This does not mean that I may not strive to serve the interests of my group. It does not mean that the decisions of the party may not in many instances coincide with my own decision; nor that, at points of disagreement, I may not on occasion choose to give greater weight to its collective judgment than to my own. It does mean, however, that for the man of faith, the man who is resolved to obey God in all his ways, party dictation cannot be substituted for responsible decision. The collective may not take the place of God in the dialogue which the Spirit conducts with mankind. Indeed, the very situation of his group, before God, lays a demand upon man, and he will spare neither himself nor his group. The man living in responsibility will make even his political decisions properly only from the ground of his being whereat he is aware of the event as divine speech to him.[312] He must not allow the awareness of this ground to be dimmed or threatened by the collective decision: he must give his own reply, even if it be in direct opposition to the party's program or command.[313] In the mass, Kierkegaard declared, responsibility is retired or fragmented; Buber counters that even in the mass there is "no hidin' place down here." Each man must accept full responsibility for his own action or inaction; he must stake his own soul.

Nor can one be certain that his answer along life's way is *the* right one. There are many pitfalls and risks; there is no absolute certainty. The risk does not ensure the truth for us; and although we live in grace, we may not expect that God will answer for us or give us the answer. He gives us the situation, the demand; He speaks the Word. Each man must give his own answer, or refuse to answer—which, indeed, is the most fatal of all answers. This is man's tragic existential situation.

It is not the "finger of God" which writes my answer correctly. It is the "finger of conscience" of which Buber is speaking. But not the routine, abused, worn out, superficial conscience, with whose discrediting has also been abolished the conviction that man must still give a positive answer. Buber is pointing to the unknown, the ever-newly-discovered conscience which is active in every decision. It is, of course, a personal certainty that is thus produced, the "uncertain certainty" of the person addressed and the one who answers.[314]

That of which Buber speaks has nothing to do with "individualism." For he considers the individual neither the starting point nor the goal of the human world. He is talking rather about the human person, the full mature self of the life of dialogue, as the focal point of the struggle between the movement of the world away from God and its movement toward God. This struggle appears to be taking place in large measure in the body politic, between groups, and more especially within groups. The decisive battles in this war of faiths, however, are being fought out in the depths of each person.[315] Time and Fate bring the problem of ultimate decision to each man, this day, now! All great ethical actions and decisions stand on the hair-line edge of personally acknowledged decision, with no safely coded *What* or *How*. There is only the fearful command: "Become what you are! Carry out God's commission which was given to you in your creation!"

Buber believes that we can now detect in youth the beginnings of a realization that their blind devotion to the party was not a genuine act of their personal life, and that in their craze for authority something precious and irreplaceable has been lost.

> They are not fully awake to the fact that their blind devotion
> to the collective springs from the fear of being left, in this age of
> confusion, to rely on themselves, on a self that no longer receives

its direction from the eternal value. . . . They do not yet realize that this devotion was an escape. . . . But there is a dawning recognition that he who no longer, with his whole being, decides what he does, or does not do, and assumes responsibility for it, becomes sterile in soul. And a sterile soul soon ceases to be a soul.[316]

It becomes increasingly clear that Buber's ethic is really an individual ethic, but one devoid of arbitrariness and subjectivity. It might be more accurate to speak of Buber's system as involving an ethic of personal values and of respect for persons, while keeping in the foreground the inter-personal nature of his personalism. The fulfillment of the individual personality is the fulfillment of the will of God, the obedience to the objective truth of being, the answer to the objective requirement of reality. This striving toward the Unconditioned, however, never achieves a pure result for life and its needs. In the last analysis, therefore, it is an ethics of grace, just as the I-Thou relation is a relation of grace. This ethic, any ethic of grace, in its denial of all the usual principles, involves a danger. It can gain its full meaning only in a moral-religious setting and goal: to realize God's Kingdom on earth. And the foundation posts on which that Kingdom must rest are Righteousness, Integrity, and the Community-Spirit of love and helpfulness as determined by fully objective thinking. More briefly, and perhaps more accurately, it means that *man shall love God* with his whole heart and mind and strength. The service of the Spirit is the eternal command to man.[317] Even though God is beyond all knowledge and all morality, even though the religious life is more than moral command, in the life of man religion and ethics must form a unity.[318] The Spirit is one and cannot be divided, but the ways of service are different and manifold. For every man there is a service in his own way. Heritage, history, culture, and bringing up will determine each his own way; but it is the way to the Spirit. No way is *the* right way. The absoluteness of the religious life remains, but the historic forms are relative—even though for those who belong to each form, it has an absolute meaning. It is, as Berdyaev has said, that in history there is no absolute, but for each man there is an absolute.

INDIVIDUALISM AND COLLECTIVISM

To get the full impact of what Buber is saying we have to recall that the great conflicts of our present era are variously conceived as conflicts between individualism and collectivism, between democracy and totalitarianism, between freedom and tyranny. More simply, on Buber's view, it is the problem of the relation of the individual to the community. Nearly all the discussions of this issue commit the fallacy of excluded middle. They either start with the individual—with his unique capacities, his freedom, his dignity and worth, his inalienable rights, etc.—and draw the conclusion of "rugged individualism" or even anarchy. Or they start with society, viewing man as a conditioned and socially determined animal, and promise man security and solidarity in a scientifically rationalized society. But this usually ends in a leveled-down anonymous generality, a collective tyranny, an impersonal omnicompetent State,—an anthill, as Dostoievski said about Europe in general.

Buber rejects both individualism and collectivism as false alternatives, and confronts us with a genuine third alternative. Neither the individual, as such, nor the social aggregate, as such, is the fundamental fact of human existence. Both individualism and collectivism understand only a part of man. Man in isolation and man in a faceless collective mass is not truly man. "With the former man's face it is distorted, with the latter it is masked." [319] Buber pleads rather for a true community of *man with man,* existing in the relation of *I* and *Thou.* The essence of human life is *what happens between* man and man in community. The opposite of bondage is not freedom, but community. "A man is truly saved from the 'One' (the mass) not by separation but only by being bound up in genuine community." [320]

Buber is not forgetting that men and societies cannot dispense with institutions and impersonal forms of organization. These he provides for in his It-world. Buber was and is a socialist, but a disappointed one.[321] For the socialist ideal which shone so brightly as a beacon of hope for Europe could not withstand the stress of the nationalistic forces joined in mortal combat in the first World War. And the unfolding of the pattern of Communist Revolution in Russia has left much to be desired. Indeed, it has lead to Leninist and Stalinist perversions of true socialism. In this New Leviathan something precious to mankind seems to be lost. The "new messiah" strangely enough writes down the value of man, forgets the relation of the individual to his own soul, tramples upon individuality and one's personal responsibility for life and the world. Modern man has become the victim of the "collective Moloch." [322] Something more is needed if man is ever to master his communal life. And Buber thinks that the truth which has power to emancipate our world from slavery to the collective Moloch is that human life finds its fulfillment in free communion, in reciprocal interchange, in mutual responsibility between man and man in personal relations. The world and attitude of *I-It* must give way to the world and attitude of *I-Thou*. Only men of the *I-Thou* world can live together. Buber's third alternative holds the promise of not deluding us, because it is based on "a primal category of human reality." The fundamental reality is *man with man*. Man does not first exist as an individual and then enter into communication with others. It is in and through communication that he is truly man. Modern man is called to the understanding of this "sphere of between," which is the guarantee and the test of man's humanity.

Under various slogans, individualism and collectivism are under attack, often indiscriminately and dishonestly, without any attempt to distinguish between what is meant and what is not meant, between what should be repealed or changed, and what spared and enhanced. There are different meanings and emphases within both "individualism" and "communism." For example, some would interpret individualism as sheer "anarchy," the atomized *I* of feelings, the absence of relation, or the stronghold of selfish isolation, yielding no genuine personal life. But it may also mean the return to the reality of the self, the place of purification, the preparation for relation, a "mode of thought of the free-born man for whom freedom is the presupposition of binding, of the true personal entry into a binding relation. . . ." [323] This latter is worth preserving in the treasure house of the spirit. Likewise, the "massed, mingled, marching collectivities" have forgotten what it is they are striving for—true community, the community built up out of living mutual relations around a living Center.[324] True community has been lost sight of, betrayed, surrendered to its false counterpart— the mass, the crowd. "Collectivity," says Buber, "is not a binding but a bundling together: individuals packed together, armed and equipped in common, with only as much life from man to man as will inflame the marching step." [325] But true community is not the being *side by side*, but the being *with* one another, a dynamic facing of one another, a flowing from *I* to *Thou*. "Collectivity is based on an organized atrophy of personal existence; community on its increase and confirmation in life lived towards one another." [326] The modern zeal for collectivism, for "regulated chaos," is really an escape from the task of community, from the commitment and testing of the person; it is a flight from vital dialogue. "Bundled together, men march without *Thou* and without *I*; hostile and separated hosts, they march into the common abyss." [327]

In this human crisis, as Buber points out, these two have become questionable: the *person* and the *truth*. These two are inevitably and crucially linked together, for only persons can make responsible response to reality and the reality of truth to which the person goes out must be there. "The person has become questionable through being collectivized." "The Truth, on the other hand, has become questionable through being politicized." [328] The basic question embedded in these two statements, the question of the real person in community, is for Buber "the question to the Single One." [329] This calls for some clarification.

The collectivizing of the person is joined historically with another movement in which, as Buber confesses, he himself participated. It was the struggle of recent decades against the idealistic concepts of "the sovereign, world-embracing, world-sustaining, world creating I." [330] The struggle of most existential thinkers against idealism was waged (among other ways) by calling attention to the "creaturely bonds" of the concrete human being which had been neglected by Idealism. It was shown following Dilthey's insight, how important it is to know that the thinker, the seeker after truth, is bound, in different degrees, to time and space, to an historical era, to the genus man, to a family, a folk, a class, a vocational group, a society, a nation—in a manifold We.[331] In other words, man is situated in a narrow creaturely and conditioned position. To know this helps a man to avoid the presumptive pride of sovereignty, as well as to realize that "being bound means being bound up in relation."

But, unfortunately, it happened that another powerful tendency gained power over the new insight, a tendency which, as we have pointed out above, "exaggerated and perverted the perception of bonds into a doctrine of serfdom." This was the tendency towards collectivism, the mass, *das Volk*, in which primacy is ascribed to the group. And the perversion comes at this point: "The collectivity receives the right to hold the person who is bound to it bound in such a way that he ceases to have complete responsibility." [332] The organic group is primary, that which really exists; the person becomes derivative and, therefore, absolved of personal response. It is just at this point that the immeasurable and unique value that constitutes man is imperilled, if not destroyed. Only a person can enter into dialogue; only a person can hear and speak to God.

Thinkers like Kierkegaard, Stirner and Heidegger insist that the connection with the mass must be overcome if self-being is to be attained. Buber agrees; it is at least half-true. In order to emerge into the world as a "self," man must cut loose from that negative nameless all-or-nothing in which modern man is immersed. But this is only one side of the coin of truth; for "the genuineness and adequacy of the self cannot stand the test in self-commerce, but only in communication with the whole of otherness." [333] This is Buber's gospel. Not the private life versus the public life, but *man with man* in the uncurtailed measure of lived-life, speaking and answering.

Not only has the person been collectivized, but truth has been politicized. The sociological theories of our age have exercised a relativizing effect on the concept of truth. In showing the dependence of thought and behavior on social processes, they have proved the connection of thought with existence. This realization, thinks Buber, was justified in so far as it linked the "truth" of a man to his immediate experience and conditioning reality. But again, this insight and its justification were perverted into the opposite when its authors omitted to draw the basic boundary line between what can and what cannot be understood as conditioned in this way. That is to say, they did not comprehend the person in his *total* reality. Buber puts it this way:

> The man who thinks "existentially," that is, who stakes his life in his thinking, brings into his real relation to the truth not merely his conditioned qualities but also the unconditioned nature, transcending them, of his quest, of his grasp, of his indomitable will for the truth, which also carries along with it the whole personal power of standing his test.[334]

We must try, urges Buber, as an inescapable duty, in the sociology of knowledge, to make a distinction between what can and what cannot be derived from the social factor, to point out what takes place "between the underivable in the recognizing person and the underivable in the object of his recognition." [335] This duty was neglected; and as a result, the political creeds of our day were able to take over the principle which was at hand and to proclaim that what benefits or corresponds to the real or supposed life of the group is sacrosanct truth.

When the individual person can no longer appeal to a truth which can be recognized and tested by him, it marks the disintegration of human faith in Truth; it marks the onslaught of skepticism, complete relativism, and the paralysis of the search for truth. We have seen that Buber contends that while Truth may never be possessed, yet it may be comprehended in an existentially real relation. The problem for modern man, therefore, is to find the reconciliation between *existential truth* and the *Absolute Truth,* to combine in personal and corporate life the dynamic of the existential with the ultimate truth and purpose of God.[336]

Stated in another way: Our question *What is man?* can never be answered, if at all, save on the basis of the totality of man's essential relations to what is—to Nature, to himself, to fellowmen, and to God. "Only the man who realizes in his whole life, with his whole being, the relations possible to him helps us to know man truly." [337] And since the depths and paradoxes of man's nature are revealed only to the man who has become "a single one," the way to the answer lies only through the man who overcomes his isolation and solitude without forfeiting his responsibility. The fundamental reality is *man with man;* freedom *and* order. Freedom is that through which man is man; but freedom must be set in ordered community.

THE SINGLE ONE

It becomes increasingly clear that both individualism and collectivism are the result of and perverse answers to the predicament of modern man, namely, the condition of cosmic and social homelessness which Buber has described so accurately.[338] The human person feels himself to be exposed, an unwanted child of the universe, a refugee in the midst of the tumultuous human world. The first reaction to the awareness of this uncanny and dreadful position is individualism; the second is collectivism.[339] In individualism man seeks relief from the despair and fear of his exposed position; he resorts to the compensatory expedient of glorifying his solitary state—and the result is anarchy and anxious isolation and egocentric defensiveness. In collectivism, man tries to escape his despair and loneliness, and the responsibility of his true aloneness, by becoming completely immersed in one of the massive group formations. But man's isolation is not thereby overcome; it is rather overpowered and numbed. For the person joined to the collective is not bound man with man. The mass neutralizes and destroys the living bonds that make him a person. Real release from isolation can be found only in personal communion with other persons. Individualism sees man only in relation to himself; collectivism does not see *man* at all, it sees only *society*. "Modern collectivism is the last barrier raised by man against a meeting with himself." [340] The inevitable meeting of man with himself is able to take place only as a meeting of man with his fellowman. He will be released from his isolation and insecurity when he knows the other in all his otherness as himself, as man. He will then realize what it means to be a human being, bound up in relation to the neighbor, suffering his destiny along with the neighbor, willing and ready to suffer it. [341]

The day of individualism is past, despite hysterical attempts at revival. Collectivism is, at the moment, in its hey-day. But it too will pass away. The third and true alternative, after the disillusionment with the other two, is the dialogic life of true relation with others in the interest of genuine community. In his *Paths in Utopia* Buber ventures to limn the pattern and the conditions for "full community" in the small organic community. [342]

There is need, then, for persons who are not collectivized and for truth which is not politicized. Human truth is thus bound up with the responsibility of the person. What does it mean, then, to be or to become this kind of "individual" person? Since Buber rejects the collective ideal and feels that the evil of our day stems, on the one hand, from the oppressive rule of the Mass and, on the other hand, from a mistaken ideal of individuality, what is his own ideal of the person (the individual, the single one, *der Einzelne*) and of the "We," the community, the corporate analog of *Thou*? Much of the answer has been given, but in order to get Buber's full meaning we must push our inquiry still a little further into the concepts of "the Single One" and of the true "We." For these concepts are basic to everything else in his thought. This will involve a certain amount of repetition, but the value outweighs the cost of some duplication.

In order to set in clear perspective his own understanding of the transformed responsible individual in the community, Buber contrasts it with two other ideals of individuality—those of Soren Kierkegaard and Max Stirner—which are radically opposed to each other and yet agree in their insistence upon the absoluteness of the individual. Out of the radicality of his own loneliness, Kierkegaard worked out in utmost detail the meaning of "the Single One" (*hiin Enkelte*) who stands in sole essential relation to God, to the exclusion of all other relations with objects or persons or body politic.[343] Max Stirner, a German Protagoras, who prepared the way for his contemporary Kierkegaard in much the same way that the Sophist prepared the way for Socrates, proclaimed the theory of absolute egoism, total selfishness, in his category of "the Unique One" or "the Only One" (*der Einzige*). We turn now to a brief analysis of *der Einzige* and *der Einzelne*.

Stirner's doctrine of the absolute and almighty Ego which is sufficient unto itself becomes clear when we examine his ideas concerning truth and responsibility. For Stirner these are both erroneous questions; he desired to destroy both concepts. Human truth is bound up with the individual's lack of responsibility. "Truth is what is mine." [344] "For me there is no truth, for nothing passes beyond me." "Truth exists only . . . in your head." You alone are the truth, for "man is the measure of all things." Everything is my own *(mein Eigentum)*; therefore real responsibility and objective truth are phantoms. Truth, independent of the ego and available to all publicly, is done away with. His theory, like solipsism, leads only to a knowing subject but not to a concrete human person. What I take as true is defined by what I am; and Buber adds: what I am is defined by my complexes, my class, my culture, etc.[345] Stirner thus becomes the involuntary founder of modern psychological and sociological relativism, which is at once both true and false.[346]

And so it is with responsibility, a concept which is denied by Stirner. "What you call responsibility is a lie." [347] Certainly it is unknown to Stirner's *Einzigen* simply because his "unique one" does not know the meaning of address and answer. He is shut off from the "ontic" and primary otherness of the other. The unique one belongs to himself. He has no essential relation except to himself. He acknowldges nothing but himself![348] There is no saying of "Thou"; no genuine relationship, otherness, or love is possible.

Buber consents to much of Stirner's attack. There is indeed a kind of responsibility which is a lie, and an idealistic conception of truth which is false. There is a pseudo-responsibility to a reason, an idea, an institution, to "all kinds of illustrious ghosts" which are not essentially "personal"; this Buber rejects because these "ghosts" cannot really call us to account—like father or mother, husband or friend, or like God. Likewise with the problem of truth. The very means with which Stirner attempts to retire objectively possessed truth are, says Buber, the proof that truth *is* conditioned by the person, by immediate experience, by existential being. But there is a Truth, declares Buber, which can never be invalidated, which one cannot possess but which one can serve, which is never quite accessible but in which man can participate and which man can prove in the living of life. "The Single One is the very truth," says Kierkegaard.[349] Herein lies the paradoxical truth of the Individual, and of Truth itself. Here Buber joins forces with Kierkegaard. To be the Single One is to be the conveyor of truth: the Crowd overlooks this fact.

Kierkegaard's "Single One" does not refer to the thinking subject, not even to "man," but to the concrete singular person who becomes aware of himself as standing alone before God. This is not only the primary condition of all religiosity; it is to be a "single one." That is why, from Kierkegaard's religious point of view, the "single one" is the category through which time, history, and the race must pass.[350] Kierkegaard denies pantheistic mysticism in which the self is lost in God, in which man can no longer say "I" or "Thou," in which man can no longer pray, or serve, or obey, or love, as is possible only between an I and a Thou. He also rejects the "only one" who exists alone. Kierkegaard knows, with Buber, that man can become whole and truly the "Single One" only in virtue of a relation to another. *But Kierkegaard restricts that essential relation to God.* At least he knows the reality of God and the relationship to God; he knows what love and obedience are; he knows that there is no room for self-love. Stirner obeys no master, hears no call, feels no contact and repulsion. But Kierkegaard repeats the age-old, misused, desecrated, yet inviolable and sacred word: Obey the Lord! When one becomes a "Single One" he will be ready and able to obey. The Many must go through the "narrow pass" and become "the Single One." And to become that one means to let God help one.[351]

Every man can and must be the single one. So, for Kierkegaard, the individual is a task. One must become a "single one"—not by a cheap "development of the personality," but by a radical act and decision, by an art, the deepest art of life, an art the execution of which may cost the artist his life.[352] One must listen, and one must obey! the very thing which is forbidden to Stirner's "unique one." In Old Testament terms: the single one materializes the "image of God." Man becomes an *I* only in relation to God as his *Thou.* Man proves truth existentially by living out in personal existence that which God has addressed to him.[353]

This relation is, according to Kierkegaard, an exclusive one, the unique, essential one which excludes all other relations as unessential. "Everyone should be chary about having to do with the 'others,' and should essentially speak only with God and with himself." [354] The Single One is alone before God.

At this point, in regard to this exclusion, Buber parts company with Kierkegaard. Buber is disturbed about two things here: first, Kierkegaard's bringing together the phrases "with God" and "with himself"; and second, the exclusion of all otherness save God. The simple experience of faith tells us that "speaking with God" is something totally different from "speaking with oneself," but it is not something totally different from speaking with another human being. "Only when I have to do with another essentially, that is, in such a way that he is no longer a phenomenon of my *I* but instead is my *Thou*, do I experience the reality of speech with another" in the irrefutable reality of mutuality.[355] Then only does the soul stand in the presence of someone who is not the soul, but yet is a Self.[356]

In his solitariness and renunciation, Kierkegaard turns away from the world of men, even from his fiancée, and says that "the Single One" has to do *essentially* only with God. Buber, the Jew, takes exception to this aspect of Kierkegaard's concept and appeals to Jesus to correct Kierkegaard, the Christian, on this point. When Jesus was asked the crucial question as to what was the "great commandment," Jesus answered by connecting the two Old Testament commandments: "love God with all your might" and "love your neighbor as one like yourself." [357] Both are to be loved—God *and* the neighbor. And the neighbor here means not man in general but the man who meets me every day in the give-and-take of life. The "other" is to be loved "as one like myself," to whom I should show love as I wish it shown to me. God and man are not rivals. To love God exclusively—"with all your heart"—means, in fact, an inclusive love, *because He is God,* loving his creation, ready to accept and include and respond to all love. Says Buber: "God limits Himself in all his limitlessness; He makes room for the creatures, and so, in love to Him, He makes room for love to the creatures." [358] "Who could suppose that God wants *Thou* to be truly said only to Him, and to all others only an unessential and fundamentally invalid word?" [359] Even though the world may be "fallen," it is still God's creation which he loves. The essential thing, says Buber, is not to separate the world from God, nor absorb the world in God, but to see things and persons *in* God. Buber finds Kierkegaard refuting himself in another place where he describes the "ethical" as "the only means by which God communicates with man." [360] If that is true, counters Buber, I am in fact forbidden to speak only with God and myself. And again, in his *Journal*, Kirkegaard wrote: "The frightful thing is that precisely the highest form of piety, to let everything earthly go, can be the highest egoism." And again: "Had I had faith I would have stayed with Regina."

"In order to come to love," Kierkegaard had said about his renunciation of Regina Olsen, "I had to remove the object." Buber thinks this is to misunderstand both God and the true human situation. For Buber, relations with objects and human beings do not obstruct, but mediate, man's relation to God. God is found in closest communion with men." "Creation is not a hurdle on the road to God; it is the road itself." [361] We are created together and for togetherness. A God reached by excluding all others would not be the God of all creation, in whom all life is fulfilled. God desires that we come to Him by way of the Reginas He has created and not by the renunciation of them. "God is not an object beside objects, and hence cannot be reached by renunciation of objects." [362] God is not to be found by subtraction, nor loved by reduction in an empty void.[363] The Single One "corresponds" to God when he, in his human way, embraces that bit of the world offered and entrusted to him as God embraces His creation in His Divine way, by saying *Thou* to all being.

Buber thus finely summarizes his own substitute version of Kierkegaard's single one:

> The single one is not the man who has to do with God essentially and only unessentially with others, who is unconditionally concerned with God and conditionally with the body politic. The single one is the man for whom the reality of relation with God as an exclusive relation includes and encompasses the possibility of relation with all otherness. . . . [364]

God is only to be found by those who take "the longest way" to Him, that is the way of active service and love to all men.[365] "In every true prayer," even if uttered alone in one's room, "it is the community that is praying." [366] "To love God truly, one must first love man." [367]

Kierkegaard declares that the Mass, the Crowd, the People is untruth; only the individual is the truth. And he renounces Regina Olsen in symbolical rejection of the body politic. But, on Buber's view, marriage is precisely the realm in which the I-Thou relation can be most ideally achieved. Married love is "the exemplary bond" in which God can best be found. Marriage, properly understood, is the institution through which man is more essentially related to the "world," to the public life, in its evil and in its goodness, in its damnation and in its salvation.[368] The person in marriage cannot escape real confrontation, real engagement, with the other; the only thing he can do is to prove himself in it, or fail in it. But he cannot pretend that the other does not exist or that his claim is limited.

For Kierkegaard, the Single one resides in the realm of Spirit, and is alien to politics.[369] So Kierkegaard turns away from the "people"; he wants nothing to do with *res publica*. Marriage is doubly to be fled because it brings one into essential relation not only with *one other,* but also with "the world." The little community of marriage and family is part of the great community, bound up with its problems and hopes and failures. The relation obtaining in happy marriage is exemplary of the relation one ought to adopt toward the larger community. And that is precisely why Kierkegaard turns away. Thus Buber interprets Kierkegaard.

Up to a point Buber agrees with Kierkegaard. But Buber cannot accept the thought that the love of God is incompatible with the love of woman or the love of other men.[370] Buber, too, is sharply critical of the collective ideal; but not to the point of abandoning the world of men. In a crowd, a man is like a stick stuck into a bundle moving with the current. And the idea of self-propulsion is an illusion. But the responsible individual in the body politic is quite different. He is bound up in relation to it, married to it, willing to suffer with it, but not abandoned blindly to any of its movements. He does what he can, with the power he possesses, to find truth and loyalty. And even in the group he seeks persons, candidates for the I-Thou relation. To him the mass is no longer a mob, but so many potential *Thous*.[371]

So Buber too recognizes the need of persons who stand with other persons in essential relation, but who never relinquish their individual responsibility. And there is need of men with faith in a truth which is independent of them, a truth which is never completely possessed but which discloses itself to the man who in responsible decision answers the demands of each hour. What that demand will be, what his answer and decision will be, no one can foretell. "One thing is essential, namely, that I expose myself to the situation as it presents itself to me, waiting for the manifestation of the Word, until hearing flows into being and I perceive what is to be perceived, and I answer to that which has been perceived." [372] "True community and true commonwealth will be realized only to the extent to which the Single One becomes real out of whose responsible life the body politic is renewed." [373]

Thus while rejecting the Mass, the Collective, Buber finds a necessary place for the "We," the corporate analog of *Thou*. A genuine *We* may arise in any kind of group in which the inner structure is right for it. By a "We" Buber means a community of several persons who have themselves reached a self and self-responsibility, for true community is impossible otherwise. "Only men who are capable of truly saying *Thou* to one another can truly say *We* with one another." [374]

In the fifth chapter of *Die Frage an den Einzelnen*, entitled "Attempts at Severance" (Trennungsversuche),[375] Buber takes final issue with those who tend to support the collective ideal as over against his doctrine of the Single One in responsibility. Buber will have none of that school of thought which gives to the political world, to the State, an exaggerated autonomy, and thereby removes it from the responsibility of the Single One who, before God, participates in it and answers for it.

Buber names in particular Oswald Spengler, the Roman Catholic Carl Schmitt, and the Protestant Friedrich Gogarten as giving support to a philosophy of the State which he opposes with his categories of the "We" and the transformed responsible Single One. Spengler's biological interpretation and what Buber calls his "trivialization" of Nietzsche's thesis attempts to establish a special sphere of the political, inaccessible to ethics, by classifying men as "beasts of prey." Political life is only a fight between packs of beasts, in which the standards of the Single One do not and cannot apply. This biological interpretation is called a "trivialization" because it does violence to the meaning of history while also over-simplifying the nature of man. To interpret human nature in biological terms abandons the true content of that which really constitutes man. Animals have no history, surely not in the unique sense which enables men to speak of "human history."

Man does have history, he makes history, because he has responsibility and relation to truth. Gogarten shares Buber's view that concrete reality resides where responsible persons confront one another in mutual relation.

Carl Schmitt, the exponent of Constitutional Law, sets forth another view of the "political" as having its own criterion,[376] namely, the distinction between *friend* and *foe,* with the implied outcome of real struggle.[377] Schmitt carries the "duel" of private life over into public life; it is the concept of the "foe" that gives to life its specifically political tension. And in such a situation there is no reconciliation or mediation: the duel situation can be resolved only in the destruction of one by the other. Buber criticizes this formula as being unstable and therefore non-constitutive. A radical friend-foe contrast appears only at those times when the common life and order are threatened, but not during times of stability and coherence. Furthermore, it takes no adequate account of the rebel, the "inner foe," the "friend-foe," who wants only to reform the political order, not destroy it.

Gogarten abandons any such notion as the "Single One," even to denying the rigor of responsibility in personal life. In his *Politische Ethik* Gogarten argues that all ethical problems derive their ethical relevance from the political problem.[378] The ethical is valid only because man is a political being. But Buber is quick to point out that if ethical problems derive their relevance from the political field, then they cannot also receive authority from the religious—with a resulting disconnected ethic. Buber is all the more critical of Gogarten because the latter is a theologian. "True as it is that he, the Single One, cannot win to a legitimate relation with God without a legitimate relation to the body politic, it is nevertheless also true that the defining force has to be ascribed not to the latter but to the former," i.e., to God.[379]

Buber also takes sharp issue with both Gogarten and Schmitt over their joint assumption of the absolute sinfulness and basic evil of man as justifying the authoritarian state. Man, being irrevocably evil, cannot know what is good; hence he must receive his ethical direction from the State. Individual liberty can only spawn further evil and confusion, for individualism is the source of sin. Buber, likewise, considers man to be "problematic" and "dangerous"; but he objects strenuously when Gogarten writes: "Whence shall the State derive sovereign power if not from the recognition of man's fallen state?" and the ethical quality of the State consists in "its warding off the evil to which men have fallen prey by its sovereign power and by its right over the life and property of its subjects." [380] Buber regards this as only a theological version of the old police-state idea; fascism in religious garb.

Buber then goes on to consider the nature and meaning of man's evil and sin.[381] In this matter, Buber is not as radical in his analysis as are orthodox Christian thinkers. In Buber's view man is essentially neither good or evil, nor simply the indeterminate possibility of either, but in a more precise sense "good and evil together." Buber refers to men, not as being sinful and fallen, but as being limited; but "the limitation is factual, it does not transform his essence or destroy God's work." [382] " God has created a world, and he has pronounced his creation to be very good—from whence then comes the evil?" [383] The primal and profound secret of Good and Evil, God has kept to himself.[384] But we know this much: Man is free to choose God or reject God. Much of the evil of life comes from man's rejection of God. Indeed, "it is not that they raise themselves against God, it is rather that they do not rise up for him." [385] In one place Buber adds: " 'Good' is the movement in the direction of home, 'evil' is the aimless whirl of human potentialities. . . . " [386] Man is ethically ambivalent, but his "fall" results from his search for redemption. "That man may fall implies that he may rise . . . he has the power to effect the work of redemption out of his own self." The opportunity for reversal or repentance is ever present.

With characteristic Chassidic forbearance, the problem of man's natural sinfulness is minimized. There is only a deep pathos and love for bungling mortals caught in the whirlpool of alternatives, and the assurance that man and God's creation can never fall beyond His loving concern. In his thought of good and evil, Buber seems to share the teachings of the Chassidim wherein we find such passages as the following two Chassidic sayings:

> But if there were no evil, there would be no good, for good is the counterpart of evil. . . . For there is no good unless its counterpart exists. . . . That fact that evil confronts good gives man the possibility of victory: of rejecting evil and choosing good. Only then does the good exist truly and perfectly.[387]
>
> Evil too is good. It is the lowest rung of perfect goodness. If you do good deeds, even evil will become good; but if you sin, evil will really become evil. How then can it contain good and evil, which are self-contradictory? But actually there is no contradiction, for evil is the throne of good.[388]

Or, again, in Buber's own words:

> What we call evil is found not only in man, it is also the Evil in the world; it is the defilement of creation. But this defilement is nothing positive, it is not an existing character of things. It is only their lack of firmness, their lack of direction, their vacillation.[389]

Evil, then, is a not standing firm. It is "the convulsive shirking of direction, of the total orientation of the soul by which it stands up to personal responsibility before God." [390] Against Gogarten and Schmitt, Buber contends eloquently that man is "fallen" only in relation to God, not to other men or to human institutions. Only before God can radical evil be ascribed to man "because God is God and man is man, and the distance between them is absolute." [391] No political institution may assume the role of intercessor between God and man. No doctrine of the State can go beyond the reality of the responsible human person in the situation of faith.

THE SELF AND THE "SPHERE OF BETWEEN"

The Spirit in its primal reality is not something that is but something that happens.[392] "We do not find meaning lying in things nor do we put it into things, but between us and things it can happen." [393] Spirit, in its beginning, is pure power to perceive the world, grasp the world, wrestle with it, play with it, participate in it. Out of this elemental and intimate participation does the "spirit" arise as a separate thing.[394] To learn what spirit really is, avows Buber, we cannot be content with investigating it where it has reached full achievement; it must also be sought out where it is still a happening—in the "sphere of 'between,' " or in the coming theophany.

In the same way that man enters into love, he enters into Spirit. Spirit is not the I, but between the *I* and *Thou*. Spirit is not like the blood which circulates within you, but like the air in which you breathe. Man lives in Spirit, whenever he can answer his *Thou*. There is no *I* in itself, but only the *I* which stands toward a *Thou* in the reality of relationship and the *I* which experiences its objects as *It*.[395] In another place, Buber compares Spirit to the sun, and explains that Spirit is to be found not so much *in* things as *between them*.[396] In every being, of course, is laid the All-Being, but it cannot develop save in connection with all else. The Divine can arise in the individual, but is fully manifested only in the relation between individuals. It follows, on

Buber's view, that the true place of the realization of the Divine is the community.

In other words, the essence of human existence is rooted in one being turning to another as particular "other," in order to communicate with it in a sphere which is common to them both but which reaches out beyond the special sphere of each. Buber called this sphere . . . the "sphere of 'between.'" This is the primal category of human reality.[397] "On the far side of the subjective, on this side of the objective, on the narrow ridge where *I* and *Thou* meet, there is the realm of 'between.'"[398] And the essence of man which is peculiar to him can be known only in living relation. The gorilla is also an individual; an ant hill is also a collective. But *I* and *Thou* exist only because man exists; and the *I* exists only through the relation to the *Thou*.

Buber goes to considerable length to underscore his conviction that "between" is not a mere fanciful construction, an auxiliary accessory, but the *real place and bearer of what happens between men*. There is, in Buber's thought, an *ontological* quality about the "between" and what happens there. It is not just a "psychological" concept; it is a reality. It comes and goes, like ebb and tide, like quanta perhaps; it is not a smooth continuum, but is periodically re-constituted whenever men *meet* with one another.[399] It may happen wherever two men fundamentally other—through fleeting glances in an air-raid shelter, through the mute understanding of two persons at a Mozart concert—create a dialogue situation which is constituted not on the basis of the two existences but out of that which has its being between them and transcends both.[400] This is the reality which points beyond both individualism and collectivism to Buber's third alternative—genuine community. Only man with man provides the complete picture. One with the other; I here, you there; *I* with *Thou!*

And even more fundamental than man with man is man with God. All doctrines of absorption overlook this. Whenever *Thou* is truly spoken to any person or object, connection or correspondence is established with the flow of Spirit that extends from man to God. "God and man, like in being, are the indissolubly real pair, the two bearers of the primal relation, which from God to man is termed mission and command, from man to God looking and hearing, and between both is termed knowledge and love."[401] A Chassidic aphorism declares: "There is no room for God in him who is full of himself."[402] And again: "Only he who brings himself to God as an offering may be called man." [403]

It can hardly be doubted that Buber is here saying that this true I-Thou relation to God and to neighbor is not simply an ideal to be attained, a command to be fulfilled. It is the "way of things." The ideal is rooted in the actual; the imperative finally rests back upon the indicative.[404] Certainly the actual conditions the manner of achieving the ideal; or perhaps one should say that the ideal is "realized" but not "completed." The Kingdom is here, among you, and yet always becoming, yet to be. I take it that the conviction expressed here is that when God created man and the world He created an order of things and of persons in relation with Himself and with each other. Only as man is part of that relational-structure of things is he distinctively *man*. If it were possible to lift a man out of it, he would on the instant cease to be a human self. As H. H. Farmer expresses it in a homely but vivid simile: "It is not that God creates a man and then pops him into the world of persons as a housewife makes a dumpling and pops it into the saucepan, both dumpling and saucepan being capable of existing apart from one another." [405] To be a man, to come into existence as a "self," is to be incorporated into this world of the personal, to be in relation with persons, divine and human. Existence as a complete human self is not possible on any other terms. In so far as I can enter into relation with the world, I am related to men. And this is not by accident; it is because of the very structure and nature of the universe. "All actuality is filled connection; nothing individual is in itself actual." [406]

Buber is not unequivocally unambiguous concerning the nature and origin of the self, and about the social nature of reality. It depends upon how we put the question to him. Buber's writings are characteristically not technical works of discursive philosophy; they are philosophical, mystical, aesthetic, poetic. He is concerned to articulate the meaning of true community in an age which desperately needs it by expressing the nature and meaning of the "personal" in such a way that it may claim a right to be taken seriously. He is not interested in working out the psychological "mechanism" of mind, self and society (as G. H. Mead is, for example, from the standpoint of experimental social psychology), but in establishing the psychic reality and actual structure of the personal world as it came forth from the creative hands of God. With Buber, therefore, it is particularly important not to conclude from his silence about particular matters that he is not concerned to elaborate.[407] He restricts himself rather closely to making the particular point which he is anxious to enforce, which is: Live the life of dialogue in the area of life that is yours, and you will find the true meaning of life. Everyone—the thinker, the statesman, the worker, the teacher, the lover—may live the life of dialogue, respond to the immediate demands of every hour, and in this dedicated life of I-Thou response and responsibility you are reaching out your hands to God and finding Him. The rest you can, and must, leave to His gracious care. For God does not leave His creation forsaken.

SUMMARY

Our discussion in this chapter has centered on the life of dialogue in a world of *I-Thou* relations, on the life of persons in a world of persons. Buber's anthropological analysis of ethics and philosophy issues in his realization of the crucial significance of relations between persons and of the fundamentally social nature of reality. The world is primarily a *Mit-welt*, a fellow-world of relations. In the give-and-take of personal encounter with neighbor and with God, in the dialogic togetherness of one open-hearted person with another open-hearted person, is to be found the origin and foundation of the meaning of human existence. The individual is "human" only because he partakes of others and can communicate himself to others. Being is in being known, and *knowing* that one is known. One learns to say "I" only because there is a "Thou" there. So one is predestined through others—in a reciprocal dependent independence. The unique inalienable character of the person is grounded in his essential otherness. Our being-for-ourselves essentially and constitutively includes being-for-others. It is in inter-personal communication that man becomes a self, a *persona*. Man is not primarily an object, a piece of the It-world; but a subject who can claim and respond, address and be addressed, who can be responsible.

Neither the solitary individual as such nor the impersonal social aggregate as such, Buber insists, is the fundamental fact of human existence. Each, considered by itself, is an abstraction. The biologica individual becomes a self in personal existence when and in so far as he steps into living relations with other selves. The social aggregate becomes a fact of human existence in so far as it is built up of respon sible living units of relations. *The fundamental reality is man wit, man.* The essence of human life is what *happens between* man and man. It is man's being-in-community that characterizes and constitutes him as a self. Speech is the sign and means for it; all achievement of the spirit has been stimulated by it. Man is made man by it.

The question what is man cannot be adequately answered by a consideration of substance, or existence, or of self-being as such, but only by a consideration of the essential existential status of the human person and his relations with all otherness. The self belongs neither to the bodily world, the spiritual world, nor the intellectual world as such, yet it belongs to all of them. It is apart from all these "worlds" to which it is bound and without which it could not exist. Buber makes little or nothing of the common distinction between body and soul, yet the "self" or "person" seems to be the unity which embraces both. The person seems to be characterized by such qualities as unity, will, purpose, desire to be expressed, capacity to create and employ speech, responsible freedom, an instinct or capacity for relation and communion, and beyond all this, a certain incommunicable essence.

Buber puts the issue this way: "I become through my relation to the Thou; as I become *I*, I say *Thou*." [408] "The individual entity makes its appearance in virtue of its differentiating itself from other entities. The person makes his appearance in virtue of his dealings with other persons." [409] There is no I taken by itself, but only the *I* of relation. "The *I* is real in virtue of its sharing in reality. The fuller its sharing the more real it becomes." [410] This suggests that some individuals never become real selves because they have never entered into a genuine *I-Thou* relation. Of course no man is pure person and no man pure individual. None is wholly real, and none wholly unreal.[411] Every man lives in the twofold world. But some men, more than others, are so defined by "personhood" that they may be called *persons* who live in the world-of-Thou, deep in reality. The test of a person's reality is his ability to say *Thou* to all otherness—and especially to God. Man most essentially needs God; but, such is the stature of man, God also needs man. Here is a mysticism, indeed, but one that is not remote from the daily concerns of men. The meeting of the *I* and the eternal *Thou* is in this world with its duties and its possibilities: man and God meet in the community. And in that meeting, man becomes most fully a self.

Relation, inclusion, experiencing from the other side, is not merely regulative, but is actually *constitutive*.[412] The self awakes when it meets the *other* as a *Thou*. Thus through the existence of real other-ness, and one's essential relation with otherness, the human being be-comes a self, what, in the context of this essay, we have called a "social self."

NOTES

1. This word is variously spelled: Hasidism, Chasidism, Chassidism. It has seemed to me that the use of "Ch" and the double-s best preserves the Hebrew pronunciation. The term is derived from the name of the "Chassidim" who were opponents of the Hellenizers in pre-Maccabean Palestine, and who were the precursors of the Pharisees, from whose ranks, some scholars main-tain, Jesus himself arose.

2. His grandfather, Salomon Buber, was one of the great figures in the Galician Haskalah, or Enlightenment. He was an erudite scholar, a patron of the arts, and a publisher of rabbinical texts.

3. See T. D. Weldon, *Kant's Critique of Pure Reason* (Oxford: Clarendon Press, 1945); Norman Kemp Smith, *A Commentary to Kant's 'Critique of Pure Reason'* (London: Macmillan, 1930).

4. Buber confesses, in rather startling terms, that as a lad, during a period of great stress when he felt the uncanny problematic of his existence, he was saved from possible madness and suicide by reading Kant's book. (*BMM*, p. 136).

5. It is doubtful, of course, that Kant would have accepted Buber's concept of "realization."

6. One is reminded of Paul Tillich's definition of man as "finite freedom."

7. See *Hasidism*, pp. 104-110; *Mamre*, pp. 108-115.

8. Here in Kant are the seeds of *Pragmatism* and *Existenzphilosophie*.

9. Of course, the idea of the worth of persons is a familiar motif in Jewish and Christian teaching. Cf. analogous concepts in Windelband, Rickert, and Münsterberg concerning the distinction between "idiography" and "nom-othetics."

    Wundt had emphasized the activity of the personality; Fechner had stressed the hierarchical arrangement of personality; Hartman pointed to the tele-ology in personality; Stern had also insisted upon the totality and dynamic character of personality, and upon the difference between *Person* and *Sache*. A. C. Watson, inspired by Mead's lectures, presented a paper, "The Logic of Religion," in which he defined religion as "the social attitude toward the non-human environment," and in which he makes a distinction between the "social" and the "mechanical" attitudes which is remarkably close to Buber's distinction between the I-Thou and the I-It attitudes. (See *The American Journal of Theology*, XX (1916), 81-101, 244-265).

10. See Hans Kohn, *Martin Buber, Sein Werk und Seine Zeit* (Hellerau: Verlag von Jakob Hegner, 1930), pp. 21-23, 59-62, 89. Between 1905-1912 Buber edited a collection of 40 monographs on social philosophy as *Die Gesellschaft*

(Rütten & Loening, Frankfurt a.M.). The foreword to the collection shows Simmel's influence on Buber. Here Buber's own ideas about the living-together of men begin to appear. Buber's expression "Zwischen-menschlichen" was here used for the first time. Here Buber is concerned with the social problem of how and why men act together as they do. Simmel's major work, *Lebensanschauung* (Munich, 1918) places him in the "philosophy of life" school. In this work he outlines his mystical-aesthetic *Lebensphilosophie* of Life-Transcendence. Cf. N. J. Spykman, *The Social Theory of Georg Simmel* (Chicago, 1925).

11. See Martin Buber, *Paths in Utopia,* for a reticent, factual, yet critical history of the Utopian and Marxian Socialist idea. See also Hans Kohn, *op. cit.,* pp. 28f, 96, 188, 200, 204.

12. The most notable group of young Jews who looked to Buber for leadership was the *Bar Kochba* Society in Prague, and included in its membership Hans Kohn and Hugo Bergmann. Max Brod and Franz Kafka were not members, but were close to this circle of friends.

13. For Buber, the myth is no mere metaphor or fable, but "an authentic record of God's revelation on earth," "any narrative of a sensibly real event in which this event is felt and represented as divine." It is the inspired expression, not of an imaginative state of mind or of mere feeling, but of "a real meeting of two Realities." Buber believes that the living force of the Jewish experience of God is not legalistic rigorism and rabbinical dialectic, but the myth which, in the Bible, tells of God's encounters with his people. (See his "Myth in Judaism," the fourth of his seven *Reden über das Judentum;* found in translation in *Commentary,* IX (June 1950), 562-566.

14. See *Ekstatische Confessionen* (Jena: Eugen Diederichs, 1909), a collection of autobiographical accounts of several ancient and modern mystics, with Buber's commentary and interpretation. In a charming autobiographical sketch, *Mein Weg zum Chassidismus* (Rütten & Loening, Frankfurt a.M., 1918), Buber relates his experiences with Chassidic life, the spell of which never left him, even though, as he sadly confesses, the movement was in his time half-degenerate. Buber also found much to admire in Nicolaus Cusa, Meister Eckhardt, and Jakob Boehme, to whom he dedicated one of his first essays.

15. See Martin Buber, *The Prophetic Faith* (New York: Macmillan, 1949).

16. Buber sums up the message of Judaism in several books and articles: *Die Jüdische Bewegung. Gesammelte Aufsätze und Ansprachen. Zweite Folge, 1916-1920.* (Berlin: Jüdischer Verlag): *Reden über das Judentum* (Rütten & Loening, Frankfurt a.M., 1923) which includes *Drei Reden über das Judentum* (1911), *Von Geist des Judentums* (1916), *Der heilige Weg* (1919), and *Cheruth* (1919). See also some of the essays now available in English in *Mamre,* in *Israel and the World* and in *Hasidism.*

17. *Die Chassidischen Bücher* (Hellerau: Verlag Jakob Hegner, 1928), p. 658.

18. See *Die Geschichten des Rabbi Nachman* (Rütten & Loening, Frankfurt a.M., 1906); *Die Legende des Baal Schem* (1908); *Der grosse Maggid und seine Nachfolge* (1922). In *Die Chassidischen Bücher* Buber has gathered together the three works listed above, plus *Mein Weg zum Chassidismus* and *Das*

Verborgene Licht (1924). In 1947–48 Schocken Books, Inc., New York, brought out in two volumes an English translation of some of this material under the title *Tales of the Hasidim*. See also *Jewish Mysticism, and the Legends of Baalshem*, trs. Lucy Cohen (London and Toronto, Dent & Sons, 1931); *Mamre* (Melbourne Univ. Press, 1946); *Hasidism* (New York: Philosophical Library, 1948). See also Jacob S. Minkin, *The Romance of Hassidism* (New York: Macmillan, 1936); Lewis I. Newman, *The Hasidic Anthology* (New York: Bloch Pub. Co., 1944).

19. *The New Palestine*, XIV (Feb. 10, 1928), 165. The Chassidic lore and legend and myth were threatened with oblivion and loss until Buber became the interpreter and evangelist of this legendary material. J. L. Perez is usually credited with first re-discovering this fountain of fantasy and wisdom, but he wrote only in Yiddish and Hebrew. Others followed—Berditchevsky, Zeitlin, Agnon, Dubow—treating of different phases of the subject. But credit for westernizing Chassidism is due to no other man more than to Buber. No other writer has treated it with such devoted care, illuminating insight, and beauty of color and diction.

20. Chassidism was not, however, an isolated phenomenon. It appears rather as a unique expression of the *Zeitgeist,* along with Protestant pietism, Catholic spiritualism, and romantic humanism. Baal-Shem-Tov was a contemporary of Count von Zinzendorf, the patron of the Moravian Brudergemeinde. They gave to the world much the same message of constant and mutual relations between God and man. Devotion to God and personal union with Him; the cultivation of mystical personal religion; belief in the presence of the holy spirit; the blending of order with liberty, individualism with community; a strong spirit of brotherhood; a joyous spiritual fervor which found expression in singing and loving deeds: these were common elements of the piety found in both the Chassidic and the Brethern communities.

The 18th century witnessed the rise of many such pietistic and evangelical movements in widely separated lands. Moravian influence aided the Wesleyan revival in England. There were similar pietistic movements led by Hauge in Norway and Rosenius in Sweden. The Quakers, the Brethern, the Mennonites, the Amish and other sects founded their settlements in America during the same period. Revivalism swept over America in the late 18th and early 19th centuries, having been first fanned into flame by Jonathan Edwards and George Whitfield. See *Die Chassidischen Bücher,* esp. pp. 657-59 and *Hasidism* for extended study.

21. "Nie hat in Europa eine grosse Volksgemeinde—nicht ein Orden Abgeschiedener, nicht ein Bruderschaft Auserwählter, sondern eine Volksgemeinde in all ihrer Geistigen und sozialen Vielfältigkeit, in all ihrer Gemischtheit—so das ganze Leben als eine Einheit auf das innerlich Erkannte gestellt." *Die Chassidischen Bücher,* p. 659. Here was not a cult, but a culture.

22. The most scrupulous observance of the 613 laws of the *Taryag Mitzvoth* was no substitute for the sanctifying of everyday life. In this sense, Chassidic pansacramentalism was "an attempt to rescue the sacramental life of man from being killed by facile routine." The release and fulfillment of the holy in each object and act is accomplished by the whole man who offers him-

self completely and directs his whole life toward God. *Mamre,* pp. 135-48; also *Hasidism,* pp. 131-144.

23. *Die Chassidischen Bücher,* p. 470; *Hasidism,* p. 100f; *Mamre,* p. 105, *passim; Menorah Journal,* XVII (1929), 52.

24. See *Jewish Mysticism, and the Legends of Baalshem.* See also Minkin, *The Romance of Hassidism,* Chap. IV, esp. pp. 92ff.

25. *Die Chassidischen Bücher,* p. 658.

26. A cardinal doctrine in late Kabbalism is that man is responsible for the fate of God in the world; in other words, man has influence upon cosmic and eternal events. The release of the *Shekinah* (literally, the indwelling divine sparks or splendor which permeate the world) can be brought about by man. It is man who accomplishes the redemptive work of re-uniting the Holy God with his world-indwelling glory. Man's action for God's sake is "messianic" action.

27. *Mamre,* p. 149. The nature of Chassidism, says Buber, is not to be found in a "teaching" but in a mode of life which had to be translated into a teaching. Therefore, the Chassidic legend is our main source of understanding it. So Buber writes (*Mamre,* p. 152), "The theoretical literature is the gloss, the legend is the text." Much of Buber's life work has been to read, interpret, and retell this treasure-trove of legendary material. Chassid legend, says Buber, is the myth of *I* and *Thou,* of man's need for God and of God's search for man.

28. See G. G. Scholem, *Trends in Jewish Mysticism* (New York: Schocken Books, 1941); S. Spiegel, *Hebrew Reborn* (London: Ernest Benn, Ltd., 1931); *The Jewish Encyclopedia,* IX, pp. 630-751. The unique achievement of Chassidism, says Scholem, was the founding of a religious community on the basis of the paradox of the mystic living in the community—"To live among ordinary men and yet be alone with God." The mystic-leader centered himself in the community and taught his secret of holy living to all men. Buber saw something of this same ideal in the Society of Friends, a society living in unity and sanctity. Many parallels are also to be found in the Third Order of Franciscans which was an attempt to carry the gospel of love and service into the domain of home and marketplace. They were pledged only to penetrate their lives with a passion for Christ, to live with joy and enthusiasm, and to make of life a radiant blessing. (See *The Little Flowers of St. Francis,* trs. T. Okey. New York: E. P. Dutton & Co.).

29. *Die Chassidischen Bücher,* p. 659.

30. See G. G. Scholem, *Major Trends in Jewish Mysticism,* p. 337.

31. Buber, *Mamre,* p. 164.

32. *Ibid.,* p. 166. See also *Hasidism,* pp. 17, 19.

33. Buber, *Tales of the Hasidim* (Early Masters), pp. 6, 8. See *Hasidism,* pp. 19-20; also *Mamre,* pp. 166-67. It should be noted that not all Hebrew scholars are as sympathetic to Chassidism and Zaddikism as Buber is. See e.g., Solomon Schechter, *Studies in Judaism* (Philadelphia, 1896), pp. 41, 43 for a typical criticism. And Buber himself (*Mamre,* p. 68) admits that by the middle of the 19th century it had become a numerically power-

ful, but spiritually dead and morally degenerative, movement. Still its ideas can live again.

34. Buber, in Introduction to *Tales of the Hasidim;* cf. also *Hasidism,* pp. 3-4; *Mamre,* p. 151; *IATW,* p. 82.

35. It is in this connection, I think, that we can understand Nietzsche's appeal for Buber. Despite the dark destructiveness of Nietzsche's influence, and despite the deep cleavage between Buber and Nietzsche on most points, they did share a romantic feeling for the creative potentialities in man. Nietzsche sang in celebration, as did Whitman, of the beautiful, vigorous, honest, willed freedom of the individual man. Buber had known these spiritual manly heroes among the Zaddikim. Buber could never condone the cult of the sword or the blond beast; but when the "superman" was translated into the realm of the spirit, Buber found meaning in what Nietzsche was saying. Nietzsche had called Jesus a "freier Geist." Buber had known such "free spirits" among the Zaddikim. But the Zaddikim knew something which Nietzsche's superman did not know: "Each life a life in itself, but as such it forms the community. . . ." "(The Zaddik) was surrounded by a community that lived a brotherly life, and who could live in this way because there was a leading person in their midst who brought each one nearer to the other by bringing them all nearer to that in which they believed." *(Mamre,* pp. 151-53. See also Hans Kohn, *op. cit.,* pp. 26-27, 36; *BMM,* pp. 73-78, 148-56). For a critical yet appreciative reappraisal of Nietzsche, see "A Symposium on Nietzsche's Centenary," in *The Journal of the History of Ideas,* VI, No. 3, 1945; Roger Hazelton, "Was Nietzsche an Anti-Christian?" in *The Journal of Religion,* XXII (1942), 63-88; E. S. Brightman, "How Much Truth in Nietzsche?" in *The Christian Century,* LXV (1948), 593-95. For a more critical estimate, see G. Morgan, *What Nietzsche Means* (Cambridge: Harvard University Press, 1941); K. Jaspers, *Nietzsche und das Christentum* (Hameln: Verlag F. Seifert, 1946); Crane Brinton, *Nietzsche* (Cambridge: Harvard University Press, 1941); Walter A. Kaufman, *Nietzsche* (Princeton University Press, 1950).

36. See Hans Kohn, *op. cit.,* pp. 81-82; cf. also Georg Koch, in *Die Kreatur,* II, No. 3, pp. 249-280.

37. Buber, *Tales of the Hasidim,* pp, 2, 10; *Hasidism,* pp. 34ff; *IATW,* p. 194.

38. *Mamre,* pp. 2, 7, *passim.* See also *IATW,* pp. 48, 49, 85f, 14, 18.

39. *IATW,* pp. 13, *passim; Hasidism,* pp. 143-44; *Mamre,* pp. 1, 88, 147.

40. *IATW,* p. 17.

41. *Idem.*

42. *Ibid.,* p. 15.

43. In a sense, this is the central theme of *Mamre,* although certain of the essays and passages deal with this problem more specifically, e.g., pp. 18-29, 67-89, 99-121, 153-175. Cf. *Hasidism,* pp. 60-94, 95-116, 6-33.

44. *Mamre,* pp. 10ff.

45. *Ibid.,* pp. 11, 141-42, *passim; Hasidism,* pp. 137ff; *Eclipse of God,* pp. 48, 120, 162, 175f.

46. *Mamre,* p. 22; *IATW,* p. 32.

47. *Mamre,* p. 38f; *IATW,* p. 71f.

48. *IATW*, pp. 21-24; *Mamre*, pp. 11-12. Buber interperts Yahweh's declaration to Moses, "I am that I am," as really meaning, "I shall be there as I there shall be." That is to say: "You need not cast a spell over me, for I am there, I am with you. . . . as I always choose to be with you." With the meaning of "I am that I am" *(ehji asher ehji)* Buber deals at length in his books *Königtun Gottes* and *Moses.*

49. *IATW*, pp. 30, 34; *Mamre*, pp. 20, 25.

50. *IATW*, p. 26.

51. *Idem.*

52. *Ibid.*, p. 27.

53. *Ibid.*, p. 25.

54. *Ibid.*, p. 24; *Mamre*, pp. 13, 141-48; *Hasidism*, pp. 137-44. Many of these same basic themes of Jewish faith are also considered in *At The Turning.*

55. *Mamre*, p. 145; *Hasidism*, p. 141.

56. *Idem.* Buber admits that there is a mystery about the unity of contraries in dialogue. But that does not disturb him, for he writes, "According to the logical conception of truth only one of two contraries can be true, but in the reality of the lived life they are interlocked." *Mamre*, p. 6; *IATW*, p. 17.

57. *Mamre*, p. 13; *IATW*, p. 24.

58. *Idem.* If I read him aright, I find in Berdyaev a similar refusal to denigrate the value of man, as he believes is done in the Anselmic jurid'cal doctrine of redemption. Redemption, for Berdyaev, is not a legal transaction, but a transforming process. It is a work of love, the goal of which is the transformation of the human into the divine-human. It is a dual, reciprocal process, in which free men may share. (See e.g., Berdyaev, *Freedom and the Spirit*, p. 172; *Slavery and Freedom*, pp. 27-28, 47-48).

59. *Mamre*, p. 147; *Hasidism*, p. 144.

60. *Mamre*, p. 25; *IATW*, p. 35.

61. *Mamre*, p. 148, *passim.*

62. *Mamre*, p. 173; *Hasidism*, p. 26f.

63. *Mamre*, pp. 28-29, 113; Cf., *IATW*, p. 37; *I and Thou*, p. 82; *Hasidism*, pp. 26, 109.

64. *Mamre*, p. 113; see also *Ibid.*, pp. 112, 28, 21, 23. An even more ecstatic (and some would say dangerously loose) "hymn to man" is sung by Berdyaev. Eastern Orthodoxy generally has made much of "theosis" and the "theandric" personality. Iraneaeus, the Eastern Fathers, and many of the mystics have employed similar terms and doctrines. Matthew Spinka, in his study of *Nicolas Berdyaev*, records that even Luther used them. Certainly Berdyaev makes much of theosis, deification, God-manhood, theanthropy, in his attempt to justify man. And he criticizes both Eastern and Western Churches for not stressing the duty of the redeemed man to help redeem the social order. (See, *The Destiny of Man*, pp. 307, 377; *Slavery and Freedom*, p. 45; *Spirit and Reality*, p. 149).

65. *Mamre*, p. 23; *IATW*, p. 33.

66. *Mamre*, pp. 4, 7, 113; *IATW*, pp. 16, 18.

67. *Mamre*, p. 114; *Hasidism*, p. 110.

68. *Hasidism*, pp. 111, 116. In Buber's idea of "filled time" there are clear resemblances to Tillich's conception of *Kairos* in which Tillich expresses both the negative meaning of historical relativism and the positive significance and responsibility of each moment.

69. *Ibid.*, p. 110.

70. *Ibid.*, p. 108.

71. See G. G. Scholem, *op. cit.*, pp. 15f. See also, *Mamre*, pp. 4, 101, 125ff; *IATW*, p. 16; *Hasidism*, pp. 96, 121ff.

72 Scholem, *op. cit.*, pp. 17-18.

73. *IATW*, p. 21.

74. *Ibid.*, p. 16.

75. It is significant, and no accident, that in the Hebrew religion there is little place for images, statues, and the religious art which adorns so many Christian, especially Roman Catholic, churches.

76. See e.g. in the Introduction to *Jüdische Künstler* (1904) and in the Introduction to *Die Geschichten das Rabbi Nachman* (1906).

77. The Greek, avers Buber, *sees* things in terms of space, form, pattern, pictorial representation. For the Oriental not the plastic arts and pictorial symbol, but music and speech appeal to him. He lives in time, in movement. There is always something beyond, always a becoming, a messianic age yet to be achieved. And God is not grasped in sensory data; He is undefinable and inexpressible. *Peake's Commentary of the Bible*, p. 172, expresses the view (supported by Robertson Smith, Davidson, Driver, McNeile, and Peake) that the name of God (*Ehyeh asher Ehyeh*, Ex. 3:14, usually translated "I am that I am") is probably more correctly interpreted as "I will be what I will be," thus denoting a becoming, activity, possibility, inexhaustibility, rather than the static Ideal Being of the Greeks. Cf. also Buber, *The Prophetic Faith*, p. 117.

78. *Die Rede, Die Lehre und Das Lied.* Drei Beispiele. (Insel-Verlag, Leipzig, 1920); *Ekstatische Konfessionen;* also *Daniel* (Insel-Verlag, Leipzig, 1913).

79. See Hans Kohn, *Martin Buber*, pp. 70-74.

80. See *Legende des Baal Schem*, p. vi ff; cf. also Hans Kohn, *op. cit.*, p. 73.

81. See *Legende des Baal Schem*, p. iii; *Commentary*, IX, 1950, 562-66.

82. *Die Chassidischen Bücher*, p. xii.

83. *Mamre*, pp. 2-8; *IATW*, pp. 14-19.

84. Buber has no monopoly on this thesis. The "philosophy of speech" had its source in Feuerbach; and prior to the publication of *Ich und Du* the same basic ideas had been written down by Ferdinand Ebner, *Das Wort und die Geistigen Realitäten* (1921), and by Eugen Rosenstock-Huessy in his letters to Franz Rosenzweig in 1916. Rosenzweig also formulated cognate ideas in "Das neue Denken," *Kleinere Schriften* (Berlin, 1937), *Der Stern der Erlösung* (Frankfurt a.M., 1921), and his *Briefe* (Berlin, 1935). Rosenstock's *Sprachlehre* of 1916 was printed in 1923 as *Aufwandte Seelenbunde*. Hints of his emerging speech-philosophy had early been suggested by Buber in his *Daniel*, in some of his addresses on Judaism, and the Chassidic writings. See also *Brief über das Wesen der Sprache*, in the communications of the International Institute for Philosophy, in Amsterdam, I, March 1918. (Ver-

lag P. Nordhoff, Groningen, 1918). See also "The Letters of Franz Rosen-
zweig and Eugen Rosenstock-Huessy" by Dorothy Emmet, *Journal of
Religion*, XXV (1945), 261-73; also the article by Alexander Altmann,
Ibid., XXIV (1944), 258-70.

85. Cf. Mead's notion of thought as inner conversation. In his discussion of
"false prophets" (*The Prophetic Faith*, p. 179f) Buber points out the dangers
of subjectivism in inner thought. It is easy to lose touch with "reality."
It is easy to listen to the subconscious "wish-deity" instead of the True God.
Thought seems not to require a hearer; but speech does, and thus points to
a relation between a man and something or someone beyond himself. But
even thought is not pure monologue; there are elements of dialogue here.
Thought requires ultimately another, a hearer. (Cf. "Dialogue" in *BMM*,
p. 26).

86. Here Buber strikes the note which he is anxious for his generation to hear,
namely, the problem of community. The little quatrain appears in German as:

> Wir sind die Laute, die der Urmund spricht,
>
> Und doch sind wir nur Wörter, Worte nicht.
>
> Wann werden wir zu Worten, die sich fügen
>
> Zu Einem Satz, dem Urspruch zu genügen?

87. See *Zwiesprache*, in *Die Kreatur*, III, No. 3, 1929; *BMM*, pp. 1-39.

88. Quoted by Hans Kohn, *op. cit.*, p. 241f from an undesignated source.

89. From *Daniel,* quoted by Hans Kohn, *op. cit.*, p. 134.

90. See e.g., *Hasidism*, pp. 32-33, 130.

91. *Daniel. Gespräche von der Verwirklichung.* (Leipzig: Insel-Verlag, 1913).
From about the same period, and dealing with the nature of the religious
life, come such other works as *Ekstatische Konfessionen* (Jena, 1909), *Reden
und Gleichnisse des Tschuang-Tse* (Leipzig, 1910), and *Die Rede, die Lehre,
und das Lied.* Drei Beispiele (Leipzig, 1920).

92. *Ich und Du* (Leipzig, 1923). *I and Thou* (Edinburgh, 1937).

93. This may seem to be an egregious instance of the "pathetic fallacy," but
surely less harmful than the same fallacy in reverse—treating persons as
things. A persistent animism remains a fact of human experience: "personality" in a more or less vague sense is commonly imputed by men to the
objects of their attention and desire. The poet and the mystic have an intensified consciousness of the subjective integrity of things such that they
can be taken up into the world of Thou. It takes the seer, the poet, like
William Blake "To see a world in a grain of sand. . . . And Eternity in
an hour." At any rate, Buber would reply that our fallible senses have
to go "beyond the broken arc" of our sight and sound "to grasp the flying
mantle of reality."

94. Buber declares with Bergson that since man's "knowledge" (orientation) is
gained by separating the part from the whole, by abstraction, it is not true
knowledge (actualization); since man's action generally expresses only a part
of himself, it is not true action, which must be the action of the whole
being, and therefore, as for Lao-Tse, non-action, or better, not action against,
but *a living towards*.

95. *Daniel*, p. 42.

96. *Ibid.*, p. 37.

97. Cf. the experience of numerous religious persons who have articulated their experience. Kierkegaard, for example, with whom Buber felt a deep kinship, associated *Angst* with man's religious response. Pascal, in an agony of spirit, felt man's exposed and uncanny position in the face of the Infinite. Rudolf Otto describes the awe-ful feeling of the "mysterium tremendum" as central to the idea of the holy. There are numerous parallel accounts in the Old Testament and in other sacred literature. Many students of the psychology of religion (Leuba, James, McDougall, Ribot) have stressed this point. The removal of the horror or fear, the sense of assurance following the dread, is also a familiar phenomenon. Awe and fear gradually turn into fascination, then into trust and love—casting out fear.

98. *Daniel*, p. 82.

99. Buber is here referring to the Kabbalistic and Chassidic notion that the Supreme Being can be actualized only through man. It is man's destiny to help in the process of creation and redemption through appropriate activity in the world. See supra, p. 126.

100. *Daniel*, p. 119.

101. *Ibid.*, p. 97. Buber feels that the Jewish soul is particularly sensitive to this tension. The "divided" soul, which all students of the psychology of religion have described, appears to Buber to be especially characteristic of the Jewish soul, thereby accounting for the Jewish genius for religion.

102. Many religious persons have this feeling for the inevitable dialectical and paradoxical nature of religion. In a sense religion worships two Gods: the God of *isness* (reality, power, law) and the God of *oughtness* (moral ideality, goodness, love). It is the character of high religion that neither side of this dynamic polarity can be completely established or surrendered. Only through loving fellowship with God and man can a living unity be achieved.

103. A suggestive analogy might be found in the field of forces in vector physics.

104. This account of a fundamental duality within the soul reminds one of similar instances reported by William James, James B. Pratt and others, as well as by the mystics themselves. Cf. also the more recent testimony of the analysts and psychotherapists concerning a fundamental duality within the human personality.

105. Buber, for himself, does not call it mysticism.

106. It is probably fair to say that Existentialism has its roots in the Romanticism of the 18th and 19th centuries. And in Buber there are echoes of Schelling's aestheticism, Bergson's intuitionism, and the voluntaristic ontologies of Fichte, Schopenhauer, and Nietzsche.

107. Cf. Schweitzer's doctrine of "reverence for life."

108. Albert Schweitzer, *Indian Thought and Its Development* (New York: Henry Holt & Co., 1936), p. 264.

109. See W. P. Montague, *Ways of Knowing* (New York: Macmillan, 1925), Chap. II, esp. p. 57; also E. W. Lyman, *The Meaning and Truth of Religion* (New York: Scribner's Sons, 1933), pp. 184-89, also Chaps. IX, V; *Journal of John Woolman* (Everyman's Library), pp. 21-29, *passim*.

110. Eckhardt was condemned by the papal Curia for pantheism, and since then Eckhardt's "pantheism" has been a subject for exhaustive study. (See e.g.,

Rudolf Otto, *Mysticism East and West* (New York: Macmillan, 1932); Raymond B. Blakney, tr. *Meister Eckhardt* (New York: Harper, 1941); and N. Berdyaev, *The Divine and the Human* (London: Geoffrey Bles, 1949), esp. pp. 26-27. Otto thinks that Eckhardt was not a pantheist nor a gnostic; Berdyaev, on the other hand, charges Eckhardt with anti-personalism, with denying the reality and value of created beings. The fact is that Eckhardt himself provides much conflicting evidence which results in the misunderstanding. Eckhardt does seem to argue for both the creatureliness of man and for an identification of man with God.

111. *I and Thou*, p. 79.

112. *DFE*, pp. 29-45; *BMM*, pp. 14, 116-17.

113. *Commentary*, IX (1950), 566.

114. Martin Buber, *The Menorah Journal*, XVII (1929), 52.

115. *DFE*, p. 16; also *BMM*, p. 43; *Eclipse of God*, pp. 127-8.

116. Cf. C. A. Bennett, *A Philosophical Study of Mysticism* which expounds a somewhat similar point of view. See also *BMM*, pp. 13f.

117. *BMM*, p. 14.

118. See *Zwiesprache* (1929); *Die Frage an den Einzelnen* (1936); *Was ist der Mensch?* (1929); *Rede über das Erzieherische* (1926). These essays are now available in English in the book *Between Man and Man*. Buber regards these as a "completion" of *Ich und Du*. Other recent works which carry forward and apply the same basic themes and purposes in a specifically Jewish framework are the miscellany of essays and lectures collected under the title *Israel and the World* (1948), and *At The Turning* (1952).

119. As a philosopher of the personal, Buber stands in close and deep kinship with Berdyaev, the best known representative of the Russian religious renascence.

120. This persistent animism, the ascribing of "intention" to events in nature, is familiar to all students of the history of religion. In this instinctive reaction to events and objects in nature, Bergson finds the origin of primitive religion. Another famous instance of this phenomenon is the description by William James of his reactions to an earthquake in California. Taken by surprise and yet fascinated by the elemental fury of nature, James apprehended the earthquake as a personal power, shouting: "Go to it!" Hocking also reports similar phenomena.

121. *I and Thou*, pp. 8, 15, *passim*.

122. *I and Thou*, p. 28; cf. also *Eclipse of God*, pp. 127-8.

123. *I and Thou*, p. 63.

124. One is reminded of the great paradox of Jesus and of his description of the "narrow way," Luke 17:33; Matt. 7:12-14. Cf. *Eclipse of God*, p. 128.

125. *I and Thou*, p. 63, *passim*. We have already noted that in *Daniel* Buber had suggested a twofold separation of life and the world into the spheres of "orientation" and "actualization." Whereas in *Daniel* this separation was largely theoretical, aesthetic, and ethical, here it takes on a metaphysical character.

126. It should be remarked here that Buber himself does not use the term "social" to describe or characterize this self-system.

127. *I and Thou*, pp. 3, 31.

128. *I and Thou*, p. 3. This is the point at which we note a close kinship with Berdyaev, who posits a similar dualism or polarity of spiritual freedom and objectified necessity. Berdyaev places the subject, the only real center of existence, over against the world of objects. Existence is prior to being; existentialism has primacy over ontology. (See his book *Solitude and Society*, the original title of which is *I and the World of Objects*). Berdyaev's central thesis is that personality, the existent subject, is primary; whereas being, the ontological object, is secondary. Or in other words, being is a product of creative thought, a rationalized concept; existence creates essence. The subject is free; the object is contingent and determined. Such considerations clearly place Berdyaev among the philosophers of *existenz*. For a full discussion of Berdyaev's existentialism, see M. Spinka, *Nicolas Berdyaev* (Philadelphia: Westminster Press, 1950, Ch. V); cf. Berdyaev, *Slavery and Freedom*, p. 76.

129. *I and Thou*, p. 3.

130. Cf. Mead's similar conception of religion as extending social relations to the universe at large, supra, p. 86, and A. C. Watson, *The American Journal of Theology*, XX (1916), 81-101. Dewey, too, has a place for "imagination" in relation of the actual, to the idea. But there is no place in Dewey's thought for a genuine "dialogue" between man and what Dewey cautiously calls God. See *A Common Faith*, p. 50, *passim*.

131. *I and Thou*, p. 6.

132. *Ibid.*, pp. 7-9.

133. *Ibid.*, p. 3.

134. *Ibid.*, p. 9.

135. A man will find his wife and children to be very awkward and intractable equations, and very difficult to predict and control on the basis of dependable laws.

136. *Ibid.*, p. 9.

137. *Ibid.*, p. 34.

138. *Ibid.*, pp. 33, 17.

139. *Ibid.*, p. 99.

140. *Ibid*, p. 33.

141. *Ibid.*, p. 79.

142. *Ibid.*, pp. 32, 33.

143. In a genuine community, responsibility can be exercised by the *We*, as well as by an *I*. See, e.g., the "we-psychology" of Dr. Fritz Kunkel as set forth in *How Character Develops* (New York: Scribner's Sons, 1940). But even in the "We," I am not relieved of my own responsible decision. Cf. also the concepts of "Gesellschaft" and "Gemeinschaft" in Tönnies, Landauer, and Simmel, which are here preserved in Buber's thought.

144. *BMM*, p. 78. See also *Good and Evil* (Scribner's Sons, 1953).

145. *I and Thou*, p. 34.

146. In this connection it is instructive to note the "diagnoses" of our times by such writers as Basil Lederer, Karl Mannheim, and Peter Drucker.

147. It appears to me that in this matter Buber over-simplifies the case. It is no doubt true that we cannot catch God in definitions and logical cate-

gories; and yet we do and must make the attempt at rational analysis, exposition, and argument (even though with fear and trembling, knowing that we attempt the impossible) or give up the enterprise of philosophy and *theologia*. Theologians who speak most confidently of the "hidden God" manage somehow to be privy to enough knowledge of God to enable them to write many heavy tomes on the subject. Moreover, although in the end it may be futile and blasphemous of men to attempt to "use" God, it is yet a fact that men have always committed the error and sin of regarding God as a sort of cosmic Public Utility upon which men might draw for the achievement of human ends. Still, men can and must call upon God for help—if God is also Person, if religion is dialogue, and if there is truth and meaning in petitionary prayer.

Even the religious person is incapable of such a radical overcoming of the I-It relation as to live constantly in the I-Thou relation with God. Just as on the human or physical level, the *Thou* of God becomes someone who is talked about in the third person, from whom we want something, or whom we would like in some sense to incorporate into our I-orbit. Here, it would seem, as in the human sphere, "The particular *Thou,* after the relational event has run its course, is bound to become an It."

148. *I and Thou,* p. 75.

149. Buber appears to part company with Barth at this point: for Buber God is "wholly Other" and the "holy Other" but He is also wholly Present.

150. The *Divine-Human Encounter,* whose German title is *Wahrheit als Begegnung.* (Philadelphia: Westminster Press, 1943).

151. *I and Thou,* p. 11.

152. *Ibid.,* p. 4.

153. *I and Thou,* pp. 62-63; Cf. *Eclipse of God,* p. 128.

154. *IATW,* pp. 78ff.

155. *I and Thou,* p. 65.

156. This, of course, is what we expect and demand from a science; but it is also the "world of It" and therefore misses the deeper wisdom of life.

157. *I and Thou,* p. 4. Cf. Emil Brunner, *op. cit.,* 85-88.

158. *I and Thou,* pp. 34, 38, *passim.* This is the meaning of "objectification" or depersonalization in Berdyaev's terminology, the treating of a person as a means, in Kant's.

159. Cf. Bergson's theory of knowledge, and his consequent demand for and exercise of a different type of awareness of reality which lies outside the operations of a sensory observation and scientific reasoning. A similar stress on mystical intuition is found in the thought of such recent thinkers as John Oman (*The Natural and the Supernatural,* pp. 120f, 142, 246f); Dean W. R. Inge (*God and the Astronomers,* pp. 174, 177, 229, 247); W. E. Hocking (*The Meaning of God in Human Experience,* pp. 95ff, 233); E. W. Lyman (*The Meaning and Truth of Religion,* pp. 165, 86, 112, 179, 183, 186, 190). It is worth noting also in this connection that many modern "theistic naturalists" (Whitehead, Bergson, Smuts, Morgan, Alexander, Wieman, etc.) make some provision for a kind of non-scientific, non-rational knowledge. Even Dewey introduces "imagination" as an appropriate approach to reality. See *The*

Quest for Certainty, Ch. X; *Experience and Nature,* p. 62; *A Common Faith,* p. 43.

160. *Ich und Du,* p. 5.
161. *I and Thou,* p. 32.
162. *Ibid.,* p. 33.
163. *Ibid.,* p. 40.
164. *Ibid.,* p. 43.
165. *Ibid.,* p. 44.
166. *Ibid.,* p. 46.
167. Cf. Mead's similar criticism of mechanistic materialism and the methodological necessity of science to reduce the world to a "knife-edged present." Supra, p. 53f.
168. *I and Thou,* pp. 51-57.
169. *BMM,* p. 78.
170. *I and Thou,* pp. 51, 53, 54. Cf. *IATW,* pp. 43-44.
171. *I and Thou,* p. 4.
172. *Ibid.,* pp. 75, 100.
173. *Ibid.,* p. 5.
174. *I and Thou,* pp. 15, 17, 18. Cf. H. H. Farmer, *God and Men,* esp. Chap. II, "The World of Persons." See also John Macmurray, *The Structure of Religious Experience* (Yale University Press, 1936) where he argues that religion has its springs in the relations between persons and must be tested in the practical world of persons.
175. *I and Thou,* pp. 11, 76.
176. *Ibid.,* pp. 9-11.
177. *Ibid.,* p. 62.
178. *Ibid.,* p. 65f. Buber remarks for example: How powerful, how lovely, how self-evident and legitimate is the I of Socrates, the I of Goethe, the I of Jesus.
179. *Ibid.,* p. 44.
180. *I and Thou,* p. 45.
181. Was it not Dostoevsky who said, "If thou love each thing, thou wilt perceive the mystery of God in all"?
182. *I and Thou,* p. 46. An echo of this same sentiment and point of view is found in Fritz Kunkel, *Let's Be Normal,* p. 125. "Love would release us from imprisonment in our ego, but how is it to come when we demand always that our partner release us? We hope for release from being-loved, and that is the exact opposite of loving. We even expect that the other release us from our ego without offending the ego, that he kill the dragon without hurting him, that he awaken the sleeping beauty without disturbing her sleep. And as long as he cannot do that, we say, 'There is no more love on earth.' "
183. *I and Thou,* p. 103.
184. *Idem.*
185. *Jeremiah* 23: 16-28; *The Prophetic Faith,* p. 179.
186. *I and Thou,* pp. 59-60.
187. *Ibid.,* p. 3.
188. *Ibid.,* pp. 8, 78.
189. *Ibid.,* p. 78.

190. *I and Thou*, p. 8.

191. *Ibid.*, p. 12.

192. *Ibid.*, p. 13.

193. *Ibid.*, p. 12.

194. *Ibid.*, p. 13.

195. We have earlier referred to Mead's dependence upon Bergson for his emphasis on freedom, flow, novelty, and creativity. Mead was busily rereading Bergson in the light of his own "philosophy of the present" at the time of his death. See *MT*, pp. 291, 325; *PP, passim*.

196. *I and Thou*, pp. 100, 115, 75.

197. Cf. H. H. Farmer, *op. cit.*, pp. 37-40; John Macmurray, *op. cit.*

198. *I and Thou*, p 58.

199. *Ibid.*, p. 9.

200. *I and Thou*, pp. 30-31.

201. Buber does not say so, but I think he might better say, "responsibility *to* a *Thou*." What he means is that each person must simply take his stand in relation to the other, needing him, surrendering to him, but not fussing over him—responsible, in a sense, *to God*, for him whom I meet.

202. *Ibid.*, p. 14. Love in the I-Thou is not unlike St. Paul's *agape*. There is nothing in the universe which we might not meet with some form of *agape*. Cf. the words of Helen Wodehouse (*Philosophy*, XX, 1945, 25). Cf. also *I and Thou*, pp. 59-60.

203. *Ibid.*, p. 75.

204. *Ibid.*, pp. 6, 75; also pp. 109, 110, 115.

205. *Ibid.*, p. 95f.

206. A similar general argument is set forth by John Oman in *Grace and Personality* (London: Cambridge University Press, 1931).

207. *I and Thou*, p. 79.

208. *Idem.*

209. *Ibid.*, pp. 6f; 101f.

210. *Ibid.*, p. 6.

211. *Ibid.*, pp. 101, 75.

212. *Ibid.*, p. 102.

213. Cf. Mead's belief that children, savages, and poets take a complete social attitude toward physical objects.

214. See Codrington, *The Melanesians*. Cf. Buber, *I and Thou*, pp. 18ff. See also Pinard de la Boullaye, *L'Etude Comparee des Religions* (Paris: G. Beauchesne, 1925); E. B. Tylor, *Primitive Culture* (New York: Holt, 1889); R. R. Marett, *The Threshold of Religion* (London: Methuen, 1914).

215. *I and Thou*, p. 20.

216. Cf. the fresh, direct greetings of certain savages: "I see you!" or "Smell me!" *Ibid.*, p. 18.

217. *I and Thou*, p. 25. Fritz Kunkel describes this stage of human development as growing out of the "primitive We" of the mother-child connection, through the break in that We (weaning), into the training period which should issue in the "maturing We" of adult relation. Cf. John Macmurray, *op. cit.*, pp. 31-34.

218. *I and Thou*, p. 27.

219. *Ibid.*, p. 28.

220. *Ibid.*, p. 26.

221. *Ibid.*, p. 27.

222. *Ibid.*, pp. 23f, 38-39.

223. *Ibid.*, p. 22.

224. In Mead, and in Royce, we noted this same process of selfhood arising from contrast-effect and "reflected appraisals" in a social matrix. In producing "social individuals" society produces selves with an even higher consciousness of *self*, self-will, even rebellious self-assertion. Cf. also Dilthey's notion that the certitude of the independence of self and other comes through resistance and opposition, and leads on to recognition and respect.

225. *I and Thou*, p. 23.

226. From *Zwiesprache*; see *Between Man and Man*, p. 23. See also his other youthful experiences with the tree, the lake, supra, pp. 132ff. I suspect that any lad who has loved a dog or a horse could confirm this story and this experience of a Thou-relation. Equally typical childish cruelties might also be accounted for in this context, although Buber never considers that possibility. He does say that genuine hate is closer to real relation than indifference.

227. *I and Thou*, p. 98.

228. *BMM*, p. 37. One recalls the story of Androcles and the Lion, and the now familiar instances in which the Air Force pilots gave affectionate personal names to their planes, and spoke with feeling about the "gremlins" which tampered with them.

229. *DFE*, pp. 52-53; cf. *BMM*, p. 61.

230. Karl Löwith's term. See his *Das Individuum in der Rolle des Mitmenschen*; p. 48f; also 71, 100, 102, 128.

231. E. Brunner, *The Divine-Human Encounter*, p. 85.

232. *Ibid.*, p. 86.

233. *Op. cit.*, pp. 69-70.

234. *BMM*, pp. 95-7.

235. *ZS*, p. 1. See also *BMM*, p. 1.

236. Cf. C. G. Jung, *Religion and Psychology* where the results of an investigation of religious dreams are reported. Jung assumes that a religious motive is the cause of this kind of dream, especially when it occurs in a series.

237. *Supra*, pp. 127-30.

238. See Franz Rosenzweig, *Letters*, p. 712. Cf. also Eugen Rosenstock-Huessy, in *Journal of Religion*, XXV (1945), 130-34.

239. *ZS*; see *BMM*, p. 3ff. Another recent author, in writing of his father, remarked: "You didn't have to talk much to visit with him."

240. *BMM*, pp. 6-8. In this connection one is reminded of the charming legend in *Little Flowers of St. Francis* according to which St. Louis, clad as a poor pilgrim, knocked at the door of a Franciscan house and asked for Brother Giles. A hint from the keeper of the convent revealed to Giles the secret that his visitor was no less a person than the king of France. Giles ran to meet his guest; they embraced and knelt together in silence. Then, without having broken the silence, Louis arose and went on his way. All the brothers re-

proached Giles for not having said anything to his royal visitor. Giles answered with fine simplicity: "I read his heart and he read mine."

241. *Ibid.*, p. 10.
242. *BMM*, pp. 8-9; see also *I and Thou*, pp. 8-9.
243. *BMM*, p. 9.
244. *Ibid.*, p. 10.
245. *Idem.*
246. *Ibid.*, p. 16f.
247. *Ibid.*, p. 14.
248. *Idem.*
249. *Ibid.*, p. 15.
250. *Ibid.*, p. 15; see also *Mamre*, p. 103.
251. *BMM*, pp. 19ff.
252. *Ibid.*, p. 20.
253. *Idem.*
254. *Ibid.*, p. 20.
255. *I and Thou*, pp. 103-104.
256. *Ibid.*, p. 104.
257. *BMM*, pp. 22f. Cf. *I and Thou*, esp. pp. 115-116 where the same attitude is considered in relation to God. See also *Eclipse of God*, pp. 99-114.
258. *BMM*, p. 22.
259. *Ibid.*, p. 21.
260. *Ibid.*, p. 25.
261. Karl Löwith, *op. cit.*, p. 12.
262. *BMM*, pp. 25ff.
263. *Ibid.*, p. 26.
264. See his treatise on *The Dual Number* (1827).
265. *Philosophie der Zukunft*, #62.
266. *BMM*, p. 27.
267. The agreement of this section with the thought of Mead is obvious.
268. *Geist and Kultur in der Sprache*, Heidelberg, 1925. Discussed also in Karl Löwith, *op. cit.*, p. 105f, (my translation).
269. *Ibid.*, quoted in Löwith, *op. cit.*, p. 106.
270. *ZS*, pp. 78-79; *BMM*, pp. 29-30. One is tempted to indicate some of the varieties of erotic man as described by Buber. "There a lover stamps around and is in love only with his passion. There is one wearing his differentiated feelings like medal-ribbons. There one is enjoying the adventures of his own fascinating effect. There one is gazing enraptured at the spectacle of his own supposed surrender. There one is collecting excitement. There one is displaying his 'power.' There one is preening himself with borrowed vitality . . . There one is warming himself at the blaze of what has fallen to his lot. There one is experimenting. And so on and on. . . ."
271. *BMM*, p. 29. The German here is worth quoting for it shows better than the English the intimate relation between language and thought It is a good example, too, of Buber's style, his play on words. "Ich gelobe es mir an und mich ihm; ich gelobe, ich glaube."
272. *ZS*, p. 79; *BMM*, p. 29. This might better be rendered "The Indwelling of

the Present Being between them" *(die Einwohnung des Seienden zwischen ihnen)* since it refers to the Shekinah of Divine Presence. This idea which is central in Buber's teaching derives from the reference in Deut. 12:11 to "the place where the Lord God causes his name to dwell."

273. Cf. Fritz Kunkel, *Let's Be Normal,* Part Four, pp. 121-158.

274. *BMM,* p. 30.

275. Cf. David Riesman, *The Lonely Crowd* (New Haven: Yale University Press, 1950).

276. This was the tragic fate of most of the "youth movements" on the continent, before and after the first World War. They were informed with a false subjectivity and sentimentality, and a desire for freedom which was only a "freeing from bonds, but not freeing to responsibility." Now they have given way to a false authority, which misunderstands genuine authority.

277. *BMM,* p. 31.

278. *Idem.*

279. *Idem.*

280. *Über das Erzieherische* in *Die Kreatur,* Vol. I; see also *BMM,* p. 101.

281. *Idem.*

282. Buber, *BMM,* p. 107.

283. *Ibid.,* pp. 96f. Cf. Mead's notion of "role-taking" and becoming an object to one's self.

284. *Ibid.,* pp. 96-97.

285. *Ibid.,* pp. 97f.

286. *Ibid.,* p. 97.

287. *Ibid.,* pp. 99f.

288. *Ibid.,* pp. 99f.

289. *Ibid.,* p. 100.

290. *Idem.*

291. *Idem.*

292. *BMM,* p. 98.

293. For a similar position see Erich Fromm, *Man for Himself,* esp. the discussions of "Productive Love and Thinking," pp. 96-112; "The Non-productive Orientations," pp. 62-80; and "Selfishness, Self-Love and Self-Interest," pp. 119-140. Cf. also Fritz Kunkel's treatment of "Objectivity" as over against "Egocentricity," in *Let's Be Normal, The Search for Maturity,* etc.

294. *BMM,* p. 20.

295. Buber appears to stand here on common ground with Peirce, Whitehead, Mead, Charles Hartshorne and others. See, for example, Hartshorne's Terry Lectures, 1947, and his article "Ideal Knowledge Defines Reality" in *JP,* XLIII (1946), 573-582. Cf. also the recent book by Prof. Hadley Cantril, *The 'Why' of Man's Experience* (New York: Macmillan, 1950).

296. *Einleitung in die Moralwissenschaft,* I, p. 85f. See also Karl Löwith, *op. cit.,* p. 71f, for a discussion of Egoism and Altruism.

297. *Philosophie der Zukunft; Feuerbach's Sammtliche Werke,* neu hrsg. von Wilhelm Bolln und Friedrich Jodl. Stuttgart: F. Frommann (1903-11), Vol. II, pp. 216, 413.

298. *The Egoist,* Modern Library, 1947; Cf. Balzac, *Lost Illusions,* Boston, Roberts Brothers, 1893.

299. *DFE,* p. 19f; *BMM,* pp. 16f, 45; *IATW,* pp. 47f.

300. This statement has, of course, to be understood in the light of Buber's insistence that responsibility is to a law or principle superior to and independent of oneself, one's class, or one's party.

301. It appears that we have here not only a reiteration of the Hebrew sense for the concrete existential hour in its historical situation, but also an expression of the Protestant doctrine of "vocation," and "election." See also *IATW,* pp. 250-51.

302. The significance of the concept of responsibility is, in a sense, the central point of *Zwiesprache,* and it is also central in the argument of *Die Frage an den Einzelnen.* As the translator rightly remarks (*BMM,* p. 206) the meaning is brought out more vividly in the German: *Wort, Antwort, antworten, verantworten,* etc., are all closely interwoven in a play of meaning in which speech and response, answering for and being responsible for are intimately related. Cf. *IATW,* pp. 239, 250, 251.

303. This is one of the reasons why Fritz Kunkel, Alfred Adler and other therapists have broken with their early teacher.

304. See *Über Charaktererziehung,* in *BMM,* pp. 104ff. The Greek word for character means "impression." "Who does the impressing?" asks Buber. And he answers: "everything does: nature and the social context, the house and the street, language and custom, the world of history and the world of daily news in the form of rumor, of broadcast, and newspaper, music and technical science, play and dream—everything together," in the interplay of all these multifarious, opposing influences. *BMM,* p. 106.

305. A similar viewpoint is expressed in the words of Fritz Kunkel, especially in his stress upon "means-end" instead of "cause-effect," in his call for responsible choice, and his whole dynamic, or "infinal" viewpoint.

306. *DFE,* p. 64; *BMM,* p. 66.

307. *BMM,* p. 68; Cf. *IATW,* p. 239.

308. In a genuine community, in a mature and essential *We,* responsibility can be exercised by the *We,* as well as by an *I.* Again cf. the "We-Psychology" of Fritz Kunkel as set forth in *How Character Develops* (Scribners, New York, 1940). But even in the We, I am not relieved of my own personal responsible decision, which at times may go counter to the collective judgment of the group. Cf. *IATW,* p. 47.

309. *BMM,* p. 69.

310. *Ibid.,* pp. 65-70.

311. *Ibid.,* pp. 66-69, also 64-65.

312. *DFE,* pp. 65, 70; *BMM,* pp. 64-69.

313. *Ibid.,* p. 68-69. Buber is saying that it is precisely in the public life, within the group, the party, the trade union, the manufacturers' association, that the struggle for human freedom and responsibility has to be fought and won. For even here, men are able to live the life of dialogue.

314. *DFE,* p. 70; *BMM,* p. 69.

315. *Ibid.,* pp. 70-71.

316. *BMM*, p. 115.
317. See e.g., *IATW*, pp. 246-251; 234-39; 13-27; 43-44.
318. *IATW*, pp. 85-88.
319. *BMM*, p. 200.
320. *Ibid.*, p. 177.
321. See his *Paths in Utopia* (New York: Macmillan, 1950), in which he carries out a serious historical and normative study of "scientific" and "utopian" socialism. A non-Marxist socialist, Buber believes that in the light of twentieth century experience, the "utopian" socialism is actually more in touch with human realities while avoiding the cruel methods of the Communists. *Paths in Utopia* ends on a hopeful note, and stresses the portent of the new cooperative village communes in Palestine.
322. *BMM*, p. 115 *et passim*.
323. See *I and Thou*, pp. 44-45, 103f; *BMM*, p. 72.
324. *BMM*, p. 31.
325. *Idem.*
326. *Ibid.*, pp. 31, 64.
327. *Ibid.*, p. 33.
328. *Ibid.*, pp. 80-81. See also IATW, pp. 45f, 234f, 246f; Cf. Julien Benda, *The Treason of the Intellectuals* (New York, 1928).
329. *Die Frage an den Einzelnen; BMM*, pp. 40-82.
330. *DFE*, p. 93f; *BMM*, p. 80f.
331. Cf. Dilthey's insistence on the importance of historical and social conditions. Both nineteenth century empiricism and idealism overlooked these facts.
332. *DFE*, p. 94; *BMM*, p. 81.
333. *BMM*, p. 178.
334. *DFE*, pp. 95-96; *BMM*, p. 81; *IATW*, p. 247.
335. *BMM*, p. 81; *IATW*, pp. 45-46.
336. Christians believe that in Jesus Christ, the Word became Flesh, the ultimate truth and existential truth became one in a person.
337. *BMM*, p. 199.
338. *Ibid.*, pp. 118-205.
339. *Ibid.*, p. 200.
340. *Ibid.*, p. 201.
341. *Ibid.*, p. 64.
342. See also *IATW*, pp. 229, 230, 252.
343. See *The Point of View for My Work as an Author*, New York: Oxford University Press, 1939, translated by Walter Lowrie. This is a remarkable autobiographical testament which comes nearer to revealing the reason for his broken engagement with Regina Olsen than anything else he wrote.
344. See *DFE*, Chap. I, and esp. pp. 19-22 for Buber's discussion of Stirner. "Truth is what is mine," says Stirner. One can hardly miss the group analogy: Collectivisms (the "group ego") simply translate this same axiom into the language of the group: "Truth is what is ours." Cf. also *IATW*, pp. 246-47; *BMM*, p. 41.
345. Stirner would be horrified with Buber's addition, but, Buber argues, it is the natural and necessary consequence of Stirner's dictum.

346. This is the basic motif of our "world-hour." In Stirner, Buber finds the early proclamation of the loss of the sense of truth and responsibility which is characteristic of our age.

347. *DFE*, p. 20; *BMM*, p. 45f.

348. *DFE*, p. 13; *BMM*, p. 41.

349. Quoted in *BMM*, p. 47. Cf. *IATW*, pp. 234, 246.

350. *DFE*, p. 11; *BMM*, p. 40.

351. *DFE*, pp. 25-26; *BMM*, pp. 49-50.

352. *DFE*, p. 25; *BMM*, p. 48.

353. *DFE*, p. 24; *BMM*, p. 48.

354. *DFE*, p. 31; *BMM*, p. 50.

355. *DFE*, p. 32; *BMM*, pp. 50-51.

356. *Idem*.

357. This rendering of Lev. 19:18 would appear to be a more precise translation of the original Hebrew; and it surely helps to keep before us the stark objectivity of the command: the other, the neighbor, whom I am commanded to love is one with a real life of his own, and not one whom I can merely "acquire."

358. *DFE*, p. 34; *BMM*, p. 52. Cf. *Ten Rungs*, p. 23 for a similar view: "God limits the godliness he has in infinity, and narrows it down to the focus of the material world in which man exists."

359. *DFE*, p. 38; *BMM*, p. 54.

360. *DFE*, p. 40; *BMM*, p. 55.

361. *DFE*, p. 34; *BMM*, p. 52.

362. *DFE*, p. 44; *BMM*, p. 58.

363. *Idem*.

364. *DFE*, p. 59; *BMM*, p. 65.

365. *DFE*, p. 35; *BMM*, p. 52.

366. A Chassidic saying which fairly reflects Buber's view. *Ten Rungs*, p. 31.

367. *Ibid.*, p. 82.

368. Buber declares that woman is the best emissary of the elemental. In comparing Kierkegaard with Augustine and Pascal, Buber recalls that beside Augustine stood his mother, and with Pascal a sister, who maintained the organic relationship to the world as only a woman can. *DFE*, pp. 11, 51f; *BMM*, pp. 40, 60f.

369. *DFE*, p. 48; *BMM*, pp. 58-59.

370. One is tempted to speculate that the ancient Jewish disapproval of celibacy, as violating the commandment to be fruitful and to multiply, may have had something to do with checking the Jewish and the Chassid saint from seeking his perfection beyond the borders of the human world. For this positive doctrinal attitude toward sex confronts him with a most crucial practical and metaphysical challenge, and turns him back to the world at precisely that point in his passion when he might be tempted to depart permanently into the deep recesses of his own soul.

371. *DFE*, pp. 57-58; *BMM*, pp. 64-65.

372. *DFE*, pp. 68-69; *BMM*, p. 69.

373. *BMM*, p. 82.

374. *BMM*, p. 175f.

375. *DFE*, pp. 73ff; *BMM*, pp. 71ff.

376. Carl Schmitt, *Der Begriff des Politischen*.

377. This view also corresponds in Schmitt's thought to criteria of other oppositions: good and evil in the moral sphere, beautiful and ugly in the aesthetic, and so on. *DFE*, p. 79.

378. F. Gogarten, *Politische Ethik* (Jena, 1932).

379. *DFE*, pp. 83-84; *BMM*, pp. 76-77.

380. *BMM*, p. 77.

381. *BMM*, p. 77f; *Hasidism*, pp. 104-110.

382. *BMM*, p. 78. See also *Good and Evil* (Scribner's Sons, 1953).

383. *Hasidism*, p. 105.

384. *Ibid.*, p. 106.

385. *Ibid.*, p. 107.

386. *BMM*, p. 78.

387. *Ten Rungs*, pp. 89-90.

388. *Ibid.*, pp. 90-91.

389. *Hasidism*, p. 105.

390. *BMM*, p. 79.

391. *Ibid.*, p. 77.

392. Buber uses the term "spirit" variously and vaguely to mean different things: self, personality, soul, meaning, the creative principle of life, reality seen under the aspect of value, human creativity, the divinely functioning factor. See *Between Man and Man*, p. 193f.

393. *Ibid.*, p. 36.

394. *Ibid.*, pp. 196-197.

395. Buber is here referring to the two basic worlds and the two basic relationships possible for an *I:* the *I-Thou* and the *I-It*.

396. See "Der Heilige Weg" in *Reden über das Judentum*.

397. *BMM*, p. 203.

398. *Ibid.*, p. 204.

399. *Ibid.*, p. 203.

400. *Ibid.*, p. 204.

401. *I and Thou*, p. 85.

402. *Ten Rungs*, p. 102.

403. *Ibid.*, p. 19.

404. Conscious of how difficult it is to persuade men of the truth of his position, especially in the absence of any common experience, Buber writes in *Zwiesprache:* "I have no authority to demand the life of dialogue. I simply record the fact that you *are able* to live the life of dialogue. . . . The life of dialogue is no privilege of intellectual activity like dialectic. . . . It begins no higher than where humanity begins. There are no gifted and ungifted here, only those who give themselves and those who withhold themselves."

405. H. H. Farmer, *The Servant of the Word* (London: The Religious Book Club, 1941), p. 38. That Farmer has come under the spell of Buber is evident in this little book on preaching, and also in his Lyman Beecher

Lectures, delivered at Yale University in the spring of 1946, and published by Abingdon-Cokesbury Press under the title, *God and Men.*

406. *Die Rede, Die Lehre, und Das Lied,* p. 42.

407. Another concept which is not absolutely clear in Buber's writings is that of the nature of God; yet I am very sure that Buber believes that God is personal, a Thou, not the pantheistic All. Buber is in this matter an "obstinate Jew" *(hartnäckiger Jude).* Perhaps more precisely, Buber is saying that God communicates with men "as a person"; God "takes on personality" in order to communicate with us. But God is not *only* a person: Buber hints at this when he refers to God as "the absolute person."

408. *I and Thou,* p. 11.

409. *Ibid.,* p. 62.

410. *Ibid.,* p. 63.

411. *Ibid.,* p. 65.

412. *BMM,* pp. 88-90, 100, 168; *I and Thou,* p. 28.

Chapter Four

Mead and Buber: A Comparison and Critique

SIMILARITIES AND DIFFERENCES

WE HAVE SHOWN how and in what ways both Mead and Buber understand man as essentially a "socius." In their different ways and in their different terminologies, they both point to the central significance of *relations* between persons and of the *social* nature of reality. The predominant motif in their thinking and writing is the conviction that all life is in essence a complex of relationships; and that on the human level it is only within a social matrix, within the field of the social act, that the "self" arises. It is in meeting, in interaction between persons, in communication with others, variously conceived, that the free, responsible, independent *human* person is achieved.

But their common view of the social self is maintained in two quite different approaches to the problem, two different *Weltanschauungen*. Remarkable points of contact there surely are. But when we consider their respective spiritual trajectories, the various categories they employ, the innermost meanings they imply, it becomes clear that their differences are as important as their likenesses. Therefore, any comparison may appear misleading at certain points.

The first basic disparity to be noted is that Mead employs a strictly genetic and naturalistic method of deriving mind and self from the bio-social process, whereas Buber starts at a different level and stands within the intuitive, existential and religious tradition. Buber is thinking on another plane; he means a different kind of reality. Because of this fact, a cogent and complete comparison becomes extremely difficult. Both men have complex and germinal minds; both men, for different reasons, are vague and unprecise in some of their concepts and terminology. Thus any simple classification and systematization of their doctrines is foredoomed.

Mead never searched for his answers in any but a secular, pragmatic frame. He was concerned with the empirical study of mind and self in their social evolution, and with the immediate problems of men in society—and he thought that that was enough. Buber, on the other hand, speaks the language of faith and revelation; he is intelligible only within a religious context, with its characteristic framework of spirituality.

The two men were rooted in traditions not at all congenial. American naturalistic-behavioristic-pragmatism was an alien viewpoint to Buber; and Mead would almost certainly have rejected Buber's aestheticism and existentialism as subjective and dangerous moonshine. Yet, on second thought, Mead might have honored Buber as a free and sensitive spirit who has used his Jewish heritage as a means for giving expression to a unique religio-social philosophy. I suspect that Mead could have read Buber, as he read Bergson, for inspiration and insight—precisely because American pragmatism (with its attack on absolutes, the "block universe," and traditional logic and metaphysics) has stated some of the same notions for which Buber and other existentialists argue—but without leaving what the pragmatists regard as the firmer ground of empirical analysis. For example, Mead's pragmatism and Buber's existentialism agree in stressing the responsible *act* over abstract *thought*.

Buber writes out of an attitude of *faith*, a faith that has never been doubted by the soul of Israel:[1] faith as pledge, as trust, as entering into a covenant with the everlasting Thou. God is ever present to his creatures, and in many garments. "The Jewish in man . . . seems to me to be the ever renewed re-discernment of God." [2] Buber has aimed at no closely-knit, rigorously logical philosophical system, nor at piling up scientifically descriptive data. His intent lies "not in the world as presented to and worked over by thought, but in the world as given to man as his material for creation." [3] His interest lies not even in God as a being who occupies a definite position in a definite system of thought, "but in God as the reality whom man meets, and to whom man can respond." [4] Buber ranges himself with Pascal in declaring that the philosopher's *idea* of the Absolute dissolves at the point where God *lives*, at the point where God *is loved*.[5] Buber is concerned with religious experience rather than with philosophical debate which might deliver his conclusions in a packet of tight logic. Religion must ever have a dimension of myth and mystery. William James could have understood Buber better than his younger pragmatist brother Mead.

Therefore, it is almost impossible to reduce Buber's work to a neat system; it is especially difficult to convert what he says into other terms and thus compare his philosophy with other systems. One can only appeal, as does Buber himself, to the experience of other men as authenticating what he says. Form and matter are inseparable in his writings. One of his translators, Greta Hort, has finely said: "He does not write about religion, because what he writes is religion, and the demand he makes is that of religion. His readers, in order to grasp his thought, must be capable of recognizing God; they must, however dimly, know what is meant by the Unity (Jichud)." [6]

What Mead gives us is a method—the method of pragmatism and research science, and their corollaries. What Buber gives us is a point of view, a faith, and a vision by which we can see and cooperate with the mysterious universe in which we live, linked by innumerable ties to God and fellowmen.

Vague though it be, then, Buber does have a metaphysics, (or so it seems to me)[7]—a theistic conception of the structure of the universe in which to place his understanding of man, and he insists upon a wider context of relatedness than does Mead.

Because of these and other rather basic differences, the temptation is to use one thinker as a foil against the other. I cannot claim to have avoided this temptation entirely, but I have not intended to sharpen any dialectical weapons on either Mead or Buber. The contrasts and conflicts, and my accompanying critical judgments, will be pointed out in due course; and while the reader will have little difficulty in detecting where my sympathies lie, I can only add that I have tried to be fair to both men and to draw only those conclusions which the internal evidence seemed to warrant.

With these thoughts in mind, we are now ready to consider the basic similarities in Mead and Buber. In the later sections of the chapter we shall return to an examination of some of the contrasts and differences.

SIMILARITIES IN MEAD AND BUBER

The Social Self.—Man is a socius, a social self grounded in essential otherness. Man is a *Mit-mensch* living in a *Mit-welt*. This is the key note in both Mead and Buber. The stress is on *relations,* on the self-other dialogue, on the self as the result of inter-personal communication. Social experience is the basic phase of all experience. Within the social matrix, through the interplay of gesture and response, address and answer, claim and counter-claim, and especially by means of the mechanism of speech, the individual comes to consciousness of himself, becomes truly human. Man's essential nature is not grasped from what unfolds in the individual's inner life, but from the distinctiveness of his relations to things and to other living beings. It appears to be the paradox of human existence that man needs others in order to be himself.

Man is no mere spectator or knower. He is the kind of knower who knows and lives the life of the other in an active meeting and passage; a social self who is mirrored in the eyes of others. Whether one loves or hates, one's spirit must adjust to the impact of another's presence. It is social inter-play, contrast-effect, resistance, reflected appraisal, a life of dialogue that turn the human organism into full selfhood.

In a strict epistemological sense, we cannot of course be sure that the "other" object or person is there at all. But in concrete lived-life, we cannot doubt the real existence of the other of whose assumed activities we are aware, who lays a claim upon us, who engages us through genuine causal impact and symbolic gesture. In this respect, at least, Mead and Buber are "realistic" like all scientists and healthy animals in their practicing epistemology. Mead especially hated the "epistemological serpent" which seduced thinkers away from a real knowledge of a real world. Both Mead and Buber insisted upon a *real other* over against oneself. Not only is real otherness involved in the true situation; but a *real other,* a *thou,* must be apprehended, indeed *intended,* as the condition of acquiring or becoming a *self.* The other is not merely an object of my thought; he is really *there* as another person. I am *I* for myself only because I am at the same time *thou* for another. Not *I,* but *I and Thou,* self and other, is the true principle of human living.

Thus, while there is a clear strain of romanticism in both Buber and Mead, both are essentially realistic and this-worldly in outlook. Even in Buber, any extreme mysticism or other-worldliness is retired along with Hegelian monism, Absolute Idealism, and the older epistemologies. Experience is social, plural, and objective, involving the given-ness and concrete reality of persons and things and happenings to other persons. The valuable, discriminating, moral agent is not possible apart from a rich and various tradition that must be socially imposed and worked out in the give-and-take of social experience. Being-for-oneself essentially and constitutively includes being-for-others. The assumption of isolated consciousness is contradicted by the whole idea of the social nature of the self.

Self and Society.—It follows, therefore, that a community of selves, an environment of communicating minds, is necessary to elicit and shape new minds and selves. And the more one participates in his group, the more one is able to take on the attitudes of his society, the more one knows of the social will, *the more highly conscious of oneself one becomes.* Independence is reached in and through relationships. Individual selfhood is never absolute nor *a priori* with respect to others; it is reciprocal "attached-detachment" and potential to relation. From this point of view, both the human fact and the human problem is how to remain oneself and develop one's own unique powers in the very process of being related.

One grows by giving and receiving within a community. The human organism is born into, nourished by, participates in, communicates with a world of persons. Thus the individual comes to full stature as a human person in the reality of relationship with other persons and things and events—and, Buber would add, with God. In the mutual recognition of other selves, like myself yet different; in response to their behavior, often unexpected and disturbing, vis-a-vis my own thought and meaning and behavior; in acknowledgment of the mutual claims which persons as persons have upon each other, the human self develops and has its being.

In both Mead and Buber, the social-ethical interest is predominant. Both had an interest in many of the same problems of men and society—a tendency characteristic of both empirical naturalism and romanticism. In other words, they were concerned to elaborate a theory and a strategy which would harmonize the individual interest with the social welfare. Furthermore, we have here not only the basis for a moral social philosophy: in the self-other relationships of man with thing there is the basis for an aesthetics, and in the man-God relation the basis for religion. It may well be questioned whether this theory

has an answer to all of life's problems, but that it is on the right lines
can hardly be doubted.

It is clear, then, that the individual grows to selfhood in an intensely
social process. The individual begins its career as a psycho-physical
organism with as yet undetermined capacities. At birth there is only
the *potentiality of socialization* in every individual. The organism is
the *given;* the self is the *given as socialized.* The individual is always
born into a group which has a culture. In this sense society and culture are antecedent to any particular person. The feral men do not
become *human personalities* except within the matrix of society, within
the warp and woof of interactional patterns and the institutional pre-
cipitates of a social history of living together.

The Social Nature of Reality.—It seems to be characteristic of both
existentialism and pragmatism that they develop their ontologies (such
as they have) in psychological, biological, or sociological terms. And
in this respect Mead and Buber are no exceptions.

What we have been saying is as revelatory of the nature of reality,
as of the self. For the total environment, including society, is the locus
and setting of all that is most active in the growth of the self. Nature
itself is "social." There is an ontological quality to Mead's "experience" and to Buber's "between." In every being is laid the All-Being,
but it cannot develop save in connection with all else. The universe
acts in ways which are characteristic of social selves; experience accords with a reality beyond itself.[8] Mead and Buber employ different
terms, but their conclusions about the social nature of reality agree.
Nature, like human nature, is socially organized.

Mead, it will be recalled, regarded nature as constituted of an organization of perspectives, in which individual acts are the units of
existence. The individual in the order of nature, as in the human order,
is a social individual. This idea came late in Mead's life, and actually
represented a projection onto Nature of the social characteristics which
Mead believed he had established as obtaining in the human social
process.[9] To accomplish this feat, Mead brought together the concepts
of emergence and relativity. By "sociality" Mead means the capacity
to occupy several perspectives at the same time, or to be several things
at once. Emergent characters produce changes in the environment;
therefore we must look to more than one system or perspective to explain the change. Furthermore, it appears that whatever reality is possessed by any act or individual within nature or history is something

achieved through the occupation of several perspectives. Both nature and history are ceaselessly progressive and emergent processes of creative advance. Emergence requires us to place an event or form in more than one system or set of relations; in other words, any emergent event or form is both determined by the old and determines the new. This is equivalent of saying that, on the human level, man is both free and determined. If man is free and able, within limits, to determine and control his future, it also means that the *future* thus determined is the *present* for some other man who is to a degree thus necessarily determined by *his present*. But this being simultaneously in different systems, this capacity to play one's own role while also taking the role of others, is precisely what Mead defines as sociality.

Buber, on the other hand, speaks of the "inborn Thou," of the "*a priori* of relation,*" of the instinct to make contact, to create.[10] In one sense relation does not exist until we have entered it, but in another sense it has been there already, potentially, waiting to be realized,[11]— like the *shekhinah* or God's "world-indwelling glory" ever waiting for release and unification. Some feature of reality, perhaps dimly seen, stands over against us; we stare and grope and wrestle with it; we try to grasp it, speak to it, while it invites and evades us. Meanwhile man tries to translate it, interpret it, make it available to his understanding.

Buber intimates that the effort to establish relation comes first; it is an elemental instinct or urge. The environment says variously: Stand and meet me; I am here, come! The beginnings of encounter and relatedness are in the natural and animal world. Buber is intensely conscious of the subjective integrity of objects in nature. The very existence in actuality of Beauty, Love, and Truth is evidence of the latent Thou-quality and Thou-relationship coming to awareness, become actualized.[12] Here again we see how Buber's religiosity gives a different turn to our concept of sociality in nature. The call to man, the creative Word, comes from beyond himself.

With his background in Judaism and Chassidism, Buber thinks that it is not at all strange that God enters into personal relationships with man as "person" and through nature and other finite persons. There seems nothing arbitrary or limiting about this. Buber believes that he is simply reporting the facts of the created world as experienced by countless men.[13] And ultimately the reason why that order is what it is lies in the inscrutable nature and intention of God, the Unconditioned. The teaching of Israel, according to Buber, is that this Infinite

Unconditioned God is both person and non-person; the unapproachable Holy of Holies is also person and meets man as person.[14] "The real God is the God who can be spoken to, because he is the one who speaks to men."[15] "God speaks to man in the things and beings which He sends him in life. Man answers through his dealings with these things and beings."[16] Why God's creation—at least on the human level— requires finite persons and things in relation to Himself and to other finite persons; why the historical process is a realm of free moral agents in relationship, it is impossible to say. If, however, as the Judeo-Christian faith affirms, God is Love, an answer becomes possible. For if, in creating man God intended a finite creature capable of sharing in some sense and degree the Creator's nature and purpose as Love, he then intended a world of finite persons in relationship—for love is meaningless apart from persons in gracious personal relations. It follows again that if love is ultimate, then persons in relation are also ultimate. Out of such considerations Buber posits the fundamentally personal and social nature of reality.[17]

Speech or Language as Constitutive.—In the thought of both Mead and Buber, *speech* is central to the origin and development of human selfhood.

Speech and deed, language and active engagement with the neighbor —these are the essential media in human relations. Both of our thinkers stress the "histrionic tendency" which seems to run through all human experience and illustrates aptly the dramatic capacity and tendency to take the role of others (personae), to speak to and for another, to project oneself over to the other and play his part.

But more than this, speech is somehow creative, constitutive. In the process of symbolic communication, in the invention and use of language, in the effort of speech—and Buber would add, in the agony and leap of prayer—man becomes or acquires a "self." Speech is the bridge between two poles, the act by which the potential between the two poles becomes actualized in a self. *Being* is not just *being known* (in Berkeley's terms), but being addressed, answering, *knowing that one is known*. The "Word," asserts Buber, is superior to "Logos." Speech is the basic, creative act of what Buber calls the Spirit. The unique and distinguishing thing about speech is that it involves true dialogue. In speech the speaker must, to a degree at least, get over into the place and attitude of the other in order to communicate his meaning. The origin of speech is to be understood only on the basis of such a turning to another. "True dialectic," wrote Feuerbach in criticism of Hegel, "is not a monologue of the solitary thinker with himself; it is a dialogue between I and Thou." Only as a *person* can one speak to others as well as to himself. And only a person can assume at one and the same time the dual-role of understanding speaker and understanding listener. Man is peculiarly a *fellow*-man, living in a world of relatedness; and the symbolic process, principally vocal gesture or language, is the chief mode of communication.

Likewise thought is the internalized conversation of gesture and symbol. By virtue of the importation or introjection of the social process of communication, the self acquires the process of reflective thought. As Mead would say: "Thinking is simply the reasoning of the individual, the carrying on of a conversation between what I have termed the 'I' and the 'me.' " [18] Buber, too, would compare thinking analogically to the dialectic encounter of two human beings, the only difference being that in thought I assume the roles of both parties to the transaction. Someone else talking to me is not essentially different from my talking to myself, i.e., thinking.

Mead, of course, is famous for his study of the "histrionic tendency" which he happily described as the tendency and ability to "take the role of the other." And probably no other theory of the symbol or of the self has done such justice to the oft-neglected social and vocal phases of mind, or has gathered such suggestive evidence to support the identification of mind with the symbolic process.[19] It is well known also that Mead opposed any attempt to locate the seat of mind in the individual brain or nervous system. For to Mead mind is not a substance of an ontal nature but simply the symbolic functioning of events, or the functioning of significant symbols, which arise in a social process. On this view, mind is an internalization of the objective social speech process. Language is the fecund matrix of mind and meaning—i.e., of selves.

The Moral as the Social.—As social philosophers, both Mead and Buber are so much concerned with moral issues that it becomes incumbent upon us to ask whether and to what extent they adequately account for moral experience. Both Mead and Buber, in their different ways, hold the view that human conduct in its true functioning contains the elements for ethical action and social progress. Mead, more explicitly than Buber, held that he could solve the moral and social problem of how to harmonize individual interest and social welfare, if he could show that psychologically the individual self is "social." For Mead, the moral *is* the social. We need, therefore, to raise the question as to whether Mead and Buber provide an adequate basis for moral obligation and moral dissent. If sociality is not just an ideal to be attained, but the real "way of things," why is it such a difficult task to "socialize" people? Why are individuals so ready to disrupt community? Where is the fulcrum for moral leverage? Are there perhaps ends, demands, standards, and sources of motivation and obligation that cannot be explained as derived wholly from social interplay and group interests? How does an ethical universalism develop from institutions already established, and perhaps vicious in character? Let us consider the answers of Mead and Buber to these and related questions.

Two conspicuous tendencies were present at the turn of the century. First, a utopian social optimism based on Spencer's social Darwinism;[20] and second, a denial of universal values and norms of absolute validity. Mead fell victim to this unduly optimistic view of human nature which created what some critics condemn as an unrealistic over-confidence in man's unaided powers. Economic and political liberalism was led astray by the uncritical assumption that individuals, pursuing their own interests, would of necessity serve the public interest. Mead, too, tended to idealize social forces, tended to find more and better meaning in social movements and in social intelligence than was actually justified. This was partly due to his generous nature, and partly due to his social philosophy. Mead sought to show that, since the self is a socius, social amelioration would flow differentially from his account of the self. "Amelioration through understanding" was a dominant note in his thought. The fact that the attitudes, values, and motivations of the microcosmic individual reflect the attitudes, habits, and values of the social macrocosm was taken as indicating that the trouble with the world is not lack of goodness or good will in the human material, but "social lag," ignorance, immaturity,[21] or lack of rigorous scientific method in attaining the human ends which appear with the means at our disposal.[22] Mead held the view that if men have the relevant facts, and if the different social interests and groups are represented, reasonable men will come up with an adequate moral judgment and social strategy.[23] This follows from the fact that, as social, the self has taken the values of others into itself; its values are indeed the values of the social process. There is then no problem as to how the self can take others and the values of others into account. The old dichotomies of egoism and altruism, self-assertion and self-sacrifice, are false alternatives and are here reconciled. Mead seemed not fully aware of the inevitable failures, frustrations, and corruptions of human reason ("creative intelligence" was his term) which pragmatism takes as its guide. Nor did he seem clearly to understand the nature and function of power, and the tendency of men to use whatever societal structures are available for purposes of self-aggrandizement and political power. In this area, too, he seemed strangely blind to the insights of depth psychology.[24]

The problem is how to get *moral* selves, not simply social selves. Mead rightly condemned "moralistic preaching," while confidently holding the view that sound morals and social policy will grow out of the progressive realization of the conditions and potentialities of variable human situations. Mead therefore believed, as did Dewey, that education, socialization, and the cultivation of free critical inquiry are all that is needed to set men on the path toward socially valuable goals.[25] So he writes: "The moral necessity lies not in the end acting from without, nor in the push of inclination from within, but in the relation of the conditions of action to the impulses of action." [26] In the moral act the motive for action is the impulse as directed toward a social end. And the impulse is "good" if it allows for the maximum satisfaction and harmony of itself and other impulses. The possibility of intelligent action awaits the discovery of the conditions and means under which that action can take place. And the statement of those conditions becomes the end. Since moral ends *are* social ends, the self, as a social being, must be concerned within and without with a social harmony of impulses, looking toward the securing of social, rather than merely private, interests.[27] No need here for God as the source and ground of values.

If Mead's thesis is true, it means at the very least that man is not and cannot be merely and essentially an egoist—short of insanity. Many, perhaps most, of his motivations, attitudes, habits, values, and responses are socially induced. But this fact, unfortunately, does not insure that man's actions, being socially conditioned, even when intelligent, will be in accord with the common welfare. For one reason, society is not—at least not yet—a single "generalized other" with a unified set of goals and values. It is divided into many groups and classes and sub-groups with conflicting goals and values. And it is usually one or more of these smaller groups, with their partisan interests, which mold the individual members. Thus the individual bears the stamp of his family, class, tribe, race, or nation, rather than that of the "great society" or the "beloved community." [28] The interests of these various groups are usually in conflict, in which case intelligent and scientific progress within an integrated group, unless guided by some ideal more universal than the socially induced patterns, will only serve to make the individuals implicated better integrated and more efficient partisans. It should be noted that war and discord are also "social" in a negative, non-moral sense. Soviet Russia is probably the most tightly integrated nation in the world, and consequently more efficient in extending her power and tyranny. Such is the ambiguous character of human nature, oscillating between self-love and self-transcendence, that sometimes a man may desert his group in order better to serve his own egoistic ends; and sometimes, happily, he is led to rise above his narrow loyalties to loyalties of a more inclusive universal community.

Still Mead is hopeful, and, if his theory is true, he is assured that this latter will eventually come to pass, because individuals and groups are participating in ever wider social acts. But it might also be argued that the considerations enumerated above suggest some qualifications of the social theory of mind and self.

In order to sharpen up this issue, let us recall Mead's position. We have already indicated that Mead was aware of this dilemma, or at least the problem of preserving the integrity of the *social individual* while assuring his participation in a wider social process. The same is true for nations groping after some kind of "League of Nations" which would reconcile the conflicting national interests. But there still remains a doubt as to how well Mead's social theory of mind enables the individual or partisan group to rise above the narrow loyalties to join the larger community. Here are two representative expressions of his views:

> The organized community or social group which gives to the individual his unity of self may be called 'the generalized other.' The attitude of the generalized other is the attitude of the whole community.[29]
>
> But only by taking the attitude of the generalized other toward himself . . . can the individual think at all; for only thus can thinking—or the internalized conversation of gestures which con-

stitute thinking—occur. . . . The self conscious human individual, then, takes or assumes the organized social attitudes of the given social group or community (or of some section thereof) to which he belongs, toward the social problems of various kinds which confront the group or community. . . . [30]

Here Mead is stressing the "me" side of the self, the social attitudes and structures which are incorporated into the self. It is important to note that Mead recognizes that it is the particular, habitual interests and attitudes and patterns of one's own little group that are thus transmitted to each individual. How, then, can Mead account for genuine ethical progress? How does an individual break through and rise above the level of his group? Mead feels the dilemma, and offers the following explanation:

> The attitudes involved are gathered from the group, but the individual in whom they are organized has the opportunity of giving them an expression which perhaps has never taken place before.[31]
>
> Take the religious genius, such as Jesus or Buddha. . . . What has given them their unique importance is that they have taken the attitude of living with reference to a larger society. That larger state was one which was already more or less implied in the institutions of the community in which they lived. Such an individual is divergent from the point of view of what we would call the prejudices of the community; but in another sense he expresses the principles of the community more completely than any other.[32]

Has Mead really succeeded here in accounting for ethical progress purely on the basis of social conditioning? It would appear, from the above, that all the ethical or religious genius can do is to work out what is already implied in the habits or institutions of the group which has shaped his own mind. For instance, it is said that Jesus generalized the conception of the community in terms of the family. True, but Jesus' mind was shaped by a community steeped in convictions about the "Fatherhood of God," and only when one has first accepted that doctrine does the notion of trust and kindliness and mutuality found in the family have any logical implication with respect to the whole human race. On any other view it is a false analogy. But ethical universalism is already implied in the idea of the Fatherhood of God. It means that God loves His whole creation. And this conclusion rests on the prior conviction that one *ought* to love all humankind. If this were not so, then, when men give up the idea of God (and the Fatherhood of God), they ought also, logically, to give up their notion that they *ought* to show good will to all men. The *moral sense* of our *obligation* to our fellowmen is, in the thought of one contemporary philosopher, the foundation of the religious feeling of the universal love of God, not *vice versa*.[33] The religious conception is a logical completion and psychological reinforcement of the moral conviction, but no more. To make it the foundation of the moral obligation would be to state a position which Mead would be quick to reject.

But what, then, becomes of Mead's claim that ethical universalism is an implication of institutions already established? Are we not forced to conclude that Mead's social theory of the mind has not wholly succeeded in explaining the origin and development of the higher moral ideas that go beyond particular group interests? One may fairly doubt that Mead has succeeded in deriving a morally free and responsible agent from a socially conditioned organism.

Commenting on this tragic loss of belief in any truth or good higher than man, Buber remarks: "In our age values and norms are not permitted to be anything but expressions of the life of a group which translates its own needs into the language of objective claims, until at last the group itself, for example a nation, is raised to an absolute value."[34] A commandment to all men is no longer observed. And of this fact, Buber says: "We are justified in regarding this disposition as a sickness of the human race."[35] Buber here recognizes two opposite dangers which threaten the good society: One is the irresponsibility of individuals and groups, and the other is the kind of idolatry that absolutizes the particular society or system. Loyalty to the community under God who transcends and judges all men and all communities appears to be the only protection against both dangers. In this respect, Buber differs from Mead and takes us "beyond conscience."[36] Ultimately, says Buber, the self-other dialogue is fruitful in moral experience only when God is included in the community. He thinks it is difficult otherwise to see how the individual self wholly immersed in the emerging flux of events can ever attain the clear perspective and sense of obligation from which to criticize it and seek to change it.[37]

THE INDIVIDUALITY AND INTEGRITY OF THE PERSON

The general drift of the argument so far has been that human existence is peculiarly characterized by the fact that man is alone and separated from the world, yet in need of relatedness and oneness. Consequently the great problem of human selfhood is how to remain oneself in the very process of being related. Mead and Buber have proposed theoretical answers to this paradox that man needs others to be himself, yet he is not identical with the other. It is relevant, therefore, to ask whether and to what extent Mead and Buber maintain the moral independence of the human self, in contrast to a part-whole identity or a solipsism which both expressly reject.

Our question now becomes: Do Mead and Buber adequately safeguard the autonomy and integrity of their "social individual" against every tendency either to make of the individual a mere function of society, to lose the individual in some Absolute Socius, or to assimilate the other (object or person) to the subject.[38] They both claim to do so and attempt to do so; but we must ask whether in fact they do safeguard true individuality and account for differentiation. There is considerable evidence that Buber succeeds in this attempt somewhat better than Mead because of his consistent religious personalism and because of his more avowed Kantian view of the knowing and acting self. Some transcendental subject, some unitary continuing *ego,* some *a priori* of relation is a necessary presupposition for Buber, even though no such ego is found in perception. On the other hand, it appears that Mead's excessive stress upon the social and cultural factors perhaps led him to minimize, though he did not neglect, the factors of uniqueness, singularity, and autonomy which Buber (and such American psychologists as Gordon Allport) would underscore. There is more than a hint that Mead, being so much a "social Hegelian," (if such a designation is appropriate) is open to the same criticism that Howison made of Royce, namely, that Royce loses the moral self in the Absolute.[39] Let us, then, review Mead's position in the matter.

In the order of nature, as in the human social order, the individual is a "social individual." Mead's position here suggests a "moderate sociological realism" which concedes a modicum of independence to the individual, while insisting that man is a social animal and that social forms have a reality of their own. Individual and social forms and structures appear to have a complementary relation.

In line with his interest in social reform, Mead was ever trying to find a formula for assuring individual expression and functional differentiation while guaranteeing social order. In a democracy, which was his model state, there must be some kind of combination of individual freedom with orderly processes, political liberty constrained by the general principle of majority rule. Democracy, properly understood, is not "individualism"; likewise it has nothing in common with a rigid caste system. Democracy involves *functional differentiation* and social participation, and thus holds the conditions and the promise of the great community.[40] Democracy is not anarchy; it should be characterized by order, discipline, restraint of the anti-social rebel in the interest of the whole.[41] But it should not, and does not, crush out individuality. Nay more, social order is the very means by which individuality is born and nurtured. So Mead writes:

> It is often assumed that democracy is an order of society in which those personalities which are sharply differentiated will be eliminated, that everything will be ironed down to a situation where everyone will be, as far as possible, like everyone else. But of course, this is not the implication of democracy; the implication of democracy is rather that the individual can be as highly developed as lies within the possibilities of his own inheritance and still can enter into the attitudes of the others whom he affects.[42]

If this be true, the democratic community grows through respecting and sharing differences. One becomes conscious of self and of self-interest through sympathetic inter-communication with one's fellowmen, by taking the place of the other. The implications in this for the meaning of justice are clear. Self-interest is roused and served through the larger social interest; self-sacrifice really leads to self-realization. Society is necessary for human fulfillment.

Mead was not unaware of the charge brought against modern civilization (and against social behaviorists, determinists, and Hegelians) that our complex society is destructive of personality. But he contended that it was precisely the reciprocal interaction between a complex social world and a social individual that offered rich possibilities for the realization of individuality. It is only in community that one can attain to selfhood, and a full free life.[43]

We have already alluded to a certain ambiguity in Mead's account. From most of the evidence presented, it may fairly be concluded that the social act is prior to the individual act, that the self is the "me" of the generalized other imported from the field of social objects into the realm of inner experience. But then Mead also says that the social act is an organization of individual acts and perspectives and has no existence apart from the discrete acts and perspectives in time which go to make it up. It is clear that Mead is trying to preserve the freedom, integrity and dignity, even the priority, of individual acts while affirming that individuals participate in and are conditioned by wider social acts. In his emphasis upon the "I" there is further evidence of his belief in both self and other, in the necessity and possibility of both organized society and individual self development.

Mead makes much of the "generalized other," yet he takes sharp issue with all those (like Cooley, Boodin, Leighton, and certain Hegelians) who hold to some notion of a "group mind" or of society or the state as having metaphysical status as an independent reality. For Mead does not see how, on that view, they could retain their concern for the preciousness of the individual spirit. Social institutions are merely the organized responses which individuals make to given acts of social stimuli. On this behavioristic view, institutions are manmade and reflect the environment in which they arise, and serve the interests of the social individuals whose social responses thus find organized expression. So he writes: "The institutions of society . . . are nothing but ways of throwing on the social screen in enlarged fashion the complexities existing inside the central nervous system." [44] Social institutions are not sacrosanct; they can be changed and are changed through the activity of individuals. There is no necessary or inevitable reason why institutions should be oppressive or rigidly conservative, or why they should not be, as many are, flexible and progressive, fostering individuality. [45]

One has the feeling at times that Mead arrives at his autonomous unified self more by assertion than by strict implication from the facts examined. More than one critic has confessed to a suspicion of "white magic" in the process by which, starting with an animal organism assuming roles, you end up presently with a well-rounded, integrated "generalized other." How can minds or selves formed by assuming conflicting roles and clashing values make harmonious the divisions that produce and constitute them? A further suspicion, not easily allayed, is that Mead seems to derive from his account of the self a method of more effective social reform than is otherwise obtainable. Actually, Mead seems to be trying to hold a middle course; he seems to be saying that man is neither the complete master of destiny nor yet its slave. He rejects explicitly any rigid determinism which would make men the slaves of fate or social institutions. Yet on the other hand, and despite his pervasive optimism about mankind and scientific method, Mead holds to no extreme voluntaristic faith which makes man simply the master. True, he does cherish the hope and faith that natural evolution and scientific progress, aided by human thought and action, will eventually work out the kinks, balance the social budget, and build a more perfect abode for mankind. Still he is properly aware of "institutional lag." Institutions, traditions, and social habits tend to "freeze" into permanent molds. But there do come and ought to come "cracking times." Mead held no brief for the *status quo*. Freedom, exceptions, functional deviations, the contributions of creative innovators should be encouraged—so long as they do not endanger the safety and stability and orderly progress of society.

Nevertheless it appears that Mead has difficulty in avoiding the stupefying, the standardizing, the de-individualizing of people through the mass pressure of the generalized other. He seems to be not cognizant of the deeper tragedy involved in the conflict of individual and social values in our time. His behavioristic treatment seems hardly adequate to protect the individual against the pressures of such modern idolatries as Nationalism, Fascism, Naziism, and Russian Communism—all social pseudo-religions, all deifying the tribe, the folk, the state. Buber, by contrast, seems to be on firmer ground to protest all forms of tyranny over personality, whether of reactionary individualism, religious orthodoxy, or of revolutionary political movements. Mead attempted to make a place for the genius, the great leader, who leaves his mark on society, who brings about fundamental changes; but, he taught, in so doing there are effected resultant changes in the personalities of the other individuals of that society.[46]

Mead would say that the genius or leader is greatly endowed with "I-reactions." But such deviation, on his terms, rests back on biological differences from heredity, on physical growth itself affected by endocrine functioning, on personal-social conditioning, and on the particular interpretation which the individual organism gives to the mass of culture that comes to him. There is a real doubt as to whether Mead's analysis adequately accounts for the mystery of genius, or how to get a unified "good" self from such a mixture of "others," both evil and good. Mead is forced once more to recognize that social facts are not the only conditioning factors in the genesis of self-consciousness. In other words, an individual need not merely assume the role of a generalized other in order to become aware of self-interest, in order to realize that he is a self. Mead himself says that the "I" is an active process of the organism, and the "me" is the content, a content or empirical other that is constructed in conformity with the impulses and needs of the "I."

We can say this much about Mead: he does reject the classical formulation of both sociological realism and nominalism. His own answer of the "social individual" suggests that self and society are laid down together: correlative aspects of the same natural experience. Selves develop only in a social context, and society exists only in and through and for individuals. Self and society are mutually interdependent and reciprocally conditioned. The universal is nothing if the particular is nothing; but the particular comes to self-awareness and effective freedom only within a complex and responsive universal. Necessity and freedom are harmonized, teleology and mechanism are reconciled,—if Mead's account be well founded.

Buber gives us a somewhat different account.

For Buber individuality is central, but for him *individuality* is a naturalistic and biological category, while *personality* is a religious and spiritual one. There are many individuals that are not "persons," yet all individuals, even trees and lakes and animals, seem to have hovering over them the potentiality of the "Thou." [47]

The basic question for Buber, as for Mead, is that of the person within the community. The person, while real and free and responsible, is correlative to society. The strange and wonderful thing about the mutual relations which obtain in Buber's I-Thou world is that the activity of one self-conscious, self-directing, unique, unprecedented person is conditioned by that of another in such a way that both remain free, autonomous, responsible. "Each life is a life in itself, but as such it forms the community." [48] Buber writes in the memory of those Chassidic communities which he knew as a boy: men of many-sided individuality and strong differences, yet each surrounded by a community that lived a brotherly life. Individual life, yes; but in the atmosphere of the true community life it became something different.

There are no living corporate or institutional persons; the community is not an organism, nor is it, strictly speaking, to be mistaken for the I-Thou relation. Buber is no sociological realist. The form-urge in the inner life of each man is the ultimate fact and mystery. The concept of the "single one" as the ground of moral responsibility which may not be repudiated is deeply embedded in Buber's thought. Selves make society and are made by it; yet each self is a unique and singular person. Like snowflakes, each individual has an unrepeatable pattern or form which forever excludes all others. When they melt and combine they disappear into formlessness. In Buber's "single one" in community there is an individual continuum that persists through all the changing states. There is always a free and sensitive core of personality which is able to transcend its culture. The self is conditioned, yet free. Buber of course realized that the concrete human being is bound to and conditioned by time and place, family, folk, nation, or people. But there ever remains the "single one," and the real other, in his existential personal standpoint, an individual, however, who is free to realize selfhood only within community. He who decides is free; he who knows decision and responsibility knows how to meet destiny. The primal category of human reality is *man with man*. It is in and through communication, in turning to the other, in being bound up in relation to real otherness, in the dialogic life of I-and-Thou, that man is truly man.

Despite his early mystical experiences and his tendency to embrace a position close to that of mystical pantheism, Buber emphatically rejects that point of view, precisely because any consistent pantheism denies and stifles the individual soul of man. The "One-without-a-second" of Eastern pantheism leaves no room for a real existential other. Time and space become a veil which hides reality, not a sacrament which reveals it. There is no place for gnosis or magic in Buber's thought.[49] "The religious life means concreteness itself, the whole concreteness of life *without reduction,* understood dialogically."[50] Man is not merely a "mode" of God's Being; man and God are existentially two. Human choice is real; man is a real partner with God. In his choice and in his action are expressed both the reality of man's being and his dependence upon grace. So Buber declares in a letter to the writer: *Kein Pantheismus!* The unification (jichud) is not contained in any pantheistic formula. Yet ultimately everything is *in* God.[51] "God is incomprehensible, but he can be known through a bond of mutual relationship." [52] When man turns to God something happens in the immediacy of the reality in which men and God are together. God has set the mark of His image upon man's nature, and "God's real commandment to men is to realize this image." [53] This is the unification and man's redemption.

Man is bound up in relation; but he is still free with respect to both society and nature. Of course, he stands in a creaturely and conditioned position; and to know this saves him from the presumptive pride of self-sovereignty. Yet he is no mere derivative of some organic collectivism, and thus absolved from personal response and morally responsible action. Buber, therefore, retires both individualism and collectivism as false idols, and as false alternatives in the systematic attempt to harmonize the two opposing viewpoints of an individualistic anthropology and a collectivistic sociology. Neither sociological nominalism nor sociological realism does justice to the data of experience. "The genuineness and adequacy of the self cannot stand the test in self-commerce, but only in communication with the whole of otherness." [54] Not the private life versus the public life, but *man with man* in the uncurtailed measure of the dialogic life. Man's way lies through overcoming his isolation without forfeiting the responsibility of his real aloneness. "Only men who are capable of truly saying *Thou* to one another can truly say *We* with one another." [55] To be free, to be responsible, to be a real person, and to be in mutual relation with all otherness—all these mean the same thing. It is the *realm of between*, where *I* and *Thou* meet, which is the genuine third alternative, the knowledge of which will bring about both genuine selfhood and the genuine community. This is Buber's gospel; and it offers strength and direction and profound insight to man in his quest for redemption.

In the course of our summary comparison of the basic similarities in Mead and Buber, we have already had occasion to note some flaws and ambiguities in their argument, along with certain differences in emphasis. We may now proceed to a further critical examination of certain contrasts and disparities in their thought.

CONTRASTS AND CRITICISM

Is Self or Society prior?—Must we assume an antecedent transempirical subject? Or does the social process precede the emergent self? Or are self and society twin-born? These questions are basic;

and they raise certain other queries as between social nominalism and social realism which cannot be avoided.

Mead's theory and contention were that mind and self develop and have their being only in and by virtue of the social process of experience and activity which is presupposed. His life-long effort was to show (1) that mind and self are bio-social emergents, generated without antecedents in a social process, and (2) that language is the mechanism of their genesis. These two propositions deserve inspection.

Mead approached social psychology from the standpoint of a qualified behaviorism in which self-conscious intelligence is considered as strictly and only a bio-social emergent which has appeared late in vertebrate evolution. Mind or self, then, is no spiritual substance or trans-empirical stuff super-induced upon a form, but rather a certain sort of behavior or set of characters arising in the relationship of an environment to an organism. But since the ultimate unit of reality (in Mead's later thought) is the *act* in time, the environment is in some sense "carved out" or determined by the selective sensitivity of the organic form. Mead's stress upon the "social" was so extreme that he seemed at times to say that *only* social facts, *only relations with other human forms,* were conditioning and constitutive factors in the genesis of self-consciousness. On his view, we must be others *before* we can be ourselves, and therefore, other selves in social environment logically antedate the consciousness of self. Furthermore, this seems to mean that only other human forms are significant and creative in the social environment of human beings. Essential social relations are horizontal and one-dimensional. There is in Mead's thought no place or need for a vertical man-God relation.

Not so with Buber. Of course, as we have seen, Buber concurs that there is no "self" by itself, but only the self which stands over against another in the reality of bi-subjective relationship. As long as individuals live in the ordinary space-time dimensional world of the I-It, they lack full reality. Only by entering and participating in the world of Spirit,[56] only by taking the I-Thou attitude, does the individual form become a fully real self. "I am here, as 'I'; but I become a self through my relationship with the world." We are and remain human in so far as we live in mutual personal responsiveness and dialogue with other men, and with God.

The decisive point here is that Buber does not restrict this dialogic life, this eternal meeting of the one with the other which is constitutive of selfhood, to the human sphere, to man's relations with the fellow-men. Buber insists upon a *threefold* living relation, including a "vertical" one with God. In this sense, man lives in three different environments: the natural, the human, the divine. Buber's religious anthropology makes it impossible for him to conceive of the universe in terms merely of man's finitude, or to imagine that man's speech with his fellows can plumb the depths of existence. Buber insists that mutual personal responsiveness occurs in the fullest sense when persons believe that God has already sought them out and addressed them and laid upon them a higher claim. Men can love God only because God has first loved them, called them into being.

Whether or not it can be maintained consistently that the empirical self is exclusively a social product, Buber would argue against Mead that human social facts are not the only conditioning factors in the development of the self: one's contact with Nature and with God must also have a share in evoking the real self. Indeed, Buber declares that man is distinctly man, in the full and definitive sense, in so far as—whether he confesses it or not—he stands in the innermost essence of his being in relationship to God in an order of persons. Man's ultimate engagement is with God.

The crucial question here is whether the individual becomes a self in and through relations, or is already a self who then enters into relations with other selves. Mead is very clear in his *declaration* that mind and self are, without residue, bio-social emergents. He is not so convincing and consistent in his *demonstration* of that fact, as we have seen. Buber, also, is not crystal clear. He appears to be guilty of ambiguity, if not equivocation, on this point—although I am not sure that it ever occurred to Buber to put the question just this way. In any event there is conflicting evidence. It is his conviction that neither the individual nor the social aggregate is the fundamental reality of human existence. The basic reality is *man with man.* Buber places the locus of reality in the "sphere of between." He shares with Ebner the thesis that in the relation between persons there is a unique spiritual reality. He seems to be saying that a person does not first exist as an individual form and then enter into communication with others. It is rather in that communication that he becomes or is a person. Yet Buber seems throughout to assume a Kantian transcendental "subject" as a prior condition of relations, and as a necessary support for the moral and religious interests at stake. Says Buber: "I am here, as 'I'; but I become a self through my relationship with the world." "To say that 'community' comes first is pure speculation." [57] "Certainly in order to be able to go out to the other you must have the starting place, you must have been, you must be, with yourself. Dialogue between mere individuals is only a sketch; only in dialogue between persons is the sketch filled in." [58] Here he seems to be positing a primary ontal status for the individual subjective ego. Relations are crucial in the personal world; but they must presuppose or infer an active and creative subject behind the scenes. Relation is not absolute; but neither is independence of the primal "I" absolute. And certainly one learns to say "I" only because a "Thou" is there. About all we can say is that *I* and *Thou* are interdependent. Man is both self and other, subject and object at the same time. On the evidence so far it seems best to conclude that self and society are twin-born.

Mead is also equivocal on this point—where we least expect him to be. Despite his exaggerated stress on pure scientific method, social behaviorism, radical empiricism, and the social category, we find Mead accepting a distinction between the "I" and the "me" which is likewise not unlike Kant in its practical effect. As an empirical scientist Mead emphasized the "me," the empirical data and organized structure of the social process. And here society is prior to the individual, the whole is prior to the part. Here Mead is a monist. But he found he must take account of the "I," the free impulsive organism; and his emphasis in this instance carried him into a monadism in which the private subjective self is intuited or assumed.[59] He escaped his dilemma, as many scientists and pragmatists do, by simply by-passing the issue, declaring that both the "I" and the "me" are only scientific postulates, fruitful for research, but not dogmas.[60] Be that as it may, Mead admits that the "I" is a necessary presupposition, a cognitive inference of an active non-phenomenal *subject* necessary to account for the evidence, and that the "me" is inconceivable without an "I." Naturally this "I" does not nor can it appear as an empirical object of knowledge, for the moment it is presented as such it becomes not a *subject* but an *object*, a *me*.[61] So while Mead denies to the "I" any ontological status, such as Buber seems to accept, he does and must accept it as a "methodological fiction." If only as a methodological fiction, Mead must provide for some trans-empirical *agency*, some creative *form*, some transcendental *center* of experience, some unitary unrepeatable *continuum* as a necessary conjunctive with the "me" or social content. He cannot consistently deny a distinction between the *attributes* and the *essence* of the self or personality. To say that we *know* ourselves only in the presence of others is not to say that we *exist* only in the presence of others. Mead's conception, it seems to me, cries out for a more concrete ontological filling that will integrate the "I" and the "me" than Mead's empiricism provides. Meanwhile his own position seems to involve a unitary, enduring and synthesizing factor not fully open to direct observation, without which human experience cannot be adequately conceived or clearly described.

It is reasonably clear, also, that Mead's axiology—which, in common with most pragmatists since James, holds to an interest theory of value akin to that of R. B. Perry[62]—encounters a similar difficulty. Mead felt that his social psychology provided an escape (epistemological, ethical, and axiological) from the egocentric predicament by getting a self which includes the standpoints and values of others. He believed, without elaborating his views in detail, that his psychology provided a fruitful basis for aesthetic theory.[63] But any interest theory of value (such as Perry's, and even Mead's with its novel bent) is embarrassed by a "subjectivism" which is incompatible with their professed empirical realism and ethical meliorism. One pardonably expects a greater realism and massiveness in values from those whose polemic was directed against idealism in epistemology. Mead's social positivism, however, prevents him from passing to a more realistic metaphysics and axiology. While this problem is related to the question of the possible intrinsic character of a knowing self, to examine it in detail would take us beyond the legitimate limits of our present inquiry. Accordingly, we here merely point to the problem, and refer the reader to certain discussions of the matter.[64]

On the evidence, then, and despite his impatient efforts to gloss over the issue as a pseudo-problem or as a purely methodological necessity, it seems that Mead gives his case away the moment he ventures into metaphysics. Even from the standpoint of epistemological analysis, Mead's view runs into serious difficulty.[65] Mead has prematurely closed the case of speculative metaphysics and dualistic theories of knowledge. Even on his own account there is, behind the scenes, a unifying principle or existing *subject* of behavior (the "I" in Mead's terms; "the transcendental unity of apperception" in Kantian jargon) which is not simply identical with the experienced "me." There are *two* correlative aspects of one enduring reality, and the distinction between them ought to be kept clear. Mead himself recognized this, when he was not too busy disavowing any trans-empirical, discontinuous factors.[66] Mead saw that the total self appears to be something in addition to the actual empirical "me," something semi-independent of the environmental data and events; but instead of seriously asking what more it might be, he cavalierly dismisses it as a "methodological fiction."

All of this is to say that Mead is always evasive in *accounting for* the *capacity* of human animals to take the roles of others and to develop and use symbolic language. I have the feeling that instrumentalism and pragmatism in general, and Mead in this instance, make ontological and value assumptions which are not clarified, and perhaps not justified even on their own account. Mead appears to be guilty of an "additive naturalism" which assumes too much. He attempts to reject all *a priori* entities and all "mere speculation," yet he appears at times to be himself guilty of smuggling in *a priori* concepts drawn from biological categories and of speculatively applying those categories to the fields of logic, ethics, sociology, religion, and psychology, and being thus guilty at times of misleading analogies and interpretations.

Different subject matters require different categories and methods. And it has not at all been proven that the *higher* can and must be interpreted in terms of the *lower*.[67] The fact that something (organism or individual) has a place in a developmental process tells us not only that it has *grown out* of its antecedents, but also that it has *outgrown* them. To interpret man in purely biological terms, or society in terms of biology or physics, must surely lead to an inadequate and distorted view. To say that man is an animal does not mean that he is only an animal. Likewise to posit "mind" as merely a product of evolution must be a gross over-simplification. Mind is surely one of the primary categories of the universe. It may very well be that mind, far from being merely a *product* of evolution, is one of its primary grounds. Has not Mead failed to make a distinction between *Mind* and a *specific mind* as a center and agent of discursive thought and symbol? A specific mind, or at least its content, obviously develops as an emergent in the social context. Few, if any, well-trained philosophers today would think of the self as a quite separate entity, sundered from nature and alien to the processes of knowing.[68] But mind is also thought of in familiar terms as including, in addition to discursive thought and intellection, such factors as feeling, will, purpose, responsible self-direction, organization, and interpretation—all modes of behavior other than those which bodies have, modes of behavior which can only with serious reservations be adequately explained as a function of some other entity. It may, then, be possible to accept Mead's empirical account of the self as a brilliant methodological postulate, solidly supported by most of the observed data, but without accepting uncritically his metaphysical naturalism as a necessary correlate, or his denial of an extra-experiential self.

Mead is not always clear as to the relation of the self to the "generalized other." This concept is also a very suggestive and felicitous *hypothesis,* rather than an empirical fact supported by observation. And there is some doubt that the view that we must be others before we can be ourselves, and that other selves logically antedate consciousness of self, can be maintained consistently. Nor has Mead himself consistently held to it throughout all of his writings. In some passages he advances the theory that the self arises in consciousness *pari passu* with the recognition and definition of other selves.[69] As a matter of fact this latter view seems rather more plausible than the former. It is like the old question of the chicken and the egg, or the famous argument between those who held that light was corpuscular and those who said it was a set of waves. So far as I know, both arguments have ended in a draw—at least for methodological purposes. Likewise this argument about the priority of self or society.[70] Social situations no doubt promote the development of self-consciousness; but it seems rather extreme speculation to contend that we are the "generalized other" *before* we are ourselves. Again it seems excessive to argue that "we cannot use our responses to others as the materials for construction of the self—this imagery goes to make up the other selves." [71]

It would seem to be nearer all the facts to seek to reconcile the two sides of this question by some such theory as F. Tönnies' version of the social group as having both organic and individualistic aspects. These two aspects Tönnies designated as *Gemeinschaft* (an organic, sympathetic, fundamental community) and *Gesellschaft* (an arbitrary collection or aggregation of individuals held together by agreement, interest or choice, and within which each seeks his own advantage). In *Gesellschaft* the individuals are separated in spite of association; in *Gemeinschaft* the individuals are associated in spite of separation.[72] In other words, both social *nominalism* and social *realism* are inadequate accounts of the true human situation. Self and Society are twin-born. The self arises *pari passu* with the recognition of, and communication with, other selves within a social field of inter-personal relations.

The Power of Speech.—Mead has shown how, in the development of the self-conscious personality, the spontaneous and meaningless gesture is defined by the responses of the other so that while our ideas and symbols are our own, the *meaning* is the contribution of others. Now, it is also Mead's own notion that human consciousness is purposive, teleological, selective of the stimuli attended to, serving as a tool in adjusting to the environment. If this be true, the meaning of one's gesture is not wholly determined from without by others. We may not presume that when a person speaks, he always speaks his mind. People like to play; they sometimes pretend and hide their feelings and their real meanings. External behavior may allow of more than one interpretation. Again, my action can hardly be conscious and purposive without having at the same time *a meaning for me* as calculated to arouse certain anticipated reactions and attitudes in others. But the meaning for me of my own act or gesture is not always the same as the responding gesture or attitude of my neighbor. Surely the meaning of my gesture (vocal or non-vocal) is not, for instance, determined by the responsive gestures provoked in a child, an insane person, or an animal. There is no inevitable connection between a concept and its verbal symbol. We may not assume, especially for learners of language, that for every word used there is an idea. Symbols do not necessarily determine the meaning of common mental images—except for insane or psychotic persons for whom the Symbol is the Object[73]— but rather mental images determine the meaning of symbols conditioned to the meaning. Even here a further difficulty is encountered, since not every idea has its appropriate word.[74] There is an ultimate loneliness of the private mind which even the powers of the speech cannot overcome. The common coin will at times misrepresent what is unique to any person. Furthermore, it is probable that we have as yet neither words nor syntax with which to express certain important truths about the world. If this line of argument is valid, we can hardly agree that all meanings are socially determined, and that social consciousness antedates physical consciousness.[75]

Likewise with respect to Buber, and despite the evidence which he adduces in support of the "inborn Thou" and the "a priori of relation," [76] his assertion that the *relational* attitude is predominant in the life of children and primitive man would be difficult of verification upon the scientific data available. Many, if not most, contemporary investigators, especially among the psychologists and anthropologists, would explain the gestures and babblings of an infant without recourse to such a theory as the "a priori of relation." [77] This, however, is not the crucial issue for Buber, nor does it invalidate his major thesis.[78]

For Buber, speech is creative at two different levels: for man and for God. On the human level Buber's meaning may be conveyed by using the analogy of spirit as a kind of magnetic field. In the world of I-It the magnetic lines of force are broken or neutralized. When the "Thou" is truly spoken, the two centers or poles of force bring about a magnetic field. "Spirit" is, then, analogous to the lines of magnetic force lying "between." [79]

We have seen that, for Buber, man is primarily and distinctively a person in a world of personal relationships. But within this relationship, and peculiarly essential to it, is the element of *speech*. Speech places at the heart of this constitutive relationship the element of claim, and the mutual recognition and acknowledgment of claims which persons as persons have upon one another, including the higher divine claim which God makes upon man. The divine claim is always related to and finds practical content in the claim of human persons upon one another.[80] Speech, the Word, personal address, is *par excellence* the mode or agency of this claim at the point where it meets a man and constitutes him distinctively a human person. For speech involves responsible answer; an answer which cannot be predicted or rehearsed. The one addressed is answerable, he is held accountable. Of course, he is free to reject the claim; he may refuse to answer. But he is still answerable, still accountable: his refusal to answer means an answer in the negative,—and it means also a kind of loss of selfhood. For something has gone wrong in that relationship which is deeply and peculiarly creative of human selfhood. He has withdrawn from that responsible encounter which makes a man a *man*. Responsibility is real only in the life of dialogue.

It is our disparate points of view which make for our contrasting claims. Therefore if I am to deal with your claim upon me, I must somehow understand it, get your point of view, grasp your meaning. This requires reasoning together, creating a community of insight and understanding. And for this kind of shared meaning within a universe of discourse, nothing is so important as communication by means of vocal symbol, i.e., language. This is the reason why *speech* is so central in the creation and maintenance of a world of *personal* relationships. Without speech and hearing one is cut off from the world of persons. "The spoken word is right within the core of the I-Thou relationship, and the written or printed word is always a poor substitute for it." [81] For the same reason a mimeographed or printed letter often seems, by comparison with a hand-written one, vaguely impersonal. Primitive peoples, perhaps even more than civilized men, have known the strange potency of the spoken word. So too H. H. Farmer declares:

> The reason why the spoken word is thus at the very heart of the world of persons in relationship of the I-Thou relationship, is that it is supremely that medium of communication wherein the three elements . . . *will and claim and shared meaning*, are, or can be, at a maximum together in a single, fused unity.[82]

Speech is full of claim and pledge. My word is my will; my will ordains it, embodies it, and directs it toward the other with objectivity, immediacy, personal claim or pledge. When I speak to you, my word and my will claims yours. I claim your attention and your answer and your truth. You may repudiate my claim, refuse an answer, or reject my vow—for claim is not compulsion. But you are not free to escape it. In refusing to respond, you prove the very point we are making. And if my claim is a right claim, rooted in the nature and reality of the I-Thou world, your rejection of it can have evil results. Here I can hardly do better than to quote again from H. H. Farmer who is in this matter greatly influenced by Buber's terminology and his whole philosophy of the personal.

> . . . In man, in whom alone appears anything that may truly be designated individuality, or personal life, the isolation of mind from mind is almost complete. . . . For man has elaborated a new method of communication, one which allows full exchange of meaning and yet respects the frontiers, the territorial integrity of the personality, namely the use of symbols, and particularly the use of speech which is a highly complex and refined way of signalling to one another. When I speak to a friend, I cannot thrust my meanings directly into his mind, however much I may be disposed to think that it would be to his advantage if I could. I can only come so far as the frontier and signal my meaning, and

the latter can only become his after he has interpreted the signals and taken up their significance into his own personal awareness. He may, however, reject their meaning, but the fact that it was first symbolized is precisely what gives him the opportunity to accept or reject it. . . . [83]

All of this is not to suggest that speech is the only medium of human communication. Music, art, ritual, dance, even silence, are also means of conveying truth and value judgments. There are indeed certain kinds of truth which transcend verbal expression and propositional form. Be it remembered, too, that speech for Buber is not the ordinary affair of words, which may or may not be communication. Speech *is* communication itself, though it be wordless. Yet everyday speech with words remains as superior to all other means of communication and therefore indispensable in the world of personal relationships.

Buber goes even further and declares that God's act of creation is speech. The world is the Word which is spoken. Buber translates both creation and theophany into speech. Out of the abyss of origin came "God's cry of creation into the void. Silence still lies brooding before him, but soon from the midst of the silence things begin to arise and give answer—their very coming into existence is answer. . . . Created stands man, a whole body, ensouled by his relation to the created, enspirited by his relation to the Creator." [84] Buber thus regards speech as "an event which grasps beyond the existence of mankind and the world." [85] Every moment is word and answer. "The world is given to the human beings who perceive it, and the life of man is itself a dialogue," [86]—a giving and a receiving.

What happens to man are signs of his being addressed; what he does is an answer or failure to answer. The whole history of the world is a dialogue between God and his creatures, "a dialogue in which man is a true, legitimate partner, who is entitled and empowered to speak his own independent word from out of his own being." [87] In a note to the present writer, Professor Buber wrote:

> The Unconditioned, in the correct sense, is only God Himself; but there is a partaking when one enters the relationship completely, unreservedly. . . . In my relationship with Him, He is a Person for my sake; only as a Person can I know Him. . . . Theophany comes singularly from above. Man behaves toward it like metal to fire, but the fire needs the metal. God needs man for material realization. . . . [88] In reality, God does not depend upon

man at all, but I have a degree of the punishment of decision; it is evident that He has given it to me. This is only comprehensible within the mystery of the relationship between God and man. One cannot argue about it logically.

And again in *Mamre* he writes:

Human choice is not a psychological phenomenon, but utter reality. . . . It is truly open to man to choose God or to cast him away. . . . Only when reality is turned into logic, when A and non-A dare not any longer dwell together, do we get determinism and indeterminism, teaching about predestination and teaching about freedom, each excluding the other. According to the logical conception of truth only one of two contraries can be true, but in the reality of the lived life they are interlocked. . . . [89] The unity of the contraries is the mystery at the innermost core of the dialogue. . . . Judaism is in earnest with the conception that man has been appointed to this world as an originator of events, as a real partner in the real dialogue with God.[90]

It is in such dialogue that man becomes truly and fully man.

The Generalized Other and the Moral Issues at stake.—Several of Mead's friends and colleagues have remarked that it is surprising that Mead nowhere suggests that his concept of the generalized or universalized other might provide the psychological equivalent for the historical and personalistic conceptions of God, or of the Absolute of the idealists.[91] But the fact is that he did not. Throughout he was the naturalist, the relativist, the pragmatist. He was concerned with the techniques for remaking values through the experimental reinterpretation of the situation in terms of the best knowledge possible. The right act or good value, on this view, is "objective" and "universal" only in the functional sense that it commands the assent of most or all rational beings in the group. Therefore, questions of right and wrong are not questions of *ends* and *values* to be judged by some ultimate standard; they are simply questions of the best means of solving the problem under prevailing conditions, or of getting an inhibited system to working again.

But Mead is not convincing at this point. Perhaps he could have corrected this failure, at least theoretically and psychologically, if he had been willing to extend his concept of the generalized other to that of a Universal Other or God, with whom men can enter into social relations and from whom men could take over some more universal ends, values, and obligations by which they themselves are judged. The conflict of narrow groups ends in expediency and casuistry unless there is some more general principle transcending those that are in dispute. When men deny that there is any objective reality to which they must submit, and insist that God or truth or even reason has no final claim upon them, there is no ethical standard left with which to judge the use of power in society. On the other hand, religious persons may often, in the name of God, fall into error; but they carry with them a self-corrective in that they point to the revelation of God in the light of whose judgment they are themselves condemned.

There is no need to deny the considerable truth and importance of Mead's theory in order to point out that the biological and the social categories may not be the *only* and *original* sources of interest and motivation, especially at the level of moral experience. For we know that men can and do transcend their partisan loyalties and group pressures to serve the larger good and the wider community. But such transcendence is in spite of the narrow group conditioning, and it is hardly possible to account for such self-transcendence or group-transcendence on the basis of a process of social conditioning, for this self-transcendence (will to the good of all, etc.,) is experienced by individuals living in groups which do not feel it or approve of it. The growing edge of society and of history is the individual who has acquired the higher insight and motivation in spite of society, its clash of interests, and its habitual traditions. Mead himself was a good example of such a person. But his treatment of the problem does not so much *explain* the "miracle" of how Mother Nature produces a noble human soul from an animal, as to *acknowledge* the fact. Mead, of course, does not deny the sense of moral or social obligation, but he seems to weaken it by explaining it as entirely due to social conditioning. Of course there are "social" impulses that demand expression, but some of those social impulses are evil and contrary to the universal good, e.g., as seen in the program of the Fascists, Nazis, and Stalinists for whom black is white, night is day, and truth and right are whatever benefits the Party or Nation. One need not see ideas in a vacuum to protest a total explanation of human relations in terms of economic and social environment.

It is, of course, obvious that much of what we call "conscience" is due to social conditioning. Many, probably most, of the everyday values-for-me are the values-for-my-group. Even my most private and critical moral ideas and practices are developed within the frame of group influence. But it appears to be both psychologically and morally mistaken to assert that *all* of my moral impulses and activities are entirely determined by social conditioning and have no authority save that of custom.[92] Simply adhering to such principles or rules will lead to difficulty unless they be somehow regarded as deductions from a general obligation which can be stated only in broad terms, i.e., the *obligation of the individual* to concern himself with the good of all. Man not only has the unique capacity for self-criticism and group-criticism, but what may be called simply "moral consciousness." It is this fundamental principle of "moral consciousness" (as interpreted most convincingly in the writings of Kant, John Baillie, and A. C. Garnett)[93] that the theory of social conditioning fails either to explain completely or to support. "It is because of its failure to explain it that the theory is psychologically unsound; and it is because of its failure to support it that the theory is morally pernicious."[94]

But Mead demurs. For him the social order is still the moral order. Morality is not a matter of following some external rule or authority, but of discovering and using intelligent scientific methods. An intelligent experimentation and consideration for the consequences will always direct our choices and actions into avenues which are socially beneficial. Such a position seems to over-simplify the facts. It just isn't true that, because minds and selves are socially derived in form and content, intelligent action will be socially valuable, that this social self will never put his own interests ahead of the common good. Mead himself seems aware that he falls short of a completely satisfactory answer as will be seen by putting in juxtaposition a few quotations.

> Ethical ideas, within any given human society, arise in the consciousness of the individual members of that society from the fact of the common social dependence of all those individuals upon one another. . . . Every human individual must, to behave ethically, integrate himself with the pattern of organized social behavior which, as reflected or prehended in the structure of his self, makes him a self-conscious personality.[95]

This passage seems to say that social communication is the whole explanation of the moral consciousness. But Mead is also trying to preserve the initiative and integrity of his social individual, so as to account for social innovation and progress. So he writes:

Any such social reconstruction, if it is to be at all far-reaching, presupposes a basis of common social interests shared by all the individual members of the given human society in which that reconstruction occurs; shared, that is, by all the individuals whose minds must participate in, or whose minds bring about, that reconstruction. And the way in which any such social reconstruction is actually effected by the minds of the individuals involved is by a more or less abstract intellectual extension of the boundaries of the given society to which these individuals all belong, and which is undergoing the reconstruction—an extension resulting in a larger social whole in terms of which the social conflicts that necessitate the reconstruction of the given society are harmonized or reconciled and by reference to which, accordingly, these conflicts can be solved or eliminated.[96]

And again:

We have not taken very seriously our membership in the human society, but it is becoming more real to us. The World War has shaken down a great many values; and we realize that what takes place in India, in Afghanistan, in Mesopotamia, is entering into our lives, so that we are getting what we term "international mindedness." We are reacting in a way that answers to the response of people on the other side of the human group.[97]

If this were true, then it would appear that the only way in which people could feel any responsibility for the welfare of, say, the Jews of Germany, the tenant farmers of the South, the peasants of China, the Negroes of Harlem is by discovering that their own interests are dependent upon or identical with the interests of these others. And, by the same token, the strength of the obligation would be relative to the importance or degree of the interests thus involved. But that means, also, that so long as it profited one group to exploit another group, the former would feel no prohibition against doing so. Prior to the development of a more universalistic ethical tradition which, like that of the early Hebrews, recognized an obligation even to slaves and strangers, no individual could recognize such an obligation as going beyond his group's narrow self-interest. Indeed, no such tradition or teaching could ever get started. Yet it is a matter of historical record and human experience that such self-transcending traditions *have gotten started*, usually in the insight, revelation, or prophetic utterance of some great individual—and proclaimed in the name of some higher

law or sanction.[98] It is true, of course, that the awareness and acknowledgment of common interests help to make us more sensitive to the
needs and claims of others. This theme is played over and over again;
and it is on this level of "enlightened self interest" posing as a moral
system that most people live their daily lives. But an obligation or
sense of community that rests on nothing higher than the self-interests
of individuals or narrow groups hardly rises to the level of *moral imperative*. It is mere prudence.

We are led to the conclusion that while Mead's social philosophy
is generous, and his social psychology probably true, the self which
results from Mead's analysis is empirically and psychologically "social"
but hardly more ethically so than the particular community which
begets it.[99] Therefore, Mead's theory tends to induce a false optimism
about human nature, while failing to explain the development of higher
and more universal moral ideas. It might even be argued that Mead's
theory of the social self, unamended, actually weakens the sense of
obligation to others, while failing to explain its most significant feature,
namely, what Professor Garnett has called "the sense of obligation to
manifest universal good will." [100] There is something to be said for
obligation to value as such, for *loyalty to loyalty*.[101] Some things are
right and wrong regardless of the majorities who may support them.
Man is social, yes; but above all, Buber would insist, he is socially
related to God—and this is the secret of all his other relations. And
it is the betrayal or rejection of this capacity and this relationship which
constitutes man's sin.

This analysis, if well founded, validates the central principle of the
Hebrew-Christian ethic, and points to some principle of *ought* and
moral will, objectively and universally valid, because rooted in the
essential nature of man. But for a religious ethic like Buber's we need
to go beyond "moral philosophy" to show that a self that is rooted
in a disinterested will to the good cannot itself have produced that
will, but must be produced by it. We must then pass from the will
to the good which is found in men to its source in the universe which
produces men.

God as a "Third" in a Triad of Relations.—In the mutual, reciprocal
conditioning of two persons or groups we have only the raw material
of a unified, harmonious moral world of trust and cooperation which
can become the world of Thou. But, as we have seen, the ideals and
interests and claims of persons and groups *clash* with one another.

Sometimes these interests and claims are reinforced by powerful drives and an ingrained self-regard. How then is any community of loyalty and cooperation to be established? One recent writer has declared that "there is no way in which it can permanently be done other than by persons acknowledging themselves to be, in their reciprocal claims, under a third and higher claim, which comprehends their claims upon one another and lays itself equally and impartially upon all in an absolute rule, the right of which to undeviating obedience neither questions." [102] Continuing, he writes, "If you and I, as we deal with one another, both acknowledge ourselves to be under one and the same higher, more comprehensive, and overriding claim, that fact at once brings our claims on one another into the same world," [103] and the basis of unity is established, despite adjustments which will still have to be made.

Along such lines can we find the answer to the moral issues: when both self and other recognize a higher claim or value which both acknowledge they ought to obey no matter how insistent the clamoring environmental or physical stimuli may be. As both acknowledge the same final claim or direction for their lives as governing their relations one with another, then a deep unity and freedom and mutuality becomes a possibility. Such a relationship is perhaps best illustrated in the relationship of married love, placed under a sacramental vow, and thereby converted into a holy vocation, responsible toward what is holy.[104]

Nothing that we have said so far in this present discussion is distinctively "religious." Men may and do accept some objective and more universal standard of values without identifying it with, say, the God of Judaism or Christianity. But the distinctively Jewish understanding of the personal world as we see it in Buber becomes significant at precisely this point. For Buber would assert that the *source* and *sanction* of this higher universal claim, in acknowledgment of which human relations can be built up into universal community, is God, the infinite personal Thou, and that only in knowledge of and right response to the Eternal Thou can man become fully *man* and human community be built. In Buber's thought the claim of the neighbor is always part of God's claim on me. God meets me most significantly in and through the meetings with the neighbor. In the perplexities and corruptions of our human world, man may know the divine claim and will, and respond to it, most clearly in the meetings with a Personal

Reality who claims him in and through and with the mutual I-Thou meetings with the neighbor. "The true community does not arise through people having feelings for one another (though indeed not without it), but through first their taking their stand in living mutual relations with a living Center, and second, their being in living mutual relations with one another." In introducing this third, higher, vertical dimension of God, it seems to me that Buber has corrected a fatal omission in Mead's theory of the social self. Only by keeping our eyes on the personal and Godlike aspects of man (including of course *other* men) can we really do justice to both the moral imperative *and* moral evil, or sin, which is the perversion of the highest in man, as Reinhold Niebuhr has reminded us.

The significant thing about the human spirit is that it is able to apprehend and relate itself to a perfection which it cannot perfectly achieve, yet to which it feels obligated. This is both man's glory and his despair.[105] The Hebrew prophets and the Christian fathers, Niebuhr insists, "saw some of the depths of life because they looked at it from the heights, and saw some of the heights because they viewed life from its depths; while the modern sees life only from the level of a complacent moralism." [106] Such a criticism would seem to apply to such as Mead who sees human nature chiefly in a single, flat dimension. Mead does not see man as both a fact in nature *and* beyond nature, as a son of God. On his account man is only a high-class animal, not as good as he might be but constantly growing better. In the light of recent history, this view strikes us as too facile to be profound and too simple to do justice to the tragic facts of human existence. Contemporary history seems to refute such an interpretation of human nature. And Mead's own account seems inconclusive as establishing an adequate ground for his optimistic meliorism. The social woof of the self is morally spotted, and the warp—about this warp, as we have already noted, Mead has little to say.[107]

Buber's theistic interpretation of moral obligations does not deny that human nature is social or that conscience is socially conditioned. Quite the contrary; his view enriches and deepens the possibility of community. Man is implicated in all manner of inter-personal relations and group relations. Selves die without community. Man *is* social; but Buber would insist that above all he is socially related to God. This is the ultimate key to all man's social relations, including (through perversion) his bad ones. It is doubtful whether Mead's description of the "I" as an agent of social change, allegedly transcending the particular social demands, offers so adequate a conception of the basis for moral obligation or the criterion of right and wrong. Men are more likely to stand firm and suffer for truth and right, if they have faith that God is on the side of Truth and Goodness, that somehow, somewhere the Universe will validate truth and virtue.

It is necessary to add that such a view in no way overlooks nor deprecates, as does Mead, the mystical element which plays so essential a role in Buber's thought and practice.[108]

THE GROUND AND END OF HUMAN EXISTENCE

We may close this comparative and critical analysis by asking what Mead and Buber have to say about what human life can be, both now and in time to come. What is their hope, their faith for a better world: Can it be well-founded? What have they to say about man's historical destiny? It might be assumed that any adequate treatment of the self must venture a consideration of the ground and end of human existence. For our present purpose, we shall try to get our bearings with respect to this problem by setting in contrast the respective views of Mead and Buber; for it happens that they represent, in broad outline, two fairly typical and sharply opposed answers given to this problem in contemporary discussions of time and its relation to any possible progress toward a brighter future.

Mead held the romantic view that man's life, set within an evolutionary natural order, is continually moving toward a higher and more intelligent good. Mead had a profound confidence in human nature and intelligence. His simple formula was: Man can if he will; and he will if he knows; but he can know only through the technique of science. His doctrine to implement the formula was a confidence in human nature to find its own best way by trusting as good its own impulses and as right whatever would solve the immediate problem. That simple optimism is today under scornful attack as being hopelessly naive and utopian. Even his student and colleague, T. V. Smith, charges Mead with romanticism—he who thought he had transcended romanticism.[109] And it must be confessed that from the vantage point of the mid-century mark, with its sober appraisal of the first half of this grim century, Mead's view of history does have a romantic quality which poorly fits the facts. Almost incredible changes there have been, but little net progress. The ongoing march of the creative forces seems slowed to a stand-still. The "faith-in-progress" cult is on the defensive and the good society seems farther away than ever.

Buber, on the other hand, bases his hope and expectancy on the faith that God is present in human history and is there creatively and redemptively at work. The ultimate meaning of man's life lies in his relationship to God. Moreover, he believes that to seek to build the City of Man on anything less than a solid faith in God and His righteous truth is to build on quicksand. Buber agrees with its critics that modern humanism (as represented by Mead) has been too optimistic about man and his progress. He believes that the Hebraic and Chassidic understanding of man and God provides a sound corrective. Faith can provide the kind of moral guidance which will sustain man's own intelligence and redemptive action within the human community. Such faith and loving community he found among the Chassidim, and Buber hopes to rekindle such faith in his readers.

We proceed now to examine somewhat more carefully the contrasting ways in which Mead and Buber describe the human adventure, define the human hope, and resolve the more immediate problems of justice and peace within the society of men. It is necessary therefore to inspect their metaphysical grounds for any philosophy of history and any hope for a better world.

Mead's Evolutionary Humanism.—Mead was typical of many in our age who are no longer capable of believing in God, the Lord of the Universe. But he could and did believe fervently in man, and in human intelligence. Man and socially derived human values were his idols. He heard only the human voice. He sang the "triumph of the purely human." Nature, as a self-contained and self-explanatory order, was the ground; whatever man could make of man, was the end. The native good in man has to be tended, to be sure, but there is in Mead's thought no notion of sin, either individual or corporate.[110] The good of man is his own happiness, here and now, and to be achieved by the realization of man's own powers, especially the power of reason and its extension into experimental science. Thus nature and human nature are on the side of human progress. And especially if the self is social, sharing the values of others, the native good will and intelligence in man will enable him to do what needs to be done.[111] Buber, in writing of "The Man of Today and the Jewish Bible," has given us a good description of such a man as Mead was:[112]

He dreams of change, but does not know transformation. He hopes that if not tomorrow, then the next day things will be better, but the idea that truth will come means nothing to him. He is familiar with the idea of development and the overcoming of obstacles, but he can realize neither that a power wishes to redeem him and the world from contradiction, nor that because of the existence of this power it is demanded of him that he turn with the whole of his being.

Modern men like Mead have lost the reality of creation in the notion of "evolution," that of revelation in the theory of the "unconscious," and that of redemption in the setting up of social or national or economic goals.

In Chapter II we saw how Mead sought to bring his social psychology into harmony with the evolutionary world view and the romantic expectation for a better world which dominated the hopes and thoughts of men at the turn of the century. The new process philosophies and cosmological speculation gave support to the doctrine of "inevitable progress." In the Christian Church a similar philosophy informed the "social gospel" with the hope in the coming of the Kingdom of God on earth.[113] The natural order, aided by human thought and action, was working toward the progressive achievement of a higher order of life for mankind. Mead's genetic account of the self had no place in it for the stark reality of moral evil in men and societies which the Christian doctrine of sin was designed to explain. Men do not need God, nor any promises of divine punishment or reward, to strive effectively against ignorance, selfishness, cruelty and injustice. If Mead were asked the questions: What has gone wrong with human life? and how can it be set right? he would have answered: Nothing that more time, education, social intelligence and moral effort cannot set right.

Mead witnessed with satisfaction the decline of the "religious man" and the enthronement of the economic and social man. This was his heritage from Hegel, Marx, Darwin, and Adam Smith. In this respect he was a child of his times. But also he became a secular prophet of the cult of the Social, and of the faith in evolutionary Progress. Building his temple on purely secular foundations, he found zest in planning and outfitting man's earthly abode. He did not claim to have the answer to all the human problems, but he thought he knew the *method* of the solution. And that method had no place for religion, which he regarded as a frustration instead of a fulfillment.[114] "We are sub-stituting," said he, "the goal of a society aware of its own values and minded intelligently to pursue them for the city not built with hands eternal in the heavens." [115] "If humanity has fled shivering from the starry spaces, it has become intimately at home in the interstices of the speck that it inhabits for an instant." [116] Man needs to take the helm in his own hands.

We recall in this connection that Mead had little use for metaphysics. Metaphysics, he thought, was a meaningless non-empirical "science" of things-in-themselves. Yet Mead had more of a metaphysics than he liked to admit. For example, his doctrines of the primacy of experi-ence and the objectivity of perspectives imply a metaphysical pluralism and a social idealism. His social positivism looked in the direction of an empirical realism.[117] And we have noted the interest which White-head, Bergson, and Dewey had for him. He has to assume or postu-late some ultimate "metaphysical" reality upon which all things depend for their being—that fundamental order which makes the world a world, which makes it more or less a cosmos, and not a chaos, and which makes it reach out creatively toward new life and new order. Late in life, while still being faithful to an empirical theory of meaning, Mead's speculative boldness outran the world that is given in any specified moment.[118] Such an emergent and naturalistic account of mind and self can hardly avoid an implicit presupposition of earlier levels of reality not open to empirical inspection. If man is a part of nature, then our conception of nature must be enlarged and enriched to include and explain man. If I mistake not, Mead's whole pragmatic problem-solving approach presupposes an unquestioned unproblematic world which surrounds the problem and with reference to which the hypothesis is tested. In Mead's terms the scientist is studying and repairing some part of an ongoing process whose existence he never questions. He was always assuming a world which extends beyond the experienced world within which experience arises. No one doubts the empirical data of evolution as descriptive of a process; but what is more important is the *interpretation* of those data. And any inter-pretation depends upon certain principles of a metaphysical character. We have already noted the failure of materialism and emergent evolu-tion to explain how something higher can emerge from something lower without being presupposed in the lower.[119] Bergson writes: "It is to social life that evolution leads, as though the need of it was felt from the beginning, or rather as though there were some original and essential *aspiration of life,* which could find full satisfaction only in society." [120] If this be true, might it not also be true that there is a still more ultimate and essential aspiration of life which can find full satisfaction only in God? It might be better to admit that evolution is at long last inexplicable without some metaphysical frame of reference. A fortuitous and gratuitous universe which builds its own laws as it goes along is rather certain to end in wreckage.

What we have before us, then, is a pragmatic attempt through social psychology to lay a firm foundation for ethical and social optimism. Mead himself seemed, at times, to sense the inadequacy of his doctrine to guarantee his meliorism. This leads him to do two things of which he was probably unaware: (1) Borrow from Adam Smith enough of the notion of a natural social harmony to support his optimism, and (2) begin to trace the outlines of a cosmology and a metaphysics which were unconsciously colored by his inconclusive attempts to provide a logical and psychological basis for social amelioration and justice. This point has been trenchantly raised by T. V. Smith who writes: "A metaphysics was emerging from his speculations to help his sociology cope with the recalcitrant warp of his psychology." [121] The pragmatic identification of reality with experience is a solace to any social thinker, especially if experience can be interpreted as "social." [122] Reality can better support our efforts for social justice if it be itself somehow social in its very texture.

Can we believe in the progress toward a more perfect society? toward some earthly counterpart of what some have called the Kingdom of God? Mead's answer was an emphatic, Yes! His pragmatic and utilitarian formula was that society gets ahead not by fastening its vision upon some distant goal, but by bringing about the immediate adjustment of itself to its surroundings. He does not know what solution may be demanded by the immediate problem, but he knows the method of the solution.[123] Our values lie in the present; past and future give us only the schedule and the plans of campaign for their realization.

The main trouble with Mead's insistence upon the intelligence and freedom of man to direct his own destiny, is the apparent assumption that this freedom and intelligence would be employed only for the good. He seemed blind to the possibility that men would almost certainly misuse their freedom and reason. On the credit side, we must in all fairness remark that though Mead exaggerated the meaning in automatic process, and failed to face squarely the fact that precious values perish in passage of time, still there are certain values in growth, change, adventure, and conflict themselves. Certainly the mere passage of time is not destructive of all values. Process may not be simply equated with progress, but it may and does produce certain gains. But are those values permanent? Is there, somehow, somewhere, a treasuring of the values of life and personality in the moving stream of time? Is there any justification for the hope in immortality as a continuing history of personality? Human experience yields no clear answer, and it might seem the part of wisdom to reserve judgment on these final matters and go about the business of today's task.

But can we simply drop the matter there, and go about our business? Human hope and morality, as Whitehead has reminded us, hinge upon "relevance in the future." [124] As men we are immersed in time and space; our experience comes to us under the form of the passage of events—past, present, future. And while we stand within time, we do in a measure transcend it. Thus far both Mead and Buber agree. Even Mead permits man to stand above time to grasp past and future in present experience. Take that capacity away, and we would cease to be selves. But Mead never was able to grasp whatever truth there is in Niebuhr's brilliant insistence upon the paradox of man's existence as a creature of nature who yet transcends nature, an eternal subject caught in the flux of time yet standing outside of time.[125]

Since Mead assumes no human "soul" nor a Source of one, he can hardly be expected to believe in immortality. Indeed, it has been the fashion of pragmatism to decry all speculation about a far future and any possible hereafter for man.[126] One life at a time, now and here. This attitude may be welcomed as a wholesome correction of an exaggerated and mawkish other-worldliness. But it may fairly be asked if this concentration on the *means* to happiness, here and now, without a single glance at some far horizon or final outcome, is truly characteristic of human experience. On the contrary, it appears to be a fundamental condition of life and of mental health that man find some meaning for his existence, some worthful enterprise in a world where nothing of value is utterly and permanently lost, some opening of himself out to the supra-human. And is there any necessary reason why the self must be anchored to the particular organism and context of the present set of relations?

In this connection it is important to recall that Mead opposed any attempt to "substantialize" the mind or locate it in the individual brain or nervous system. Mind, for Mead, is not a substance of an ontal nature but simply the symbolic functioning of events which arise in a social process. Mind or self is just a *set of relations*, as distinguished from the biological form. And he observes significantly, "We are at least able to think of a self without it." [127] It is a complex of relations, a field of social forces, a precipitate of social experience.

Now if we argue consistently with Mead and Buber that the self is not the product of the individual organism alone, but of a process of interaction between a number of organisms—a process, indeed, with which the whole of nature and the whole cosmic environment may conceivably enter as a final, mutual, and supremely determining factor,— is there any reason why we cannot argue further that the self becomes less and less dependent on the organism and more and more dependent upon the wider environment? And how or where shall we set limits to the wider environment? Mother's womb, home, school, community, nation, humanity, the world of ideas, the cosmic order—where is the final frontier of the fully matured self? Man seems finally to be related to society, history, cosmos, all otherness. May it not be a legitimate hope and expectation that all mankind, together with all precious personal values, will be gathered together with all other sentient creatures into One Great Society whose unity is the life of God? Those who live with the assurance of God's love can see beyond the years without knowing *how* God's care for His creation will be expressed. But to go further into the land of speculation in this matter is beyond the scope of this essay. It is not amiss, however, to raise the question conditionally and to point out that the evidence that we now possess is not conclusive either way. It is surely premature of Mead, or anyone else, to close a question of such difficulty and far-reaching import for human life. If such an inquiry were part of our present purpose, we could point out many reasons—historical, logical, practical, moral, philosophical, and religious—in defense of the hope for immortality or some ultimate treasuring of personal values. It may be that the welfare of man and the welfare of the universe require us to give credence to the elemental longing and profound conviction of most of mankind that man's true and final dwelling is in the life of God.[128]

Buber's Biblical Humanism.—To the question of a possible ground and end of human existence Buber, as we have come to expect, gives a different and favorable answer. He takes his stand on what he calls Hebrew humanism,[129] by which he means not Greek or Latin or Renaissance humanism, but *humanitas*. More specifically, he speaks of "biblical humanism," because of the normative values of the human pattern displayed in the Bible, and because it distinguishes between "what is conditioned by the times and what is timeless." Buber is not content with Mead's man-sized cosmos; and he is suspicious of all such neatly devised schemes. Man is distinctively a person in a world of personal relationships. In this, Buber and Mead agree. But Mead denies what for Buber is the central figure in this personal world, the eternal personal reality, the Alpha and Omega of all being, whom men call God. Buber's metaphysics—which is certainly theistic, and probably realistic, personalistic, and holistic—is exceedingly vague;[130] but he never forgets that *"In the beginning God!"* Strongly rooted in the Jewish tradition, the most concrete, earthly, and matter-of-fact tradition in our western heritage, Buber's existentialism has notable points of contact with pragmatism;[131] but Buber affirms against all naturalism that, first and last, man stands in personal relation to God. Of course, he stands in relation to other men and to nature as well. But his relation to the eternal Thou is the primary and ultimate relationship which constitutes him *man!* And consciously to reject that relationship means to sin, to delay the coming of the Kingdom, and to fall short of what God intended him to be when he created man. Where Mead saw only continuity, progress and rational activity, Buber sees also discontinuity and paradox—though not so unrelieved as in Kierkegaard. It would hardly be fair to call Mead a naive optimist, yet he felt pretty confident and secure in the natural processes and in the power of human thought— one of his inheritances from Hegel. Buber, however, feels deeply the inward suffering and problematic of human existence. Buber's confidence lies elsewhere—in the bed-rock fact of God and the Biblical conception of the Kingdom of God. This means, among other things, that man must never be understood merely in the light of his present being, knowledge, and condition, but also in the light of his prophetic destiny. Only from this perspective can man truly understand himself, since only in God does man become truly himself, perceive the truth about himself, and also the great perversion we call sin.

The basic difference between Buber and Mead lies in the fact that in comprehending the relation between decision and destiny, Buber finds the religious conception of God more compatible with all the complexities of the human situation than the naturalistic faith of Mead. In Buber it is entirely clear, as it is not in Mead, that *society* is not the end of man. And the reason is that Mead was formulating a social philosophy which is concerned with the society now present or possible in any earthly future, whereas Buber is *also* concerned with the Kingdom of God and the redemption in preparing for which man has a part but which at last is taken up into God's atonement.

Thus Buber interprets human life and history as running their course within and under the reign of God. Buber's religious philosophy has its roots in the great central convictions of Judaism which have to do with "the meaningfulness of history, the sovereignty of spirit, the verifiability of truth, the power of decision ensuing from personal responsibility, the spontaneity between men, and faith as the engagement of one's entire life to the Lord of the one voice, who wishes to be recognized in each of his manifestations." [132] God has made it possible for men to believe in the working and ultimate victory of His redemptive power. We see its beginnings, for every holy act performed with *kawwanna* is messianic action. But the victory is not yet won. Man's moral responsibility is interpreted in relation to the faith that God's grace is operative both creatively and redemptively in life and history. That responsibility has its source peculiarly in the people which at the very commencement of its world journey, at the Red Sea, made the Lord of the world their King in a song of redemption.[133] The spirit of that people Israel is the spirit of fulfillment and of realization. Fulfillment of what? "Fulfilment of the simple truth that man has been created for a purpose. There is a purpose to creation; there is a purpose to the human race, one we have not made up ourselves, or agreed to among ourselves. . . . No. The purpose itself revealed its face to us and we have gazed upon it." [134] That purpose is to upbuild and demonstrate a life of unity and peace, of righteousness and justice, among the peoples and nations. That charge is not addressed to isolated individuals but to a people. "The people of Israel was charged to lead the way toward this realization." [135] And from age to age the people of Israel has preserved its heritage, which is this mandate. But, remarks Buber, the Jewish nation did not meet the test. And then he adds: "Only one great attempt was made to create . . . a concrete social life, the fraternal life of sons of the One God living together. That was the attempt of Hasidism, and even it did not pierce to the vital, the essential problem, but crumbled away after a time." [136]

In the Hebrew prophetic faith all history is understood as the working out of God's redemption of a world which he has created good, which has somehow fallen away from Him, and which He is pledged faithfully to redeem from sin and death. From the creation of the world by God's creative Word, to the consummation of all things (whether within or beyond history) the Bible describes man's pilgrimage as a series of events which taken together constitute a dialogue of man with God and a story of God's continuing creation, revelation, and redemption—ending in the establishment of the Kingdom of Love and Peace in which God's will is regnant. It is especially in the experience of one people, Israel, that this dialogue is most clearly heard, and the story is told with dramatic power.[137] That story is one of divine creation and judgment, of healing and mercy, recognizing the Lordship of the righteous God over all life. Yet there is a tragic side to the story which no one, not even the great prophets of Israel nor the philosophers since, has satisfactorily explained. Christianity sought, thinks Buber, to overcome this tragic dilemma by combining revelation and redemption in one historical event,—in Christ. But Buber cannot accept the Christian answer that the redemption has taken place,[138] for it seems obvious to him that redemption has *not* occurred. In the Jewish soul is the deep consciousness that "God's redeeming power is working everywhere and at all times, and that yet nowhere and at no time is there a state of redemption."[139] To bring all of man's life—his freedom, his ethical task, his daily round, yes, and death itself—into one religious unity is the vocation and the fulfillment of man. "The task of man," writes Buber out of his deep understanding of Judaism and Chassidism, "is to affirm the world and himself for God's sake and by this very means to transform both."[140]

Buber wishes to avoid commitment to any metaphysical or theological system. So he writes:

> I have occasionally described my standpoint to my friends as the "narrow ridge." I wanted by this to express that I did not rest on the broad upland of a system that includes a series of sure statements about the absolute, but on a narrow rocky ridge between the gulfs where there is not sureness of expressible knowledge but the certainty of meeting what remains undisclosed.[141]

This is clearly the profession of an existentialist—but of a religious existentialist. While giving up any dogmatic knowledge about the ground of being, Buber surely stands within the general theistic tradition of Judaism.

Whereas Pascal denied the God of the philosophers, Buber also discards the logicized God of the theologians. Only those who have never met the Eternal Thou in the spontaneity, freedom, and exclusiveness of the I-Thou encounter have any need for a systematic metaphysics or an institutionalized dogma. God cannot be grasped in time, space, or doctrine—but must be *met* in the lived-life, for life is a dialogue. Reason and empirical observation have here proved inadequate. Reason itself is questionable and ambiguous, even though it be the highest power of man. Its own origin and meaning are obscure. Man cannot explain himself from within himself. He must listen to God.[142] For, in Böhme's words, "the centre of man's soul came out of eternity."

The sharpest criticisms against Buber came at this point, because as a mystic and an existentialist Buber appears to minimize reason. For example, Jacob Agus writes: "That devotion uncontrolled by reason is a greater danger to society than selfishness, history proves abundantly." [143] We are asked to listen to God; but how are we to know that the call comes from God? Perhaps it is the voice of some "demonic Thou" which man hears. Basically, this criticism stems from the vagueness of Buber's metaphysics, his theory of knowledge, and his idea of God.[144] And it must be confessed that Buber is vulnerable in these areas. Buber is remiss in not formulating more explicit principles of guidance, clearer norms for determining the true world of Thou, and more reliable criteria for judging what aspects of the environment we choose as the *Thou* of our self. For without a clearer principle of selection and direction may not our devotion to persons and things become idolatry? In practice, and for those without Buber's own discriminating ethical and religious sensitivity, may not the views of Buber lead to provincialism, nationalism, statism, and various kinds of "chosen people" ideologies? Even love may become capricious and clannish. On such grounds Buber's critics conclude that his teachings cannot be recommended as in themselves sufficient to guide the destinies of men.

For such misgivings I have respect. A wholesome regard for empirical observation, and a modest skepticism about the irrational are not amiss. We need not make a God out of Reason in order to hope to retain whatever hold on reason we have gained. Some mystics and some existentialists have made excessive claims. Also there is an extreme school within the "dialectical theology" which, in its avowed renunciation of reason and its stress upon stark revelation, comes very close to reducing to the vanishing point man's capacity to receive and to respond to revelation, and to keep faith relevant to ethical action.

In Buber, however, there are no such extremes, either of mysticism or existentialism. Yet one wishes that Buber could be more definite and explicit in his theory. Some feel that he follows too closely the tradition of German and Chassidic mysticism. There is, indeed, a mystical, and some would say a perfectionist, outlook. This charge is not without its measure of truth, although it overlooks several correlative truths including the one that Buber recognizes no sharp dividing line between the religious and the mundane, between the worlds of I-Thou and I-It. But to charge, as Agus does, that lack of precision in these matters "renders his philosophy of life rudderless and adrift," [145] is surely an unwarranted accusation. As a matter of fact, Buber provides his own corrective to the extremes of both mysticism and existentialism. For Buber believes that existentialism, when Christian as in Kierkegaard, tends toward an other-wordliness, the negation of community, and an ethical conservatism; and when atheistic, as in Heidegger, it leaves man with only anxious solicitude and self-consciousness.[146] For all his vagueness, Buber's thought stands deeply rooted in and patently informed by the great historical and moral realism of Hebraism, and he shares the sharp discrimination and the acute ethical tension of the prophetic faith. His perceptive type of intuition seizes upon the significance of persons as unique individual reals, set in this world with its duties and responsibilities. He starts therefore with the existence of concrete man and finds the meaning of life in a responsive and responsible fellowship with God which includes the world and fellowmen. The meeting and mutual address of the finite I and the infinite Thou takes place "neither in the Heaven of Heavens, nor in the Holy of Holies, nor in the Heart of Hearts: man and God meet in the community." [147] Buber also takes the "imago Dei" seriously: it is precisely God's sameness and nearness, though real otherness, that makes possible a meaningful reciprocal encounter with the Eternal Thou.[148] It is this revelation of God in the community, in the natural environment, in the things that happen to men and claim men everyday, that becomes the source of man's decision and conscience. God is still God in all His God-ness; but conversation and prayer are possible.

Buber's "mysticism" is a receptive and apperceptive attitude toward the universe which is achieved by an abandonment of the egocentric attitude and a complete turning in readiness to devote one's energies to the creative task of hallowing every act and every moment. "The place where this treasure can be found is the place on which one stands." [149] This kind of openness, creative intuition and faith has a vital part to play in religion, for it gives fresh penetrations into truth and reality, a heightened awareness and functioning of the total self, and ethical illumination and empowerment.

Mystical leadings and intuitions are of course not infallible. There can be mistaken intuitions, just as there can be illusory perceptions and fallacious arguments. Buber would not deny that intuition must meet the further test of congruity with the rest of man's experience, or that vital religious experience must achieve an interpenetration of intuition and reason. Reason has a role to play in completing the work of creative intuition, in order that the mere feeling of certitude be not taken as proof of certainty. I think that Buber would agree that high religion is at once mystical, aesthetic, ethical and rational. Intuition, faith, imagination, rational synthesis, and moral faithfulness must all play their part in the knowledge of Divine Reality.[150] Mysticism and intuition need not be contrary to the spirit of inquiry. All that Buber is saying is that concrete temporal existence is too subtle and various to yield to complete logical analysis. Man and his versatile nature, and surely God, can never be fully encompassed in neat rational propositions. Every rational system ever devised by man ends in some paradox or absurdity. Beyond that, Buber is saying that mysticism affords insights into spiritual truth not otherwise gained, and especially the kind of understanding that "may confirm that there is meaning in the world." [151]

Without faith and revelation, all that reason can discover or demonstrate will be less than enough for man's salvation. Faith and reason together must aspire after the true goal of wisdom and blessedness. Logically coercive knowledge of these things we do not have. Faith, rather than logical proof, seems what we may hope for here. If, for example, one try to say dogmatically and concretely what God is like and what his purposes are, we must confess that only God can know. We can only inquire, believe, and affirm in faith that God's purpose is the realization of the good, of the Kingdom of God. By such a term we surmise the whole of what God's nature portends for the universe: love, truth, beauty, goodness, justice.

No concept of ours can adequately encompass the range of God's being and purpose. God's being and purpose are things that we cannot accurately define. But we can believe with the prophets, Jesus, Plato, Spinoza, and Buber that God is good, the author and conserver of good to man. In ways we know not of, God acts in wisdom and power and love faithfully to make the world good.

In sum: Buber does not minimize reason; he simply regards it as only a *part* of the whole man. Reason should fulfill its own part and no more. And as for the charge that he is vague in his theory and remiss in not formulating clearer criteria for determining the true world of Thou, let Buber speak in his own defense. In a recent note to me apropos of these matters, he writes:

"I had and have only the choice between silence and saying just so much as I say. . . . Not being the bearer of direct revelation in this matter, I would be obliged to derive such criteria from the world of I-It, and this would mean to destroy the authentic spontaneity of the I-Thou relation! The I-Thou relation as such does not procure objective criteria. . . . Insecurity is an inherent element of human existence. Faith means decision, venture, unfathomable risk; Pascal was near to this knowledge." "All of my existence means just standing on the Boundary, on 'the narrow ridge'."

The danger here is that in any critique of Buber one tends to assimilate his ideas to a certain accredited standard of thinking and, where this proves to be impossible, to see a flaw or a vagueness where silence is imposed by the very character of the I-Thou knowledge, experience and decision which are the basis of all that Buber has to say. Perhaps this is a difficulty which can never be completely overcome.

We would like to venture one more observation about Buber's metaphysics,—even though he denies that he has a metaphysics. Surely it lacks any clear and adequate elaboration. But this much is certain: Buber is a Jew, and the Creator-Redeemer God of Hebrew religion is involved in the basic structures which underlie everything that has being. Buber's God is both transcendent and immanent, the source of all being and good, present in every moment of history, unconditioned yet available to men, entering into personal engagement and interaction with men whose freedom is not destroyed. Furthermore, Buber's "social" philosophy means that to be a real entity is to be an active functioning reality entering into relations with all otherness. With this in mind, Buber could perhaps find metaphysical support for his philosophy of nature, man and God in a metaphysics of *process*.[152]

This category of process permits of richer meaning and value in history than is true of the metaphysics of static being. This philosophy makes it possible, indeed more intelligible, to conceive of God as the living personal Will who acts in history, the Thou who speaks His word to man, the caring saving Father of the Bible, the universal creative power which sustains all things. The older doctrine of the immutability and impassivity of God seems rather to hide from man the creative and redemptive Father than to reveal His face. Moreover, this new process philosophy appears capable of resolving many ancient problems like the problem of transcendence and immanence, and the problem of how God deals with man and the world. For, in line with Buber's doctrine of the social self, this view permits every individual being (including the personal being of God) to enter into mutually determinative relations with everything else. Such a view seems to agree with Charles Hartshorne when he writes: "According to current metaphysics every individual is immanent in and transcends all others, and the transcendence and immanence of God is the supreme case of this double relation." [153] Buber's existentialism enables him to express the biblical hope for God's redemptive work in history without falling into Mead's error of too simply identifying process with progress, and while still affirming that the natural processes can be loci of God's activity. Buber is also able to make a radical distinction between God and men without falling into the Barthian error of making a complete separation between God and his creatures.[154]

Buber has no simplicist notion that the achievement of the divine intention is easy or inevitable. He recognizes full well the fact of conflict and tragedy in history, and of man's freedom to rebel against God and the moral good. In rejection of any kind of determinism (Iranian, Hegelian, Marxian, Freudian, or scientific) he adds: "There is, of course, no historical process that is necessary in itself and independent of human resolve." [155] Man is always confronted with a decisive *choice!* The prophets did not warn against a predetermined event, but against that which will happen if those who are called to turn do not turn.[156] Judgment and destruction are visited upon those who defy Truth and Right. There is, warns Buber, a *reality of history* and a *Truth* which is not illicit fiction.[157] Truth is Truth, because God is!

We do not own this truth—rather it is our task to set the stamp of this truth on all the various facets of life where we are. Our final defeat would be to give up this truth. And he adds: Zion cannot be built and the Torah fulfilled save with justice (bemishpat. Isa. 1:27). God will refuse to receive His sanctuary from the hands of the devil. Then Buber concludes eloquently:

> For Judaism is the teaching that there is really only One Power which while at times it may permit the sham powers of the world to accomplish something in opposition to it, never permits such accomplishment to stand. But whatever is done in the service of that power, and done in such a way that not only the goal but the means to that goal are in accord with the spirit of justice, will survive, even though it may have to struggle for a time, and may seem in great peril, and weak compared to the effective sham powers.[158]

The Jew, says Buber, feels the unsaved world, and he feels salvation happening. Since no savior with whom a new redeemed history has begun has yet appeared to him, he is turned toward the coming of that which is to come.

> The Jew feels, perhaps more intensely than any other, the world's lack of redemption. . . . He feels this lack of redemption against his skin, he tastes it in his tongue, the burden of the unredeemed world lies on him. . . . Because of this almost physical knowledge of his, he cannot concede that the redemption has taken place.[159]

But because of the basic consciousness that God's redeeming power is at work everywhere and at all times, the really Hebraic prophetic eschatology (as distinguished from the apocalyptical belief compounded of elements of Persian dualism) promises a consummation of creation and fulfillment of God's creative will. Thus evil is continually being transmuted into new good. God's forgiveness is not just for special occasions; it is a continuing quality in life without which none of us could live. And there is a human counterpart to this divine forgiveness to be found in loving relations within the community of persons.[160] Man can thus be free from self-concern.

Buber seems to favor a gradualistic program of redemption which includes man's messianic assistance over any apocalyptic plan which for him smacks of Iranian dualism or magic theurgy. God is faithfully and continually redeeming his promises to his people in this present world. He calls for men and peoples to serve him. But he is not dependent on their service, save as he wills to be so. Buber seems not so concerned as, for instance, Berdyaev with a salvation beyond history. His stress is rather on an existential this-worldly salvation. He is content to trust God and await his final restoration; and does not seek "to expose what will be disclosed to us in its own time and disposition." [161]

Buber's emphasis is on the grace of God rather than on the wrath of God. This appears to be a corollary of his immanentism, pan-sacramentalism and the Kabbalistic world view which were taken up and modified by Chassidism. So while Buber's theology is really a theology of grace and anticipation, he counsels man to concern himself "less about the other side, but about our side; not about grace, but about will." [162] This "will" is in man's domain. The ground of election is not an utterly one-sided affair. The result of these considerations is an ethic of hope, rather than of despair. It is an ethic centered in the hallowing of God, rather than being obsessed with man's sin. It is an ethic of faith in God, rather than of confidence in man. "The men of the Bible," writes Buber, "are sinners like ourselves, but there is one sin they do not commit, our arch sin: they do not dare confine God to a circumscribed space or division of life." [163] They have not the insolence to draw boundaries around God's creative and redemptive activity. It is all God's universe, and He is the Lord of history—past, present and future. The important thing is to cleave unto God and love the neighbor here where one stands. The way of man is to perform, with holy intent, the tasks which belong to his daily round: For "there is no thing in the world which does not point a way to the fear of God and to the service of God." [164]

Pursuing this point Buber writes: "Some religions do not regard our sojourn on earth as true life. . . . Judaism, on the contrary, teaches that what a man does now and here with holy intent is no less important, no less true . . . than the life in the world to come." "Israel professes that the two worlds are essentially one and shall in fact become one." [165] How and when no one knows. Nor does Buber; so he writes in paradoxes:

> God's grace consists precisely in this, that He wants to let himself be won by man, that he places himself, so to speak, into man's hands. God wants to come to his world, but he wants to come to

it through man. This is the mystery of our existence, the super-human chance of mankind.[166]

God, then, wills to be Lord not only *over* man; He wills to be Lord *of* man. God wills to be acknowledged Lord in freedom and full fellowship with another subject who in free personal decision acknowledges Him as Lord. Where, then, is the dwelling of God? *God dwells wherever man lets him in.*

It remains to underline two significant features of Buber's thought which now become clear. The first is that the *eschaton* in Buber's thought is no shere futurity, but is a present expected reality as well as a future event. "There is no obedience to the coming one without loyalty to his creature." [167] "Fulfillment in a Then is inextricably bound up with the fulfillment in the Now." [168] There is, then, no meaningless drift. History is neither chance nor fatality. Something happens in what happens.[169] There is a meaning which we are to live, not to formulate. What is incumbent upon men and nations is the turning, the commencement, the beginning of the preparation of the world in readiness for the Kingdom. It follows therefore (this is the second point which Buber asserts with what may appear to be daring boldness) that God needs man.[170] "Judaism regards each man's soul as a serving member of God's Creation which, by man's work, is to become the Kingdom of God." [171] The object is not just the saving of one's soul, "but for the sake of the work which it is destined to perform upon the world." [172] Man turns the world into a sacrament and aids in the world's redemption by bringing God into the human community, by loving God in the world, by every innocent and holy act. "You need God, in order to be," Buber points out, "and God needs you, for the very meaning of your life. . . . The world is not divine sport, it is divine destiny." "The man who prays pours himself out in unrestrained dependence. . . . 'Thy will be done,' he says, and says no more; but truth adds for him 'through me whom Thou needest.' " [173] There is a Truth, a Spirit, which is not dependent upon us, but we upon it, and which nevertheless needs us in order to become something concrete, something historic. And it is not as if man were capable of accomplishing anything, but because the world was created for the sake of man's "turning," his "beginning." [174]

Buber is quite aware of the unique character of biblical-prophetic literature in its attitude toward future history. Through all the vicissitudes of Israel, there remains an aura of expectancy, pointing toward the final Lordship of God and the triumph of His just and merciful purposes. Of the development of this theme, Buber is summarized in one place:

> The synthesis of individual and cosmic salvation, on the one hand, and the purely Jewish element, on the other, begins only with the disintegration of the Second Commonwealth. Kabbalah especially comes to unite these alien elements, including the Gnostic conception of the redemption of the Divine Essence itself, with Jewish religion into one system whose core is Israel's hope of redemption. But the philosophy produced by this synthesis is the "esoteric teaching" which . . . in its very nature cannot penetrate the religious life of the many, of the folk. It is only through Hasidism that the philosophy of salvation comes to dominate the psychology of ordinary men. Not merely because in Hasidism this philosophy achieves its popular formulation, but because here the individual Jew is assigned an active part in the salvation of the world.[175]

This idea, running through traditional Jewish literature, is simply that to the extent that every Jew strives for self-perfection, he not only brings himself closer to personal redemption, but he also aids the group, Jewry, in its gradual advance toward redemption. And by his own acts, the individual Jew enhances or vitiates the endeavors of the whole world to attain to a state of perfection, that state in which God Himself, as it were, will have returned to His own domain. These three phases of redemption are ultimately to be achieved through Israel's return to the land God has given Israel. Jewish tradition has always known the insoluble bond of people, land, and God.[176] For the individual Jew and for Israel as a people, existence *in* God, knowledge *of* God, and choice *before* God are the same: man's highest being consists in knowing that he is known before God.

Buber says nothing specifically about a doctrine of immortality, but one gets the impression very definitely that his doctrine of time and messianic redemption includes the salvage of the precious personal values of life out of the perishing of time and death. Death is not a purely biological fact for one who is made in the image of the eternal. Without God and man's sturdy faith in God, man's doctrinaire optimism becomes a ghastly pessimism, such as we find in the atheistic existentialists.[177] Either we believe, or we despair, and despair in our despair. Either we believe there is meaning in life, or we are engulfed in the

tragedy of human existence. So Buber speaks of the Coming, remind-
ing men that the life of faith is a certain "quality" of eternal life, lived
in terms of this tension and expectation. In the eternal Thou there is
a treasuring for all time of the momentary goods of life. Somehow,
somewhere, the personal value which the love of God bestows on persons will be preserved. In the hour of his death, the Besht said: "Now
I know the purpose for which I was created." And when Rabbi Bunam
was dying, he comforted his wife, saying: "Why dost thou weep? All
my life has been given me merely that I might learn to die." All of
life is taken up into death, and death is taken up into life. The end
explains the beginning. And if Aristotle is right, the meaning of life
is found ultimately in the meaning of death. Biblical eschatology is
the outcome of such a faith. The eschaton involves some "Day of the
Lord"—some day of judgment and of fulfillment, and of full revelation
of God's purpose in history. The Present Age, with its woe and failure
and sin, will give place to some Age to Come, which will be in some
sense the Lord's doing. The Kingdom of God is at the hand of man,
and ever anticipated, yet it stretches out beyond our sight into the far
reaches of time and eternity,—in God. Meanwhile within and above
all is God's undefeatable love.

The above paragraph is, of course, my own interpretation of Buber's
point of view. It is not in Buber's own words, but it is near to his
thought. He hesitates to speak of such matters because he does not
know anything about time going on after one's death. "I believe," he
writes, "that dying I shall enter eternity, and eternity means something utterly different from time, something unimaginable and even
unthinkable." Furthermore, he believes that the use of such apocalyptical terms as the "Age to Come" is a kind of illegitimate simplification.
Thus again: "I am opposed to all the simplifications of the eschaton,
although I understand very well that man again and again cannot
do without them." [178]

In their different ways, both Mead and Buber center their thought
and their hope on the prospects for a better world. They both contend
that there is legitimate expectation of good in every human situation.
Yet the quality of their respective hopes is very different. Mead's hope
lies in his faith that human thought and action are alone fit instruments for perfecting our world, and that process is progress. He had
faith that from his account of the self would flow differentially a humane
sociology and social reconstruction. Buber obviously would find in

Mead's philosophy no adequate ground for his optimism regarding amelioration. Buber's optimism flows from his faith in God and in the capacity of man's God-given spirit to grow in love to God and neighbor. God's grace is real and immanent. In every particular human good, in every human victory over evil, in every loving act, in every particular Thou-relation, man gets a glimpse through to the eternal *Thou*. Every situation and deed may be the starting point of creative and messianic activity. The nature of the task will be made clear in the historical hour and situation itself. Such acts make us real; such acts help God to create and redeem the world. "Our faith that God is the Lord of history may sometimes appear ludicrous; but there is something secret in history which confirms our faith." [179] This is the ultimate purpose: to let God in.

NOTES

1. *Mamre*, pp. 1-17; *IATW*, pp. 13-52; *The Prophetic Faith, passim.*
2. *Mamre*, p. 20; *IATW*, p. 30.
3. Greta Hort, in Translator's Introduction to *Mamre*, p. x.
4. *IATW*, pp. 53-54, *et passim*; *I and Thou*, pp. 75ff, *et passim.*
5. *IATW*, pp. 53-54. Pascal remarked: "The entire religion of the Jews consisted only of the love of God."
6. See the Translator's Introduction to *Mamre*, p. xii.
7. See our discussion of this point in Chap. IV, pp. 273-87.
8. See e.g., Charles Hartshorne, *The Divine Relativity* (New Haven: Yale University Press, 1948) where he argues with acute logical analysis for a personal God who "has social relations, really has them, and thus is constituted by relationships and hence is relative. . . ." See also Hartshorne, *Beyond Humanism* and *Man's Vision of God.*
9. *PP*, pp. 49, 63-67, *passim.*
10. *I and Thou*, pp. 27-28, 9-10, 14-15.
11. *Ibid.*, p. 8.
12. *Ibid.*, pp. 27, 65-66.
13. Cf. the studies on mysticism by C. A. Bennett, Rufus Jones, Evelyn Underhill and others who accept God as the basic premise.
14. *I and Thou*, pp. 66-67; *IATW*, pp. 13-40. Buber asserts that the great achievement of Israel is that "it has taught men that this God in very reality hears when they speak to him, that men can be natural with him, that we human beings can stand face to face with him, that there is communion between God and man." "It was only Israel who conceived life itself as a being spoken to and giving answer. . . ." It was Spinoza's error that he undertook to deprive God of his approachableness. Spinoza's *deus sive natura* is God purified of all limitation, of all taint of approachability. That which could be spoken to was not pure, not divine enough. See *Mamre*, pp. 100-102; *Hasidism*, pp. 96-97.

15. *Mamre*, p. 101; *Hasidism*, p. 96.

16. *Hasidism*, p. 99.

17. Cf. H. H. Farmer, *God and Men;* also Alan Richardson, *The Gospel and Modern Thought* (Oxford: Oxford University Press, 1950), pp. 73ff, 140ff.

18. *MSS*, p. 335.

19. Because of the prominence given the vocal gesture in Mead's theory of symbols and of mind, it is often called the "social-vocal" theory.

20. See e.g., John H. Hallowell, *Main Currents in Modern Political Thought* (New York: Holt, 1950); cf. C. Howard Hopkins, *The Rise of the Social Gospel in American Protestantism* (New Haven: Yale University Press, 1940).

21. Cf. the recent book by H. A. Overstreet, *The Mature Mind* (New York: Norton, 1949), the thesis of which is basically that it is immaturity that makes men fail to do the right thing; hence, *grow up!* and you will act right and be decent. It is a valuable and useful book, but it over-simplifies the human problem.

22. It must be noted, however, that Mead never went so far as the romantic naturalists like Rousseau in over-estimating the goodness of man or the evil of social institutions. He bluntly declared that there is no given emotional basis for a generous extension of community. (*IJE*, XXXIX (1929), 400).

23. Mead, *IJE*, XVIII (1907–08), 318.

24. Mead was influenced by Freud, but he seemed to overlook the *dynamic* aspects of the depth-psychology. Mead appropriated what he wanted from Freud in accord with his own bias. The two things in Freud which exerted the most influence on Mead were (1) the doctrine of the "unconscious" which served to establish the necessary link between the physical and the social sciences, thus making possible the application of scientific method to the whole of life, and (2) the idea of the emotional catharsis furnished by intelligence and understanding in the social field.

25. Mead's papers on education include: "The Relation of Play to Education," *University of Chicago Record*, I (1896-97), 140-145; "The Teaching of Science in College," *Science*, XXIV (1906), 390-97; "Educational Aspects of Trade Schools," *Union Labor Advocate*, VIII (1908), 19-20; "Moral Training in the Schools," *Elementary School Teacher*, IX (1908–09), 327-28. These papers express Mead's conviction that education can and should build moral selves (i.e., intelligent, socialized selves) through play, manipulatory activities, common linguistic tools, and shared meanings.

26. *IJE*, XVIII (1907–08), 316.

27. Cf. John Dewey, *Human Nature and Conduct*, pp. 326-27. "For Right is only an abstract name for the multitude of concrete demands in action which they impress upon us, and of which we are obliged, if we would live, to take some account. . . . If we had desires, judgments, plans, in short a mind, apart from social connections, then the latter would be external and their action might be regarded as that of a non-moral force. But we live mentally as physically only in and because of our environment. Social pressure is but a name for the interactions which are always going on and in which we participate, living so far as we partake and dying so

far as we do not. . . . Accordingly failure to recognize the authority of right means defect in effective apprehension of the realities of human association, not an arbitrary exercise of free will."

28. Cf. Josiah Royce, *The Philosophy of Loyalty* (New York: Macmillan, 1908), and *The Hope of the Great Community* (New York: Macmillan, 1916).

29. *MSS*, p. 154.

30. *Ibid.*, p. 155.

31. *Ibid.*, p. 198.

32. *Ibid.*, p. 217, *passim.*
   See also *PP*, p. 194, where Mead deals with this problem of extending the bounds of one's community. Here he confesses that any self is restricted to the group whose roles it assumes, and will not abandon this self until it finds a way of entering into and maintaining itself within the larger society, such as the League of Nations, etc.

33. This is the point of view presented so attractively by Prof. A. C. Garnett in *A Realistic Philosophy of Religion* and *God in Us,* both published by Willett & Clark, Chicago. One need not endorse Garnett's whole position in order to recognize its pertinence in the present argument. See also his long paper, "Philosophical Ideas and World Peace," read before the Fourth Conference on Science, Philosophy, and Religion, and published in *Approaches to World Peace* (New York: Harper, 1944), pp. 572-608.

34. *BMM*, p. 109.

35. *Ibid.*, p. 110.

36. *Ibid.*, pp. 110-112. Cf. T. V Smith, *Beyond Conscience* (New York: McGraw-Hill, 1935)

37. For a discussion of this point, see R. L. Calhoun, *God and the Common Life* (New York: Scribner, 1935), pp. 170ff.

38. These are, respectively, the alleged errors in Absolute Idealism and subjective idealism.

39. Josiah Royce, Joseph Le Conte, G. H. Howison, and Sidney E. Mezes, *The Conception of God* (New York: Macmillan, 1897), esp. pp. 108ff, 193ff, 266ff, 272ff. Howison contends strongly that Royce, for all his assertions to the contrary, failed to save the reality of human individuals, and reduced them to mere aspects of the Absolute. Furthermore (agreeing with Fichte and disagreeing with Lotze) Howison argued that a plurality of selves is an indispensable condition of self-consciousness. There is no ego without an alter. Be it noted in passing that, in certain respects, the criticism is more cogent in Mead's case than in that of Royce. This question in the instance of Royce has been most recently and closely examined in an unpublished dissertation by Prof. Paul Ramsey, "The Nature of Man in the Philosophy of Josiah Royce and Bernard Bosanquet," Yale University, 1943.

40. *MSS*, p. 326.

41. Adam Smith, too, would turn in his grave at the thought of being held up as the apologist for unbridled self-interest. With his doctrine of "sympathy" and his ideas of the moral law and of the social good, he thought he had reconciled the ethics of the individual and society.

42. *MSS*, p. 326. See also pp. 318, 208, 281ff, 318-327; also *IJE*, XXXIII (1927), 238.

43. See *MSS*, pp. 22-222, 208, 243; *PP*, p. 169.

44. *MSS*, p. 242.

45. *Ibid.*, p. 261.

46. I suspect that the very glorification of the strong individual, the leader, and the almost hysterical emotion centered upon "personalities in the news," reflect the feeble hold so many of us have on our own selfhood.

47. *I and Thou*, pp. 7-9, 101-103, *passim*.

48. *Mamre*, p. 151; *Hasidism*, p. 3.

49. *Mamre*, p. 10f; *IATW*, p. 21f; see also *Eclipse of God*, pp. 112f, 116f, 119f, 162, 175.

50. *IATW*, p. 19.

51. Aber letzlich ist alles *in* Gott! Even for Spinoza, nature and mind are only two of an infinite number of attributes. We have already noted Buber's rejection of Spinozism, precisely because Spinoza makes God unapproachable as a real Other, and unduly softens the duality between God and man.

52. *IATW*, p. 32.

53. *Ibid.*, p. 31.

54. *BMM*, p. 178.

55. *Ibid.*, p. 175.

56. Spirit seems to mean for Buber, or at least to include, the capacity to perceive the total world, grasp the total world, play with it, participate in it—the capacity to become a free, self-transcending person. See e.g., *Israel and the World*, pp. 43-44.

57. Martin Buber in a letter to the writer.

58. *BMM*, p. 21.

59. Of course, Mead's monads have "windows."

60. One strongly suspects, however, that Mead held to some of his postulates so firmly that they assumed almost the force of dogma. Most pragmatists have more metaphysical assumptions than they realize. I fear that Mead, eschewing metaphysics, allowed his whole doctrine to be vitiated by surreptitious and uncriticized presuppositions not always justified by the facts.

61. *JP*, IX (1912), 406; same journal, X (1913), 374.

62. *General Theory of Value*, New York: Longmans, 1926.

63. "The Nature of Aesthetic Experience," *IJE*, XXXVI (1926), 382-92.

64. See Cornelius Kruse, "Is Subjectivism in Value Theory Compatible with Realism and Meliorism?" in *The Nature of Religious Experience* (New York: Harper, 1937), pp. 136-55; C. W. Morris, "Pragmatism and Metaphysics" in *PR*, 1934; W. P. Montague, *Belief Unbound* (Yale University Press, 1930), esp. p. 33; D. C. Macintosh, *The Problem of Religious Knowledge* (New York: Harper, 1940); *Religious Realism* (New York: Macmillan, 1931); *The Pilgrimage of Faith* (University of Calcutta, 1931).

65. See A. O. Lovejoy, *The Revolt Against Dualism*, exp. pp. 12-15, 78, 267-302.

66. See the acute and persuasive arguments of R. L. Calhoun in his article, "The Semi-Detached Knower," in *The Nature of Religious Experience* (New York, 1937), pp. 156-182, where he argues on purely epistemological grounds

for the reality of substantial selves, existentially other than God. Calhoun follows the argument in Kant's *Kritik der Reinen Vernunft*, A 99-110, 115-130, and B 155ff. See also Norman Kemp Smith, *A Commentary to Kant's Critique of Pure Reason* (1918), pp. l-lii, xliv-xlv. Calhoun speaks of a "semi-detached knower" as "including one or more factors not identical with nor completely determined by object, datum, nor cognitive act, and not fully open to observation." The most forthright defense of the reality of substantial souls to be found in recent literature is that of F. R. Tennant in *Philosophical Theology*, Vol. I (1928), pp. 82-104, 366-68, *passim*.

67. John Olif Boodin, himself an evolutionary theist, contends against emergent evolution that it can never explain how something higher can emerge out of something lower without being presupposed in the lower. He therefore introduces into his theory of evolution "an eternal hierarchy of levels." See his *Cosmic Evolution*, pp. 85, 99ff, 43, and his *God*, pp. 69, 128, *et passim*.

68. See e.g., R. L. Calhoun, *op. cit.*; J. M E. McTaggart, "Society as an Organism," *Studies in Hegelian Cosmology* (Cambridge, 1918), pp 177-195; also F. H. Heinemann, "Man Without Mind," *Hibbert Journal*, XLIX (1950), 54-61.

69. In his essay "Psychology of Social Consciousness Implied in Instruction," *Science*, XXXI (1910), 691-92; also "The Objective Reality of Perspectives," *Proceedings of the Sixth International Philosophical Congress*, 1926, p. 81.

70. See Prof. Morris Cohen, *Preface to Logic*, p. 75: "We must be on our guard against the universal tendency to simplify situations and to analyze them in terms of only one of such contrary tendencies. This principle of polarity is a maxim of research. . . . It may be generalized as the principle . . . of the necessary co-presence and mutual dependence of opposite determinations."

71. *JP*, IX (1912), 406.

72. F. Tönnies, *Gemeinschaft und Gesellschaft* (Leipzig, 1923).

73. See Count Alfred Korzybski, *Science and Sanity* (Lancaster, Pa., Science Press, 1933), and the work of the Institute of General Semantics, Chicago.

74. Cf. Susanne K. Langer's discussion of the power and peril of language, "The Lord of Creation," *Fortune*, January, 1944. See also Stuart Chase, *The Tyranny of Words* (New York: Harcourt, Brace & Co., 1938), pp. 1-17, 79-82, 206, 359, *et passim*.

75. A similar point of criticism has been made by C. J. Bittner in *Sociology and Social Research*, XVI (1931), 19-20.

76. *Supra*, pp. 159-61.

77. See e.g., Levy-Bruhl, *How Natives Think;* Fraser, *the Golden Bough;* Tylor, *Primitive Culture;* Ralph Linton, *The Study of Man* and *The Cultural Background of Personality;* Margaret Mead, *Coming of Age in Samoa*.

78. Buber's main theme is that there are possible more than one form of consciousness in which reality may be apprehended; and that one of these forms of awareness may, from time to time, displace the normal common-sense consciousness of man. This conclusion finds support in the evidence of nearly all students of the psychic and religious life.

79. See *I and Thou*, p. 93.

80. Cf. I John 4:7-21; also *Ten Rungs*, p. 82.

81. H. H. Farmer, *The Servant of the Word*, p. 41; *God and Men*, Chap. II.

82. *The Servant of the Word*, p. 46 (italics mine).

83. *The Servant of the Word*, p. 53; cf. also Farmer, *The World and God*, pp. 70-72.

84. *IATW*, p. 27.

85. *Ibid.*, p. 16.

86. *Idem.*

87. *Idem.* Cf. Ibid., pp. 78-79.

88. The verb Buber uses here is *brauchen* which means both *need* and *use*. Buber accents the Chassidic conception of messianic redemption as being prepared by men through the sanctification of the deeds of everyday. "The intention of the divine revelation is to form men who can work for the redemption." If this suggests that God *needs* man's help, it does not mean that God could not have redeemed the world without man's help, but that God "wills to have need of man." Cf. the passage in Alan Richardson, *The Gospel and Modern Thought*, p. 143, where he is considering the Trinity in contrast to a unitarian concept of God: "(God) could not be a God of love until he had a world to love. Before the world was made, this kind of a God was incomplete, dissatisfied. . . . Thus, on this kind of theory, God had to make a world in order to complete his own perfection. The world is as necessary to God as God is to the world."

89. Here is expressed the paradoxical, dialectical, existential character of religion with which we have become familiar in the writings of Barth, Brunner, Niebuhr, Tillich, etc.

90. *Mamre*, pp. 5, 6, 7; see also 113, 114, 173. Man's actions may be such as to prepare for the messianic fulfillment. "He who does a *mizwah* (fulfills a commandment) with complete *kawwanah*, that is completes the act in such a way that his whole existence is gathered in it and directed towards God, he works on the redemption of the world, on its conquest for God." Cf. *IATW*, pp. 17-19.

91. See e.g., C. W. Morris in his Introduction to *MSS*, pp. xxx, xxiv. E. S. Ames also differed with Mead on this point.

92. Unless we are prepared to include God, Christ, or some such Universal Other in the community who then, on occasion, becomes the *Alter* in the *ego*, and confronts the ego as the agent or epitome of the universal community.

93. See e.g., *The Critique of Practical Reason*, and other essays (trs.) Lewis W. Beck (University of Chicago, 1949); John Baillie, *The Interpretation of Religion* (New York: Scribner, 1928); A. C. Garnett, *Approaches to World Peace; A Realistic Philosophy of Religion*, etc.

94. A. C. Garnett, *op. cit.*, p. 587.

95. *MSS*, p. 319f.

96. *Ibid.*, p. 308.

97. *Ibid.*, p. 270.

98. See the general argument in Bergson's *Two Sources of Morality and Religion*.

99. See a similar judgment of Mead by T. V. Smith, "The Social Philosophy of George Herbert Mead" in *The Am. Jr. of Soc.*, XXXVII (1931), 368-85.

100. *Loc. cit.* Cf. *IATW*, pp. 45ff, *passim*.

101. Recalling Josiah Royce, *The Philosophy of Loyalty* (New York: Macmillan, 1908).
102. H. H. Farmer, *God and Men*, p. 59.
103. *Idem.*
104. Cf. *IATW*, pp. 173-182.
105. This makes highly significant the assurance of grace in the Hebrew and Christian faiths, for through grace and forgiveness man's failure to achieve the perfection he envisages is made tolerable. It is out of this tension, out of this divine-human encounter, so long as man does not repudiate it, that the moral and spiritual power of life is generated.
106. *The Christian Century* (June 7, 1933), 748.
107. Cf. T. V. Smith, *AJS*, XXXVII (1931), 380.
108. Cf. Rufus Jones, *Studies in Mystical Religion* (New York: Macmillan, 1909); *The Journal of John Woolman* (New York: Macmillan, 1922); E. W. Lyman, *The Meaning and Truth of Religion* (New York: Scribner, 1933); Henri Bergson, *Two Sources of Morality and Religion* (New York: Holt, 1935).
109. *AJS*, XXXVII (1931), 368-85. A more recent and sustained attack on naturalism is to be found in Eliseo Vivas, *The Moral Life and the Ethical Life* (University of Chicago Press, 1950). His strictures are directed to John Dewey, Santayana, R. B. Perry, C. I. Lewis, etc., but the implications for Mead's doctrines are clear, and the more telling since Vivas, until very recently, was a confident exponent of naturalism.
110. Recalling Rauschenbusch's concept of "The Kingdom of Evil" or the social sin incorporated into social institutions. See *A Theology for the Social Gospel* (New York: Macmillan, 1917). I find only one place where Mead discerns clearly the moral limitations of natural affections and spontaneous good will, and the social institutions arising from the two. ("National-Mindedness and International-Mindedness," *IJE*, XXXIX, 1929, pp. 385-407). There he writes: As for the sexual passion, it "isolates those whom it consumes"; the resulting family life "segregates us" (p. 400); as for business partners, "we protect ourselves even against our partners, associates, and employees with contracts and agreements defended with penalties" (p. 393); as for "good manners," they are "means of keeping possible bores at a distance" *(idem.);* and as for nationalism, "the more unintelligible the issue is [he is speaking of the influence of the Monroe Doctrine] the more it emphasizes the unanimity of the community." (p. 398). "We cannot depend upon feeling ourselves at one with our compatriots, because the only effective feeling of unity springs from our common response against the common enemy." (p. 400). In short, "the hostile attitude is peculiarly favorable to social cohesion." To summarize Mead's view of the moral inadequacy of the feelings, we quote from *IJE*, XXXIX, p. 399, "There is nothing in the history of human society nor in present-day experience which encourages us to look to the primal impulse of neighborliness for such cohesive power." Fortunately, Mead contends that creative intelligence is strong just where the emotions are weak. It is strong in that its whole function is to consolidate, and integrate; it provides the objective factor.

Creative intelligence informs the scientific and evolutionary method by which science, nature, and social organization transform the individual, problematic, inharmonious situation into a harmonious working unity.

111. See e.g., *PP*, pp. 89-90.

112. *IATW*, p. 101.

113. See e.g., Walter Rauschenbusch, *op. cit.*; C. Howard Hopkins, *The Rise of the Social Gospel in American Protestantism.*

114. Actually there was, I think, more of a residue of Christian idealism (as also of Hegelian idealism) than he suspected. After all, he was brought up in a Congregational parsonage; and the social solicitude in Christianity had a profound appeal for Mead. In a sense, Mead was attempting to implement scientifically the Golden Rule by showing that man is by his very nature adapted to practice brotherhood. This is the way of things; this is not prescription but description.

115. *PP*, p. 90.

116. *IJE*, XXXIII (1923), 234.

117. Cf. C. W. Morris, "Pragmatism and Metaphysics," *PR* (1934), also "Peirce, Mead, and Pragmatism," *PR*, XLVII (1938), 109-27.

118. See his *PP*, The Paul Carus Lectures, Chicago, 1932, esp. pp. 87-88, where he clearly indicates that the stretch of the present within which self-consciousness finds itself stretches beyond the immediate perceptual horizon. In *PP* we find Mead's daring extension of the "social" into what may be fairly called a "metaphysics," a philosophy of nature.

119. So far at least I understand certain philosophically minded biologists. Professor E. G. Conklin, for example, writes in *The Christian Century*, LXV, July 1948, pp. 680-83: "No purely mechanistic hypothesis ever proposed has been able to account for the origin of such purposive and psychic phenomena from dead and senseless matter." Such hypotheses go far beyond the natural selection of Darwin as explaining the course and cause of nature, and the origin of psychic phenomena in animals and men. Darwin himself confessed to a sense of "the extreme difficulties or rather impossibility of conceiving of this immense and wonderful universe, including man with his capacity of looking far backward and far into futurity, as the result of blind chance or necessity." Whitehead also, in company with many other philosophers and scientists, finds in matter and energy the promise and potency of all life. Starling and Cannon, two of the world's greatest physiologists, have spoken of the purposive structures and functions of higher animals and man as "the wisdom of the body." Biologists like W. E. Agar and R. S. Lillie find that matter is a psycho-physical entity. Cf. J. E. Boodin, *Cosmic Evolution.*

120. *Mind-Energy*. Lectures and Essays. Trs. H. Wildon Carr. London: Macmillan Co., 1920, p. 33. Italics mine.

121. *AJS*, XXXVII (1931–32), 384.

122. See John Dewey, "Social as a Category," *Monist*, XXXVIII (1928), 161-77, and Mead's *PP.*

123. *IJE*, XXXIII (1923), 247. "We don't know where we are going, but we are on our way."

124. *Process and Reality* (New York: Macmillan, 1936); Cf. Berdyaev, *The Destiny of Man* (New York: Scribner's Sons, 1937), p. 317, *passim.*

125. Reinhold Niebuhr, *The Nature and Destiny of Man* (New York: Scribner's Sons, 1941–43), 2 vols.

126. Perhaps the most careful and complete study from this point of view is that by Corliss Lamont, *The Illusion of Immortality* (New York: Philosophical Library, 1950).

127. *MSS*, pp. 139-40.

128. For some recent discussions of this issue, see John Baillie, *And The Life Everlasting* (New York: Scribner's Sons, 1933); A. E. Taylor, *The Christian Hope of Immortality* (London: The Unicorn Press, 1938); F. C. Grant, *Can We Still Believe in Immortality* (Louisville: The Cloister Press, 1944); R. H. Charles, *Eschatology: Hebrew, Jewish, and Christian* (London: Black, 1913); C. D. Broad, *The Mind and its Place in Nature* (New York: Harcourt, Brace, 1929); H. H. Farmer, *op. cit.*, pp. 143ff, 163ff; A. S. Pringle-Pattison, *The Idea of Immortality* (London: Clarenden Press, 1922); Harold Bosley, *A Firm Faith For Today* (New York: Harper, 1950), Chap. XII; and the Ingersoll Lectures, Harvard University Press, by E. W. Lyman, J. S. Bixler, W. E. Hocking, W. P. Montague, J. H. Holmes, etc., etc.

129. "Hebrew Humanism," *IATW*, pp. 204ff.

130. In a note written to me after this manuscript was prepared, Professor Buber declares that he has no metaphysics; for "metaphysics," on his definition, "is (necessarily) putting the absolute (idea) in any form in the place of God,—just what I refuse to do."

131. E.g., its anti-intellectualism; its functional active theory of knowledge; its stress upon the act or deed; its accent on the social; its taking time and process seriously; its insistence upon the unity of theory and practice, inner idea and outer deed; the element of faith, venture, and immediate experience.

132. *IATW*, p. 52.

133. *Ibid.*, p. 194.

134. *Ibid.*, pp. 185-6.

135. *Ibid.*, p. 187.

136. *Idem.*

137. Buber's *Königtum Gottes* (Berlin: Schocken Verlag, 1936) is the first of three projected volumes under the general title *Das Kommende*, an inquiry into the historical origins of the messianic faith. The present volume attempts to display the sources of biblical eschatology and myth in Israel's early history, and deals with the Theocracy, especially as these factors are related to the prophecy of the coming and of the last things. The second volume is to deal with the messianic Person; the third with the eschatological tension and expectation.

138. Needless to say, the idea of a creative and redemptive God working in human history, acting relevantly and purposively in the human situation, would be repugnant to Mead's secular mind. Yet it is the grand central affirmation of Judaism that God is a Thou who acts and seeks and claims men.

139. Therefore, until the Messiah comes "the Jew is to the Christian the incomprehensibly obdurate man, who will not see what has happened; and the

Christian is to the Jew the reckless man, who in an unredeemed world affirms that its redemption is accomplished." See *Mamre*, pp. 25-31; *IATW*, p. 40.

140. *The Way of Man According to the Teaching of Hasidism* (London: Routledge & Kegan Paul, 1950), p. 6. Used by permission of The Seabury Press, Greenwich.

141. *BMM*, p. 184.

142. Cf. Pascal, *Pensees,* Chap. X, sec. 1; XXV, sec. 18.

143. Agus, *Modern Philosophies of Judaism* (published by Behrman House, Inc., 1261 Broadway, New York), p. 276.

144. We have already noted (*supra,* p. 295 n130) that Buber insists that he has no metaphysics. For similar reasons, he believes it is presumptuous of man to think he can have an adequate idea of God or submit God to the laws of human logic. Be it remembered, too, that Buber's philosophy involves a theory of knowledge in which the old subject-object relationship can no longer be taken as primary.

145. *Op. cit.,* p. 279n.

146. *Eclipse of God,* Chaps. v-vii, contains a recent discussion of these themes.

147. Joseph L. Blau, *The Review of Religion,* November 1948, p. 64.

148. *I and Thou,* p. 79.

149. *The Way of Man,* p. 41.

150. See the studies of W. E. Hocking, D. C. Macintosh, L. T. Hobhouse, W. P. Montague, E. W. Lyman, Henri Bergson, Rufus Jones, all of whom recommend a synthesis of methods of knowing, especially in religious knowledge. Surely such an attempt to keep faith and reason together in some fashion without impoverishing either can find room in Buber's mature method and outlook, which is opposed to the merely creedal and formal aspects of religion.

151. *I and Thou,* p. 115.

152. This new metaphysical orientation finds most explicit expression in the various cosmological speculations of Whitehead, Bergson, Wieman, Charles Hartshorne, Daniel Williams and others, especially in contemporary Protestant theology, in which the ideas of process, evolving life, and dynamic relations are held to be fundamental to anything we know about the scheme of things. I suspect, for example, although we have no recent statement, that Prof. R. L. Calhoun's metaphysics comes very close to this general position, since he earlier (*God and the Common Life* (1935), and *Christendom,* Vol. I and II (1936–37)) claimed company with Tennant, Whitehead, Bishop E. W. Barnes, Lloyd Morgan, Hobhouse, and von Hügel. Cf. especially Daniel D. Williams, *God's Grace and Man's Hope* (1949) and Charles Hartshorne, *Beyond Humanism* (1937), *Man's Vision of God* (1941) and *The Divine Relativity* (1948).

153. *Beyond Humanism,* p. 6.

154. This interpretation of Barth is, of course, Buber's (as well as my own and that of many others). It may be too sweeping a statement, but it seems to be an accurate reading of a very strong tendency in Barth toward an "infinite qualitative distinction." It may only mean that the relation between God and the world is established *by* God and on *his* terms, and

not in accord with man's schemes or hopes. Still it seems to leave no place for redemption *in* history, but only at the "end."

155. *Paths in Utopia*, p. 14.

156. *IATW*, p. 37. Cf. *The Book of Jonah*.

157. *IATW*, pp. 234-39, 45-46.

158. *Ibid.*, p. 237f.

159. *Ibid.*, p. 35.

160. Buber finds this in the community of Israel; Christians find it within the Church. Cf. J. Royce, *The Problem of Christianity* (New York: Macmillan, 1914), Esp. Vol. I, Lecture VI.

161. *I and Thou*, p. 92.

162. *Ibid.*, p. 76.

163. *IATW*, p. 247.

164. *The Way of Man*, p. 20.

165. *Ibid.*, p. 44.

166. *Ibid.*, p. 45.

167. *BMM*, p. 7.

168. *IATW*, p. 239.

169. Thus Buber would answer Mead, for whom there is no beginning and no end, no creation, no redemption, and hence no present revelation, and also the Greeks for whom history was a cycle with the Golden Age in the past. Cf. *Israel and the World*, p. 96f, and Franz Rosenzweig, *Stern der Erlösung*.

170. *I and Thou*, p. 82f; *Mamre*, p. 112f; *IATW*, pp. 170f, 188, 192f.

171. *The Way of Man*, p. 37.

172. *Idem.*

173. *I and Thou*, pp. 82, 83.

174. *IATW*, p. 21.

175. Quoted in Simon Halkin, *Modern Hebrew Literature* (New York: Schocken Books, 1950).

176. See "The Land and Its Possessors," *Israel and the World*, pp. 227-233. For a fuller discussion see also *Israel and Palestine* (New York: Farrar, Straus, and Young, 1952).

177. See Marcel's criticism of Sartre in *The Philosophy of Existence* (London: Harvill Press, 1948), pp. 32-66. Cf. H. Kuhn, *Encounter with Nothingness* (Hinsdale, Ill.: H. Regnery, 1949), and Marjorie G. Grene, *Dreadful Freedom* (Univ. of Chicago Press, 1948).

178. See *Königtum Gottes*, Vol. I of *Das Kommende* (Berlin: Schocken Verlag, 1936).

179. *IATW*, p. 239.

Chapter Five

The Validity and Value of the Social Self

A SUMMARY AND SOME CONCLUSIONS

WE HAVE NOW identified the motif of the "social self" and have reviewed the ways in which two quite different but first-rate minds have tried to formulate the problem of the human self in the light of this concept. In the writings of Mead and Buber we have two foci in which the concept comes to explicit and persuasive, if not always clear and consistent, expression.

The dialectic between these two standpoints will and should go on because, as I believe, there is truth on both sides. Yet the conviction has been growing throughout our study, and apparent to the reader, that Mead's formulation of the problem needs amendment in the direction of Buber's theocentric personalism as being the richer, fuller, truer statement of the total human situation. But despite their radically different methods of approach, their empirical accounts of the self are remarkably similar—the major differences being that Buber provides a firmer metaphysical anchorage for the self and wider dimensions of relatedness than does Mead. To change the metaphor, we might say that Mead provides a scientific *floor* and Buber a metaphysical *ceiling* for man's abode.

We may now, in this concluding chapter, attempt to draw together the strands of our argument, review the way we have come, suggest some of the residual difficulties, and illustrate something of the extent and effect of this new concept and perspective in contemporary thought. This, we believe, will further demonstrate the validity and practical value of the concept of the social self by showing some of its fruitful applications and meanings—ways in which the idea is serviceable as the starting point of further reflection and analysis.

It will help guide us through this summing up if we list briefly the major agreements and conclusions of Mead and Buber touching upon the essentially social nature of the self.

1. *The Self as Socius.*—The primary category to which Mead and Buber point is that of the social self. Human nature and selfhood are social through and through. The individual person is not, to use Mead's phrase, "an intradermal self," nor a self-sufficient atom. But neither is the self a mode or function of some Absolute. The self is the human individual who, in an ego-alter dialectic, in a dialogic meeting with the other, comes to know himself as a self. We become or acquire selves when we know ourselves to be known, when we are apprehended and valued by self-disclosing others, when we reply to others who have spoken "themselves" to us. Each man finds himself in every other man; each man finds his own good in every other man's good.

This means that (1) "selfhood" is a *human* category; (2) the self in this dialectic is subject and object at the same time, caught, prehended in the act of the other's knowing it; (3) man needs others to be himself, yet he is not identical with any other; (4) the self is both transcendent and empirical, a unique event in space-time—no general statement that ignores the unique self-feeling and solitariness can be adequate; (5) but—and here is the paradox and mystery of human selfhood—there is an equally inevitable sociality. The same thing which makes a man a person, also places him in community, in *coincidentia oppositorum;*[1] bound up with the life of every son of man in a mutual inter-meshed fabric of giving and receiving. There must be an other, or even morality is only a kind of unblessed onanism.[2] Man is a *Mitmensch* whose *Umwelt* is also a *Mitwelt*.

2. *Self and Society are correlative terms.*—"All existence is co-existence."[3] The world is what I share with others. Man, the individual, is incomplete; therefore, he is set in families and communities as the condition of his being. His very unique reality is, paradoxically, discovered and developed in and through community. As Daniel Williams has it: "Every individual in so far as things enter into mutually determinative relations, enters into the determination of the constitution of everything else."[4] Or as Eduard Heimann writes: "Freedom

is that through which man is man. But there cannot be personal freedom without there being order in the life of the community." [5] This is to say that the dependence of freedom and order, self and society, are dialectical. Man's essence resides in his being-in-community; and this further implies "existence-in-responsibility." [6] The "between" thus becomes both the basis of unique and precious selves and the bond of social cohesion.

3. *Speech and role-taking as the techniques of self-realization.*—This is by now familiar doctrine, and I think sound doctrine. The capacity for speech seems to be the basis of man's selfhood. Only a man turns and speaks to another as a being existing for himself as well in independent otherness, and therefore capable of genuine conversation,[7] of "personal correspondence." [8] Speech is a journey to the dwelling of other men. "The Word unlocks person to person." [9] Language is the mark of man. We are literally talked into self-hood. The human fish swims in a sea of signs and symbols, as Charles Morris has it. Or to change the figure, through language the self becomes "dressed in social clothes," looks at itself in a social mirror, approves or disapproves of itself through social eyes.[10] Man's being, in the deepest sense, is *respons*-ible.

4. *The Social Nature of Reality.*—Not only man, but all existence has a social structure, is qualified and conditioned by social relations. From cells upward in the ascending scale of emergence—and up to God, if Buber is correct—the social-relational aspects of reality assume a more prominent role. Nature, self, and society are alike "fields" of forces, organizations of perspectives, occasions of mutually determining lines of influence. And if "person" means being related to other persons in a world of persons, then God is the supreme case of personality, and is related to all otherness by sympathetic concern. If God is love, then He must be personal and social. Even if we exclude God, we can still assert with Mead that "social psychological process is but an instance of what takes place in nature, if nature is an evolution.[11] Sociality and relativity are to be understood as special cases of a process that takes all nature for its province. We can here appeal to some of the greatest philosophers from Plato to Whitehead who have held, with varying degrees of explicitness and consistency, that "social structure" is the structure of all existence. Fechner and Whitehead, even Peirce, not to mention many recent thinkers like Charles Hart-

shorne, have held that deity is the supreme case of the social category, rather than an exception of it.[12]

What we have before us (I think in both Mead and Buber) is a philosophical anthropology which affirms that man and reality are "social" in essentially the same way—with the same sociality. There is convincing evidence to show that their metaphysics, such as it is, is derived from their conception of man. The universe, as real, is a generalization from their doctrine of man. This is perhaps clearer in Mead than in Buber; but it has even more remarkable implications if we can hold with Buber that the Other can be or can include the infinite Thou.

5. *Levels of Selfhood.*—There appear to be *levels* of selfhood, stages in the achievement of selfhood; and if we may include Buber's religious dimension, man is not truly and fully a self or person in all the rich meaning of those terms unless and until he knows himself before God. "My life shall be real," cried St. Augustine, "because it is full of Thee." [13] In this context, also, we may think of "soul" as the self when apprehended in the knowledge of God. And knowing that such knowledge means reciprocal relation, knowledge and choice of one's self before God, we can understand the full meaning of St. Augustine's prayer: *Domine, noverim me, noverim Te*—as though to pray, "Lord, may I know myself in my relation to Thee." [14]

6. *Similar theories from different methods.*—The obvious agreements thus far between Mead and Buber reveal how similar descriptive social and psychological theories can be arrived at by radically dissimilar methods, out of different philosophical traditions, and independent of their differing metaphysics. Mead reacted from Hegelian monistic idealism to his statement of the empirically dialectical self.[15] Buber drew back from his youthful pantheistic mysticism to the firmer dialogic conception of the I-Thou self. I believe the fuller truth lies with Buber. I share with Buber his view that (borrowing a phrase from David E. Roberts)[16] "human beatitude is dependent upon an uncoerced alignment between man's own resources and divine power," while agreeing with Mead that scientific method and its hypotheses are justifiable and useful *qua* hypotheses, and may indeed contribute to the theological understanding of man. In any event, the definition of the self as social gains cogency from the fact that it can be expressed in two such divergent forms.

7. *God in the Community.*—Man is also *homo religiosus*. He has gods; he worships. *Der Mensch hat immer Gott oder Abgott*, said Luther. Consequently, when we raise the question of how far the community of personal relations can or should extend, we find Mead too narrow in his interpretation. He seems to think of the self as existing in only one society (the generalized other) and in only one flat dimension (the human-social). Here Buber is the more dependable guide for he recognizes that the self lives in many communities, relations, and dimensions, including the vertical dimension in which a God of revelation confronts man as the most general and supreme Other.

All this we have learned from our study. And before we look forward to note the fertile applications of these lessons, let us quickly summarize what these investigations have contributed to our understanding of human nature. First of all, the individual knows that he is a single one. But he also knows that his personality rests on social fellowship, that knowledge of oneself is pre-eminently knowledge of oneself in relation to others. This human interdependence gives a rational and psychological basis for ethics, political loyalty, and loving community both secular and religious. Man learns the possibility of verbal communication and the wordless communion of the mystic. He realizes that there is a tension between the adequate expression of his immediate emotional experiences and the consistent work of reason. His search for spontaneity and creative freedom only serves to remind him once and again of his enslavement to the systems; yet when he seeks to free himself, to transcend the systems, he confronts the paradox that structure and discipline are necessary to freedom. In fleeting moments he is aware that there is a deeper core of selfhood incommunicable within the human fellowship. Even when he achieves a certain inner harmony, there is a restless discontent which tells him that there is a higher harmony, that the life of man, "always roaming with a hungry heart," may be transformed and finally be at home only by the apprehension of and response to a Spirit which is divine. Then he knows with the prophets that the universe is dynamic, that time is real, and that God works actively in nature and history. He also then recognizes the social and historical character of his ideas and values yet can hold to the belief in a Truth and a Goodness which is universal, and will not fail. Prayer is the natural language of this realm of experience. "Because (God) is immanent, we can find him. Because he is also transcendent, we can trust him. Because he is both, we can work with him for the coming of his kingdom." [17]

APPLICATIONS OF THE CONCEPT OF THE SOCIAL SELF

If the considerations and analysis by which Mead and Buber establish the "social self" as a valid doctrine have been well founded 'in their thought and in this exposition, the concept will be seen to apply fruitfully in numerous directions and contexts. The importance, relevance, and urgency of the view that the self is a "self-other system" are to be measured by the fertility of its practical and theoretical applications and by the disaster of forgetting it.

One of the remarkable impressions which come from even a cursory inspection of a wide range of contemporary literature in many fields—theological, philosophical, psychological, educational, and sociological—is the productive and illuminating employment of this concept of the social self by a host of writers in many areas. Many of these writers explicitly acknowledge their indebtedness to Mead or to Buber, or to both; but whether or not there is conscious dependence upon or parallelism with Mead or Buber, it is only too apparent that this motif is a part of *Zeitgeist* and finds fertile meaning and implications for many disciplines. Indeed, it is difficult to trace this idea to any one thinker or school. It is something new in the spirit of the age which has opened up new vistas and fresh possibilities for further advance. Mead and Buber now stand forth as prophetic and pioneering figures in this new movement of thought; the seeds of their germinal ideas are scattered, wind-borne in many directions.

One thing is clear: There is a striking convergence of opinion toward the general conclusion at which this present study has also arrived—a convergence indicated by the numerous authorities we have cited throughout our investigation, and which we can now more explicitly illustrate by the work of many writers who have used these new notions of the nature of the self as the starting-point of their reflections.

Let us begin with a rapid survey of representative thinkers in ten or a dozen fields who seem to pursue this new line or display something of its influence. We will offer a more extended treatment in one or two areas to show in more detail how this new insight into the problem of the self opens up fresh ground. Such a summary does not pretend either to completeness of scope or to equal competence in exposition in all of these fields. Its intention is mainly to illustrate areas of significant application of the central theme of this study which lie outside its central focus.

We may begin the survey with a look at the field of social psychology. Mead, in particular, has helped to mold the philosophical point of view of a large number of the present leaders of American social and philosophical inquiry, particularly in the colleges and universities of the Midwest. He is especially well known and honored among the students of social psychology and, among modern social philosophers of first rank, is probably most quoted and least criticized. John Dewey attributes to Mead "the chief force of this country in turning psychology away from mere introspection and aligning it with biological and social facts and conceptions." [18] Professor A. E. Murphy has said that "in depth and originality Mead's contribution to philosophy equals anything that America has yet produced." [19] A judicious and probably just estimate of Mead may be found in the following summary encomium by C. W. Morris:

> Whatever be the fate of the democratic ideal, George H. Mead's extraordinarily fertile ideas have not merely given him a secure place among the creators of social psychology, led to social and ethical theories of intrinsic interest, and provided a matrix for a significant expansion of pragmatism in the form of "the philosophy of the act," but they give every indication of having within themselves the power to enrich the concepts of the social sciences, to suggest new avenues of empirical investigation, and to open new horizons for philosophical interpretation.[20]

One would indeed have to list many, if not most, of the prominent names in the contemporary field of social psychology in order to indicate how widely Mead's germinal ideas have found rootage. Van Meter Ames has said: "He published no books, but for years books will appear of which he is the author." The list is long of those who find in "symbolic interactionism" the view best calculated to bring order and meaning into the data of social psychology. The processes that are distinctively human and rational appear only at the level of the social. It therefore requires a *social*, or a bio-social, not a simply physiological psychology to do justice to them. This view, of course, finds in the use of language the distinctive basis of both self and society. Speech takes its character from being the common endeavor of at least two centers of activity engaged in the social act of intercommunication.[21] This view has become the fundamental postulate of the Chicago School of social psychology and finds clearest exposition in the work of Faris, Kimball Young, Blumer, Bernard, and Charles Morris.[22]

In the field of general psychology the same bio-social approach to origins and structures informs scores of recent books of which we may cite as examples Professor Gardner Murphy's *Personality*,[23] Gordon Allport's *Personality*,[24] Hadley Cantril's *The Why of Man's Experience*,[25] and *The Open Self* by Professor Charles Morris.[26] This last is, in effect, a popular application of Mead's ideas which makes much of the theory of signs and symbols as pivotal to a scientific understanding of man. For Morris, as for Mead, language is social and provides the framework of the personality. Therefore it is important to know what are the life-symbols, the "big words" which a given society develops and employs.

In the adjoining fields of biology and anthropology[27] the investigations of such workers as Abram Kardiner, Ralph Linton, Margaret Mead, and Ruth Benedict are outstanding. In his book *The Psychological Frontiers of Society*, Kardiner and his associates are concerned to track down the social forces which shape the *basic personality*.[28] Margaret Mead, in her *Sex and Temperament in Three Primitive Societies* concludes that temperament and value judgments are the result of cultural conditioning and education evolved in the order of the social, for it is in that order that man becomes human.[29] Ralph Linton[30] and Ruth Benedict[31] are also interested in the inter-relation of personality to culture and hold that individual personalities and personality types cannot be understood without constant reference to the cultural and social environments in which they develop and operate.

In view of the excessive stress on competition and struggle for survival in our world, the ill effects of which we have noted earlier, it is interesting to discover that more recent research establishes the fact that inter-dependence or fellow-feeling or mutuality is at least as fundamental in life as competition. Professor W. C. Allee now declares that cooperation, mutual aid, and social integration are as important in the evolutionary process as hostility.[32] An Ashley-Montagu has only recently brought together the leading, scientific data in support of the principle that cooperation, not conflict, is the natural law of life.[33] He builds an impressive case by mustering evidence from the most up-to-date findings in biology, psychology, and the social sciences.

Further, he offers proof that all living things are so constituted as to demand satisfaction in terms of cooperation and love; that the central conception of "natural selection" has long been misinterpreted—that it is not to be understood in terms of competition, but in terms of cooperation. Ashley-Montagu has little to say of conflict, frustration, hatred and the breaking of community; in particular he does not make clear what it is that gives birth to these, except to suggest that they are abnormal and neurotic phenomena. But his study does marshall an impressive array of data in support of the conclusion that community is at least as primordial as the individual, cooperation as basic to the natural order as competition, and that man's social nature places inexorably before us the choice between competition and cooperation. Here also may be mentioned such other inspiring students of social life as Pitirim A. Sorokin,[34] Alfred Adler,[35] Sir Charles Sherrington,[36] John E. Boodin,[37] Margaret Ribble,[38] and William Goldfarb.[39]

Lawrence K. Frank has also pointed out that the "costs of competition" have become so excessive, so wasteful of human values, so destructive of mental health, that mankind must work toward a more cooperative social order not based on competition or else suffer the further disintegration of the structure of civilization itself.[40] The spectacular experimental studies of Kurt Lewin on the processes of democracy almost force the conclusion that persons function better in a cooperative than in a competitive or authoritarian situation.[41] Fellow-feeling and mutuality appear to be more productive of human happiness and social welfare than aggressive attitudes. Now comes Gardner Murphy reporting that Psychic Research has turned out to be largely a study of inter-relations of persons.[42] From Europe comes the arresting observations of a great physical scientist upon some of the themes with which we have been dealing—Dr. C. F. von Weizsächer. His book *The History of Nature* is full of the *I* and *Thou* problem, and his final verdict is that knowledge without love will lead mankind to destruction. And that battle is now raging. The new understanding of the problem of philosophical anthropology and ontology begins, as we have seen, with Ebner, Buber, and Gogarten. Our task appears to be one of integrating the human family while preserving the integrity of the individual members. Certainly all this evidence points to the conclusion that the human self is better understood when it is seen in terms of membership in the social group. "No man is an island," sang

John Donne, echoing the words of St. Paul that "we are all members one of another."

Turning to the psychology of religion we find that such early investigators as George A. Coe, Harrison Elliott, and Hugh Hartshorne have found Mead's social-functional-democratic pattern illuminating about the purposes and methods of religious education and the nature of religious experience. A more recent but representative worker in this field who also acknowledges the inspiration he has drawn from Buber is Professor Paul E. Johnson. His point of view is avowedly "dynamic," and "interpersonalistic." Of his *Psychology of Religion* he writes:[43]

> This is *interpersonal psychology*. It is my conviction that interacting persons are the field of psychology. Nothing less than personality is an adequate functioning unit for psychology. Yet persons are what they are always in social context. . . . Isolation is impossible, for the solitary person is unreal, abstract, artificial, abnormal. . . . Individualism leads to selfishness and anarchy; collectivism, to totalitarianism, oppression and exploitation. But inter-personalism does justice both to the individual and to society. The interacting units are persons; the interacting process is society.
>
> Religion is social reference to social realities by social responses for the sake of social values reinforced by social cooperation. . . . Psychology of religion is inevitably a social psychology of inter-acting persons.

This interpersonal and I-Thou influence is even more in evidence in his latest book *Christian Love* in which he undertakes a social and psychological study of Christian love.[44] From the standpoint of interpersonal psychology—"the scientific study of persons interacting with other persons"—the author analyzes the problems and possibilities of Christian love in sex and marriage, the family, in the community, and in national and international affairs. It is instructive to note Professor Johnson's statement of the central emphases in interpersonal psychology:

(1) Persons are the central focus of this psychology.

(2) Persons confront each other in I-Thou relationships.

(3) Personal motives are responses to significant persons in one's social orbit.

(4) The desires and efforts of persons are aimed toward goals valued by other persons.

(5) Persons work for values in order to share them with, or keep them from, other persons.

(6) From defensive tactics come fear, rivalry, and poverty; from sharing come mutual confidence, cooperation, and growth.

(7) The health of persons and societies depends upon the kind of relations persons develop toward each other; when interpersonal relations are insecure, hostile and predatory, the society declines and its members suffer nervous disorders; when interpersonal relations provide security, love, and mutual aid, the society prospers and its members mature in creative wholeness.

Perhaps in no other field, with the exception of religion, has there been so much attention given and such contributions made to the social character of the self as in the field of psychoanalysis and psychotherapy. With the exceptions of Anton T. Boisen and Seward Hiltner, I find no specific and declared dependence of these analysts on Mead or Buber; but the recent work of such therapists as Karen Horney, Harry Stack Sullivan, W. A. White, Erich Fromm, Fritz Kunkel, Rollo May, Harry Bone, and Ian D. Suttie share the central themes of Mead and Buber at crucial points even though the lines of influence are obscure and indirect.[45] This idea has now become a powerful and pervasive vector in psychological analysis and its seeds have produced a rich harvest especially in the theory and therapy of the American "cultural analysts,"[46] concerned as they are with hostility, isolation, loneliness, and anxiety and how they affect the growth of the self.

Boisen has found Mead's point of view the best key to the understanding of the personality disorders which confront the therapist as well as of certain types of religious experience.[47] He holds that the social response which is the basis of the personality is not just to others in general but to those we love and admire and whose authority we accept, those who for the religious man are associated with his idea of God. In his work as Chaplain of the Elgin (Illinois) State Hospital and as founder and consultant of the Council for Clinical Training of theological students, Dr. Boisen has been particularly interested in developing services of worship for group therapy and worship materials which would mediate the loyalties, energies, comforts, memories, and symbols of the Hebrew-Christian religion to persons in whom the better self is struggling to gain control.[48]

The recent development of pastoral counseling takes advantage of the constant and intimate personal relationships that exist between pastor and parishioner and the dynamic resources available in the religious meanings and fellowship of a church. Of the many recent books which attempt to bring the facts and theory, the insights and techniques of psychotherapy to the aid of the pastoral ministry, we may consider Seward Hiltner's *Pastoral Counseling* as an up-to-date discussion of this whole development.[49] He regards counseling as a relationship of a person who seeks help and a helper. His approach is called *eductive,* to indicate a sharing with the patient or parishioner in drawing or leading out the unfolding insights and decisions of growth in the person himself. He holds that counseling must be a permissive relationship in which there is mutual respect but no coercion or condemnation. Yet the multiple tasks of the pastor all unite in the role of representing God's faith in and forgiving love for every person.

A number of theologians are now at work on clarifying the relationship between psychotherapy and Christian theology. Among these we may mention two: David E. Roberts and Albert C. Outler. It is not hard to see that the notions of Mead and Buber have found their way into the thinking and writing of these two young theologians.[50]

Karen Horney and the group who follow her leadership have reformulated their doctrines in terms of interpersonal relations, explaining all neurotic reactions not as repressed sexuality or instinctual trends, but as conflicts between the tendencies to "move toward," "move away from," or "move against people."[51] This group now regards psychoanalysis as essentially the "science of human relations," rather than merely the scientific study of instinctual dynamics. Neurosis is the total inwardly estranged or contradictory reaction of a given character-structure or self-system to present-day culture. In other words, neuroses and anxieties are generated by disturbed personal relationships in which our normal responses to people become exaggerated by fear and hostility into compulsive ways of searching for security and love. Compliance, aggression, and detachment are forced and alien exaggerations of our normal movements toward, against, and away from other persons in our society.

Harry Stack Sullivan also defines psychiatry as the *study of interpersonal relations.* "This made psychiatry the probable locus of another evolving discipline, one of the social sciences, namely social psychology." [52] Psychiatry as the specialized preoccupation of doctors with the mentally ill now becomes the study of processes that involve or go on between two or more people, "only one of whom need not be illusory." The focus of psychoanalysis is thus directed to the *social basis* and the *social morphology* of the self. On this view the person is seen as a dynamic "self-system" composed of the developing sum of "reflected appraisals," and thus can be fruitfully studied only in the total dynamic "situation." Of necessity, Sullivan attaches great importance to the relations between patient and therapist, since the disturbance which brings the patient to the therapist was a failure of inter-personal relations between the patient and significant "others," and a cure can be effected only by a skillful and "gracious" handling of the inter-personal relations which accords to the patient a real sense of security, recognition, confidence and freedom. Love, for Sullivan, means that state which exists "when the satisfaction or security of another person becomes as significant to one as is one's own satisfaction or security." [53] Sullivan's approach is clinical and psychiatric; yet it obviously has far-reaching reverberations for any general theory of what human beings are, how personalities are formed, how they react to group life and significant adults, and in what direction lie health, growth, and happiness. This is a far cry from the mechanistic presuppositions of Freud, and corrects his lack of any social philosophy and the inadequacy of his "free association-transference" techniques in therapy. It would seem to me that at all crucial points Sullivan comes very close to the earlier work of William Alanson White who is regarded by many as the greatest leader to date in American psychiatry.[54]

Sullivan's use of verbalization as usually, if not always, necessary to insure permanent benefits to the patient provides opportunity in this connection to mention two other workers who have developed unique systems of therapy which employ dramatization, "acting out," and other extra-verbal devices for the solution of mental disorders. David M. Levy, in his "release therapy" of problem children has worked out a technique of this sort.[55] And J. L. Moreno uses the same principle in his "psychodrama" technique in which the patient acts out under more or less controlled conditions a dramatization of persons and performances connected with his conflicts.[56]

Many others might be listed here; but any complete roster of contemporary psychotherapists who have made notable contributions would include the names of Fritz Kunkel who, while oriented to Jung's point of view, has gone on to develop his own distinctive "We-psychology,"[57] and Erich Fromm, himself a social psychologist, who brings to his understanding and practice of psychoanalysis a wide knowledge of sociology, economics, history, and philosophy.[58] He clearly perceives the influence of society and culture on the character structure of the self, and shows how man's neurotic suffering in our age springs very largely from the loneliness and estrangement which have seized him. Modern man is sick because he is isolated. Accordingly, says Fromm, "the fundamental approach to human personality is the understanding of man's relation to the world, to others, to nature, and to himself." [59] Then he adds:

> We believe that man is primarily a social being, and not, as Freud assumes, primarily self-sufficient and only secondarily in need of others. . . . In this sense, we believe that individual psychology is fundamentally social psychology or, in Sullivan's terms, the psychology of interpersonal relationships; the key problem of psychology is that of the particular kind of relatedness of the individual toward the world, not that of satisfaction or frustration of single instinctual desires.[60]

It is important to note that the theory and practice of Fromm, Horney, Kunkel, and Sullivan recognize that every neurosis is a character disorder, that treatment involves the problem of morals and requires absolute honesty on the part of both therapist and patient. No therapist can be lastingly helpful who does not really believe in the possibility of the patient's fulfilling his own potentialities and no patient can be cured who is not ready to pay the price of constructive action and re-training.[61]

It is manifest that Fromm's concept of "character and the social process" comes close to the thought of Mead and Buber respecting the social perspectives of the individual and the dynamic adaptation of human nature to the structure of society. Fromm has a clear recognition of the meaning of Buber's I-It orientation and alienation as over against the world of I-Thou.[62] On this view "conscience" is often the voice of "social demands" which have assumed the dignity of ethical norms. And the role of education is crucial.

A great many educational books and the writers of those books have been influenced by the social psychology of Mead and/or Buber, particularly by Mead's account of the role of the "significant symbol" in the genesis of mind, and the role of the "other" in the development of the self. I think it would be well within the facts to assert that the "philosophy of education" dominating the Teachers' College of Columbia University is largely shaped along the lines laid down by Mead and Dewey. Dr. W. H. Kilpatrick in *Selfhood and Civilization*[63] makes extended use of Mead's view of the nature and genesis of the self. John L. Childs is much indebted to Mead in his recent book, *Education and Morals*.[64] Professor Childs holds to a bio-social functional view of the self, and shows a preference for a certain type of group and personal living which provides for the full development of the capacities of individuals in a life of "organized freedom" within a free society. He is concerned for both the child and society, with social and moral "ends" as well as with educational procedures and means. Education, he says, has to do with values that appear only at the level of the conscious, purposeful human life set within a physical and cultural environment in which the behaviors that are mind are elaborated. Thus method in education is a *moral* as well as a pedagogical affair. Dr. A. S. Clayton's book, *Emergent Mind and Education*[65] is entirely devoted to the educational implications of Mead's ideas.[66] Considerable use of Mead's views are also found in a Yearbook called *The Improvement of Practical Intelligence* by Raup, Axtelle, Benne and Smith, four leaders in American philosophy of education.

In England Herbert Read and John Macmurray have found the thought of Buber illuminating about the purpose and methods of education. Dr. J. H. Oldham has also expressed his profound debt to Buber. In one place he writes: "It may well be that the main conflict between Christian faith and the secular interpretation of life will have to be waged in the field of public education." [67] John Macmurray, although technically a philosopher, displays in all his writings and broadcast talks his concern for understanding life in personal terms. In *Interpreting the Universe*[68] he contrasts the three ways of interpreting the world in terms of mechanism, of organism, and of personality, and works toward the conclusion that the supreme reality in human life is the reality of persons in personal relation to one another. Macmurray also gives an analysis of "sin" as *isolation* and of "salvation" as *community* which recalls what Royce, Kunkel, Fromm and Boisen affirm. Genuine education of character is education for community. Communal righteousness within a "we-group" is as much a divine imperative as is personal integrity.

To show further how thoroughly the themes of Mead and Buber have penetrated the thought of our time, let me quote from Kurt Riezler, writing on public opinion:[69]

"I and Thou are the eternal cells of any living body social. . . . Looking at things, they look at each other, mutually assume their roles and, responding to each other, take into account each other's perspectives. In so doing, they do not pile up, but organize, their opinions in a more or less consistent body."

Continuing, he writes:

Response is not reaction to stimuli. The language is wiser than its usage. The original meaning of *respondeo* is: 'I, too, in my turn dedicate a libation to the Gods.' Responsiveness of an I to a You assumes responsibility toward some god. The man of behaviorism, the ideal object for techniques of manipulating the conditioned responses of emotional masses, does not respond: he reacts. Response includes even the element of possible surprise: If Eves were no longer able to surprise their Adams, and the Adams knew in advance and perfectly what their Eves would say, they would not deserve to be called a society, though to many a social dreamer they might seem an ideal society.[70]

The themes of Mead and Buber have fertilized the thought and writing of many contemporary writers in the fields of social and political philosophy. From this perspective, the problems and institutions of the democratic state, politics, and industry are seen in a new light; and many are saying that in going beyond the individual to the "we," in organizing common attitudes and values, lies the hope of democracy or any workable moderate socialism. The problem is how to secure the position of the state as the bond which holds the community together —responsible for fostering the good life of the community as a whole— and at the same time assure that the power of the state will be used not to suppress and oppress the people.

Among the many whom we might cite as being in debt to Mead or to Buber, or as moving along similar lines, we may name only a few typical writers. John Macmurray, already listed above, has extended his thinking about the reality of personal relations to theories of the state, of marriage and family life, and of economics. Gregory Vlastos has addressed himself to the task of theoretically reconciling the increasing organization of society, which science, technics, and the control of economic forces have rendered inevitable, and which is itself under modern conditions the indispensable basis and safeguard of liberty, with the freedom of thought and action which is essential for a truly human life.[71] He holds that responsible self-determination and communal inter-dependence are not in principle antagonistic; rather they are complementary. To deny this leads either to pure anarchy or to pure despotism. The values of the group are both the common *and* the personal values of those who make up the group, unless the group becomes a "crowd" in which the members have sacrificed the very thing which is constitutive of personality, namely, responsible self-determination. One cannot surrender such responsible decision to anyone else without forfeiting one's status as a personal being. This ultimate reality and dignity of the person-in-community, in the I-Thou relation, is the only basis for the moral justification of democracy.

We may again cite Dr. Oldham as having drawn from Buber much of the inspiration for his studies of our social and economic institutions and for his leadership in the field of "practical" Christianity and the ecumenical Church movement. This influence is clear and explicit in *Church, Community and State*,[72] where he declares that the Christian Church is committed by its central affirmations to the belief that the life of man finds its meaning and fulfillment in a community of persons living in mutual personal relations. The religious life should be the life of free personal response to the claim of persons, human and divine—a life of trust and loyalty, of mutually dedicated faith and love, within community.

Another notable effort in this direction is *Freedom and Order*, by Eduard Heimann,[73] in which he tries to strike a proper balance between freedom and order so that neither will become a menace. He shows that just as there cannot be genuine individual liberty unless there is order, there cannot be a stable order without a certain genuine liberty. The principle that keeps the two in equilibrium is justice. And they must be kept in balance or we shall end up in the unregulated anarchy of laissez-faire capitalism in which there is no order or genuine community or in the ruthless tyranny of Stalinism.

The distinguished French Roman Catholic philosopher, Jacques Maritain sets forth a Thomistic personalism as applied to the problem of the relation of the individual to society and to God. The central thesis in *The Person and the Common Good* is that the person is never, even to God, a mere object, "a mere cog in the machinery of the world." It is in the person and not in society that the image of God is to be found. Actually, he says, the struggle in every life is between *individuality* and *personality*, between the cry for freedom without responsibility and the spirit of expansive generosity which includes understanding of self and others. Evil results when individuality overcomes personality. Society exists not for the individual but for the maximum development of persons. Yet society is subordinate to the person because each person has supra-temporal aspirations. Yet neither society, nor the person, nor the common good suffer from this kind of subordination. The implications of such personalistic principles for totalitarianism, bourgeois liberalism, and communism are clear. The implications for religious freedom are not so clear as one might wish.[74]

Another answer to the economic and political evils of our times which bears striking resemblance to Buber's positive proposals in *Paths in Utopia* is Samuel Seabury's *The New Federalism*,[75] namely that of leaving people free to conduct their social and economic affairs according to the principle of decentralized and federalized self-government. Seabury stresses—as the condition of justice—the necessity of a widening social and economic federalism, in which small autonomous local cooperative groups will voluntarily affiliate with regional, national, and then international groupings. Thus men, living in small organic communities, can have some control over their lives, not only on election day, but every day through the bonds they forge and the joint decisions they make in their families, unions, cooperatives, fraternal organizations, and trade associations.

An English writer, J. B. Coates,[76] also commends personalism as a social philosophy for those who, believing the old orthodoxy of liberal individualism to be bankrupt, are yet unwilling to see a Marxist or fascist collectivism installed as its official receiver. Coates follows Buber in asserting the autonomy, freedom, and spirituality of the *person* over against materialism, scientism, the State, and other institutions, while insisting that personality involves an organic relation to other persons and to society at large. The political outcome seems to be an optimistic form of socialism.

These references to personalism, and its exposition by these various writers, suggest metaphysical assumptions to which reference needs to be made.[77] For personalism is, first of all, a metaphysic and a world view in which to set human personality. Personalism, as it is interpreted in the works of Edgar S. Brightman and his students is (1) a holistic and social theory of personality, (2) an ethic of personal values and respect for persons, (3) a theistic-idealistic philosophy of religion, and (4) a personalistic metaphysic—i.e., all reality is in, of, and by persons.[78] Brightman and other personalists are increasingly articulate about interpersonalism and interactionism as basic to their position. There seem to be traces of it in James Ward and in White-head's "prehensions." This becomes clear, as we have already noted, in the new metaphysical orientation which finds varied expression in the philosophies of Whitehead, Bergson, Hartshorne, Wieman, Williams, Calhoun and others.[79] These contemporary process philosophies aim to be consistent with our best scientific knowledge of the world; and they appear to be capable of being harmonized with our theme of dynamic interpersonal relations.[80]

In the field of epistemology a number of writers have made use of the new view. Professor John Baillie presents an especially striking treatment of the new attitude. Says he: "There is no more hopeful element in the philosophy of our time than the reopening of the question of the nature of our knowledge of one another." [81] This knowledge of other minds becomes the key to his study of *Our Knowledge of God.* Some anticipation of this new direction is found in W. E. Hocking's *The Meaning of God in Human Experience.*[82] In 1920 there appeared Samuel Alexander's Gifford Lectures on *Space, Time and Deity,*[83] and C. C. J. Webb's *Divine Personality and Human Life.*[84] Then in 1930 Professor Webb published his *Our Knowledge of One Another.*[85] And a further contribution was made by Professor A. A. Bowman in his *Studies in the Philosophy of Religion.*[86] It was, however, in the German speaking lands, and influenced more or less by Kierkegaard, that this new movement of thought found its richest development in the work of Ebner, Buber, Barth, Brunner, Gogarten, Heim, Grisebach, Kroner, and others. In general epistemology, this same influence may be found at work in the philosophies of Martin Heidegger, Karl Löwith, Karl Jaspers, and M. Jean Wahl. In Barth the new view of our knowledge of other mind is represented in the conceptions of the Word, Revelation, and God as Subject. This same influence is manifest in the writings of Friedrich Gogarten,[87] and in those of Eberhard Grisebach,[88] who has worked out the ethical significance of the ideas made familiar to us by Buber, but without Buber's notion of the eternal *Thou* who guarantees the human *Thou* to us and also directly addresses us. Gogarten employs the distinctive terminology and the thesis of Buber to clarify the relation of faith to history. The concrete reality, for him, as for Buber, is the situation where responsible persons confront one another in living mutual relation: history is constituted where two or more persons meet. This same understanding is summarized by Baillie in these words: "All our knowledge of God is given us 'in, with and under' our knowledge of one another. . . . Only when I am in *fellowship* with my fellow men does the knowledge of God come to me individually." [89] This suggests the necessity of the historic Church; or in Brunner's words: "God will not bind me to himself on any other terms than these, that he binds me at the same time to my brother." [90] Professor H. Richard Niebuhr has employed a similar notion in making a distinction between the inner and outer history of a historical fellowship,[91] and he develops his idea of "external history" and "internal history" in terms of Buber's distinction between the I-It world and the I-Thou world respectively.

In sum, knowledge of the "other" is not just an inference drawn from solipsistic self-consciousness or from knowledge of the external world. This view is steadily realistic, and insists that *self*-consciousness in the first instance can not arise in advance of recognition of and relation with other selves. The old subject-object orientation of experience is retired in favor of a subject-subject situation in which I find myself confronted with what claims to be another center of experience—a being in the knowing of whom I myself am known. Yet self-consciousness is perhaps no more obviously socially conditioned than is our consciousness of the external world. For it is a public world, the world I share with others. In Hocking's words: "I do not first know my physical world as a world of *objects,* and then as a world of *shared* objects: it is through a prior recognition of the presence of Other Mind that my physical experience acquires objectivity at all. The objectivity of nature is its community." [92]

No record of the fertile applications of the idea of the social self would be complete without some reference to its uses for ethics. The meanings in this realm are various and clear, but we shall resist the temptation to fuller exposition and content ourselves with one notable example of the relation of the self-other dialectic to the problems of *conscience*: the familiar experience of a duality in the self in which one is judged, commanded, approved, condemned, or consoled by an *alter* in the *ego*. Reflecting the influence of Mead's and Buber's analysis of the self, Professor H. Richard Niebuhr has developed a kind of "socio-theology" which uses the I-Thou and the self-other motifs as being more adequate as tools of criticism than the part-whole, lower-higher patterns of idealism. In the only published statement of this development in Niebuhr's moral philosophy,[93] he discusses such problems as who the *self* is in this moral dialogue, who the *other* is (e.g., Smith's "impartial spectator," society, Christ, God, etc.), the authority and sanction in such moral experience, the validity and verification of this inner legislation, and the relation of a good conscience to the forgiven conscience.

In his lectures in Christian ethics at the Yale Divinity School, Niebuhr speaks more in terms of a "trialogue" or a "trialectic" of persons or personal elements. This seems to suggest the influence of either the Christian doctrine of the Trinity as a "Self-system" involving three persons, or an analysis of the theory of knowledge akin to that of Baillie, namely, that no one of the subjects of our knowledge—ourselves, our fellows, the corporeal world, and God—is ever present to us except in conjunction with the others.[94] In other words, our knowledge of ourselves, our fellows, and God is not *direct,* but a *mediated immediacy.* We know God *with* the world. We know God *with* the neighbor.[95] The ethical God-man relationships must be inclusive of the neighbor, suggesting a man-God-man, or a man-man-God pattern. I love the neighbor in and with God; I love God in and with the neighbor, in community. Even in my relations with my fellows there is always a third factor: some object, task, idea, art form related to or having personal and public meanings. The *It* may become a *Thou,* and it always stands between as a common object for human beings.

Nowhere has Buber's message had so marked an influence as in contemporary European religious thought—both Jewish and Christian. "Wherever on the continent of Europe Jews are deeply concerned over the character and fate of their people, the name of Martin Buber is a power." [96] So wrote Ludwig Lewisohn some years ago; and Ronald Gregor Smith, the translator of several of Buber's books, says: "In view of this influence alone, it may be affirmed that *I and Thou* will rank as one of the epoch-making books of our generation." [97] In England, as on the continent, it has entered deeply into theological and philosophical discussion, and has left a deep impress upon twentieth century religious thought, particularly Protestant theology. Commenting on this influence, H. H. Farmer says: "I regard this as the most important contribution that has been given to us of recent years towards the reflective grasp of our faith." [98] We turn, therefore, to the ways in which the I-Thou motif has found fruitful application in theology and religion. Here, too, the same tendencies are at work, for they seem to be a part of "the world-hour." [99]

The last three decades have witnessed a significant revival of creative theology,[100] which makes abundant use of the themes which Buber and Mead have made familiar. This new theology is especially concerned with the nature and status of man vis-a-vis God and man's own culture. Its beginning can be conveniently symbolized by the publication, in 1919, of Karl Barth's *Römerbrief*.[101] The great truths of the Christian religion, Barth holds, are paradoxes and beyond the power of human reason to grasp unaided by revelation as found in the Biblical "Word of God" in Christ. God is unknowable by man—He is the "hidden God"—yet man may know what God knows if man accepts His point of view, and sees himself as God sees him and judges him. Man knows the love of God when, out of his wretchedness and failure, he turns back to the Father. There man's sin is met and redeemed by grace. Only through such faith, and with God's gracious help, can man come to God, meet God across the gulf between, hear God's address to man as it is proclaimed through Christ in the Church.

We must resist the temptation to engage in a full and genetic account of this so-called "neo-orthodox" theology, and simply state that it is a strange and varied blend of anti-rational, paradoxical, existential, personalistic, and dialectical tendencies. It manifests a distinctly Hebrew-Christian concern for persons as whole persons brought face to face with God, the eternal Other. Faith is a meeting, a decision, a commitment—an act of man, yet paradoxically a gift of God. Only in such a dialectical situation can man really know himself. This line of thought emphasizes the quite *sui generis* nature of persons and their relationship to one another, the two-way, bi-subjective character of every genuine religious experience, the involvement of the whole man in the situation, and the impossibility of leaving God outside the situation. Buber's phrase "I-Thou" most accurately characterizes this dialogic nature of high religion. Out of this divine-human encounter in which man confronts God across the abyss between man and God are faith and spiritual tension generated. Neither reason nor mystic union can resolve this tension. Thus, especially in neo-Protestant theology, both rationalism and mysticism are rejected. Only when reason recognizes the limits of reason,[102] can man meet God in the decisive encounter of faith.

In other places we have mentioned the "social gospel," [103] and it is important to note that nearly all of these neo-orthodox theologians of whatever communion are social radicals wrestling with the dilemmas within the present crisis which baffle both liberalism and Marxism. Many of them are or have been members of socialist parties.[104] Certainly these theologians are not hermits, rejecting social Christianity as did Kierkegaard. In Europe their criticism of contemporary culture took the form of the Christian Socialist Movement in Germany and Switzerland;[105] in America it took the form of a radical prophetic message which goes beyond the older liberal "social gospel." [106] This realistic theology seeks a deeper foothold for its understanding of the Christian imperative in an ecumenical consciousness and a deepened appreciation of the scriptural and historical nature of Christianity. But it remains anti-capitalist and anti-totalitarian; it seeks an adequate Christian social philosophy which will guarantee a maximum of both freedom and community.

The concept of the radical "otherness" of God makes possible an acute appreciation of the meaning of human sin and moral evil. This, perhaps more than any other aspect of the new theology, has become its familiar "hallmark." [107] Man's inordinate pride in his own reason, his efforts to deny or transcend his creatureliness, his egocentricity, his tendency to love himself instead of God, his rebellious self-will and lack of love for the neighbor—these suggest a primal and radical perversity in human nature. Man's "sin" stands for the other side of man's capacity for self-transcendence in reason, aspiration, and moral freedom, and constitutes both a tragic limitation and a source of corruption of that capacity. This is the reason, say these theologians, why the Kingdom of God may never be identified with historical progress or any earthly social order.

Reinhold Niebuhr, combining the insights of both Marx and Freud, perhaps more clearly than any of the other neo-orthodox leaders, points out the ambiguities in all of man's achievements, the self-deceptive ways in which human motives are idealized, and the self-interest in all human ideals. Yet the Kingdom of God, Niebuhr holds, is relevant to human striving, it breaks through into human existence, becoming the source and judge of moral effort.[108] The final elimination of evil is impossible for man in time; that is possible only "beyond tragedy"

in God's Eternity. In other words, Niebuhr contends that human existence and history are dynamic and meaningful, but not ultimately
redemptive. Here, so the claim is made, is a religious Utopianism that
can resist corruption, a theologically based social gospel which can face
and deal with the harsh realities of life without either naive optimism,
self-deception, or despair.

Buber's pioneering work prepared the way, in many respects, for the
"new" theology and anthropology which have come from the pen of
such Protestant theologians as Brunner, Barth, Heim, Gogarten, H. H.
Farmer, John Oman, and John Baillie. Some of these—e.g., Brunner,
Heim, Gogarten, Farmer, and Oman—have developed entire theological
systems which echo or parallel the themes of Buber and Mead; and
the same tendencies have helped many others, such as Baillie, the later
Barth, Cave, Dickie, the Niebuhrs, Tillich, and Williams to formulate
their understanding of God and man in "social" or "inter-personal"
terms.[109] As Brunner and Farmer have clearly shown, there is hardly
an article of faith or doctrine in Biblical theology which may not be
freshly illuminated by the I-Thou motif. From the doctrines of the
triune God, creation and revelation, through those of Church, sin and
sacraments to final redemption, the Biblical category of "personal correspondence" or the "divine-human encounter" are central.[110]

Religion is defined as the continuous dialogic meeting in history of
God and man. The Bible is the record of that dialogic experience,
culminating (in Christian doctrine) in the Word being made flesh in
Christ. The relation of the covenant-God with Israel is the content
of its history. History is that which takes place between the personal
God and his people. For these reasons the life of the people of Israel
was and is conceived in personal I-Thou terms. Only thinkers like
Brunner, Barth, Gogarten and Ebner, echoing the prophets, and now
Buber, never a Greek, I suspect, could have understood such a thesis.[111]
Faith is not just trust in a gracious God; it is, as Sydney Cave reminds
us,[112] a *meeting* between God and man, a glad *response* on man's part
to God's gracious self-revealing initiative, a bi-polar uncoerced relationship not entirely at the disposal of the will of either person. God is not
purely transcendent; he is also immanent and world seeking.[113] Faith
means both human dependence and freedom,[114] obedience to and fellowship with a living Person and Lord.[115] True faith occurs only through
a coincidence between God's will and man's will.

This movement of the "divine turning" (grace, agape, revelation) has been given a subtle and profound interpretation by H. Richard Niebuhr in his Taylor Lectures, *The Meaning of Revelation*. There he writes:

> The only word in our vocabulary which does justice to the knowledge of persons or selves is 'revelation.' . . . In the knowledge of other selves both the relationship and the related terms are different. . . . We cannot know here save as we are known. . . . No amount of initiative on our part will serve to uncover the hidden self-activity. It must make itself manifest or it cannot be known. . . . Where there is no response it is evident that there is no knowledge. . . . Loving and hating selves must reveal themselves.[116]

Selves are known in this act of address and reply, initiative and response, choosing and being chosen, or not at all. In such meetings the I is changed. The I is no longer just a knower, a thinker, an impersonal doer; this I is a *person*, a particular subject, implicated with another particular subject. This is true of God as well as of men.

Buber's assertion (and Mead's) concerning the creative nature of speech is reflected in Barth's and Brunner's doctrine of the Word of God, which is active and manifest in Creation, the Covenant, and the Incarnate Christ, in all of which the Lord confronts man and claims him as his God and Redeemer.[117] Barth's theology is a theology of the revealed and proclaimed Word of God, the first principle of which is: *Thus saith the Lord!*

This interpersonal conception makes it possible for the theologians to interpret the *imago Dei* in *relational* rather than in rational or substantial terms.[118] The important thing, thinks Brunner, is not that man as he is bears God's likeness, but rather that man is created for and called to a particular *relation* and fellowship with God.[119] So Paul Lehmann, also, who places the stress on that which differentiates men from the rest of nature, on that which essentially characterizes man as a human being: the fact of *relationship with another*.[120] Man is made in God's likeness: this means that man is *like unto God*, i.e., related to God as God is related to him—a relation of self-giving, seeking, and responding. In similar fashion, Paul Ramsey interprets the *imago Dei* in his recent book, *Basic Christian Ethics*. "The image of God is rather to be understood as a relationship *within which* man sometimes stands, whenever like a mirror he obediently reflects God's will in his life and actions." [121]

This view points to an interpretation of "sin" as the destruction of this "image," or relationship. If man is a person standing in essential relation to God and fellowmen, and constituted a self by these relations and claims, sin may then be defined, as it is by the theologians, as a breaking of the faith-ful fellowship with the divine Other and with the neighbor. It arises out of the tension between freedom and determinism, between self and community,—from the fact of man's capacity for self-transcendence. Sin is then not merely bodily passion, ignorance, or finitude as the idealists and moralists would have it. Sin is irresponsiveness, the self-sufficient loving of oneself, the irresponsible and proud absolutizing of the finite self before the holy and infinite. Thus variously do Brunner, Barth, Niebuhr, Farmer and others define sin,[122] while insisting that somehow or other it is universal, total, inevitable, and responsible. Mead's and Buber's emphasis upon the social self-in-community lends support to the view that "I-isolation," "loss of community," and "withdrawal" define sin in the sense of denial of and rebellion from the loyal fellowship with others, and especially self-chosen alienation from God.[123] Sin is still a relation to God, of course; but now a negative, perverted one. The face-to-face relation is broken; the finite-infinite nature of man is perversely employed; and the result is self-contradiction within man, as well as estrangement of man from God and his fellows.

The analysis of the self as a "self-other" system permits the interpretation of sin as rebellious self-will. It is a division within himself which robs man of his true selfhood. And if this self is composed of the "reflected appraisals" of other persons, it means that society is constantly training up children who may, and do, rebel against society.[124] If the analysis of Mead and Buber be correct, we become selves in a process which *arouses and heightens self-will*. Men are psychologically built upon trouble, for society is inevitably breeding its own enemies. In such a social world of interacting individuals, it is hardly possible for one to become a self without at the same time becoming a sinner. If this be the human predicament, the doctrines of the Fall and Original Sin become useful symbols of this fact and also of the solidarity of the human family.

Furthermore, if this account be true, there is what Brunner calls a "solidarity in sin"—as an inevitable characteristic of group life, a corporate character of sin which shows up in group life.[125] The social nature of the self makes it essential to take into account the effects of one man's sins upon another, and the cumulative evil of any society which becomes incorporated into massive structures of evil which might well be called the Kingdom of Evil, as Rauschenbusch so aptly put the matter. If community is essential to personality, evil in either the self or the group must affect the other.[126]

Brunner introduces one doctrine not found in Buber:[127] that of the "Orders"—the forms of community in which men must live out their days—family, state, economic life, school, culture, church. But the "orders," says Brunner, are one of the inevitable conditions of sin, yet without relieving man of responsibility for his sin. It would appear that Brunner has here run into trouble, for the "orders" are divinely ordained, while yet predisposing man inevitably to sin. Brunner is in difficulty at another point, also, for he rightly holds the inevitability and responsibility together, but at the expense of any rational explanation. Sin, for Brunner, is inexplicable—the one great negative mystery.[128]

Since sin is a kind of "treason" which banishes the self from his true homeland, it is irrevocable in the sense that he can never forgive himself for such a traitorous deed: he must be saved by an act of "grace," from beyond himself. This is the work of the Mediator, the Redeemer—the act and self-communication of God, the God who approaches man in self-giving love to restore the broken relationship, to forgive the rebellion, to persuade the alienated one to repentance and self-surrender, to reconcile the lost self to a new two-sided fellowship. This means a kind of re-birth of the true self. Here we see that the I-Thou relation is the basis of Brunner's ethic as well as his doctrine of salvation; and a similar situation obtains for the other theologians under consideration. If man is both free and responsible, and if communion is a two-sided happening, there are implications not only for sin but for redemption. For while redemption is a gracious gift of God rather than a human achievement, it is "offered" to rather than irresistibly "forced" upon man. Thus while grace is God's "turning" to man in love, it always respects man as subject; it is not an arbitrary action, but a personal communion. Man is so conquered by God's love in Christ that he returns God's love in reciprocal love, in uncoerced obedience.[129]

The view that sin is "social" and the self a "social self" passes easily into the view that salvation is also social in two senses: (1) full deliverance from the isolated, estranged ego is achieved only when the forgiven self is united with the Other, and (2) no one is saved by himself alone, but within some group which becomes to him a "channel of grace." Perhaps he, too, is not truly saved until he himself becomes a "mediator" of saving influence to others in his society. Thus man is a forgiven sinner who forgives; the other (be he neighbor or Holy Spirit) may become, as Professor Niebuhr has so finely said, "a source of consolation, and of inspiration toward the keeping of the principles which have been transgressed." [130] And from an unexpected source comes support for this view of the social structure of selves and of sin:

> It may be that the acts and sufferings of great archetypal individuals such as Adam and Christ are ours, not by legal fiction, metaphor, or causality, but in some much deeper fashion. . . . Legal fiction, adoption, and transference or imputation of merit and guilt could never have played the part they did play in theology if they had always been felt to be so artificial as we now feel them to be.[131]

The preaching of repentance is therefore the first task of the Church. And while Barth and Brunner make much of "preaching" the Word of God as the prime function of the Church,[132] I want to mention H. H. Farmer as one who has expounded most attractively the conception of the preaching ministry in terms of Buber's description of the personal nature of real life.[133] His series of lectures are cast throughout in terms of the I-Thou relationship and make eloquent use of the notion of speech as so indispensable to the world of personal relationships, especially the idea of encounter, challenge, claim and offer. His two main theses are that God's personal encounter with man is never apart from his I-Thou relations with his fellows, and speech is supremely the medium wherein the direct confrontation of will with will through claim and shared meaning can be at a maximum. In the Church's preaching ministry God's demand and God's succour are fused together.

One of the charges most frequently brought against Protestants is that they have no doctrine of the Church and the Sacraments. But a survey of recent theological literature indicates that, by making full use of the doctrine of the social self and similar themes, many Protestant Christians are turning more and more toward a corporate, sacramental, and churchly conception of Christianity. The contemporary revolt against liberal individualism,[134] the social gospel movement,[135] the stress on the social origin and character of religion,[136] the ecumenical movement,[137] the recovery of corporate liturgical worship and symbolism,[138] the "cell" movement,[139]—all of these influences, whether cause or effect, show a renewed interest in the historical Christian Community as the Body of Christ and in the communal nature of salvation.[140] The Christian is first of all a member of a historical fellowship, a member of God's Family, members one of another.

This influence was also prefigured by Josiah Royce.[141] The "holistic" and "organismic" philosophies of Smuts, Boodin, Whitehead, Morgan, and Hartshorne give the movements of social collectivism metaphysical expression and support. Now come such theologians as L. S. Thornton, P. T. Forsyth, Dietrich von Hildebrand, Gregory Dix, W. Norman Pittenger and others with impressive works on the doctrine of the Church and its Sacraments. Scholasticism is also enjoying a renaissance, in the form of neo-Thomism. In its philosophical and social realism and its doctrine of law, it supports an organic spiritual society as opposed to the nominalism and individualism of liberal Protestantism.

It is important to underline the fact that the conceptions of prayer and the sacraments involve the notion of the "real presence" of the Spirit in a communal, two-sided, personal correspondence. The revival of liturgical worship also brings support to the neglected doctrine of the priesthood of all believers. The doctrine of the "real presence" is again prominent as an assertion that the Spirit of God in Christ is actually present in the corporate worship of the fellowship. Whether this be expressed in terms of transubstantiation or consubstantiation, this doctrine becomes central, and is related to the other doctrine of the Church as the mystical Body of Christ. This makes possible, indeed explains, the combination, often observed, of a "high church" sacramentalism with a radical social ethic.[142]

This survey of the manifold influence of Buber's and Mead's thought may be concluded with a reference to Tillich's belief that Buber's philosophy of religion points a way beyond both liberal and ultra-orthodox theology.[143] In a remarkable article in *Commentary* Tillich does two things: (1) He traces the common sources of himself and Buber in:

(a) The prophetic message of social justice as the criterion of political thinking and acting within some radical group;

(b) The mystical tradition, especially of Boehme and Schelling;

(c) The participation in the philosophical and educational movements of Germany after the First World War.

and (2), he sets forth what he thinks is Buber's significance for Protestantism as follows:

- (a) Buber's existential interpretation of prophetic religion;
- (b) His rediscovery of mysticism as an element within prophetic religion;
- (c) His understanding of the relation between prophetic religion and culture, especially in the social and political realms.

RESIDUAL DIFFICULTIES

We have seen how both Mead and Buber establish a philosophical anthropology which conceives of man as a "self-other" system comprising a duality of an *alter* in the *ego* in which the self is both subject and object at the same time. The finite individual self is mutually dependent upon and mutually determinative of other selves. This social concept of the self is further expressed in the doctrine that the discovery and continuity of selfhood is inseparable from community and social continuity; that speech or language is the chief and constitutive mechanism of the developing human psyche; and that all existence is social in the same general sense in which finite selves are social—the world itself being also a network of mutually supporting, dynamic, interacting relations.

Beyond that we have shown the valid and fertile contributions of this theory of man as being a self-other structure in many directions and in many different disciplines. This notion of the self which tries to do justice to the factors of duality and polarity in human nature comes near, as we have seen, to the issues in which modern social ethics, epistemology, metaphysics, psychotherapy, and Protestant theology are interested. These contributions come particularly at the point of viewing the self either (1) as an inter-personal and self-transcending movement of the self toward the other (perhaps even to an Infinite Other), or (2) as an individuating, obligating, controlling, judging, forgiving, and redeeming movement of the other (or Other) upon the self. It remains for us only to consider summarily some of the residual difficulties.

We have said all along, and shown specifically, that Mead and Buber are not always clear or consistent in their formulation of their theory. And we have seen that the inconsistent and inadequate elements in their doctrine of man are for the most part, but for different reasons, associated with their methodologies. We need therefore only to clarify and summarize where those difficulties and failures lie in the areas of social psychology, sociology, epistemology, metaphysics, ethics, and religion.

The philosophies of both Mead and Buber have more loose ends than most systematic thinkers would consider permissible. But this does not disturb either Mead or Buber: not because they are careless or indifferent thinkers; for they are very acute thinkers. But Buber sees no great virtue in strict logical consistency or in following one's argument to the bitter end. He is not afraid to speak of "mystery." His intuitionism and his distrust of neat rational systems permit him to walk the "narrow ridge" of religious experience, of the living concrete moment, rather than of theological debate. He is compelled to use prose to express ideas which are inherently poetic, mythical, aesthetic, mystical—some would say irrational. But life, experience, the soul of man, and man's deep hunger and need can scarcely be confined within the sober lines of prose or logic or tight system. Academic research, scientific analysis, and animal psychology cannot give man the eternal meaning and the immortal soul he wants; nay more, they tend to destroy with doubts the soul which he does have.

There is, however, one general criticism of the whole existential school, and of mysticism in general, which must be considered, and admitted with respect to Buber, for the possible errors in Buber's philosophy lie chiefly in this area of his existentialism and mysticism. In throwing the weight of truth upon the existential decision or the inner mystical vision, and removing the content of that decision or vision from rigorous rational scrutiny, Buber[144] had perhaps unwittingly been a forerunner of the nihilism and the revolt against reason which in the recent past have swept away so many of our cherished values. Thus he inadvertently gave support to the demonic idolatries and parochial movements that lack no existential intensity of decision and commitment, but which have directed their ruthless volitional drive toward the destruction of western civilization.

Without quarreling with the conclusion that the way of a practical mysticism,—checked by reason, living experience, and pragmatic consequences, and issuing in appropriate and imaginative moral action— is one of the roads on which man may find God and truth, and without which we cannot live, we are perhaps entitled to ask of one who is so sure of the road that he give further and clearer particulars which might assist other seekers in finding the way and walking in it. Buber fails to provide needed specific principles of guidance and definition for detecting true theophanies of God, or for distinguishing between "personal" relations with things and "personal" relations with persons. Without such clearly defined standards, most men will never attain them. Those without Buber's sensitive spirit, religious awareness, and discriminating conscience may be only doomed to seek, and not to find.

On his part, Buber feels that he has done all that any human being can possibly do to give concreteness and particularity to these I-Thou criteria and standards—especially in his dialogical essays, in his Biblical exegesis, and in his Chassidic commentaries—for example, *The Way of Man*.

While we may agree with the protest against the claims of science to an omnicompetent *objectivity,* we may still raise the query as to whether there may not also be such a thing as an enslaving *subjectivity?* While Buber may be vulnerable at this point, he also has some weapons of defense. His recognition of the naturalness of the It-world, and his insistence upon the reality of the other, make clear the error of treating all objectivity as enslaving and evil. His appeal to the Thou is for him no warrant to wallow in subjectivity. He is simply saying that man lives in two worlds and that when he tries to make his home in one alone something goes wrong with him. Consequently, the imputation of subjectivity to which his mysticism, romanticism, and personalism might appear vulnerable is evaded by maintaining its sharp duality and polarity and its view that all persons are united in a common relationship to God, or to Objective Value. Some objective otherness and over-againstness of the world is ever stepping up to his soul and laying its demands upon him. Mind is transcendent of the present perceptual field, but never to be simply identified with it, explain it as you will. One can appreciate the meaning of the I-Thou encounter without wishing or needing to repeal Kant's *Critiques.* But it should also be remembered that Buber's I-Thou relationship is something quite different from the familiar subject-object relationship.

Mead, too, was embarrassed by a persistent subjectivism,—an unadmitted residue of his early training in idealism, as well as of his empiricism and pragmatism. His realism and process naturalism rejected the logic and metaphysical rationalism of idealism, but he never really understood idealism's doctrine of man and so substituted his own doctrine of man for another. Mead was excellent for analysis, but he was always embarrassed and confused by his efforts to fit his analysis into the dogmas of naturalism and evolutionary biology. Therefore his subjectivism remains as much a rigid framework for him as his naturalism.

Meaning, for Mead, exists between subjects, not in their common relation to objects. Thus Mead persists in what we might call "inter-subjective" idealism.

Mead's great contribution is that he tried to show *how* the organism becomes a self within the social matrix, *how* society shapes the mind and personality of the individual member. Whatever the virtues or defects of Mead's theory, this is a real advance over the mere assertion that it does. In this connection we may point out several lacunae in Mead's method. He failed to make clear whether the *mechanism* which generates language and subsequently the self is the same mechanism or relation required for the development of the mature stages of the self. He failed to indicate the difference between "role-taking" and "role-learning." In other words, probably due to his preoccupation with the "me," Mead failed to give full acknowledgment of and adequate consideration to the place in the development of the self of the unique creative achievement of the individual self-transcending human spirit. Furthermore, Mead's description of role-taking leaves insufficient room for the influence of the general environment (nature, intelligible forms, God, etc.) upon the development of the individual. Finally, Mead gave all too little heed to the *dynamic* concepts developed by abnormal psychology, psychotherapy, and by the Freudian psychology. Had he done so, it might have helped him to account for the hostility and community-breaking aggressiveness in men. It is indeed strange that so fertile and hospitable a mind did not "strike gold" in psychoanalysis. Mead seems almost pre-Freudian; a fact to be explained largely by his preoccupation with behavioristic and genetic psychology, and perhaps by the early Freudians' disregard of the social factors in personality development. This is all the more remarkable in one who held such a dynamic, interpersonal, social interpretation of personality; for the work of psychotherapy has shown with increasing clarity that the sense of guilt, anxiety, and other such elements in functional illness have to do with the internalized sense of isolation and estrangement. They are often due to the presence of desires and attitudes and actions which can neither be renounced nor acknowledged for fear of condemnation. Buber, as another geographer of the social map, does more justice to these phenomena by his idea that God, the Universal Other, stands for the fellowship of the best by which the estranged or rebellious self judges himself, consoles himself, and to which he transfers his ultimate loyalty. This sense of isolation and alienation poses a problem for any social theory of personality for which Mead has no adequate answer.

Mead recognized hardly any limits beyond which science, and particularly scientific sociology, might not go in its cure for the ills of life. He seemed unaware that science cannot save the world, since it must serve and cannot lead. And he hardly considered seriously the question of who is to guide or control the scientist. His own sociology had religious presuppositions which he did not recognize or admit: it could take humaneness and democracy for granted. Likewise his social ethics had a regard for ideas of human worth which came from an ethical religion. Recent years have shown abundantly the moral neutrality and lack of social control of science which have been turned to horribly destructive ends. The instrumentalism, functionalism, and operationalism of Mead's science are deficient because they go too far. Concepts cannot be completely defined in terms of operations, since the operations themselves are meaningless apart from a certain theory (i.e., apart from concepts). Nor has it been demonstrated that we must give up talking about experience *of* reality and talk only of experience *as* reality.

But credit where credit is due! Man's pride in and use of reason and science can be blameworthy only if it has become the rival of something nobler: if, for example, science or reason is put in the place of God. We can surely assert with Mead the values of the scientific method *within its own sphere.* Furthermore, moral questions cannot be solved by moralizing alone, but by implementation. Any separation of "means" and "ends" inevitably permits a form of moral escapism. It permits the theologian to talk about moral ends without necessarily finding moral means toward those ends. Both ends and means are partly technical and partly valuational problems. Mead's error lay in assuming that the means at our command also delineated the ends and the basic standards of value. Science cannot tell us how to act, for it is not the moral standard; indeed, it can only be defined and measured in terms of a value standard beyond itself, as for example when a judge interprets existing statutes by the "rule of equity," or where constitutions and bills of rights serve as checks upon arbitrary power. Science cannot tell us *why* human personality is valuable, *why* justice is better than tyranny, or *why* we should be for democracy or humane ends; but if we are for these things, science and reason can do very much to tell us how to transform life through ethical conviction. Mead was correct in insisting that human values, wherever derived, are answerable to the pragmatic court of human experience which knows a good tree by its fruit.

So long as Mead and Buber hold to a self-other, I-Thou structure of the self, they are on fairly safe ground as regards the charge of extreme subjectivism, or of denying the self-transcending capacity of the human spirit from which their dialectic and metaphysics arise.

They would be on even firmer ground if, as Professor Richard Niebuhr points out, they employed a triadic or a trialectic formula which involves not just a meeting and a meaning between two subjects, but a meaning and a meeting of relation of two subjects to a common object or a third subject. Buber is a safer guide here because of his third dimension of God: man's relation to man must always be inclusive of God, and man's relation to God must always include the neighbor.

Mead and Buber are social philosophers endeavoring to elaborate a social psychology and philosophy which will do justice to both the individual and society, individual freedom and the common welfare. They reject the extremes of both individualism and collectivism, of sociological nominalism and sociological realism, and seek instead a middle axiom in the social self in which self and society are correlative terms.

Mead rejected idealism as primarily either a dualistic epistemology or an absolutistic and intellectualistic metaphysics; but he adapted much of the social theory of Hegelian idealism to an empirical evolutionary naturalistic method. And it is our conviction that it is this aspect of his thought (quite as much as his empiricism and pragmatism) which confuses his thought. He begins with an empirical and genetic analysis of human nature, and gives us an anthropology couched in the terms of a behavioristic social psychology which regards man more as a "self-system" than as a mind, and seeks to establish a conception of self-other symbolic relations as being more essential to an understanding of man's nature and situation than a part-whole identity. But there is some evidence to make us believe that he never outgrew his Hegelian legacy, with the result that his doctrine of the self includes both the part-whole and the self-other patterns.

Buber responded differently and for somewhat different reasons, but he achieved a very similar result in his doctrine of man's I-Thou, finite-infinite nature. Buber came close to pantheism in his youthful mysticism, with the attendant threat of losing the finite self in the Unconditioned Absolute. But he resisted the temptation to either pantheism or solipsism, disparaging neither the independent reality of the finite subject nor the Infinite Subject. He rejected both Spinozism, with its tendency to represent man as absorbed in God, and subjective idealism, with its tendency to assimilate the object of knowledge to the subject. His Jewish awareness never permits him to remove the existential duality between God and man. And his consistent personalism and his philosophy of speech, with its inevitable dialogic character, enable him to affirm that God and man stand over against one another in that bi-polar tension of independent wills without which a genuine personal relationship cannot exist.

Despite all this there is a fair certainty that Mead (and perhaps Buber with him) was beguiled by his generous nature as well as by his social optimism into regarding an acknowledged noble ideal as an operative social force. For if "sociality" is the real way of things, why is it such a task to "socialize" people? Why do men remain such stubborn individualists? Why do the aggressive centripetal, self-regarding drives of the self seem so much more powerful than the centrifugal? If man as "social individual" is actually in harmony with the law of life how shall we account for the constant rupturing of the human community? Here is the unsolved problem of human relations.

Let us admit that the self is social. For it is beyond dispute, I think, that to be anything real is to enter relations. A purely isolated individual self is nothing at all. One may not rightly consider himself, psychologically or morally, and perhaps metaphysically, a completely separate being. But the mere social nature of the self obviously does not suffice to guarantee the desired result of either integrated selves or a social good when the self is molded as much from social conflict and clashing roles as from social harmony. We have to seek further for the answer. And there are several questions which we meet on the way to any satisfactory answer.

For example: Granted that the "social" is a great deal, is the "social" all there is? Does mental phenomena develop *only* in gestural give-and-take? Are not one's memory and purposes, one's physical nourishment, and one's world of natural objects and forces also vital and necessary to one's consciousness of selfhood? Or again, are activity, behavior, adjustment, and social experience the only reals? Perhaps there is too much stress on the "social." Is there not some danger that we make an *idola tribus* of Society, creating "a type of individuality whose pattern of thought is enduringly marked by consensus with others?" [145] May we not create a culture in which persons are mere fragments and functions of public opinion? We are tempted to rejoice in all this "social-mindedness" as an indication of the growth of brotherly love, without recognizing the deep peril here; for the "bond between" can be turned into chains of slavery. The truth is, unhappily, that there is hardly a hint of the truly "personal" in much that passes as "social." The struggle in our time to create true humanity in and among the masses has led not to a "community of saints" but to a savage solidarity of state or clan. "We are," says Fromm, "a herd believing that the road we follow must lead to a goal since we see everybody else on the same road." [146] Perhaps it is time now, before it is too late, to remind ourselves that in order to correct the old-fashioned "rugged individualism" we need not develop bitter animus against true individuality. In the caustic words of Glenn Morrow: "The fashion of attributing everything to 'society' is happily passing— together with the extreme reverence for 'the social' which character-ized Mead's generation. We can now recognize the importance of the 'social process' (in some sense of the term) without making it the sole factor in the life of mind." [147] Buber realized all this, but too late to stem the tide of the new tyrannies which collectivize the individual and relativize the truth.[148] Mead's theory gave support to the rising collective world; his view is dangerously unprotected against the con-clusion that society is the chief or only locus of values.

Since the moral and religious interests of man demand integrity and responsibility in the individual self, it is fitting to review briefly the question as to whether and in what measure Mead and Buber maintain the autonomy of the self. It should be noted at once that both Mead and Buber rejected the position of speculative idealism because it seemed to destroy both true individuality and true com-munity. Individuality, especially, constitutes a serious problem for the absolute idealists, since it is almost impossible on their account to assign ultimate significance to the individual. Mead and Buber make a genuine effort to preserve the status for the individual within the community. But how well did they succeed?

It must be admitted that Mead neglected the "I," because of his pre-occupation with a scientific, behavioristic, empirical account of the mind and self. His attention was centered on the empirical data (the "me"), on the activity of forms, rather than on the subject-knower. Yet his whole theory is full of *assumptions* which suggest idealistic and

Kantian antecedents: the analytic and constructive activity of the I; the doctrine of the "form of the social object"; the amorphous nature of sense experience; the centered position of the act (or self); the "importation" and organization and interpretation of the social data, etc. How can the self import and organize experience without some continuing subject or trans-empirical ego as agent of such activity? Yet nearly all of Mead's critics charge him with neglect of the factors of uniqueness and autonomy in the self. Mead indeed seems to oscillate between an idealistic position in which the self is lost in the Socius or Absolute Experience, and a radical empiricism which represents the self as merely a "moment" or "mode" in the general flux of pure experience. Either position tends to jeopardize the real independence of the self. The self as subjective and private, while admitted by Mead, is really a means to an end: it performs its function by forfeiting its life. "The proudest assertion of independent selfhood is but the affirmation of a unique capacity to fill some social role." [149] Buber likewise appears somewhat ambiguous on this point; but his consistent theocentric personalism and his persistent accent on the bi-subjective polarity of the I-Thou relation appear to be the predominant notes which enable him to retain a genuine integrity for his self—albeit a social self. Both Mead and Buber, let it be said again, *intend* to affirm the ultimate reality of the individual self. The whole is a society of selves; the self is a derivative member of society. The result: a social self.

There seems to be an impregnable citadel of self-being and self-feeling which any true general statement may not ignore. And no glorification of the "social" or even the self-other relationships should blind us to the fact that we shall not solve the social problem by enthusiastically huddling together. Surely that is a most evil bondage. We have seen that responsibility is closely related to personality; yet much of group life in our day requires of individuals that they surrender their responsibility, private conscience, tolerance, and private decision. It is unhealthy for persons to hide behind "organizations." The rights and freedoms of individuals are in danger without duty and discipline and responsibility lodged in the private souls of men. Moreover, the health of states is also undermined as soon as individuals and minority groups are subjected to influences which inhibit, through intimidation, mendacity and violence, the free operation of individual thought and conscience.

Conscience must be something more than the "inside of custom" [150] or the "outpost of society." Of course, Buber and Mead have seen this, and have attempted to give theoretical support to a high degree of individualization *within community* and *without anarchy*. Their intention is to *individualize* and *socialize* at the same time. They understand "shared experience" to be a very great good—but perhaps not the only human good. But we must conclude that Mead, especially, has not been entirely successful, since he surrenders the "private" on grounds moral, epistemological, and metaphysical. In spite of Mead's effort to take account of the "I," it seems fairly certain that he over-emphasized the *public* and the *social* at the expense of the genuinely *private*. Obviously we are social; that is clear to all. It is not so clear in Mead's account that we are also *private*, that each one of us is or has a private self capable of responsible choice and action. Perhaps mentality is not all social. The reasons for Mead's failure here seem to stem from his monistic naturalism (involving necessary implication and organic relations) and from his failure to push his pragmatism far enough. The pragmatic evidence for private mind is: (1) I have private feelings and states of mind: I *know* how *I* feel! No one else can feel as I do. (2) There is the *fact* of moral obligation and responsibility; no one else can absolutely take my place. (3) I initiate my own acts and anticipate the results. Everyone believes that, theory apart, he has an independent, private self. You *have* to live by that belief: Mead lived by it too; just as you *must* take reality for granted—or die! This is the proof of realism. Those who deny the privacy of thought keep their privacy so real that you cannot tell what they are thinking. When you cannot act at all except on a certain hypothesis, that hypothesis is, in so far, true. One need not refer all meaning to a mysterious transcendental realm beyond ordinary human experience, in order to insist that *some* of the meanings of men are *private*. [151]

Mead, especially, is in trouble here. Positing more metaphysically and morally than does Mead with respect to the particular responsible self, Buber is not so unprotected as is Mead. We *know* ourselves and become persons in a real sense only in relation to another; but Buber never affirms on this ground that ontologically the individual *exists* only in the presence of another—unless that other be God. Accordingly, society only qualifies and conditions the individual; and it is especially God's address to man which makes him man. But in Mead's thought society *constitutes* the self through the psychological technique of gestural and symbolic experience. The self carries within its psychic morphology the whole social order. As in structure we are social, Mead decided that the *intent* and influence of the self must be toward a harmonized society: the old moral contrast between egoism and altruism is allegedly retired. But just here the trouble begins. How can the organism wholly immersed in the flux of social events attain the clear perspective from which to criticize it or seek to change it? How does an "in-group" ever transcend its own group loyalty to achieve justice with respect to an "out-group"? Here again Mead's pragmatism seems to confuse his social psychology as a completely adequate basis for moral reform. For the pragmatic account of social reform makes it depend upon dissatisfaction with the established order. But, in Mead's account, it is this present order with its injustice and disorder and stupidity which formed our minds. How can a mind or conscience formed by assuming conflicting and disorganized roles have value for harmonizing the disharmony which produced it? How, in other words, can a self so constituted ever achieve a unity, or introduce unity into the social order? Mead appears to *assume* a unified self, because only thus could he hope for a unified society. But, by his own theory, to get such a self would require a unified society in advance. And moreover, he seems to assume, while denying it, some continuing core of selfhood to do the organizing.

Or again: Let us admit that society molds the self. But which society? Individuals belong to many groups, have many interests— often anti-social, special interests which conflict with or cancel out others. What may appear as altruism in the family or gang or other primary group, may be quite unsocial with respect to the larger society. Indeed, group-egoism is more destructive of social order than that of individuals. What we have, instead of Mead's generalized other, is a confused medley of generalized others which constitute the self. Mead's generalized other is not unified nor always good. And it is so "generalized" as to have little efficacy in competition with smaller, intimate generalized others. The self may be social, even integrated, and yet be committed to narrow loyalties and vicious group-egoisms. Simply to demonstrate the self as "social" does not license a harmony-producing miracle. To assert that a self so derived is *descriptively* social is not to prove that it is *morally* social.[152] Buber saw all this very clearly. Mead saw something of this,[153] but never really faced its implications. Therefore his account is full of gaps, ambiguities, semantic confusion, and ultimately is inconclusive at the point of deriving a morally free and responsible self from a socially conditioned organism. He seems to presuppose that which he wants to attain, a morally responsible self.

We seem to be right where we started: the problem is precisely that of getting a *moral self*, not simply a social self. This was the egregious error of thinkers like Sumner who held that morals are only mores. The only way this could possibly be true would be to posit the society which constitutes the self an "ideal" society; but that has metaphysical implications which Mead would not espouse.

If these considerations be sound, and if we correct Mead in the direction of Buber, we are permitted to draw certain conclusions respecting the moral aspects of a doctrine of the social self. (1) Intelligence and scientific progress are not necessarily socially valuable. (2) Scientific method alone will not serve to correct all our moral and social ills. (3) Reason is not the intrinsic nature of the self (nor the *imago Dei*) but an organ in its employ. The self transcends any natural or moral law which reason may apprehend. (4) Similarly, biological and social categories are not the only sources of interest or motivation especially at the level of moral experience. (5) Mead, especially, fails to develop an adequate concept of conscience chiefly because his concept of the "other" is at once too generalized and too narrow, and takes no acount of a Holy Other who may enter into the self as an unbidden judge, who confronts one as the Universal God for whom justice and mercy are more than sacrifice. (6) We are not justified in equating the "moral" with the "social." (7) Pragmatism and instrumentalism are prone to bring about the dissolution of all final criteria of truth and goodness and therein lies a danger to society. (8) The ethical test of man or community lies not in the mere fact of social integration but in the range and level of integration, in the goodness and truth of the interests integrated. (9) Selfhood is not a birthright, but an achievement. (10) All of this means that the self can fulfill itself only by finding ends that are beyond itself—ultimately in God. Here the self-other dialectic or the I-Thou dialogic pattern is very useful as an instrument of analysis. For it provides for self-transcendence and for judgment by some "other" who stands for the universal community. (11) The only way a unity of loyalty and cooperation can be established is by persons acknowledging themselves to be, in their reciprocal and perhaps conflicting claims, under a third and higher and more comprehensive claim.

The weakness of a merely humanistic or social ethic is that there is no provision for the redemptive and transcendent transvaluation of a personal or social scale of values such as occurs in a genuine religious conversion. And it provides no adequate dynamic to break out of narrow self-concern or group egoism. Loyalty to the community under God who transcends and judges the community is a protection against the twin dangers of the irresponsibility of individuals and groups, and the idolatry that absolutizes the particular group. "The belief in God . . . is the local presupposition of an objective or absolute morality. . . . Our moral ideal can only claim objective validity in so far as it can rationally be regarded as the revelation of a moral ideal eternally existing in the mind of God." [154] A conviction that human worth roots in God supports equally the realization of the intrinsic worth of others and of one's own worth.

In this connection it can be said that Mead, and to a lesser extent Buber, is too optimistic about the nature and status and prospects of man and of society. Mead was aware of socially disruptive forces, but his central theories of an emergent universe, creative intelligence powered by science, and his social philosophy inevitably induced an optimistic, almost utopian, view of human nature and social progress through an extension of role-taking and education.[155] Mead fails to deal realistically with the ever-present tragedy of sin which no plan or program seems able to banish. Typical of Mead's over-simplification of a knotty problem is his solution of race relations. Said he: "The most fundamental attack that can be made upon race prejudice is through the careful and scientific application of the intelligence test." [156] Mead may be right. Perhaps longer vistas of history are needed to settle the issue; but this much seems certain: As a latter-day prophet of evolutionary progress, Mead never took a realistic view of that stain of imperfection, that ugly rent in human nature, which the theologians have called sin. Buber's account of man has both deeper and higher dimensions than that of Mead. Yet from the standpoint of orthodox Christianity, Buber is perhaps overly optimistic when he writes: "that man may fall implies that he may rise . . . he has the power to effect the work of redemption from *out of his own self.*" [157]

Buber is here writing of the Hasidic message, but I believe that it also comes near to his own ideas. In this connection, it has seemed to me that Buber's optimism about human nature and human culture fits in rather poorly with his acute comprehension of Hebrew prophecy and with his own feeling for man's finitude and turmoil. And in the light of his devastating polemic against the human self-postulation found in the Sophists, in Sartre and Heidegger, it is strange that he is unable to apprehend the full meaning of the Christian doctrine of sin, which involves, I take it, the deliberate and presumptuous usurpation of the moral role of God.

Mead thought that he had rid himself of the "philosophic riff-raff known as epistemology." Therefore, in a sense, everything he said was in intention ontological (though he denied this also). But he had to deal with the "contents" of cognition. So he gives what professes to be an objective account of cognition in which cognition is simply a phase of conduct and any distinction between *content* and *form, attribute* and *essence* is erased. But here again we must report a failure of technique when we examine the process by which a biological organism becomes or acquires a self. I think we can, indeed we must, agree that something like Mead's descriptive path to selfhood does take place. But it appears, on closer inspection, as though Mead employed "mirrors" or "sleight of hand"; he *assumes* some kind of a self in order to tell *how* the self came to be. For what or who is it that begins to take the role of others, import the social data, and by responding to its own vocal gesture as the others respond to it become as other to itself?[158] Mead says it is only the biologic organism. But note: He calls it an "I," and it is an organism *capable* of assuming roles, capable of speech and symbolic communication. There are other organisms living in human communities, with vocal equipment and ears that can hear their own sounds,—yet they never learn to become selves. This means that the human organism brings with it into the world a *capacity* which is a *sine qua non* of the selfhood which through social-symbolic relations he is to become. The normal human infant is predestined to become a self—and surely through some process as Mead describes. But to say that the self is thus socially constituted is only half the story. There seems to be some original, primordial, trans-empirical element that plays a creative role of its own in the very process of role assumption and persists throughout the history of the self in its social experience. Mead recognizes this, but dismisses it as a "methodological fiction," a necessary hypothesis for the solution of his riddle. But that seems too neat a trick. For so crucial a role does this antecedent, "semi-detached," element play in the "fabric" of selfhood that rather than being so blithely taken for granted it might better be described as the "warp" of the self into which is woven the "woof" of the social content.

All the evidence seems to require a concept of the self sufficiently distinct from the role of the other and sufficiently distinct also from organic response to provide it with more permanency, privacy, and integrative creativity than Mead's concept provides. I recognize Mead's point that the "I" becomes a "me" just as soon as it begins to think about itself, but it would seem that the "generalized other" must have its counterpart in some generalization of the individual's own role. Mead has not successfully avoided falling back into idealism or phenomenalism or subjectivism, any more than he has completely avoided the psycho-physical dualism against which he rebelled so boldly. His cognitive meanings and judgments are "subjective" in so far as they relate to properties which are dependent upon a "standpoint" or "percipient perspective" of the I. Meanwhile, by his doctrine of "objective relativism" and "perspectives" he claims to make objective judgments about objects by asserting something which is not relative to a standpoint. At best, he achieves a complex mixture of epistemological objectivity and subjectivity. A residue of dualism of some sort seems impossible to avoid without contradicting either the implications of realism or of admitted facts. Mead himself recognized that he had not won his battle. Even after continued and repeated assaults upon the bastions of dualism, he had regretfully to confess to failure.[159]

In this respect Buber is on safer ground because he posits an irreducible minimum of the non-social Kantian subject inside every self. "Something" is affirmed to exist in advance of the incidence of the social relatedness upon it. Buber's self is not just an "outpost" of society, but the result of I-Thou dialogic relations. Certainly selfhood signifies or involves relations with the whole environment. The self is in a very real sense related to all accessible otherness. But Buber seems nearer to the facts of both poles of the I-Thou dichotomy by his less dogmatic suggestions that I-Thou relations in the community, which includes God, *fulfill* and *complete* and *embellish* rather than *create* selves. The human self is a structure of free, responsible self-transcendence according to which the transcending, knowing subject (the I) always eludes itself and is not identical with the self that is transcended, known (the me). He has the spiritual urge to go beyond any actual self he has attained. This structure of self-transcendence and freedom is the spiritual element in man (*the imago Dei*) and is related to the transcendent God. Buber, the Jew, is more concerned with whether the nature of this relationship is one of faith or rebellion than he is with elaborating a metaphysical blueprint of the ground of the relationship.

A similar negative conclusion is reached when we turn to the metaphysical aspects of this problem. There is something inconclusive about the whole account. It simply will not do to dismiss metaphysics, since it deals with the structure and substance of the ultimately real. Nor does Mead eventually. But the moment he ventures into metaphysics, his account becomes even less satisfying and less convincing in trying to account for mind and self and the peculiar properties we normally associate with those terms as not being entirely dependent upon a physical system nor a function of any other entity. Not only is Mead's materialism or naturalism inadequate in general, but also in the particular instance of accounting for minds and selves. Neither in their nature nor in their laws are minds and selves equal to or reducible to physical changes. And in the case of Mead's account of how the "I" assumes roles, as we have already seen, Mead takes for granted an antecedent, trans-empirical subject who creates, organizes, interprets, purposes, endures in or from his own unique perspective. The role or roles assumed is some modification of itself; and as a part of itself, it is at least to a degree private. There is something of a paradox, if not a mystery, here. And we may as well admit it. In any event, Mead's case for man is weakened for lack of a satisfactory metaphysical basis. Mead has failed to show *by virtue of what* in the natural order minded selves appear and function effectively in that order. How is it to be understood that there is such an animal as man? His statement of the integral relation of mind to the natural order is even less convincing if we adopt his evolutionary teleological view of the late appearance of mind.[160]

A metaphysics is involved whenever we attempt to characterize the ultimate ground and content in which natural and human events take place. In this respect Buber corrects Mead. For I believe that Buber has from the start a metaphysics (vague though it is and despite his denial of it),—a conception of the universe in which he can place his understanding of human personality: a theistic conception rooted in the rugged faith of the Hebrew people about the unity of God with

His world and the concrete polar conditions under which God and man can speak to one another. In Buber, man as an existent real is derived from God, not the other way round. Some world purpose and master power is the basis of world unity and of the appearance on the world stage of "a being who knows the universe as a universe, its space as space, its time as time, and knows himself in it as knowing it." [161] Buber's vague holism, it seems to me, is his attempt to bridge the gaps in the polarity of relationships without falling into a part-whole identity of idealism or pantheism.

The lapses and difficulties in Mead's theory point the need for revision toward a view which might include a more "substantial" self and a more transcendent reference. Believing in human control by human effort in accordance with human ideals, Mead cannot well account for the self-transcendence of the human category. With God excluded, man is merely a part of nature; and how shall he lift himself above nature and the animal world, if he is only a part of that world himself? The corruption of our moral values is recognized only by a "revelation" from without in which we are made to see ourselves as the Great Other sees us, as when Nathan of old in condemning David, and Elijah in judging Ahab, pointed the "finger of God" at them and said: Thou art the man! Nor will it do to substitute Man or Society as the moral equivalent of God. If religion or ethics must substitute Man or Society for God as the object of worship, they will die of disillusionment; for one does not need to be a cynic or a pessimist to feel that man is a poor substitute for God. Man has feet of clay; and Society, when worshipped, becomes a Tyrant. Moreover, when we try to do without God, God is not thereby successfully denied, but is actually, though unwittingly, implied or required. Something like God must be assumed in order to lend any dignity to man, to assure an ultimate optimism and hope with respect to man's destiny, and to believe that nature is metaphysically and morally a progressive and purposive creation. How are we to have any assured faith in human life, while supposing that the cosmic background is unpurposive and insensible? That is what Professor Hocking has called "the valor of ignorance." In such a universe, good deeds as well as bad will eventually produce the same nullity. Nothing is better or worse for our having lived. And where in a universe without God, is the moral demand to use our freedom for good ends and where the justification for the faith that our efforts will bear their fruit in a meaningful world? It appears that we do need God in order to be quite at home in the world.

The most serious weakness of Mead's view of the self stems from his failure to consider man as a theological creature who is most adequately known and realized only from beyond himself in God. Mead tries heroically to escape the part-whole identity of idealism. But his self-other relation does not include God as Other Self, and so falls short of a completely accurate report of the total human situation. Buber's theism permits him to set the self-Other system free from the part-whole identity, and thus achieves a more adequate statement of the self. His theological anthropology, however, does not claim to have solved all the theoretical or practical problems of man, because his religious philosophy is fundamentally a conception of the mystery and problematic of man. The most serious objection which some make against Buber in this connection is his perhaps too ready willingness to reify "the between" and to personify God in more than an analogical sense.[162] In trying to avoid cosmic immanence, the theologian may fall into a social immanence. It can be said, I think, with fair certainty that Buber avoids this pitfall; but he makes no apology for conceiving of man's relationship to God in "personal" terms as the only adequate way to speak of God's ways with man. God meets man "as a person," but God is not *only* a person. He is not thus limited.

Mead, somewhat like Marx, foresaw a liberated, humane, and united humanity, possessed of its own meaning and destiny, reconciled with itself and the universe, living in fulfillment and peace. Actually this is not so different from the Biblical promise. But Mead, it appears, made the same mistake which Marx made: by believing that, to be attainable, the ideal must be stripped of all transcendent reference and realized only in time, they deny its conditions and render it inconsistent. The consequences of an attempt to find the whole meaning of man's life within the temporal and the material are becoming increasingly and tragically evident. If man is not made in the image of God, he has to be made in the image of society. He becomes a function of society, the instrument of impersonal ends. In the end he ceases to be man. Life loses its sacredness. And when the interests of the state seem to require it, the individual may be ruthlessly sacrificed. Only if man lives for God, and for a goal beyond all men, is there a valid ground for objection to the tyranny of State, Party, or *Volk*.

The problem of consciousness and conscience remains about where it was. Real problems cannot be killed though pseudo-problems can be retired. It may be that the "substance" theory of the mind (at least in the older sense) is dead, or dying—at least more difficult to defend. But there is still massive evidence to show that something denoted partially by the terms "mind," "self," or "spirit" does persist. It may well be that just that which cannot be translated into the language of the "me" is the most distinctive and valuable part in man. It seems to be a bit premature to dismiss the concept of "mind" or "self" as the bearer of knowledge and with non-phenomenal gifts of self-direction and organization which persist through a period longer than a single "specious present." It seems quite possible, even probable, that antecedent mind, and trans-empirical subject, are not "wholly redundant," "postulational rejects." [163] We must conclude that Mead has not succeeded entirely either in demonstrating his technique or in laying the basis for moral and social community through the very genesis of the private self. His lapses seem to suggest revision in the direction of a view that might include at least a "semi-detached," partly hidden, primary center of selfhood, and a Universal Other (God) which Buber's philosophy less ambiguously provides.

Finally, I venture one or two suggestions in the direction of a possible resolution of the difficulty. Mead's empirical concept of the self takes seriously Hume's criticism of the self as a substance. The self Mead posits is near to the Whiteheadean "event"—not an enduring substance or absolute self-identity in the traditional sense of Leibniz or Aquinas, different, yet the same in its cumulative, *ongoing* history. Moreover, Mead's definition of "structure" and "process" seem to be not inconsistent with Aristotle's definitions of "substance" and "form," or the Thomistic doctrines of "primary matter" and "substantial form." Professor W. H. Sheldon, for example, defines "substance" as the *tendency of anything to act in a certain way.* In the newer process philosophies substance is not a static inert stuff, and one might fairly argue that "mind" or "self" is "substantial," in the sense that it always behaves in a certain way. If this be an acceptable definition of substance, it seriously qualifies, if it does not retire, Mead's life-long warfare against the concept of antecedent substance in the idealistic and scholastic systems.

Again, Hartshorne's treatment of the new cosmology suggests that the self possesses a measure of real independence which prevents any domination by other things or selves. But every individual self enters into reciprocal and mutually determinative relations with other selves and with all otherness. To transcend something is to be independent of it; to be immanent in something is to have one's own being enter into the constitution and determination of that thing. And if, with Buber, we may introduce God into the process, we can speak of God as the supreme instance of this double relation. It appears also that Buber's philosophy could be supported fairly consistently by this new process metaphysics. For both high religion and process metaphysics teach that man has a definite kinship and relation with the whole world of nature—space, time, events, things, other persons—which he cannot ignore if he would be true to his own nature as a social self.

In conclusion, we must venture some remarks about the general practical effectiveness of Mead's and Buber's ethics. We have earlier observed that their ethical and social philosophy issues in a kind of optimistic democratic socialism. Of peculiar interest is Buber's suggestion of the importance of the Jewish cooperative settlements in Palestine. Buber continues his polemic against the Marxist-Leninist theory of a highly centralized state, and he reasserts his conviction that the first step in the renewal of Community should be the formulation of a *communitas communitatum*, a confederacy of various small organic and social unities, each of which would be autonomous in its given sphere.

Be it remembered that neither Mead nor Buber attempts to give us a blueprint. They have only pointed to the solidarity of men, bound together as members of the body politic. And they recommend a "middle way" between the extremes of individualism and collectivism. But they chart no clear path through the middle, nor limn the topography of the *civitas terrena* which no man has seen at our destination. Mead offers a method of progress; Buber a glimpse of the towers of New Jerusalem shining above the clouds. They do not consider directly the economic or political means for achieving the harmonious common good in a very complex social order. They only urge our participation in the continuing task of building that fairer world by the systematic application of the theoretical principles which they espouse.

The most serious reservations arise at the point of asking whether the intensity of I-Thou attitudes and "we-feeling" can be maintained in any but primary groups whose size permits direct face-to-face relations? Here lies the crux of our problem in the twentieth century:

How adapt the I-Thou theory to the practice of a River Rouge plant, of a city like Pittsburgh or New York, or of a highly industrialized nation like England or Germany? It seems to be a remedy which, like William James's "moral equivalent for war," cannot be taken by the patient until he is already well. Communities incorporating the I-Thou attitude and the utopian socialism of Buber cannot be manufactured to order—except perhaps in a small new land like modern Israel, or at certain plastic points within the established order, there to work as yeast in the lump.

Specifically, we see difficulties in at least two directions. (1) We have established the fact that without free, responsible selves society itself withers at the roots. Communism, Fascism, and National Socialism, in their mistaken endeavors to correct the extreme individualism of the past and the gross inequalities of capitalism, have tended in practice to destroy all individual freedom and responsibility. As one observes even the experiments of the British Labor Party with Fabian socialism, doubts arise as to whether any thorough-going "p'anned economy" of any size can be set up that will not eventuate in vast restrictions upon human freedom, even in a despotism of the state. How are we, then, to have freedom *and* order, liberty *and* justice, individuality *and* social cohesion? Can we establish social justice and serve the common weal without placing the entire productive and distributive system under centralized management? Such vast authority over the common life is still exercised by individuals; in a collective world individuals have both greater power and wider sweep for their stubborn self-interest.

(2) In the other direction, a thorough-going application of Buber's utopian socialism of decentralized organic groups, while attractive in theory, may lead to the conclusion that an ethic based on the primary group attitudes and relations (love, trust, mutuality, kindness, loyalty) tends inevitably to become pietistic and separatist. Certainly the history of all such movements (and history abounds in the records of such attempts) shows that they present serious difficulties for fellowship and mutuality in the larger body, like the state or nation. And some would add that it leads to a dualism in ethics between justice and love. Professor Aubrey, for one, has shown that the sects are needed to enrich the larger community. But he goes on to point out that the objectionable feature of sects is not their deviation from the patterns, but their exclusiveness, maintaining their distinctiveness

through isolation rather than through cooperation and functional differentiation.[164] We conclude that the small sectarian group is always
an answer for the few; it does leaven the larger lump; and it should
be extended as far as possible in the direction of a decentralized and
functionally differentiated economy. But that it is applicable to great
industrial aggregates, or that the present social order can be re-struc-
tured along those lines, is very dubious. While not excluding the wider
spread of small, functional, autonomous groups of all sorts, as both
desirable and possible, the solution for our present society seems
rather to lie in the careful attention to the political means of holding
responsible a government which takes overall representative action
for the common welfare in major economic and social affairs.[165]

Buber is sensible to all of this. Still he favors a rebirth of the com-
mune,[166]—the warm, friendly togetherness of the small organic community—as the unit in some sort of representative Commonwealth.
Perhaps Buber is right. Perhaps it can be done—by men of faith with
a common relation to a Centre. The answer appears to be so simple
as to be baffling. For the first thing to do is to enter the I-Thou relation and attitude, live in the I-Thou world, wherever you are, hallowing every natural act. Certainly the habit of seeing one's neighbors,
near and far, in the I-Thou dimension would take the poison out
of personal relations. But Buber is not very specific as to how this
habit is to be acquired and strengthened. And he fails to take full
cognizance of man's destructive and stubborn self-preference, and the
evil structures into which this sin is built in society. Thus to many
Buber's program will sound naive, "utopian." And in the light of
many logical considerations and present historical facts perhaps it is.
Yet it is often the "realistic" theories that have proved to be out of
touch with human realities and the utopian ideals the more practical.
And some such plan and program mankind must find and follow—or
perish! Furthermore, "fellowship in the Spirit" is a fellowship of power
as well as of ideals,—and we dare not dogmatize upon what the
Spirit can and cannot do. In an earlier dark era it was said, and
truly, of the despised Christian fellowship: "They hold the world
together." [167] Since the world is somehow a continuous dynamic
unity, one with many parts, cooperation gives us the clue to what is
deepest and truest in life. When cooperation is informed with imagination and sustained by faith in God, the result is love. "And love
never faileth." Or in Buber's words: "The true victories, won in

secret, sometimes look like defeats. True victories happen slowly and imperceptibly, but they have far-reaching effects. In the limelight, our faith in God as the Lord of history may sometimes appear ludicrous; but there is something secret in history which confirms our faith." [168]

MAIN CONCLUSIONS: A RECAPITULATION AND SUMMARY

1. There are striking and significant similarities in the thought of Mead and Buber, often where we would least expect to find them.

    (a) The Social Self. Both Mead and Buber have established an empirical and anthropological foundation for man as essentially a "socius." Man is a "Mit-mensch" in a "Mit-welt"; he comes to self-consciousness, becomes a person, only in relation with others.

    (b) Self and Society are twin-born. Neither self nor society is the fundamental fact of human existence. The individual and the community are equally primordial and correlative entities. The more fundamental fact is *man with man* in a self-other dialogic communal relation. The self is a being-in-community.

    (c) Speech, dialogue, is the chief mechanism constitutive of selfhood.

    (d) Reality itself has a social structure, is constituted of and mutually conditioned by relations.

    (e) Selfhood is not simply a birthright, but an achievement; and there appear to be levels of achievement up to full true selfhood.

    (f) Both Mead and Buber attempt to preserve the integrity of their "social individual." Both reject atomistic individualism and organic monism, but Mead is less convincing at this point because of the residue in his thought of Hegelian social idealism. Man is both conditioned and free, subject and object, transcendent and immanent. While the self develops as a reflection of the social structure, the social structure has no existence apart from the selves which reflect it.

    (g) The self, then, is essentially a self-other system rather than a mind. Mead's view is somewhat qualified in that it includes part-whole relations as well. Buber's view is less ambiguous because his self-other system is also a finite-infinite system.

(h) The social and political philosophy of both Mead and Buber lends support to an essentially democratic or moderately socialistic view of society and the state. Mead tends more than Buber to an organic realistic interpretation of society, but he avoids any extreme statism by insisting that the generalized other to be complete must include the perspectives of all the individual acts.

(i) Both reject Hegelian Absolutism and Rationalism, and the older logic and epistemology. Both are realists, or at least semi-realists, in their practicing epistemology; yet neither entirely escapes the suspicion of subjectivism.

(j) Mead's pragmatism and Buber's existentialism agree in stressing the *act* over *thought*: truth is related to doing and being.

(k) The social and ethical interest is predominant in both. Mead, however, identifies the "moral" with the "social," whereas Buber finds a place for an objective and transcendent reference for the moral sanction, and therefore seems on safer ground.

(l) There appear "Kantian" transcendental elements in both Mead and Buber: frankly admitted by Buber, assumed as methodological fictions by Mead—and thus the source of some embarrassment to him. Mead's naturalism and pragmatism are not entirely consistent, and there is evidence of a tendency in the direction of idealism.

(m) Both are optimistic, perhaps too much so, concerning the ability of human action to build the great community of good on earth. Buber seems more realistic about the stubborn difficulties present.

(n) Both stress the reality and dynamic quality of time, one result of which is to give metaphysical support to human hope for a better world.

(o) Both systems appear capable of finding metaphysical support in a metaphysics of process, in contrast to one of static being.

2. There are significant differences between Mead and Buber.

    (a) The chief differences concern motivation, methodology, temperament, and metaphysical presuppositions.

        (1) Mead employs a strictly genetic method of deriving mind and self from the bio-social process, whereas Buber starts at a different place and level of reality.

        (2) Mead stresses a secular, scientific, pragmatic method; Buber stands in the existential, intuitive, and religious tradition. He speaks the language of faith and revelation.

    (b) With respect to the nature of the "other," Mead too narrowly stresses a single flat dimension and man's involvement in the human society only. Buber conceives of man as living in many communities: at least three—the natural, the human, and the divine.

    (c) For Mead, moral values are equated with the social: they are relative, relevant only to human life, and have no cosmic rootage. Buber believes there are certain absolute, or at least objective and eternal values, and that man stands responsible to a Being or Reality or Truth superior to man and society. Mead holds, however, that men arrive at "objective" standards, or universals, which approximate practical absolutes.

    (d) Both Mead and Buber are vague and ambiguous in their metaphysics. Indeed, until late in life, Mead eschewed formal metaphysics. Still he has metaphysical assumptions throughout which are naturalistic, temporalistic, and allegedly realistic—derived eventually from his view of human nature as social. His social positivism prevented him from achieving a clear philosophical realism. Buber, by contrast, is clearly and avowedly theistic; though he likewise rejects metaphysics and never achieves a closely-knit and consistent philosophical system. Both Mead and Buber would gain by a more clearly developed metaphysics; as it stands, they are equivocal, if not irresponsible, with respect to their metaphysics.

3. The social doctrine of the self can be developed and elaborated empirically, independent of the underlying metaphysical assumptions. In other words, the similarities between Mead and Buber are such as to warrant the conclusion that this social concept of the self may be formulated independently to their divergent metaphysical positions.

4. The dialogic relationship of man to his world, as found in the doctrine of the social self, provides the basis for an ethical and social philosophy, and for religion, which is superior, at one and the same time, to the older individualistic view of the self and to the new collectivist dogma. Mead and Buber have succeeded in formulating a theory and strategy which can better harmonize the individual interest with the social good, liberty with order, freedom with necessity, mechanism with teleology, and God with man.

5. The self-other motif, with its effort to do justice to the factors of duality and polarity in human nature, becomes germane to the problems in which modern ethics, education, social theory, psychotherapy, and Protestant theology are interested. Its fertile applications in such diverse fields show the concept to be a valid and valuable instrument of analysis in helping us to understand the human situation.

6. Perhaps the most fruitful contributions of this theory to an understanding of man are those features which are associated with the finite-infinite interpretation found in Buber, either as a self-transcending movement of the self toward the eternal *Thou,* or as a constituting, obligating, judging, consoling, and saving movement of the infinite Other upon the finite self.

7. The inconsistent and inadequate elements in Mead's doctrine are associated with his romantic biological evolutionism, his naturalistic rejection of a sound metaphysics, or the vestigial residue of Hegelian monism. The imbalances and ambiguities in Buber's thought stem largely from his vague metaphysics and from his mystical existentialism.

8. Both Mead and Buber attempt to maintain the ultimate autonomy, freedom, and integrity of the finite "social individual," but the internal evidence suggests that Mead is less successful than Buber because of his social idealism and his radical empiricism.

9. Both Mead and Buber attempt to provide an adequate basis for moral obligation and moral dissent from the social patterns, which may become rigid and vicious, while also preserving social order. Again Buber seems to present sounder and more adequate grounds for a moral imperative beyond the community which begets the self, and thus accounts more adequately for moral reformation and progress. He is able to do this because he brings God into the "community" as a higher and more inclusive loyalty.

10. A reconstruction or amendment of Mead in the direction of Buber's personalistic and religious philosophy is permissible, if indeed not necessary, if we are to do full justice both to their theory and to the facts of the human situation.

(a) Mead's too great stress on the social and cultural factors led him to minimize the factors of uniqueness, singularity, and autonomy which Buber underscores.

(b) Mead's biological romanticism and evolutionism induced a false optimism about human nature and social progress not justified by the stern facts of life.

(c) In the absence of a firmer metaphysics, Mead's naturalism never accounts for the *capacity* of the human animal to develop language, take the role of others, and envisage values. He therefore assumes a self in order to get a self. Metaphysically and epistemologically, Mead appears guilty of begging the question.

(d) Mead denies the existence and necessity of God, again oversimplifying the human situation. Mead was unable or unwilling to see the religious implications of the Generalized Other. Moreover, he saw no necessity of explaining the order, organization, values, apparent design, and teleological emergence in nature on any other basis than that of a self-existent and self-sufficient nature. He appears to be guilty of an unwarranted addition in order to account for man's freedom and creative intelligence.

(e) Mead equates the "social" with the human and moral, whereas Buber's self stands in a three-fold relation to nature, other men, and God. He thus provides a moral authority, sanction, and transcendent judgment of more urgency and radicality than is to be found in Mead's merely human and societal "other." Mead's self is not more ethical than the social group which molds the self. And Mead fails to show how to get a harmonious integrated self from a discordant and multifold society, especially if there is no nuclear permanent center.

(f) Buber's theocentric personalism provides a firmer ground for an ultimate optimism concerning the end of human destiny.

(g) Buber's notion that the "other" might be God, the eternal Thou, provides the basis for a doctrine of creation and redemption, grace and forgiveness not found in a purely secular and social morality. Man can thus know the blessedness of forgiveness while responding to the lure of the infinite moral demands of the Infinite Other. Buber's inclusion of God as a "third" in the community also suggests a *triadic* pattern of relations which seems better to fit the facts than a purely dialectical pattern.

1. Emil Brunner, *Der Mensch im Widerspruch* (Berlin: Furche Verlag, 1937); tr. *Man in Revolt* (New York: Scribner's Sons, 1939), p. 289, *passim.*

2. *Icheinsamkeit*, solitude of the self or self-love as Ebner has it. Cf. Brunner, *The Mediator* (Philadelphia: Westminster, 1947), p. 209, *passim.*

3. *Alles Dasein ist Mitsein*. Martin Heidegger, *Sein und Zeit*, p. 117.

4. *Op. cit.*, p. 44.

5. *Freedom and Order* (New York: Scribner's Sons, 1947), p. vii. Cf. William Temple, *Christianity and Social Order* (Penguin Books, 1943).

6. Brunner, *Man in Revolt*, pp. 50, 278-9, *passim.*

7. Buber, *I and Thou*, p. 96f; *BMM*, p. 22f; *The Hibbert Journal*, XLIX (1951), 111. The German language which Buber uses enables one to employ several expressive compound words to denote this peculiar characteristic of human selfhood. So Buber, Ebner, Brunner and Barth speak variously of the *Ansprechbarkeit* and *Wortmächtigkeit* of man, and assert that the true man is *angesprochene Mensch* and *wortempfängliches Wesen*.

8. Used so frequently by Brunner in *The Divine-Human Encounter*.

9. Brunner, *The Divine-Human Encounter*, p. 67. Cf. Helen Keller's observation about her deafness: "It is a silence which isolates cruelly, completely."

10. Charles Morris, *The Open Self*, p. 48f.

11. G. H. Mead, *PP*, pp. 173-4.

12. Precisely this point, and this whole point of view, is the subject of rigorous and incisive treatment in Hartshorne's Terry Lectures, *The Divine Rela-*

tivity. See also his *Beyond Humanism* and *Man's Vision of God*. One need not share Hartshorne's idealistic theory of knowledge in order to find his treatment of deity trenchant, suggestive, and reverent.

13. *Confessions*, X, xxviii. On this point, see also the able and sensitive treatment from the standpoint of a liturgical and sacramental Christianity by Dietrich von Hildebrand, *Liturgy and Personality* (New York: Longmans, Green, 1943).

14. F. C. Copleston has developed this theme in an article, "Know Thyself! But How?" *The Hibbert Journal*, XLI (1942–43), 12-17.

15. But he never outlived the idealistic influence, and his subjectivism remained as rigid as his naturalism—what we might call an inter-subjective idealism, or simply a social idealism.

16. *Psychotherapy and a Christian View of Man* (New York: Scribner's Sons, 1950), p. 147.

17. E. E. Aubrey, *Recent Theological Tendencies*, p. 205.

18. "George Herbert Mead As I Knew Him," Memorial Address in University of Chicago *Record*, XVII (1931), p. 175. Dewey also confesses, "I dislike to think what my own thinking might have been were it not for the seminal ideas which I derived from him." In all important respects Mead's general position is the same as Dewey's. Mead learned much from Dewey— and most that is sound in Mead is also in Dewey. But Dewey does not raise the question about the self as such.

19. See his Prefatory Remarks to *PP*, p. xl. This estimate is one with which A. N. Whitehead agrees.

20. See his Introduction to *MSS*, p. xxxv.

21. Cf. M. C. Otto, "Speech and Freedom of Speech," *Freedom and Experience* (ed.), Sidney Hook and Milton Konvitz (Cornell University Press, 1947).

22. Charles Morris is, of course, Professor of Philosophy at the University of Chicago; but perhaps more than any of Mead's former students and colleagues Morris has continued the many and diverse interests of his teacher.

23. New York: Harper, 1947.

24. New York: Holt, 1937.

25. New York: Macmillan, 1950.

26. New York: Prentice-Hall, 1948.

27. There is much cooperative work going on between sociologists, anthropologists, biologists, and psychotherapists. To mention a few names: there are among the psychotherapists and analysts Karen Horney, Erich Fromm, H. S. Sullivan, W. A. White, F. Alexander, W. A. Healy, and Adolf Meyer; among the social psychologists Dollard, Horkheimer, and Lasswell; among the anthropologists Kardiner, Benedict, Mead, Hallowell, and Linton.

28. New York: Columbia University Press, 1945.

29. New York: William Morrow, 1930. See also her *Coming of Age in Samoa* (1928).

30. Ralph Linton, *The Cultural Background of Personality* (1945) and *The Study of Man* (1936), New York: Appleton-Century.

31. Ruth Benedict, *Patterns of Culture* (Boston: Houghton Mifflin, 1934).

32. W. C. Allee, *The Social Life of Animals* (New York: Norton, 1938); also "Cooperation Among Animals," *AJS*, XXVII (1931), 386-98. Cf. Prince Petr Kropotkin, *Mutual Aid,* now available in the Penguin Books series, 1939. See also the studies of Albert Schweitzer dealing with his conception of the ethics of "reverence for life."

33. Ashley-Montagu, *On Being Human* (New York: Henry Schuman, 1950).

34. See his massive work *Cultural and Social Dynamics* (New York: American Book, 1937). See also *The Crisis of Our Age* (New York: Dutton, 1942); *Man and Society in Calamity* (New York: Dutton, 1942); *The Reconstruction of Humanity* (Boston: Beacon Press, 1948); *Altruistic Love* (Boston: Beacon Press, 1950).

35. A. Adler, *Social Interest: A Challenge of Mankind* (New York: Putnam, 1938).

36. C. Sherrington, *Man on His Nature* (New York: Cambridge University, 1941).

37. J. E. Boodin, *The Social Mind* (New York: Macmillan, 1939).

38. Margaret Ribble, *The Rights of Infants* (New York: Columbia University Press, 1943).

39. W. Goldfarb, "The Effects of Early Institutional Care on Adolescent Personality," *Journal of Experimental Education,* XII (1943), 106-129. Here may also be cited Leo Loeb, *The Biological Basis of Individuality* (Springfield, Ill.: Thomas, 1944); S. S. Sargent and M. W. Smith (editors) *Culture and Personality* (New York: Viking, 1949); D. G. Haring, *Personal Character and Cultural Milieu* (Syracuse University Press, 1949); James West, *Plainville, U.S.A.* (Columbia University Press, 1945); D. Leighton and C. Kluckhohn, *Children of the People* (Harvard University Press, 1947); and James Plant, *Personality and the Cultural Pattern* (New York: Commonwealth Fund, 1937).

40. "The Costs of Competition," *Society As The Patient* (New Brunswick: Rutgers University Press, 1948); also *Human Conservation* (National Resources Planning Board, 1942).

41. Kurt Lewin, *A Dynamic Theory of Personality,* tr. Donald K. Adams and Karl E. Zener (New York: McGraw-Hill, 1935); *Resolving Social Conflicts* (ed.), Gertrud Weiss Lewin (New York: Harper, 1948); *Studies in Topological and Vector Psychology* (University of Iowa, 1944); also *Twentieth Century Psychology,* pp. 175-181, 200-230.

42. "Man and His Destiny," *The Nature of Man* (ed.), A. W. Loos and L. B. Chrow (New York: The Church Peace Union, 1950).

43. P. E. Johnson, *Psychology of Religion* (New York and Nashville: Abingdon-Cokesbury, 1945).

44. New York and Nashville: Abingdon-Cokesbury, 1951.

45. See e.g., Karen Horney, *Our Inner Conflicts* (1945); *The Neurotic Personality of Our Time* (1937); *New Ways of Psychoanalysis* (1939); and *Self-Analysis* (1942), all issued by Norton. Harry Stack Sullivan, *Conceptions of Modern Psychiatry* (Washington, D.C., William A. White Foundation, 1947); W. A. White, *Foundations of Psychiatry* (New York and Washington: Nervous and Mental Disease Publishing Co., 1921); Erich

Fromm, *Escape from Freedom* (New York: Farrar Rinehart, 1941); *Man For Himself* (Rinehart, 1947); Fritz Kunkel, *In Search of Maturity* (New York: Scribner, 1943); Rollo May, *The Art of Counseling* (New York: Abingdon-Cokesbury, 1938); *Springs of Creative Living* (1940). See also Franz Alexander, *The Psychoanalysis of the Total Personality* (New York and Washington: Nervous and Mental Disease Publishing Co., 1930), and *Psychoanalytic Therapy* (New York: Ronald, 1946) with Thomas M. French; Seward Hiltner, *Pastoral Counseling* (New York and Nashville: Abingdon-Cokesbury, 1949); John S. Bonnell, *Pastoral Psychiatry* (New York: Harper, 1939): Ian D. Suttie, *Origins of Love and Hate* (London: Kegal Paul, Trench, Trubner, 1948).

46. By this term I refer particularly to the groups of American depth therapists who split off from the main stem of orthodox Freudian psychoanalysis: one group under the leadership of Karen Horney (the Association for the Advancement of Psychoanalysis) and another large group who followed William A. White and Harry Stack Sullivan to form the Washington School of Psychiatry. Clara Thompson (*Psychoanalysis: A History of its Development*, Hermitage House, 1950) is the leader of the New York section of this latter group. There had been other offshoots and schisms from the orthodox Freudian group, especially those under the leadership of Alfred Adler, Carl G. Jung, Otto Rank, Franz Alexander, and Fritz Kunkel.

47. Anton T. Boisen, *The Exploration of the Inner World* (Chicago: Willett & Clark, 1936). This book sheds a flood of light on the meaning and dynamics of the sense of isolation.

48. See *Hymns of Hope and Courage* (New York: Harper, 1937); also "The Service of Worship in a Mental Hospital: Its Therapeutic Significance," *Journal of Clinical Pastoral Work*, II, No. 1.

49. Among others who have made notable contributions to the theory and practice of pastoral counseling we may mention Rollo May, Russell L. Dicks, Charles T. Holman, Otis R. Rice, John S. Bonnell, Leslie Weatherhead, and Carroll A. Wise.

50. See David E. Roberts, *Psychotherapy and a Christian View of Man;* "Psychotherapy and the Christian Ministry," *Religion in Life*, Spring, 1945; "Theological and Psychiatric Interpretations of Human Nature," *Christianity and Crisis*, Feb. 3, 1947. Cf. Albert C. Outler, *A Christian Context for Counseling*, Hazen Foundation Pamphlet, 1947, and *Psychotherapy and the Christian Message*, to be published by Harper & Brothers, 1954.

51. See especially *Our Inner Conflicts* and *The Neurotic Personality of Our Time.*

52. *Conceptions of Modern Psychiatry*, also published in *Psychiatry*, Feb. 1940. See also his posthumous lectures, *The Interpersonal Theory of Psychiatry* (W. W. Norton, 1953), which may well turn out to be the most seminal book in this field in this decade. His interest in Brightman's personalism and Edward Sapir's studies of language is clear.

53. *Op. cit.*, p. 20.

54. W. A. White, *Twentieth Century Psychiatry* (New York: Norton, 1936).

55. "Release Therapy," *Psychiatry*, I (1938), 387-90.

56. Jacob L. Moreno, *Psychodramatic Treatment of Psychoses* (New York: Beacon House, 1945); *Psychodrama* (1946); *Psychodrama and the Psychopathology of Inter-Personal Relations* (1945). In a private conversation, Dr. Moreno confided to the writer that he knew Martin Buber and had taken inspiration from the implications of the I-Thou motif for his own "psychodrama."

57. Fritz Kunkel, *Let's Be Normal* (New York: Ives Washburn, 1931); *In Search of Maturity* (New York: Scribner, 1943); *How Character Develops*, with Roy E. Dickerson (Scribner, 1940). Kunkel was for a time the leader of the Adlerian School in Germany which developed a dynamic theory of personality. This "Individual Psychology" stressed freedom and responsibility as the significant characteristics in man, and the goals sought as the source of behavior. And being a socialist, he believed that "social feeling" and love are of the greatest importance for human well-being.

58. Erich Fromm, *Escape From Freedom* and *Man For Himself*.

59. *Escape From Freedom* (New York: Rinehart, 1941), p. 290.

60. *Idem*.

61. Fromm's *Man For Himself* is the fullest discussion of ethics and therapy.

62. See esp. *Escape From Freedom*, pp. 118ff, 164ff, 279, *passim*.

63. New York: Macmillan, 1941.

64. New York: Appleton-Century-Crofts, 1950. Childs is associated with the progressive wing in American education, believes that democracy is the most significant pattern in American life, and further that a child is a *person* and should be so treated.

65. New York: Teachers College, 1943.

66. The major themes which Mead elaborates in his articles on education are: (1) The prime importance of school in providing common meanings and linguistic tools; (2) the central place of scientific studies in the curriculum; (3) the necessity of manipulatory activities; (4) the importance of play in providing natural opportunities for taking the roles of others; (5) the aim and duty of the school to develop moral selves.

67. *Church, Community and State* (London: S.C.M. Press, 1935), p. 17.

68. John Macmurray, *Interpreting the Universe* (London: Faber & Faber, 1932); see also *The Structure of Religious Experience* (Yale University Press, 1936); *Reason and Emotion* (New York: Appleton-Century, 1936); *Freedom in the Modern World* (London: Faber & Faber, 1932).

69. "What is Public Opinion?" *Social Research*, XI (1944), 397-427. Cf. H. D. Lasswell, "The Person: Subject and Object of Propaganda," *Annals of the American Academy of Political and Social Science*, May-July, 1935, pp. 187-193.

70. *Ibid.*, p. 403.

71. See G. Vlastos, *Christian Faith and Democracy* (New York: Association Press, 1939). Professor Vlastos is at present working on a new book dealing with this problem; his series of addresses before the Hazen Conferences are as yet unpublished.

72. See esp. pp. 36ff.

73. New York: Scribner, 1947. Cf. William Temple, *Christianity and Social Order* (Penguin Books, 1943).

74. J. Maritain, *The Person and the Common Good* (New York: Scribner, 1947). See also *Scholasticism and Politics*. Actually Marxism and liberalism are both more alarming to the Vatican in principle than is the organic doctrine of the state. Maritain's "Organic Democracy" is the ideal of a good organic society, which is true also of humane organic thinkers like Bradley and Bosanquet. But history also seems to show that organic states, even when their aims are noble, even when they are under the sponsorship of the Church, are at least as likely to enforce the morals of Hitler or Franco as those of T. H. Green. For a full discussion of this and other relevant topics see T. D. Weldon, *States and Morals* (New York: Whittlesey House, 1947).

75. New York: Dutton, 1950.

76. *The Crisis of the Human Person* (London: Longmans, Green, 1950).

77. Personalism is the name given to a number of philosophies which have in common their correlation of the conceptions of personality and value, which conceive of personality as a unique entity in every human being which has a movement towards value. But the term is too often used indiscriminately to designate thinkers and systems which have in common only their concern for persons, while overlooking sharp divergencies.

78. It would appear that Buber is personalistic in senses (1) and (2), but it is not clear where he would stand with respect to (3) and (4). Buber has not worked out his metaphysics clearly, but it would appear to incline to a semi-realism. Surely his "narrow ridge" is not fully idealistic. Just what it is, he declines to say, denying that he has a "metaphysics."

79. In listing these thinkers in the same company I am well aware that radical distinctions are possible and necessary between the different kinds of "process" and of "personalism" they represent. The same can be said for Berdyaev, Mumford, Mannheim, Laski, Aldous Huxley, C. S. Lewis and others who have in common only the fact that in varying degrees they are exponents of, sympathizers with, a "personalist" point of view in ethics and social theory.

80. See esp. C. Hartshorne, *The Divine Relativity*, in which he speaks of God as Supreme, yet indebted to all; of God as Absolute, yet related to all; and of the divine attributes as types of social relationship. Cf. A. N. Whitehead, *Process and Reality*, and Daniel D. Williams, *God's Grace and Man's Hope*.

81. *Our Knowledge of God* (New York: Scribner, 1939), p. 201.

82. Yale University Press, 1912.

83. London: Macmillan, 1920.

84. New York: Macmillan, 1920.

85. London: Milford, 1930.

86. London: Macmillan, 1938.

87. *Ich Glaube an den Dreieinigen Gott* (1926), and *Glaube und Wirklichkeit* (1928).

88. *Gegenwart: eine kritische Ethik* (1928). Grisebach translates the Kantian imperative to read, "Never reduce the I-Thou relationship to the I-It relationship." "Never treat another subject as a mere object."

89. *Op. cit.,* p. 179.

90. *God and Men,* p. 127.

91. *The Meaning of Revelation,* esp. Chap. II.

92. *Op. cit.,* p. 210.

93. "The Ego-Alter Dialectic and the Conscience," *JP,* XLII (1945), 352-359.

94. See John Baillie, *op. cit.,* pp. 178ff.

95. Cf. Emil Brunner, *The Divine-Human Encounter,* pp. 103ff; *The Mediator,* pp. 209ff.

96. Ludwig Lewisohn, *Menorah Journal,* XII, Feb. 1926, p. 65.

97. See his Introduction to *I and Thou,* p. v.

98. *The Servant of the Word* (London: Religious Book Club, 1941), p. 26.

99. This is a phrase of Wilhelm Michel in *Martin Buber, Sein Gang in die Wirklichkeit* (Frankfurt a.Main, 1926).

100. Variously labelled as "crisis theology," "dialectical theology," "realistic theology," "existential theology," "neo-orthodox," or as neo-Reformation theology, since in Protestant lands, in the hands of thinkers like Barth, Brunner, Niebuhr, and Tillich, it has meant a re-working of the Reformation tradition of Luther, Calvin and Zwingli. But it has also had significant developments in the Eastern Orthodox Church in the thought of Berdyaev and Bulgakov, and in the Roman Catholic communion in the neo-Thomist Christian Humanism and Personalism of J. Maritain, and in the Catholic existentialism of Marcel and Rousselot. In Judaism there are Buber and Rosenzweig.

101. See the English translation *The Epistle to the Romans* (London: Oxford, 1933). It should be noted, however, that the Catholic revival in France predates the First World War, and Buber had been writing of the I-Thou dialogue of man with God before the familiar form of existential philosophy appeared.

102. Thus Reinhold Niebuhr defines a paradox: a rational contradiction which points to a truth which logic cannot embrace.

103. It is the compound of utopian sociological thinking, the hope of the Kingdom of God on earth, and the equalitarian and democratic ideals of the nineteenth century which gives us the social gospel. Its classic American expression is Walter Rauschenbusch's *A Theology for the Social Gospel.* Its story has been well told by C. H. Hopkins, *The Rise of the Social Gospel in American Protestantism.*

104. This means that they all accept much of the Marxian theory that man's "sin," suffering and estrangement are the results of economic maladjustment and social evils. Man is flesh as well as spirit; he is social as well as individual. Accordingly, their notion of sin and redemption has been enlarged to include economic and social ills. It is perhaps worth noting that there is a socially reactionary streak in the later Barth that is sometimes shocking in its irresponsibility, and this despite his recently renewed concern with worldly institutions.

105. Barth and Brunner in Switzerland were influenced by the religious socialism of Kutter and Ragaz; Tillich and Heimann belonged to the fellowship of Socialist Christians in Germany; Berdyaev and Bulgakov were both Marxists, although they also draw inspiration from the Orthodox concept of *Sobornost* which means community or free union. Buber is also a utopian socialist and fraternized with Tillich's group in Germany.

106. In America nearly all of the important figures in this movement were members of the Fellowship of Socialist Christians, now re-named Christian Action, which publishes the little journal *Christianity and Society,* and is much less Marxist than it was in its early years. They reject at one and the same time the extreme economic determinism and materialism of Marxism and its political utopianism. They believe that modern Stalinism is not only a corruption of early Marxism but in some sense a natural consequence of Marxist errors and illusions about man. They are still concerned with the social dimensions of the Christian faith, believing that all human enterprises stand under the judgment and fulfillment of God.

107. It should be remarked, however, that the social gospel also produced a "realistic" social doctrine of sin in terms of a solidaristic society. Central to the thought of Rauschenbusch, Ross, Royce and Ritschl (How's that for a case of alliteration's artful aid?) is the concept of corporate or social sin, "the super-personal forces of evil" which become embedded in social institutions and have a corrupting influence on the growth and well-being of individuals. The Social Gospel also included a note of crisis, activism, missionary urgency, and criticism of a materialistic profit-grubbing culture.

108. This theme runs through all of Niebuhr's writings, but has found most recent expression in his *Faith and History* (New York: Scribner, 1949). See also *The Nature and Destiny of Man* (1939-41), esp. Vol. II, Chap. VII. A somewhat more optimistic view is held by Daniel D. Williams, *God's Grace and Man's Hope* (New York: Harper, 1949).

109. Characteristic works are Emil Brunner, *Man in Revolt* (New York: Scribner, 1939); *The Divine Imperative* (London: Lutterworth, 1937); *The Divine-Human Encounter* (Philadelphia: Westminster, 1943); *The Mediator* (London: Lutterworth, 1934); *Dogmatik* (Zurich: Zwingli verlag, 1946-50, 2 vols.); Karl Barth, *The Doctrine of the Word of God,* Vol. I/1 of Church Dogmatics (New York: Scribner, 1936); *Die Kirchliche Dogmatik,* Bd. II/1 and Bd. III/1 (Zollikon: Evangelischen Buchhandlung, 1940); Karl Heim, *God Transcendent* (London: Nisbet, 1935); F. Gogarten, *Glaube und Wirklichkeit* (Jena: Diederichs, 1928); *Ich Glaube an den dreieinigen Gott;* John Oman, *Grace and Personality* (New York: Macmillan, 1925); John Baillie, *Our Knowledge of God* (New York: Scribner, 1939); Sydney Cave, *The Christian Estimate of Man* (London: Duckworth, 1944); E. P. Dickie, *The Obedience of a Christian Man* (London: S.C.M. Press, 1944); Reinhold Niebuhr, *The Nature and Destiny of Man;* H. R. Niebuhr, *The Meaning of Revelation* (New York: Macmillan, 1941); Paul Tillich, *The Religious Situation* (New York: Holt, 1936), *The Protestant Era* (University of Chicago, 1948); N. Berdyaev, *The Destiny of Man* (New York: Scribner, 1937), *The Divine and the Human* (London:

Geoffrey Bles, 1949), *Solitude and Society* (New York: Scribner, 1937);
E. E. Aubrey, *Present Theological Tendencies* (New York: Harper, 1936);
H. R. Mackintosh, *Types of Modern Theology* (New York: Scribner,
1937); W. M. Horton, *Realistic Theology* (New York: Harper, 1943);
L. S. Thornton, *The Common Life in the Body of Christ* (Westminster:
Dacre Press, 1942); J. E. Fison, *Blessing of the Holy Spirit.*

110. These are Brunner's phrases in *The Divine-Human Encounter.* Professor
Buber tells me that on the fly-leaf of the copy of this book which Brunner
sent to Buber, Brunner calls him the man without whom he would not
have been able to write this book.

111. Cf. Brunner, *Man in Revolt,* pp. 448, 546, *passim.*

112. *Op. cit.,* p. 223.

113. See E. P. Dickie, *op. cit.,* p. 59f. These theologians differ among themselves as to the nature and degree of the divine immanence, but most
of them (Barth and Nygren being apparently the more extreme in their
insistence upon the divine transcendence) hold that the initiative remains
in some way with God without destroying man's freedom and responsibility.
To deny this is to conceive of a "personal" relation in impersonal terms.
God and man are not mechanical opposites, however wide the gap between them. Grace means a gracious personal relation as Oman has it.
If we stress God's distance from men by asserting His Otherness alone,
and do not realize at the same time the truth of His Presence in the
I-Thou relation, we are bound to reduce the idea of Transcendence to a
sub-human category, and to take refuge in the paradox of the impassability
of the gulf between God and men. Cf. Cave, *op. cit.,* pp. 209, 222f.

114. See e.g., Brunner, *The Divine-Human Encounter,* pp. 73ff, 148ff. Cf. Oman,
op. cit.

115. See Dickie, *op. cit.,* p. 60; Barth, *The Doctrine of the Word of God,* pp.
441, 466.

116. New York: Macmillan Co., 1941, pp. 144, 145, 146.

117. Brunner, *The Mediator,* p. 209, *passim; Man in Revolt, passim; The Divine-
Human Encounter,* pp. 52, 60f, 74ff. Barth is so repetitious that one may
find these themes treated anywhere and everywhere throughout his massive
and tedious works, but they are especially treated as follows: Creation in
the *Dogmatik,* III/1 and II/1; Covenant, in III/1; the Incarnation and
God's loving approach in II/1. The Doctrine of the Word of God, being
I/1 of the *Dogmatik* deals primarily with Revelation and the Proclamation
of the Word of God, of the Triune God.

118. E. Brunner, *Man in Revolt,* pp. 91ff; *The Divine-Human Encounter,* pp.
127-130.

119. Such an interpretation would seem to make it possible to reconcile the
doctrine of the Incarnation and the *imago Dei* (the Christian source and
analogy of the liberal doctrine of individual liberty and natural rights) with
the doctrine of the Church as Community.

120. Paul Lehmann, *The Intercollegian,* Feb. 1947, p. 15.

121. *Basic Christian Ethics* (New York: Scribner), p. 255. See esp. Chap. VIII.

122. Brunner, *Man in Revolt*, pp. 114-165; *The Divine Imperative*, pp. 61ff, 154f; Farmer, *God and Men*, Chap. III; Barth, *The Doctrine of the Word of God*, pp. 466ff.

123. Brunner, *The Divine-Human Encounter*, pp. 133-36; *Man in Revolt*, pp. 139ff.

124. It is noteworthy that Josiah Royce sets forth a very similar interpretation of sin as self-will in *The Philosophy of Loyalty* (New York: Macmillan, 1908) and *The Problem of Christianity* (New York: Macmillan, 1913), Vol. I, *passim*.

125. The whole question of the social nature and structure of sin has been recently examined in an unpublished dissertation by Prof. James L. Martin, Yale University, 1950.

126. Cf. H. R. Niebuhr, *op. cit.*, pp. 166ff.

127. Unless we can legitimately include the Orders in Buber's I-It world.

128. See *Man in Revolt*, p. 132.

129. *Ibid.*, p. 541; cf. *The Divine-Human Encounter*, pp. 131-133.

130. H. R. Niebuhr, *JP*, XLII (1945), 359.

131. C. S. Lewis, *The Problem of Pain* (New York: Macmillan, 1943), pp. 75-76.

132. K. Barth, *The Doctrine of the Word of God*; E. Brunner, *Man in Revolt*, p. 66ff; *The Divine Imperative*, pp. 555ff; *The Divine-Human Encounter*, pp. 149-50.

133. H. H. Farmer, *The Servant of the Word*.

134. See e.g., W. M. Horton, *Theology in Transition* (New York: Harpers, 1943); H. P. Van Dusen, *World Christianity* (New York: Abingdon-Cokesbury, 1947); Justin Wroe Nixon, "The Liberal Returns to the Church," *Religion in Life*, VIII (1939), 200-212; Samuel McCrea Cavert, "The New Place of the Church in Protestant Thinking," *Religion in Life*, VIII (1939), 14-24.

135. See C. H. Hopkins, *op. cit.*; Rauschenbusch, *op. cit.*; D. D. Williams, *op. cit.*

136. E.g., George A. Coe, *Social Theory of Religious Education*; John Macmurray, *The Structure of Religious Experience*; Joachim Wach, *Sociology of Religion* (Chicago: University of Chicago Press, 1944).

137. W. M. Horton, *Toward a Reborn Church* (New York: Harper, 1949); see also the reports of the Oxford Conference on Life and Work, of the Amsterdam meetings of the World Council of Churches, etc.

138. F. Heiler, *The Spirit of Worship* (New York: Doran, 1926); Dom Gregory Dix, *The Shape of the Liturgy* (London: Dacre Press, 1944); Dietrich von Hildebrand, *Liturgy and Personality* (New York: Longman, Green, 1943); Norman Pittenger, *Sacraments, Signs and Symbols* (Chicago: Wilcox, Follett, 1947).

139. See Elton Trueblood, *Signs of Hope* (New York: Harper, 1950); Harvey Seifert, *Fellowships of Concern* (Nashville: Abingdon-Cokesbury, 1949).

140. See L. S. Thornton, *The Common Life in the Body of Christ*; P. T. Forsyth, *The Church and Sacraments*.

141. Josiah Royce, *The Philosophy of Loyalty*, *The Problem of Christianity*, and *The Hope of the Great Community*.

142. But it also raises some questions: (1) As Buber points out (*Mamre*, 137) in the strife between Luther and Zwingli over the Holy Communion, Luther noticed, what Zwingli overlooked, that by a merely symbolic presence

the worshipper is not met, laid hold of, and claimed in the whole of his personality. And Brunner points out clearly the difficulties this doctrine has for infant baptism in which there can be neither faith, assent, or response (*The Divine-Human Encounter*, pp. 178ff).

143. "Martin Buber and Christian Thought," *Commentary*, V (1948), 515-521.

144. The same holds true for Kierkegaard and others of like persuasion. Something of this same distrust of the existential claim is what has caused Barth to renounce his early dependence upon Kierkegaard. Any such taint is now rejected by Barth as "anthropocentric,"—the word Barth uses to club opponents with.

145. Quoted in Barbara S. Morgan, *Individuality in a Collective World* (New York: Norton, 1935), p. 251.

146. E. Fromm, *Man For Himself* (New York: Rinehart, 1947), p. 248.

147. See Morrow's review of *MSS*, in *PR*, XLIV (1935), 588.

148. *BMM*, pp. 80-81.

149. *IJE*, XXXIX (1929), 395.

150. See William Graham Sumner, *Folkways* (Boston: Ginn, 1907).

151. Thackeray once described Addison as one who liked "to mingle in that great club of the world, sitting alone in it somehow." One recalls in this connection, too, that Beethoven went on "hearing" melodies and composing immortal songs when he was deaf. And Franz Rosenzweig, paralyzed so that he lost his voice and the ability to move his limbs, went on with the work of his mind, and wrote entire books with the help of his devoted wife.

152. See the similar judgment and discussion of this point by T. V. Smith, *AJS*, XXXVII (1931), 382. Cf. William Miller, "A Catholic Plan for a New Social Order," *Social Action*, Feb. 15, 1951, esp. pp. 23-38.

153. *BMM*, pp. 108-111, *passim*. Cf. Mead, *IJE*, XXXV (1924–25), 276.

154. Hastings Rashdall, quoted by Widgery in his 1946 edition of Sidgwick's *History of Ethics* (New York: Macmillan, 1946), p. 334.

155. The dogma of inevitable progress is for Buber the abdication of man before the world of It.

156. *PA*, p. 510.

157. *Mamre*, p. 112f (italics mine); *Hasidism*, p. 108f.

158. Cf. a similar view as expressed by Bertrand Russell in *The Analysis of Mind* (London: Allen & Unwin, 1949), p. 17, where he speaks of "collecting thoughts into bundles." By whom? How are thoughts collected into bundles?

159. "Proceedings of the Sixth International Congress of Philosophy" (1926). Reprinted in *PP*, pp. 161-175. See also A. Lovejoy, *The Revolt Against Dualism*, esp. Chaps. III and IV.

160. See William Temple, *Nature, Man and God* (London: Macmillan, 1934), Chaps. V and VIII.

161. *BMM*, p. 155.

162. E.g., Helmut Kuhn in a review article, *JP*, XLVI (1949), 75-79.

163. See John Dewey and A. F. Bentley, *Knowing and the Known* (Boston: Beacon Press, 1949), p. 141.

164. E. E. Aubrey, *Man's Search For Himself*, p. 105.

165. Cf. E. S. Schattschneider, "Our Unrecognized Governmental Crisis," *Social Action*, October 15, 1950.
166. *Paths in Utopia*, p. 136f.
167. "Epistle to Diognetus," in J. C. Ayer, *A Source Book for Ancient Church History* (New York: Scribner, 1913), p. 29.
168. *Israel and the World*, p. 238.

Bibliography

The following bibliographical items will serve as suggestive and representative examples of works by authors other than Mead or Buber, but who are likewise concerned with the same or similar problems of ego-alter communication, of inter-human or I-Thou relation. Many of these writers make specific reference to Mead or Buber. They are indications of a flourishing literature in many related fields by scholars and workers who find themselves, in theory or practical point of view, near to Mead and/or Buber.

THE MAJOR WRITINGS OF GEORGE HERBERT MEAD

The Philosophy of the Present. The Paul Carus Foundation Lectures. Edited with an Introduction by A. E. Murphy and Prefatory Remarks by John Dewey. Chicago: Open Court Pub. Co., 1932.

Mind, Self and Society. Edited with an Introduction by Charles W. Morris. Chicago: Univ. of Chicago Press, 1934.

Movements of Thought in the Nineteenth Century. Edited with Introduction by Merritt H. Moore. Chicago: Univ. of Chicago Press, 1936.

The Philosophy of the Act. Edited with Introduction by Charles W. Morris, in collaboration with John M. Brewster, A. M. Dunham, and David L. Miller. Chicago: Univ. of Chicago Press, 1938.

ARTICLES AND OTHER WRITINGS BY
GEORGE H. MEAD
(Arranged Chronologically)

Review of K. Lasswitz, *Die moderne Energetik in ihrer Bedeutung für Erkenntniskritik,* in *Psychological Review,* I (1894), 210-13.

Abstract. "Herr Lasswitz on Energy and Epistemology," *ibid.,* pp. 172-75.

Review of C. L. Morgan, *An Introduction to Comparative Psychology,* in *Psychological Review,* II (1895), 399-402.

Abstract. "A Theory of Emotions from the Physiological Standpoint," *ibid.*, pp. 162-64.

Abstract. "Some Aspects of Greek Philosophy," *University of Chicago Record,* I (1896-97), 42.

"The Relation of Play to Education," *ibid.*, pp. 140-45.

Review of Le Bon, *Psychology of Socialism,* in *American Journal of Sociology,* V (1899), 404-12.

"The Working Hypothesis in Social Reform," *ibid.*, pp. 367-71.

"Suggestions Toward a Theory of the Philosophical Disciplines," *Philosophical Review,* IX (1900), 1-17.

"The Definition of the Psychical," *Decennial Publications, University of Chicago,* III (1903), 77-112.

"The Basis for a Parents' Association," *Elementary School Teacher,* IV (1903-4), 337-46.

"Image or Sensation," *Journal of Philosophy,* I (1904), 604-7.

"The Relations of Psychology and Philology," *Psychological Bulletin,* I (1904), 375-91.

Reviews of D. Draghicesco, *"Du rôle de l'individu dans le déterminisme social,"* and *"Le probleme du déterminisme, déterminisme biologique et déterminisme social,"* in *Psychological Bulletin,* II (1905), 399-405.

"The Teaching of Science in College," *Science,* XXIV (1906), 390-97.

"The Imagination in Wundt's Treatment of Myth and Religion," *Psychological Bulletin,* III (1906), 393-99.

"Science in the High School," *School Review,* XIV (1906), 237-49.

"Editorial Notes," *ibid.*, XV (1907), 160, 164.

Review of Jane Addams, *The Newer Ideal of Peace,* in *American Journal of Sociology,* XIII (1907), 121-28.

"Concerning Animal Perception," *Psychological Review,* XIV (1907), 383-90.

Abstract. "The Relation of Imitation to the Theory of Animal Perception," *Psychological Bulletin,* IV (1907), 210-11.

"On the Educational Situation in the Chicago Public Schools," *City Club Bulletin,* I (1907-8), 131-38.

"Industrial Education and Trade Schools," *Elementary School Teacher,* VIII (1907-8), 402-6.

"Policy of the *Elementary School Teacher,*" *ibid.*, pp. 281-84.

"The Philosophical Basis of Ethics," *International Journal of Ethics,* XVIII (1908), 311-23.

"The Social Settlement: Its Basis and Function," *University of Chicago,*

Record, XII (1908), 108-10.

"Educational Aspects of Trade Schools," *Union Labor Advocate*, VIII, No. 7 (1908), 19-20.

"Industrial Education and the Working Man and the School," *Elementary School Teacher*, IX (1908-9), 369-83.

"On the Problem of History in the Elementary School," *ibid.*, p. 433.

"Moral Training in the Schools," *ibid.*, pp. 327-38.

"Social Psychology as Counterpart to Physiological Psychology," *Psychological Bulletin*, VI (1909), 401-8.

"What Social Objects Must Psychology Presuppose?" *Journal of Philosophy*, VII (1910), 174-80.

"Social Consciousnesss and the Consciousness of Meaning," *Psychological Bulletin*, VII (1910), 397-405.

"Psychology of Social Consciousness Implied in Instruction," *Science*, XXXI (1910), 688-93.

Review of B. M. Anderson, Jr., *Social Value, a Study in Economic Theory*, in *Psychological Bulletin*, VIII (1911), 432-36.

Review of Warner Fite, *Individualism: Four Lectures on the significance of Consciousness for Social Relations*, in *Psychological Bulletin*, VIII (1911), 323-28.

"Remarks on Labor Night," *City Club Bulletin*, V (1912), 214-15.

"Exhibit of City Club Committee on Public Education," *ibid.*, p. 9.

"The Mechanism of Social Consciousness," *Journal of Philosophy*, IX (1912), 401-6.

A Report on Vocational Training in Chicago and in Other Cities, by a committee of the City Club, George H. Mead, Chairman. (Chicago: City Club of Chicago, 1912), pp. 315. Reviewed by Judd, *Elementary School Teacher*, XIII (1912-13), 248-49.

"The Social Self," *Journal of Philosophy*, X (1913), 374-80.

"A Heckling School Board and an Educational Stateswoman," *Survey*, XXXI (1913-14), 443-44.

"The Psychological Bases of Internationalism," *ibid.*, XXXIII (1914-15), 604-7.

Philosophy, XII (1915), 141-55.

"Natural Rights and the Theory of the Political Institution," *Journal of*

"Madison—The Passage of the University through the State Political Agitation of 1914; the Survey by Wm. H. Allen and His Staff and the Legislative Fight of 1915, with Indications these offer of the Place the State University Holds in the Community," *Survey*, XXXV (1915-16), 349-51, 354-61.

"Smashing the Looking Glass, Rejoinder," *ibid.*, pp. 607, 610.

"Professor Hoxie and the Community," *University of Chicago Magazine,* IX (1916-17), 114-17.

The Conscientious Objector, Pamphlet No. 33, "Patriotism through Education Series," issued by National Security League, New York City, 1917.

"Josiah Royce—A Personal Impression," *International Journal of Ethics,* XXVII (1917), 168-70.

"Scientific Method and Individual Thinker," *Creative Intelligence* (New York: Henry Holt & Co., 1917), pp. 176-227.

Review of Edith Abbott and Sophonisba P. Breckinridge, *Truancy and Non-Attendance in the Chicago Public Schools,* in *Survey,* XXXVIII (1917), 369-70.

"The Psychology of Punitive Justice," *American Journal of Sociology,* XXIII (1917-18), 577-602.

"Retiring President's Address," *City Club Bulletin,* XIII (1920), 94.

"A Behavioristic Account of the Significant Symbol," *Journal of Philosophy,* XIX (1922), 157-63.

"Scientific Method and the Moral Sciences," *International Journal of Ethics,* XXXIII (1923), 229-47.

"The Genesis of the Self and Social Control," *ibid.,* XXXV (1924-25), 251-77.

"The Objective Reality of Perspectives," *Proceedings of the Sixth International Congress of Philosophy* (1926), pp. 75-85. Reprinted in *The Philosophy of the Present* (Chicago, 1932).

"The Nature of Aesthetic Experience," *International Journal of Ethics,* XXXVI (1926), 382-92.

"A Pragmatic Theory of Truth," *Studies in the Nature of Truth, University of California Publications in Philosophy,* XI (1929), 65-88.

"The Nature of the Past," *Essays in Honor of John Dewey* (New York: Henry Holt & Co., 1929), pp. 235-42.

"National-Mindedness and International-Mindedness," *International Journal of Ethics,* XXXIX (1929), 385-407.

"Bishop Berkeley and His Message," *Journal of Philosophy,* XXVI (1929), 421-30.

"Cooley's Contribution to American Social Thought," *American Journal of Sociology,* XXXV (1929-30), 693-706.

"The Philosophies of Royce, James, and Dewey, in their American Setting," *International Journal of Ethics,* XL (1930), 211-31. Also in the co-operative volume, *John Dewey: The Man and His Philosophy*

(Cambridge, Massachusetts: Harvard University Press, 1930), pp. 75-105.

"Philanthropy from the Point of View of Ethics," *Intelligent Philanthropy,* edited by Faris, Lane, and Dodd (Chicago: University of Chicago Press, 1930), pp. 133-48.

"Dr. A. W. Moore's Philosophy," *University of Chicago Record,* N. S., XVII (1931), 47-49.

"The Philosophy of John Dewey," *International Journal of Ethics,* XLVI (1936).

WRITINGS ABOUT GEORGE H. MEAD

"George Herbert Mead: An Appreciation," Van Meter Ames, *University of Chicago Magazine,* XXIII (1930-31), 370-72.

"George Herbert Mead," John Dewey, *Journal of Philosophy,* XXVIII (1931), 309-14.

George Herbert Mead. Memorial Addresses and a biographical note by his son. Chicago: University of Chicago Press, 1931.

"George Herbert Mead As I Knew Him," John Dewey, *University of Chicago Record,* XVII (1931), 174-75.

"G. H. Mead's Social Concept of the Self," C. J. Bittner, *Sociology and Social Research,* XVI, September 1931, pp. 6-22.

Obituary, *Philosophical Review,* XL (1931), 410.

"Social Philosophy of George Herbert Mead," T. V. Smith, *American Journal of Sociology,* XXXVII (1931), 368-85.

"George Herbert Mead and the Philosophy of Philanthropy," T. V. Smith, *Social Service Review,* VI (1932), 37-54.

"Notation on the Problem of the Past with special reference to George Herbert Mead," A. Tonness, *Journal of Philosophy,* XXIX (1932), 599-606.

"The Religious Bearings of a Secular Mind—George Herbert Mead," T. V. Smith, *Journal of Religion,* XII (1932), 200-13.

"Work of George Herbert Mead," John Dewey, *New Republic,* LXXXVII, July 22, 1936, p. 329.

"Social Psychology of George Mead," E. Faris, *American Journal of Sociology,* XLIII (1937), 391-403.

"Peirce, Mead and Pragmatism," C. W. Morris, *Philosophical Review,* XLVII (1938), 109-27.

Basic Factors in the Growth of Mind and Self: Analysis and Reconstruction of George Herbert Mead's Theory. Herbert Kessler. Abstract of Ph.D. Dissertation, University of Illinois, 1940.

Social Philosophy and the Social Mind: A Study of the Genetic Methods of J. M. Baldwin, G. H. Mead, and J. E. Boodin, Eugene Clay Holmes (New York: privately printed), 1942.

"Genius of Pragmatic Empiricism," B. W. Brotherton, Journal of Philosophy, XL (1943), 29-39.

"G. H. Mead's Conception of the Present," David L. Miller, Philosophy of Science, X (1943), 40-46.

Emergent Mind and Education. A. S. Clayton. New York: Teacher's College, Columbia University, 1943.

George Herbert Mead: Philosopher of the Social Individual. Grace Chin Lee. New York: King's Crown Press, 1945.

"A Behavioristic Account of the Logical Function of Universals," John A. Brewster, Journal of Philosophy, XXXIII (1936), 505-514; 553-547.

"George H. Mead's Metaphysics of Time," Maurice Natanson, Journal of Philosophy, L (1953), 770-782.

"Zen and Pragmatism," Van Meter Ames, Philosophy: East and West, IV (1954), 19-33.

"Mead and Husserl on the Self," Van Meter Ames, Philosophy and Phenomenological Research, XV (1955), 320-331.

"The Concept of 'the Given' in Peirce and Mead," Maurice Natanson, The Modern Schoolman, XXXII (1955).

"Phenomenology From the Natural Standpoint," Maurice Natanson, Philosophy and Phenomenological Research, XVII (1956), 241-245.

The Social Dynamics of George H. Mead. Maurice Natanson. Introduction by Horace M. Kallen. Washington, D.C., Public Affairs Press, 1956.

"Mead and Sartre on Man," Van Meter Ames, Journal of Philosophy, LIII (1956), 205-219.

"Zen and American Philosophy," Van Meter Ames, Philosophy: East and West, V (1956), 305-320.

"Mead's Principle of Sociality," Frank M. Doan, Journal of Philosophy, LIII (1956), 607-615.

"Mead's Conception of Simultaneity," Frank M. Doan, Journal of Philosophy, LV (1958), 203-209.

"Zen to Mead," Van Meter Ames. Presidential Address before the Western Division of the American Philosophical Association. Proceedings and Addresses of the American Philosophical Association, XXXIII (1959-60), 27-42.

"Psychology, Theology, and the Social Self," Hobart O. Mowrer, in The Crisis in Psychiatry and Religion, Chap. 10, pp. 130-155. New York and Princeton: D. Van Nostrand Company. 1961.

THE MAJOR WRITINGS OF MARTIN BUBER
(Arranged Chronologically)

Daniel. Leipzig: Insel-Verlag, 1913.

Vom Geist des Judentums. Leipzig: Kurt Wolff, 1916.

Die Jüdische Bewegung. Gesammelte Aufsätze und Ansprachen. Zweite Folge. Berlin: Jüdischer Verlag, 1916-20.

Ereignisse und Begegnungen. Leipzig: Insel-Verlag, 1917.

Mein Weg zum Chassidismus. Frankfurt a.M.: Rütten & Loening, 1918.

Cheruth. Wien: R. Löwit Verlag, 1919.

Der heilige Weg. Frankfurt a.M.: Rütten & Loening. 1919.

Die Rede, die Lehre, und das Lied. Drei Beispiele. Leipzig: Insel-Verlag, 1920.

Ich und Du. Leipzig: Insel-Verlag, 1923.

Reden über das Judentum. Frankfurt a.M.: Rütten & Loening, 1923.

Das Verborgene Licht. Frankfurt a.M.: Rütten & Loening, 1924.

Rede über das Erzieherische. Berlin: Lambert Schneider Verlag, 1926. (Vorher abgedruckt in *Die Kreutur,* 1. Jahrg., 1 Heft.).

Die Chassidischen Bücher. Gesamtausgabe. Hellerau: Verlag Jakob Hegner, 1928.

Zwiesprache. Die Kreatur, III. Jahrg., 3 Heft, Berlin: Lambert Schneider Verlag, 1929.

Jewish Mysticism. Translated by Lucy Cohen. London: J. M. Dent & Sons, Ltd., 1931.

Kampf um Israel. Berlin: Schocken Verlag, 1933.

Die Frage an den Einzelnen. Berlin: Schocken Verlag, 1936.

Königtum Gottes. Vol. I of *Das Kommende.* Untersuchungen zur Entstehungsgeschichte des Messianischen Glaubens. Berlin: Schocken Verlag, 1936.

I and Thou. Translated by R. Gregor Smith. Edinburgh: T. & T. Clark, 1937.

For the Sake of Heaven. (A Novel.) Philadelphia: The Jewish Publication Society of America, 1945.

Moses. Oxford: East & West Library, 1946. Harper Torchbook, 1958.

Mamre: Essays in Religion. Translated by Greta Hort. Melbourne: Melbourne University Press, 1946.

Between Man and Man. Translated by Ronald Gregor Smith. London: Kegan Paul, Trench, Trubner & Co., 1947.

Dialogisches Leben; Gesammelte philosophische und pädagogische Schriften. Zurich: G. Müller, 1947.

Ten Rungs: Hasidic Sayings. New York: Schocken Books, 1947.

Tales of the Hasidim. Vol. I. *The Early Masters:* Vol. II. *The Later Masters.* New York: Schocken Books, 1947-48.

Das Problem des Menschen. Heidelberg: Verlag Lambert Schneider, 1948.

Hasidism. New York: Philosophical Library, 1948.

Israel and the World. New York: Schocken Books, 1948.

The Prophetic Faith. Translated by Carlyle Witton-Davies. New York: Macmillan Co., 1949. Harper Torchbook, 1960.

Paths in Utopia. Translated by R. F. C. Hull. New York: Macmillan Co., 1950.

The Ways of Man According to the Teachings of Hasidism. London: Routledge & Kegan Paul, 1950.

Zwei Glaubensweisen. Zurich: Manesse Verlag, 1950.

Two Types of Faith. Translated by Norman P. Goldhawk. London: Routledge & Kegan Paul, 1951. Harper Torchbook, 1960.

At the Turning. New York: Farrar, Straus & Young, 1952.

Eclipse of God. New York: Harper & Brothers, 1952. Harper Torchbook, 1957.

Israel and Palestine. New York: Farrar, Straus & Young, 1952.

Images of Good and Evil. Translated by Michael Bullock. London: Routledge & Kegan Paul, 1952.

Right and Wrong: An Interpretation of Some Psalms. Translated by Ronald Gregor Smith. London: S.C.M. Press, Ltd., 1952.

Zwischen Gesellschaft und Staat. Heidelberg: Verlag Lambert Schneider, 1952.

Good and Evil: Two Interpretations. (Includes *Images of Good and Evil* and *Right and Wrong*). New York: Charles Scribner's Sons, 1953.

Einsichten. Aus. den Schriften gesammelt. Wiesbaden: Insel Verlag, 1953.

Hinweise. Gesammelte Essays (1910-53). Zurich: Manesse Verlag, 1953.

Gottesfinsternis. Zurich: Manesse Verlag, 1953.

For the Sake of Heaven. Second edition with new Foreword. New York: Harper & Brothers, 1953. Paperback edition—Meridian Books, 1958.

Die Schriften über das dialogische Prinzip. Heidelberg: Verlag Lambert Schneider, 1954. A collection of familiar Buber works, but includes several essays not previously published in book form.

The Legend of the Baal-Shem. Translated by Maurice S. Friedman. New York: Harper & Brothers, 1955.

Der Mensch und sein Gebild. Heidelberg: Verlag Lambert Schneider, 1955.

Tales of Rabbi Nachman. Translated by Maurice Friedman. New York: The Horizon Press, 1956.

Pointing The Way: Collected Essays. Translated by Maurice S. Friedman. New York: Harper & Brothers, 1957.

Ich und Du. Nachworterweiterte. Heidelberg: Verlag Lambert Schneider, 1958.

Hasidism and Modern Man. Edited and translated by Maurice Friedman. New York: Horizon Press, 1958.

The Writings of Martin Buber. Edited, with Introduction, by Will Herberg. New York: Meridian Books, 1958.

The Origin and Meaning of Hasidism. Vol. II of *Hasidism and the Way of Man.* Edited and translated by Maurice Friedman. New York: The Horizon Press, 1960.

The Kingship of God. New York: Harper & Brothers, 1962.

Stationen des Glaubens. Aus dem Schriften gesammelten. Wiesbaden: Insel Verlag, 1960.

WORKS TRANSLATED OR EDITED BY MARTIN BUBER

Die Gesellschaft. Sammlung sozial-psychologischer Monographien. Frankfurt a.M.: Rütten & Loening (40 Bde. 1906-1912).

Ekstatische Konfessionen. Jena: Eugen Diederichs, 1909.

Gustav Landauer: Sein Lebensgang in Briefen. Under Mitwirkung von Ina Britschgi-Schimmer herausg. von Martin Buber. 2 Bde., Frankfurt a.M.: Rütten & Loening, 1929.

Die Kreatur. Vierteljahrsschrift. Herausg. von Martin Buber, Viktor von Weizsacker, und Joseph Wittig. Berlin: Lambert Schneider Verlag, 1926-29.

ARTICLES, LECTURES, AND OTHER WORKS BY MARTIN BUBER

"Über Jakob Böhme," *Wiener Rundschau*, 5 Jahrg., Nr. 12, 15 Juni, 1901.

"Brief über das Wesen der Sprache," in den *Mitteilungen des Internanational Institute für Philosophie* in Amsterdam, Nr. 1, Marz 1918, Groningen: Verlag P. Nordhoff, 1918.

"Rabbinic Wisdom," *The Reflex,* IV (May, 1929), 65-67.

"Sayings of the Baal-Shem-Tov," translated by Clifton P. Fadiman. *Menorah Journal,* XVII (1929), 52-55.

"The Spiritual Pattern of Judaism," in *Rebirth, A Book of Modern Jewish Thought.* Edited by Ludwig Lewisohn. New York: Harper & Brothers, 1935, pp. 90-108.

"The Beginnings of the National Idea," *Review of Religion,* X (1945-46), 254-65.

"Our Reply," *Towards Union in Palestine: Essays on Zionism and Jewish-Arab Cooperation.* Edited by Martin Buber, Judah L. Magnes, and Ernst Simon. Jerusalem: Ihud Association, 1945, pp. 33-36.

"The Philosophical Anthropology of Max Scheler," *Philosophy and Phenomenological Research,* VI (1945-46), 307-321.

"Myth in Judaism," the fourth of the seven *Reden über das Judentum.* Commentary, IX (1950), 562-566.

"Remarks on Goethe's Concept of Humanity," *Goethe and the Modern Age.* Edited by Arnold Bergstraesser. Chicago: Henry Regnery Co., 1950, pp. 227-234.

"Distance and Relation," *The Hibbert Journal,* XLIX (1951), 107-113.

"Education of Character," *Cross Currents,* I, No. 2 (1951), 16-25.

"On the suspension of the Ethical," Translated by Maurice S. Friedman. *Moral Principles of Action,* edited by Ruth Nanda Anshen. Vol. VI of Science of Culture Series. New York: Harper & Brothers, 1952.

"Religion und modernes Denken," *Merkur,* VI (February, 1952), 101-120.

"Letters to Franz Rosenzweig on the Law," in Franz Rosenzweig, *On Jewish Education.* Edited by N. N. Glatzer. New York: The Noonday Press, 1954.

"Christus, Chassidismus, Gnosis. Einige Bemerkungen," *Merkur* (Berlin), VIII (1954).

The William Alanson White Memorial Lectures, 4th Series, 1957. "Distance and Relation," "Elements of the Interhuman," "Guilt and Guilt Feelings," reprinted in *Psychiatry,* XX, (No. 2, May 1957), 97-129.

"Hasidism and Modern Man," Journal of Religion, XXII (1957), 109-120.

"Israel and the Command of the Spirit," trans. by Maurice Friedman. *Congress Weekly,* XXV (Sept. 8, 1958), 10ff.

Schuld und Schuldgefuehle. Heidelberg: Verlag Lambert Schneider, 1958.

"What is Common to All," trans. by Maurice Friedman. *Review of Metaphysics*, XI (1958), 359-379.

WRITINGS ABOUT MARTIN BUBER

Lewisohn, Ludwig. "Martin Buber," *Menorah Journal*, XII, February, 1926.

Michel, Wilhelm. *Martin Buber: Sein Gang in die Wirklichkeit*. Frankfurt a.M.: Rütten & Loening, 1926.

Lewisohn, Ludwig. "Martin Buber," in *Cities and Men*. New York: Harper & Bros., 1927, pp. 200-212.

Der Jude. Sonderheft zu Martin Bubers 50. Geburtstag. Redigiert von Robert Weltsch. Berlin: Jüdischer Verlag, 1928.

Kohn, Hans. "The Personal Aspect of Zionism: A Study of Martin Buber," *The New Palestine*, February 10, 1928.

Simon, Ernst. "Martin Buber: An Appreciation on the Occasion of His 50th Birthday," *New Judea*. Feburary 3, 1928.

Kohn, Hans. *Martin Buber: Sein Werk und Seine Zeit*. Hellerau: Jakob Hegner Verlag, 1930.

Tepfer, John J. "Martin Buber and Neo-Mysticism," *Yearbook*, Central Conference of American Rabbis, XLIV (1934), 203-19.

Maringer, Simon. *Martin Buber's Metaphysic der Dialogue in Zusammenhang neuerer philosophischer und theologischer Strömungen*. Köln: Buchdruckerei Steiner, 1936.

Kohn, Hans. "The Religious Philosophy of Martin Buber," *Menorah Journal*, XXVI (1938), 173-85.

Martin Buber und Sein Werk. Anlasslich seines sechzigsten Geburtstags überreicht. Berlin: Schocken Verlag, 1938.

Agus, Jacob B. *Modern Philosophies of Judaism*. New York: Behrman's Jewish Book House, 1941, Chap. IV, pp. 213-79.

Wodehouse, Helen. "Martin Buber's 'I and Thou,'" *Philosophy*, XX (1945), 17-30.

Pfuetze, Paul E. "Martin Buber and Jewish Mysticism," *Religion in Life*, XVI (1947), 553-67.

Smith, R. Gregor. *The Thought of Martin Buber*. (Burning Glass Paper No. 18.) Shorne, Kent: Ridgeway House, 1947.

Smith, Constance I. "The Single One and the Other," *The Hibbert Journal*, XLVI (1947-48), 315-21.

Blau, Joseph L. "Martin Buber's Religious Philosophy," A review article, *The Review of Religion*, XIII (1948), 48-64.

Pfuetze, Paul E. "The Chasid Maggidim," *Crozer Quarterly*, XXV (April, 1948), 144-53.

Werner, Alfred. "Buber at Seventy," *Congress Weekly*, XV (Feb. 13, 1948), 10f.

Simon, Ernst. "Martin Buber: His Way Between Thought and Deed," *Jewish Frontier*, XV (Feb. 1948), 25-28.

Tillich, Paul. "Martin Buber and Christian Thought," *Commentary*, V (1948), 515-521.

Schulweis, Harold. "Crisis Theology and Martin Buber," *Review of Religion*, XIV (1949), 38-42.

Herberg, Will. "Has Judaism Still Power to Speak," *Commentary*, IX (May, 1949), 447-457.

Simon, Ernst. "Religious Humanism," in *Goethe and the Modern Age*, edited by Arnold Bergstaesser. Chicago: Henry Regnery, 1950, pp. 304-325.

Tillich, Paul. "Jewish Influences on Contemporary Christian Theology," *Cross Currents*, II (Spring, 1952), 38-42.

Schulweis, Harold. "Martin Buber: An Interview," *The Reconstructionist*, XVII (March 21, 1952), 7-10.

——————. "The Personalism of Martin Buber," *The Personalist*, XXXIII (April, 1952), 131-134.

Kaplan, Mordecai M. "Martin Buber: Theologian, Philosophy, and Prophet," *The Reconstructionist*, XVII (May 2, 1952).

Wolf, Ernst M. "Martin Buber and German Jewry, Prophet and Teacher to a Generation in Catastrophe," *Judaism*, I (Oct., 1952), 346-352.

Cohen, Arthur A. "Revelation and Law: Reflections on Martin Buber's Views on Halakah," *Judaism*, I (July 1952), 250-256.

Hartshorne, Charles and Reese, William L. *Philosophers Speak of God*. Chicago: The University of Chicago Press, 1953, pp. 302-306.

Friedman, Maurice S. "Martin Buber's New View of Evil," *Judaism*, II (July, 1953), 239-246.

——————. "Martin Buber and Christian Thought," *Review of Religion*, XVIII (Nov., 1953), 31-43.

——————. "Martin Buber at Seventy-Five," *Religion in Life*, XXIII (Summer 1954), 405-417.

——————. "Martin Buber's View of Biblical Faith," *Journal of Bible and Religion*, XXII (Jan. 1954), 3-13.

——————. "Martin Buber's Theory of Knowledge," *Review of Metaphysics*, VII (Dec. 1954).

————. "Revelation and Law in the Thought of Martin Buber," *Judaism*, III (Winter, 1954), 9-19.

————. "Symbol, Myth, and History in the Thought of Martin Buber," *Journal of Religion*, XXXIV (Jan. 1954), 1-11.

————. "Martin Buber: Prophet and Philosopher," *Faith Today*, I (1954-55).

Pfuetze, Paul E. "The Concept of the Self in Contemporary Protestant Theology," *Journal of Religious Thought*, XII (1954-55), 5-16.

Smith, Ronald Gregor. "The Theology of Martin Buber," *Theology Today*, XII (1955), 206-215.

Friedman, Maurice S. *Martin Buber: The Life of Dialogue*. Chicago: The University of Chicago Press, 1955. New York: Harper Torchbook, 1960.

————. "Healing Through Meeting: Martin Buber and Psychotherapy," *Cross Currents*, V (Fall 1955).

————. "Martin Buber's Theory of Education," *Educational Theory*, VI (April 1956).

Mullahy, Patrick. "Interpersonal Psychiatry, versus the Philosophy of I-Thou and I-It," *Psychiatry*, XIX (1956), 401-408.

Farber, Leslie H. "Martin Buber and Psychiatry," *Psychiatry*, XIX (1956), 109-120.

Farber, Leslie H.; Friedman, Maurice S.; Howe, Reuel L. "Martin Buber and Psychotherapy," *Pastoral Psychology*, VII (Dec. 1956).

Friedman, Maurice S. "Martin Buber's Concept of Education," *Christian Scholar*, VL (June 1957).

Cohen, Arthur A. *Martin Buber*. Studies in Modern European Literature and Thought. New York: Hillary House, 1957.

Wasmuth, Ewald. "Martin Buber: Prophet in verdunkelter Zeit," *Die Neue Rundschau*, IV, 1957.

Farber, Leslie H. "The Therapeutic Despair," *Psychiatry*, XXI (1958), 7-20.

Pfuetze, Paul E. "The Concept of the Self in Contemporary psychotherapy," *Pastoral Psychology*, IX (Feb. 1958), 9-19.

Jones, Edgar. "Man in Society: Some Aspects of the Thought of Martin Buber," *Congregational Quarterly* (London), XXXVI (1958) 155-161.

Murchland, Bernard G. "Buber's Pursuit of the Holy," *The Commonweal*, LXVIII (1958), 469-471.

Trapp, Jacob. Editor. *To Hallow This Life*. An Anthology of Martin Buber's Writings. New York: Harper & Brothers, 1958.

Herberg, Will. Editor with Introduction. *Four Existentialist Theologians.* New York: Doubleday Anchor Books, 1958, pp. 169-253.

Friedman, Maurice S. "Martin Buber's 'Theology' and Religious Education," *Religious Education,* LIV (Jan.-Feb. 1959).

——————. "Martin Buber and the Social Problems of Our Time," *Yivo Annual,* 1959.

——————. "Martin Buber's Biblical Judaism," *CCAR Journal,* No. 24, January 1959.

——————. "Martin Buber's Life and Thought," Vol. III, *Modern Jewish Thought,* and "Martin Buber Anthology," Vol. IV, *Modern Jewish Thought,* B'nai B'rith Great Books Series. New York: Farrar, Straus & Cudahy, 1960.

——————. "Dialogue and the 'Essential We': The Bases of Values in the Philosophy of Martin Buber," *American Journal of Psychoanalysis,* XX (May 1960).

Diamond, Malcolm. *Martin Buber: Jewish Existentialist.* New York: Oxford University Press, 1960.

Rome, Sidney C. Editor. *Interrogations of Contemporary Philosophers.* New Haven: Yale University Press, 1961.

Schilpp, Paul A., and Friedman, Maurice S., Editors. *The Philosophy of Martin Buber,* volume of *The Library of Living Philosophers.* New York: Henry Tudor, 1961.

Pfuetze, Paul E., "Martin Buber and American Pragmatism," in *The Philosophy of Martin Buber,* volume of *The Library of Living Philosophers,* edited by Schilpp, Paul A., and Friedman, Maurice S. New York: Henry Tudor, 1961.

Stahmer, Harold M., Jr., "The Role of Language in the Dialogical Approach to Religious Truth." A Study of the role of language in the thought of Martin Buber. A Doctoral dissertation, University of Cambridge, 1960, soon to be published.

THE MEAD MATERIALS listed above are fairly complete. But no attempt has been made to provide a complete bibliography of Martin Buber's works or of works about Buber. I have tried, rather, to include here a carefully selected list of important books, articles, and anthologies readily available to most readers of this book, and especially those in English or in English translation. Most of the important Buber materials are now in excellent translations, for which we owe a vast debt of gratitude to Maurice Friedman and Ronald Gregor Smith. They have given us skillful translations which retain in a remarkable way the flavor and graceful phrasing of Buber's German style.

In his early biography *Martin Buber: Sein Werk und Seine Zeit,* Hans Kohn has provided a complete bibliography up to 1930. *Martin Buber: The Life of Dialogue* by Maurice S. Friedman, Harper Torchbook, TB 64, 1960, contains the most complete up-to-date bibliography available to American readers.

For other general references basic to this study, the interested reader may consult the items in the footnotes of this book, and the recent files of such journals as the following (whose pages are full of the themes and concerns of this book):

The American Journal of Sociology
American Sociological Review
Journal of Social Psychology
Sociology and Social Research
International Social Science Bulletin
Psychiatry
Pastoral Psychology
Journal of Religion
Group Psychotherapy
Child Development
Human Relations

WORKS OTHER THAN MEAD'S OR BUBER'S, BUT CONCERNED WITH THE SAME OR SIMILAR PROBLEMS OF INTER-PERSONAL OR I-THOU RELATION

Barth, Karl. *Die kirchliche Dogmatik,* Vol. III, *Die Lehre von der Schöpfung.* Zurich: Evangelischer Verlag, A. G. Zollikon, 1948, esp. "Die Grundform der Menschlichkeit," pp. 265-340.

Berdyaev, Nicholai. *Solitude and Society.* London: Geoffrey Bles, 1938.

Brunner, Emil. *The Divine-Human Encounter.* Philadelphia: The Westminster Press, 1943.

Clarke, Fred. *Freedom in the Educative Society: Educational Issues of Today,* edited by W. R. Niblett. London: University of London Press, 1948.

Coates, J. B. *The Crisis of the Human Person.* London: Longmans, Green & Co., 1949.

Cullberg, John. *Das Du und die Wirklichkeit. Zum ontologischen Hintergrund der Gemeinschaftskategorie.* Uppsala: Uppsala Universitets Arsskrift, 1933, Vol. I, A. B. Lundeqvistska Bokhandeln, 1933.

Duhrssen, Alfred. "The Self and the Body," *Review of Metaphysics*, X (1956-57), 28-34.

──────────. "Tools, Symbols, and Other Selves," *Review of Metaphysics*, XI (1957-58), 215-223; 411-425.

Ebner, Ferdinand. *Das Wort und die geistigen Realitäten*. Innsbruck: Brenner-Verlag, 1921.

Erikson, Erik H. *Childhood and Society*. New York: W. W. Norton & Co., 1950.

Farmer, H. H. *The Servant of the Word*. New York: Charles Scribner's Sons, 1942.

Fison, J. E., *The Blessing of the Holy Spirit*. London: Longmans, Green & Co., 1950.

Friedrichs, Robert W. "Alter versus Ego: An Exploratory Assessment of Altruism," *American Sociological Review*, XXV (1960), 496-507.

Fromm, Erich. *The Sane Society*. New York: Rinehart, 1955.

──────────. *The Art of Loving*. New York: Harper & Brothers, 1956.

Gogarten, Friedrich. *Glaube und Wirklichkeit*. Jena: Eugen Diedrichs Verlag, 1928.

Grisebach, Eberhard. *Gegenwart. Eine kritische Ethik*. 1928.

Guardini, Romano. *Welt und Person*. Würzburg: Werkbund-Verlag, 1950.

Hazelton, Roger. "Religion as Encounter," *Journal of Religious Thought*, XIV (1957), 129-140.

Häring, Bernard. "The Master Idea of Christian Morality," in Burghardt & Lynch: *The Idea of Catholicism*. New York: Meridian Books, 1960, pp. 42-54.

Heider, Fritz. *The Psychology of Interpersonal Relations*. New York: John Wiley & Sons, 1958.

Heim, Karl. *God Transcendent*. New York: Charles Scribner's Sons, 1936.

Herberg, Will. *Judaism and Modern Man*. New York: Farrar, Straus & Young, 1951.

Hiltner, Seward. "The Social Self," editorial in *Pastoral Psychology*, IX (Feb. 1958), 7-8.

Howe, Reuel L. *Man's Need and God's Answer*. Greenwich, Conn., The Seabury Press, 1952.

Jones, M., *The Therapeutic Community*. New York: Basic Books, 1953.

Löwith, Karl. *Das Individuum in der Rolle des Mitmenschen*. Munich: Drei Masken Verlag, 1928.

Macmurray, John. *The Structure of Religious Experience*. Terry Lectures. New Haven: Yale University Press, 1936.

——————. *The Self as Agent* and *Persons in Relation,* The Gifford Lectures 1953 Vols. I and II. New York: Harper & Brothers, 1958-1961.

Marcel, Gabriel. *Being and Having.* Translated from *Etre et Avoir* by Katherine Farrer. Westminster: Dacre Press, 1949. Forthcoming Torchbook.

Montagu, M. F. Ashley. *The Biosocial Nature of Man.* New York: Grove Press, 1956.

Mowrer, O. Hobart. *The Crisis in Psychiatry and Religion.* New York and Princeton: D. Van Nostrand Co., 1961.

Murphy, Gardner. *Personality: A Biosocial Approach to Origins and Structure.* New York: Harper & Brothers, 1947.

Niebuhr, H. Richard. *The Meaning of Revelation.* New York: Macmillan, 1941.

Niebuhr, Reinhold. *The Self and the Dramas of History.* New York: Charles Scribner's Sons, 1955.

Oldham, J. H. *Real Life is Meeting.* New York: The Macmillan Co., 1947; London: The Sheldon Press, 1947.

——————. *Life is Commitment.* New York: Harper & Brothers, 1952.

Parsons, Talcott. "Social Structure and the Development of Personality," *Psychiatry,* XXI (1958), 321-340.

Paul, Leslie Allen. *The Meaning of Human Existence.* Philadelphia: J. B. Lippincott Co., 1950.

Pfuetze, Paul. E. "The Concept of the Self in Contemporary Psychotherapy," *Pastoral Psychology,* IX (Feb. 1958), 9-19.

Read, Herbert. *Education Through Art.* New York: Pantheon Books, 1945.

Rosenstock-Huessey, Eugen. *Angewandte Seelenkunde.* Darmstadt: Roethenverlag, 1924.

——————. *Der Atem des Geistes.* Frankfurt a-Main: Verlag der Frankfurter hefte, 1951.

Rosenzweig, Franz. "Das neue Denken," *Kleine Schriften.* Berlin: Schocken Verlag, 1935.

——————. *Der Stern der Erlösung.* Heidelberg: Verlag Lambert Schneider, 1954.

Scheler, Max. *Nature of Sympathy.* New Haven: Yale University Press, 1954.

Sullivan, Harry Stack. *The Interpersonal Theory of Psychiatry.* New York: W. W. Norton & Co., 1953.

——————. *Conceptions of Modern Psychiatry*. New York: W. W. Norton & Co., 1953.

Taguiri, Renato and Petrullo, Luigi. *Person Perception and Interpersonal Behavior*. Stanford, Calif., Stanford Univ. Press, 1952.

Tillich, Paul. *Biblical Religion and the Search for Ultimate Reality*. Chicago: The University of Chicago Press, 1955.

Turner, Ralph. "Role-taking, Role Standpoint, and Reference-Group Behavior," *American Journal of Sociology*, LXI (1955-56), 316-328.

Witzleben, Henry D. von, "On Loneliness," *Psychiatry*, XXI (1958), 37-43.

Index

World of It, 141-49, 161, 182-83
  contrasted with the World of Thou,
    147, 161
  the world of science, space, time and
    causality, 147-49
World of Thou, 141-45, 150-65, 183
  characteristics of the I-Thou relation,
    153-57
  the "sphere of between," 202
Wundt, W., 38, 59, 64, 68, 72, 119,
  206 n9
  and the concept of imitation, 68
  and the gesture, 64, 111 n149
  on language, 72, 111 n149

Y

Young, Kimball, 306

Z

Zaddik, Zaddikim, 121, 122, 123, 131,
  210 n35
Zeitgeist, 21, 208 n20, 304
v. Zinzendorf, Count, 208 n20
Zionist movement, 119-20
Zwingli, Ulrich, 364 n142

HARPER TORCHBOOKS / The Bollingen Library

HARPER TORCHBOOKS / The Academy Library

HARPER TORCHBOOKS / The Science Library

HARPER TORCHBOOKS / The Cloister Library